Caesar, Rome and Beyond

ROME STUDIES
ARCHAEOLOGY, HISTORY, & LITERATURE

Editorial Board

Trine Arlund Hass (Founding Editor), *Aarhus University*
Rubina Raja (Founding Editor), *Aarhus University*
Henriette van der Blom, *University of Birmingham*

Advisory Board

Christopher Hallett, *University of California, Berkeley*
Sine Grove Saxkjær, *Aarhus University*
Christopher Smith, *University of St. Andrews*

VOLUME 4

Previously published volumes in this series are listed at the back of the book.

Caesar, Rome and Beyond

New Research and Recent Discoveries

Edited by

Jan Kindberg Jacobsen, Rubina Raja,
and Sine Grove Saxkjær

BREPOLS

British Library Cataloguing in Publication Data

A catalogue record for this book is available from the British Library.

© 2023, Brepols Publishers n.v., Turnhout, Belgium

All rights reserved. No part of this publication may be reproduced,
stored in a retrieval system, or transmitted, in any form or by any means,
electronic, mechanical, photocopying, recording, or otherwise,
without the prior permission of the publisher.

D/2023/0095/248
ISBN: 978-2-503-60344-5

Printed in the EU on acid-free paper

CONTENTS

List of Illustrations vii

Introduction

1. Caesar, Rome and Beyond: New and Old Sources
JAN KINDBERG JACOBSEN, RUBINA RAJA, and SINE GROVE SAXKJÆR 1

Caesar and Rome

2. Sensing Change: Late Republican Architecture in Rome
PENELOPE J. E. DAVIES 7

3. Find a Lover in Augustan Rome: How Ovid's *Ars amatoria*
Became a Criticism of Augustus's Moral Politics
ERIC M. MOORMANN 27

The Archaeology of
Caesar's Military Ventures

4. The Archaeology of Julius Caesar: New Research on the Gallic Wars
NICO ROYMANS and MANUEL FERNÁNDEZ-GÖTZ 51

5. Across the Rubicon to Rome: New Elements
for the Identification of Caesar's Military Camp
ANNALISA POZZI and CRISTIAN TASSINARI 71

6. Caesar in Britain: Britain in Rome
A. P. FITZPATRICK and COLIN HASELGROVE 97

New Discoveries

7. Excavating the Forum Iulium: The Danish-Italian Excavations between
Longue Durée Perspectives and High-Definition Narratives
LAURA DI SIENA, JAN KINDBERG JACOBSEN, GLORIA MITTICA,
GIOVANNI MURRO, CLAUDIO PARISI PRESICCE, RUBINA RAJA,
SINE GROVE SAXKJÆR, and MASSIMO VITTI. 119

8. The So-Called Aquinum Portrait of Julius Caesar:
From its Discovery to Research Development
GIUSEPPE CERAUDO 141

9. The So-Called 'Caesar' of Aquinum: A Preliminary Analysis
GIOVANNI MURRO 161

10. L'immaginario cesariano tra visioni classicistiche e ideologie nazionalistiche:
il caso di un ritratto emerso dalle acque del Rodano
MARIO DENTI 173

New Contributions on Caesar and Historiography

11. Julius Caesar and the Forum Caesaris: World History, Historiography, and Reception
Investigated through Danish Biographies of Caesar from the Early Twentieth Century
TRINE ARLUND HASS and RUBINA RAJA. 189

12. Past Research Perspectives and Narrated Space: The Incident When Caesar Did Not
Rise for the Senate, according to Georg Brandes (1918) and Hartvig Frisch (1942)
TRINE ARLUND HASS 211

Index. 227

List of Illustrations

2. Sensing Change: Late Republican Architecture in Rome — *Penelope J. E. Davies*

Figure 2.1.   Scale comparison of Republican temples. 9

Figure 2.2.   Temple of Castor and Pollux, Phase II, *c.* 117 BC. 11

Figure 2.3.   Temple of Castor and Pollux, Phase I, *c.* 496 BC. 11

Figure 2.4.   Sanctuary of Magna Mater, restored *c.* 102 BC (?). 11

Figure 2.5.   Sanctuary of Magna Mater, restored *c.* 102 BC (?). 11

Figure 2.6.   *Substructio* on the Capitoline saddle, 78 BC, actual state. 11

Figure 2.7.   *Substructio* and temples on the Capitoline saddle, 78 BC. 11

Figure 2.8.   *Substructio* and temples on the Capitoline saddle, 78 BC. 15

Figure 2.9.   Galleries under the forum pavement, 78–74 BC (?). 15

Figure 2.10.   Theatres of M. Scribonius Curio, 53 BC. 16

Figure 2.11.   Theatre of Pompey, *c.* 61–52 BC. 16

Figure 2.12.   Theatre-Portico Complex of Pompey, *c.* 61–52 BC. 18

Figure 2.13.   Circus Maximus, actual state. 18

Figure 2.14.   Forum Iulium, begun *c.* 54 BC, actual state. 18

Figure 2.15.   Forum Iulium, begun *c.* 54 BC. 20

Figure 2.16.   Forum Iulium, begun *c.* 54 BC. 21

3. Find a Lover in Augustan Rome: How Ovid's *Ars amatoria* Became a Criticism of Augustus's Moral Politics — *Eric M. Moormann*

Figure 3.1.   Rome at the time of Augustus. The monuments discussed
in Ov., *Ars am.* 1.67–176 and some more complexes. 28

4. The Archaeology of Julius Caesar: New Research on the Gallic Wars — *Nico Roymans and Manuel Fernández-Götz*

Figure 4.1.   Gaul: tribal groups and major regional subdivisions on the eve of the Gallic Wars. . . .53

Figure 4.2.   Statue of Vercingetorix at Alesia, erected in 1865. 53

Figure 4.3.   Topographical sketch map of the Siege of Alesia. 53

Figure 4.4.   Location of key sites mentioned in the text. 54

viii

Figure 4.5.	Map of the Caesarian military camp at Hermeskeil.	54
Figure 4.6.	Gaul at the time of the Roman conquest, with the distribution of the cases of genocide/ethnocide described by Caesar in his *Commentarii*.	55
Figure 4.7.	Topography of the Late Iron Age fortification at Thuin, including the location of gold finds and Roman lead sling bullets.	56
Figure 4.8.	Roman lead sling bullets from the Late Iron Age fortification at Thuin.	57
Figure 4.9.	Palaeogeographic reconstruction of the Meuse–Waal confluence at Rossum in the early first century AD.	58
Figure 4.10.	Human remains from a battle-related find complex dredged from the River Meuse at Kessel-Lith (The Netherlands), probably linked to Caesar's massacre of the Germanic Tencteri and Usipetes in 55 BC.	59
Figure 4.11.	Tribal map of the 'Germanic' frontier zone in the Caesarian period and the Augustan/Tiberian period.	61
Figure 4.12.	Five test regions with good settlement evidence for the investigation of demographic trends during the Late Iron Age and earliest Roman period.	62
Figure 4.13.	Diagram of the period of use of excavated settlements, cemeteries, and cult sites from the Late Iron Age and earliest Roman period in the Meuse/Demer/Scheldt region.	63
Figure 4.14.	Distribution of some Late Iron Age gold coins that were in full circulation in the conquest period.	65
Figure 4.15.	Scheers 31 gold staters, ascribed to the Eburones, from the hoard of Amby.	65

5. Across the Rubicon to Rome: New Elements for the Identification of Caesar's Military Camp — *Annalisa Pozzi and Cristian Tassinari*

Figure 5.1.	The Arno-Rubicon frontier river system and the main rivers of central-northern Italy.	71
Figure 5.2.	Geographical location of Gatteo with indications of the minor locations mentioned in the text.	72
Figure 5.3.	Areas of archaeological and historical interest.	73
Figure 5.4.	Main pre-Roman evidences.	74
Figure 5.5.	Villanovan finds in the territory controlled by Verucchio.	75
Figure 5.6.	Stretch of the Roman road, recognized by the lateral ditches.	75
Figure 5.7.	Gatteo. Sector A (warehouse area and east car park) evidence from the Late Latenian/Early Roman period.	76
Figure 5.8.	Comparison (at the same metric scale) between Structure 9 and some ritual complexes found in Celtic territory.	77
Figure 5.9.	General plan of the Roman remains.	77

LIST OF FIGURES ix

Figure 5.10. Aerial view of the rectangular building, Structure 147, located in the internal part of the eastern closure. 78

Figure 5.11. The layout at the crossroads in the first century AD. 78

Figure 5.12. View of the timber buildings from the north-east. 79

Figure 5.13. Remains of moats and palisades in Sector B1. 80

Figure 5.14. General plan of Sector B2. 80

Figure 5.15. View from the west of the tower and the double palisade. 81

Figure 5.16. View from the north of the eastern gate. 82

Figure 5.17. Aerial view of the southern part of the officer's housing district. 83

Figure 5.18. View of the courtyard with brick fragments floor and a view of the well. 84

Figure 5.19. Comparative table between the neighbourhoods of some earth-and-wood camps. . . .85

Figure 5.20. Current hydrography and Roman roads in the territorial area of the Rubicon River. 86

Figure 5.21. Roman stone bridge over the current Rubicon River. 87

Figure 5.22. Section of the *Tabula Peutingeriana*. 89

Figure 5.23. Northern Italy in the early stages of Romanization. 90

6. Caesar in Britain: Britain in Rome — A. P. Fitzpatrick and Colin Haselgrove

Figure 6.1. Selected sites and places mentioned in the text. 98

Figure 6.2. Gallo-Belgic E coin found at Pakenham, Suffolk. Mid-first century BC. 99

Figure 6.3. Visualization of the warrior found at North Bersted burial, West Sussex. 100

Figure 6.4. View of Dover harbour. 101

Figure 6.5. View along Walmer Beach looking north towards Deal. 102

Figure 6.6. Model of a Roman galley of the first century BC or AD. 103

Figure 6.7. Timeline of the fleet's crossing to Britain, 4–5 July 54 BC, in Caesar's own words. . . 104

Figure 6.8. Lidar model of the topography of north-east Kent and the location of selected places mentioned in the text. 105

Figure 6.9. The Ebbsfleet enclosure looking east towards Pegwell Bay and the chalk cliffs at Ramsgate. 106

Figure 6.10. The defensive ditch at Ebbsfleet under excavation. 107

Figure 6.11. Gaulish Coolus type helmet found with a cremation burial at Bridge, near Canterbury, Kent. 107

Figure 6.12. The Iron Age hillfort at Wallbury, Essex, considered to be the most likely site of the decisive battle in 54 BC. 108

7. Excavating the Forum Iulium: The Danish-Italian Excavations between Longue Durée Perspectives and High-Definition Narratives — *Laura Di Siena and others*

Figure 7.1.   Small coins minted in Singapore in 2016. 120

Figure 7.2.   Modern carved wooden turtle. 120

Figure 7.3.   Aerial photo with an indication of the current excavation area at the Forum of Caesar. 121

Figure 7.4.   View of the Forum of Caesar and the Temple of Venus Genetrix seen from the south. 123

Figure 7.5.   Profile in the *domus terrinee* area showing a direct transition from early medieval layers to Archaic layers. 123

Figure 7.6.   Small Etruscan bucchero jugs during excavation and after conservation. Sixth century BC. 124

Figure 7.7.   *Doppia olla* graves found during the excavation in 2021. Sixth century BC. 124

Figure 7.8.   Map with an indication of the sixth-century BC phases in the eastern part of the 1998–2000 excavation and within the current excavation field. 125

Figure 7.9.   Sixth-century BC contexts with postholes in Area A. 126

Figure 7.10.   Bucchero fragments from bowl and cup. Sixth century BC. 126

Figure 7.11.   Granite columns, eastern part of Caesar's Forum. 127

Figure 7.12.   Caesarean sewer with fill. 128

Figure 7.13.   Mud deposits inside the Caesarean sewer. 129

Figure 7.14.   Archaeological material from Renaissance infills datable from the Roman period to the second half of the sixteenth century. 131

Figure 7.15.   Fragment of marble frieze with a depiction of a Nike figure. Late second century AD. 132

Figure 7.16.   Renaissance ceramics found in walls of the Alessandrino phase. Second half of the sixteenth century. 133

Figure 7.17.   Vertical sewer in Area A. 133

Figure 7.18.   Minor, personal objects, coins, and medicine vessels from the medical dump. Second half of the sixteenth century. 134

Figure 7.19.   Vessels from the basin in Area B. Latter part of the seventeenth century and first half of the eighteenth century. 135

Figure 7.20.   Chinese porcelain plate. Reigns of Emperor Kangxi (1662–1722) or Yongzheng (1723–1735). 136

LIST OF FIGURES

**8. The So-Called Aquinum Portrait of Julius Caesar:
From its Discovery to Research Development — *Giuseppe Ceraudo***

Figure 8.1.   Aerial views of Aquinum in the Castrocielo area in comparison................. 142

Figure 8.2.   Perspective aerial view from 2022 of the southern sector of the
Triumviral colony of Aquinum... 143

Figure 8.3.   Schematic representation of the urban layout and the
main monuments of Aquinum. 143

Figure 8.4.   Schematic representation of the urban layout of Aquinum
by Giuliani (1964) and by Sommella (1988)................................ 144

Figure 8.5.   View of the non-orthogonal intersection of two urban road axes
identified at the modern Casale Pascale................................... 144

Figure 8.6.   Vertical aerial view from 2017 of the central section
of the urban map of Aquinum north of Via Latina........................ 145

Figure 8.7.   Extract from the Archaeological Map of Aquinum
prior to the start of the excavation campaigns............................. 146

Figure 8.8.   Oblique aerial view from 2005 with the traces of four *decumani*
north of the Via Latina. 148

Figure 8.9.   Oblique aerial view from 2012 of the north of the field
owned by the Municipality of Castrocielo................................. 148

Figure 8.10.   Aerial zenith view from 2018 of the access from 'Via delle Terme'
to the women's sector of the Terme Vecciane.............................. 149

Figure 8.11.   Perspective aerial view from 2018 of the Balneum of M. Veccius............... 149

Figure 8.12.   Perspective aerial view from 2018 of the theatre and
the continuation towards the west of 'Via del Teatro'...................... 150

Figure 8.13.   The intersection of 'Via del Teatro' and Cardo Maximus..................... 150

Figure 8.14.   Zenith aerial view from 2015 of a sector to the west of the theatre............. 151

Figure 8.15.   Detail of Fig. 8.14 in which two clear linear traces
can be seen at an angle and parallel to each other......................... 151

Figure 8.16.   Zenith aerial view from 2016 of the central sector
of the city north of the Via Latina...................................... 152

Figure 8.17.   The discovery of the three marble heads from the southern *crepidoma*
of 'Via del Teatro'.. 153

Figure 8.18.   The portrait head attributed to Julius Caesar. 153

Figure 8.19.   The north-eastern corner of the porticus duplex. 154

Figure 8.20.   Plan of the structures excavated to the west of the theatre................... 155

Figure 8.21.   Perspective aerial view from 2018 of the central sector of the city
along the Via Latina... 156

Figure 8.22.   The field south of the Via Latina. 156

9. The So-Called 'Caesar' of Aquinum: A Preliminary Analysis — *Giovanni Murro*

Figure 9.1.   Aquinum, aerial view of the porticus duplex west of the theatre. 162

Figure 9.2.   Plan of the excavation of the porticus duplex. 163

Figure 9.3.   Sima slab with leonine protome coming from the collapsed layers
of the roof of the porticus. 163

Figure 9.4.   The context of the discovery of the marble heads
along the paved road north of the porticus. 164

Figure 9.5.   Fragment of the head of Hercules, right part. 164

Figure 9.6.   Fragment of the head of Hercules, left part. 164

Figure 9.7.   Marble head of a young adult with his head covered (*velato capite*). 164

Figure 9.8.   Marble head of the so-called 'Caesar' of Aquinum, front view. 164

Figure 9.9.   Marble head of the so-called 'Caesar' of Aquinum, right side view. 164

Figure 9.10.   Portrait of Julius Caesar from Tusculum. 165

Figure 9.11.   Portrait of Julius Caesar 'Chiaramonti-Pisa'. 165

Figure 9.12.   Presumed portrait of Julius Caesar, National Roman Museum. 165

Figure 9.13.   Portrait of Julius Caesar on a modern bust,
National Archaeological Museum of Naples. 166

Figure 9.14.   Presumed portrait of Julius Caesar kept at the
Musée départemental Arles antique in Arles. 166

Figure 9.15.   Portrait of Julius Caesar, Opera del Duomo Museum, Florence. 166

Figure 9.16.   Portrait of Pompey the Great, Augustan copy of an original from 70–60 BC. 166

Figure 9.17.   Portrait of the so-called 'Julius Caesar or Nerva',
National Archaeological Museum of Naples. 166

Figure 9.18.   Male portrait, British Museum of London. 166

Figure 9.19.   Male portrait from Palestrina, National Roman Museum. 166

Figure 9.20.   Male portrait, Museo Gregoriano Profano. 166

Figure 9.21.   Male portrait from Rome, via Prenestina, Museo Nazionale Romano. 166

Figure 9.22.   Male head from Dalmatia, Ny Carlsberg Glyptotek. 167

Figure 9.23.   Male head, probably from Venice, Ny Carlsberg Glyptotek. 167

Figure 9.24.   Denarius of Lepidus and Octavian from 43 BC. 168

Figure 9.25.   Denarius of Lepidus and Octavian from 42 BC. 168

Figure 9.26.   Denarius of Lepidus and Octavian from 42 BC. 168

LIST OF FIGURES

10. L'immaginario cesariano tra visioni classicistiche e ideologie nazionalistiche — *Mario Denti*

Figura 10.1. Busto maschile in marmo, vista frontale, Arles, Musée départemental Arles antique. 182

Figura 10.2. Busto maschile in marmo, lato, Arles, Musée départemental Arles antique. 182

Figura 10.3. Busto maschile in marmo, non finito, Aquileia, Museo Archeologico. 182

Figura 10.4. Busto maschile in marmo, non finito, lato, Aquileia, Museo Archeologico. 183

Figura 10.5. Busto maschile in calcare, lato, Treviso, Museo Civico. 183

Figura 10.6. Busto maschile in marmo, vista da tre quarti da sinistra, Arles, Musée départemental Arles antique. 183

Figura 10.7. Ritratto maschile in bronzo, Verona, Museo Archeologico al Teatro Romano. . . . 184

11. Julius Caesar and the Forum Caesaris — *Trine Arlund Hass and Rubina Raja*

Figure 11.1. Forum Romanum viewed from the east featured in Brandes's *Cajus Julius Cæsar*. 191

Figure 11.2. Reconstruction of the Forum Romanum as featured in Brandes's *Cajus Julius Cæsar*. 192

Figure 11.3. Map of the Imperial fora with the excavation field. 193

Figure 11.4. View of the Forum Iulium towards the south-west. 193

Figure 11.5. The demolition of the Alessandrino Quarter and the construction of Via dell'Impero, 1933. 194

Figure 11.6. Anaglypha Traiani (from the south). 204

Figure 11.7. Anaglypha Traiani (from the north). 205

INTRODUCTION

1. Caesar, Rome and Beyond: New and Old Sources

Jan Kindberg Jacobsen
Accademia di Danimarca (jan_jacobsen@hotmail.com)

Rubina Raja
Department of History and Classical Studies and Centre for Urban Network Evolutions (UrbNet), Aarhus University (rubina.raja@cas.au.dk)

Sine Grove Saxkjær
Centre for Urban Network Evolutions (UrbNet), Aarhus University (klasgs@cas.au.dk)

The work done within the framework of the Danish-Italian Caesar's Forum Project sparked the idea for this volume. An idea which pivoted around bringing together some of the scholars who have done recent work on remains and sources from the time of Caesar and about Caesar in later times, in order to tease out potential new perspectives on this central figure and his doings and the interpretations of these in the time after his death.

For some years, the Caesar's Forum Project has been going on in the heart of Rome, right next to Rome's monumental avenue, Via dei Fori Imperiali and directly below the Capitoline Hill. The excavation area lies between the monumental road, laid out during the reign of Mussolini as a parade road, and the part of Caesar's Forum which is open to the public already and recently has been connected directly with the Roman Forum and the Forum of Trajan, making it possible for visitors to transverse these spaces for the first time since the Middle Ages. The team has been working in the south-eastern part of Caesar's Forum, where an excavation area of about 1000 m² has already provided an incredible amount of new information about the long history of Rome.[1] It is a privilege to work in such a central area — central to the archaeology and history of Rome, but also to the broader world in terms of global history and cultural heritage. Therefore, a project like this comes with obligations and a responsibility to undertake archaeology of the highest quality as well as to make the results available as fast as possible to both the research community and the general public, so others can benefit from the new knowledge which has come out of the ground so to speak.

Via dei Fori Imperiali, running from Piazza Venezia to the Colosseum, was inaugurated on 28 October 1932 by Benito Mussolini. Originally the street was named Via dell'Impero and was used as a means to celebrate the fascist regime's ideology, whilst connecting it to the ancient Roman past. The inauguration of the monumental street was the culmination of a large-scale demolition of the entire area between Piazza Venezia and the Colosseum, which until then had held a sprawling residential neighbourhood where more than four thousand people lived. It was in the years before the layout of the street that the Imperial fora were partly uncovered to support the fascist ideology by merging the material remains of the Roman Empire's heyday with that of the fascist regime. It was immense amounts of accumulated cultural layers, which were moved within a very short time. Today we would not call what went on archaeology, but rather demolition and clearing out of a large area to make space for new building projects.

The area in which the Danish-Italian project has been working is most famous for having housed Caesar's Forum, but it saw an immense amount of development taking place over thousands of years, which has rarely been acknowledged as important in scholarship. Therefore, the project has from its initiation taken a longue durée perspective, taking into consideration all chronological phases encountered in the excavation.[2]

---

[1] For the most recent publications from the project see: Boschetti and others 2022; Corsetti and others 2020–2022; Egelund 2018; Jacobsen and Raja 2018; Jacobsen and others 2019–2020; 2020; 2021; 2022; Raja and Rüpke 2021; Sauer 2018; 2020–2022; 2021; Saxkjær and Mittica 2018. Also see the contribution by project members in this volume.

[2] Jacobsen and others 2021. See also Di Siena and others (in this volume).

This has already been reflected in the state of publications from the project, which among other things has cast entirely new light on the Renaissance and later phases.[3] However, we cannot get around the fact that this site is usually seen as the area in which Caesar had his forum built, his monumental public space, laid out right next to the main public space in Rome, the Roman Forum, situating Caesar and his political programme in the very heart of Rome and its world far beyond the city itself as well.

Originally Caesar's Forum was known as the Forum Iulium, the forum of the Julian family, of Caesar's forefathers and -mothers. In the Late Republican period, Rome was undergoing monumental changes, and numerous large building projects were undertaken in the city: projects financed by rich and politically strong individuals all competing for power in Rome. At the same time, it was a period in which wars were being fought in territories beyond Rome and new territories were becoming part of the Roman realm. Caesar was one of the central persons in the fluid and fast-changing political and military alliances and he made several moves toward making himself the centre of power.[4] We all know that the story ended with the murder of Caesar on the Ides of March, which ironically paved the way for an even stronger centralization of power in the Roman world, culminating in Octavian coming to power and later being bestowed the title of Augustus — becoming the first Roman emperor in a string of many.

In an earlier volume in this series edited by Trine Arlund Hass and Rubina Raja, numerous topics relating to Caesar — both in his time and after — were already tackled in a broader perspective than in this volume.[5] Here we aim to focus on fewer aspects that were closely connected to Caesar as an individual — both in terms of his person as described in sources, the material remains of his time, and the events in which he was involved.

The volume opens with the contribution by Penelope J. E. Davies entitled 'Sensing Change: Late Republican Architecture in Rome'. Davies, a specialist on Late Republican Rome, takes us through examples of the radical rescaling of building projects in Rome in the time of Caesar. She argues for a shift of perspective when reading Late Republican architectural building projects, and shows the ways in which we can read a heightened

awareness or more conscious use of spaces as places which embodied much more than just the physical scale present and to a larger extent held numerous and complex messages conveyed subtly or not so subtly through the architectural layouts and decorations of the complexes. Eric M. Moormann's 'Find a Lover in Augustan Rome: How Ovid's *Ars amatoria* Became a Criticism of Augustus's Moral Politics' takes us into the texts of the time and reminds us that while we look at the remains of architectural spaces in archaeology, we must not forget that these spaces were inhabited by people and that people had different intentions and that the same spaces, therefore, could be used in very different ways. In many ways, despite their different points of departure, these two contributions nail it down: so much of what we would like to know about ancient Rome in Caesar's time is inaccessible to us, and we rely on scattered and certainly also often biased sources. Caesar was a contested individual — both in his time and thereafter, and this is reflected in the source material available and the interpretation of it. It is not easy to stay objective when most sources have strong opinions. So setting these two contributions in the same section serves the purpose of reminding us of the variation in the sources as well as the opinionated nature of generally later sources.

The volume's second section turns to three contributions on the archaeology of Caesar's military ventures. The first contribution, written by Nico Roymans and Manuel Fernández-Götz is entitled 'The Archaeology of Julius Caesar: New Research on the Gallic Wars' and takes us through some of the archaeology of Julius Caesar's military campaigns, which have gained renewed attention in recent years, through new archaeological discoveries and readings of the source materials. The authors take us on a tour de force and give a solid historiographical overview of the research done over more than the last century, beginning with the interest Napoleon III took in the figure of Caesar and his military doings outside of Rome. They integrate new archaeological evidence, which gives entirely new perspectives on old stories about expansion and military practice, enslavement, murders, and the suppression of local societies — all themes that go directly back to Roman centralized war strategies in foreign territories. In the contribution 'Across the Rubicon to Rome: New Elements for the Identification of Caesar's Military Camp' Annalisa Pozzi and Cristian Tassinari tackle new archaeological evidence from Gatteo excavated between 2018–2020, which might allow for a better understanding of the crossing of the Rubicon by Caesar in the late

---

3 Jacobsen and others 2020; Corsetti and others 2022; Boschetti and others 2023.

4 See, for example, Gruen 2008. Also see Raja and Rüpke 2021.

5 Hass and Raja 2021.

40s BC. The authors connect the architectural remains with military activities, such as being a military camp underlining the expansionist Roman approach. They suggest this location at Gatteo to have been the place where the reunion between Caesar and the troops stationed along the banks of the Rubicon took place. A. P. Fitzpatrick and Colin Haselgrove contribute with an article entitled 'Caesar in Britain: Britain in Rome' in which they revisit the evidence for Caesar's expeditions to Britain. His crossing to Britain in 55 BC was the first time that this part of the ocean was crossed — as the authors underline — a fact which has not been acknowledged enough until now in our readings of the evidence for Caesar's campaigns in Britain, which usually in the popular perception are viewed as having been military failures. Through a close reading of the sources and a re-evaluation of them and the archaeological evidence, they advocate that — at least in Rome — Caesar's expeditions were considered major events and that this indeed shines through in the evidence, in particular in the imagery of the crossing of the ocean from the continent to Britain. The contribution gives us a refreshing re-reading of evidence and reminds us that trends in research and pushes for new lines of enquiry often bring the possibility of viewing old evidence in a new light.

The third section in the volume tackles some new discoveries. The first contribution by Laura Di Siena, Jan Kindberg Jacobsen, Gloria Mittica, Giovanni Murro, Claudio Parisi Presicce, Rubina Raja, Sine Grove Saxkjær, and Massimo Vitti entitled 'Excavating the Forum Iulium: The Danish-Italian Excavations between Longue Durée Perspectives and High-Definition Narratives' outlines the archaeological work undertaken within the Danish-Italian Caesar's Forum Project. It focuses on the ways in which the longue-durée perspective has been brought in close conversation with the snapshot narratives from closed contexts available to the excavators through the work done on the material findings. They highlight the possibilities that new methods and full quantification not only give us but also underline the challenges experienced within urban archaeological projects undertaken in living city environments where numerous agendas are at play, including accessibility for the public as well as the immense costs of keeping central parts of the city closed in connection with the movement of machinery and finds. The next two contributions both focus on finds from Aquinum — partly addressing one of the same objects, namely the Aquinum portrait. The contribution by Giuseppe Ceraudo entitled 'The So-Called Aquinum Portrait of Julius Caesar: From its Discovery to the Research Development' gives an overview of the excavations and some of the finds as well as insight into the excavation strategies. It contextualizes the finding of the Aquinum portrait, which by some has been interpreted as depicting Caesar. In the contribution by Giovanni Murro entitled 'The So-Called "Caesar" of Aquinum: A Preliminary Analysis' an in-depth analysis of the portrait and comparative material is given, situating it firmly within portrait studies of its time. In the contribution 'L'immaginario cerariano tra visioni classicistiche e ideologie nazionalistiche: il caso di un ritratto emerso dalle acque del Rodano' by Mario Denti we move on to discussions about the so-called 'Caesar' portrait found in the Rhône River outside of Arles. Denti takes us through the discovery of the portrait and its circumstances as well as the research leading to the identification of the portrait, seen by some as a depiction of Caesar. He re-evaluates the evidence and highlights the pitfalls, which should be evident to all scholars of ancient portraiture, that often we are driven by historical narratives and the desire for sensation when attributing ancient portraits to well-known individuals of their time.

In the concluding section, two contributions, one by Trine Arlund Hass and Rubina Raja entitled 'Julius Caesar and the Forum Caesaris: World History, Historiography, and Reception Investigated through Danish Biographies of Caesar from the Early Twentieth Century' and one by Trine Arlund Hass entitled 'Past Research Perspectives and Narrated Space: The Incident When Caesar Did Not Rise for the Senate, According to Georg Brandes (1918) and Hartvig Frisch (1942)', take us to Denmark and Danish cultural heritage. Both contributions focus on the much later writing about Caesar in Danish literary contexts and aim to disentangle the ways in which Caesar was seen by Danish male writers of the nineteenth and twentieth centuries. The contributions remind us that despite much research undertaken on the historiography of Caesar's perception in art and literature, there is still much more to explore and put forward.

With this volume, we hope to bring new impetus to research on Julius Caesar and his time and inspire researchers to revisit the sources available to us in light of the newest pieces of evidence that have emerged over the last decades.

Acknowledgements

We thank the funders of the Caesar's Forum Project. The excavation project is conducted as a collaboration between the Sovrintendenza Capitolina ai Beni Culturali in Rome, the Danish National Research Foundation's Centre of Excellence, Centre for Urban Network Evolutions (UrbNet) at Aarhus University, and the Danish Institute in Rome. The project, which is jointly directed by Jan Kindberg Jacobsen, Claudio Presicce Parisi, and Rubina Raja, has been funded by the Carlsberg Foundation since 2017 and by Aarhus University Research Foundation since 2019 through a flagship grant. Further support comes from Centre for Urban Network Evolutions, under the grant DNRF119. We thank research assistant Nikoline Sauer for editing. We also thank Rosie Bonté from Brepols Publishers for handling the publication process, Tim Barnwell for the copyediting, and Martine Maguire-Weltecke for the layout of the volume. We appreciate their professional handling of the manuscript at all stages.

Works Cited

Boschetti, C. and others. 2022. 'Glass in Rome during the Transition from Late Antiquity to the Early Middle Ages: Materials from the Forum of Caesar', *Journal of Heritage Science*, 10.95: 1–14 <https://doi.org/10.1186/s40494-022-00729-y>.

—— 2023. 'Disease Control and Disposal of Infectious Materials in Renaissance Rome: New Evidence from the Excavations in the Area of Caesar's Forum', *Antiquity*: 1–17. doi:10.15184/aqy.2023.34.

Corsetti, F. L. and others. 2020. 'The Danish-Italian Excavations on Caesar's Forum 2021. Report', *Analecta Romana Instituti Danici*, 45: 267–80.

—— 2022. 'The Last Days of the Alessandrino District', *Journal of Contemporary Archaeology* <https://journal.equinoxpub.com/JCA/article/view/22264> [accessed 25 January 2023].

Egelund, L. 2018. 'A Space for Caesar: The Heart of Rome and Urban Development', in R. Raja and S. M. Sindbæk (eds), *Urban Network Evolutions: Towards a High-Definition Archaeology* (Aarhus: Aarhus University Press), pp. 45–50.

Gruen, E. S. 2008. 'Caesar as a Politician', in M. T. Griffin (ed.), *A Companion to Julius Caesar* (Chichester: Wiley-Blackwell).

Hass, T. A. and R. Raja (eds). 2021. *Caesar's Past and Posterity's Caesar*, Rome Studies, 1 (Turnhout: Brepols).

Jacobsen, J. K. and R. Raja. 2018. 'A High-Definition Approach to the Forum of Caesar in Rome: Urban Archaeology in a Living City', in R. Raja and S. M. Sindbæk (eds), *Urban Network Evolutions: Towards a High-Definition Archaeology* (Aarhus: Aarhus University Press), pp. 21–25.

Jacobsen, J. K. and others. 2019–2020. 'Excavating Caesar's Forum: Present Results of the Caesar's Forum Project', *Analecta Romana Instituti Danici*, 44: 239–45.

—— 2020. 'Practicing Urban Archaeology in a Modern City: The Alessandrino Quarter of Rome', *Journal of Field Archaeology*, 46: 36–51.

—— 2021. 'High-Definition Urban Narratives from Central Rome: Virtual Reconstructions of the Past and the New Caesar's Forum Excavations', *Journal of Urban Archaeology*, 3: 65–86.

—— 2022. 'Digging Caesar's Forum: Three Thousand Years of Daily Life in Rome', *Current World Archaeology*, 113: 32–39.

Raja, R. and J. Rüpke. 2021. 'Creating Memories in and of Urban Rome. The Forum Iulium', in T. A. Hass and R. Raja (eds), *Caesar's Past and Posterity's Caesar*, Rome Studies, 1 (Turnhout: Brepols), pp. 53–66.

Sauer, N. 2018. 'The Archaic Period on the Forum of Caesar: The Urbanisation of Early Rome', in R. Raja and S. M. Sindbæk (eds), *Urban Network Evolutions: Towards a High-Definition Archaeology* (Aarhus: Aarhus University Press), pp. 39–44.

—— 2020–2022. 'The Forum of Caesar: A Historiographical Review', in T. A. Hass and R. Raja (eds), *Caesar's Past and Posterity's Caesar* (Turnhout: Brepols), pp. 213–41.

—— 2021. 'Looking for Domestic Architecture in Archaic Rome', *Analecta Romana Instituti Danici*, 45: 7–41.

Saxkjær, S. G. and G. P. Mittica. 2018. 'Caesar's Forum: Excavating Italian Iron Age', in R. Raja and S. M. Sindbæk (eds), *Urban Network Evolutions: Towards a High-Definition Archaeology* (Aarhus: Aarhus University Press), pp. 35–38.

CAESAR AND ROME

2. Sensing Change: Late Republican Architecture in Rome

Penelope J. E. Davies

Department of Art and Art History, The University of Texas at Austin
(pjedavies@austin.utexas.edu)

Old Approaches, New Approaches

Like most classicists, scholars of Late Republican architecture are collectors of materials and methods. Mining *in situ* remains, as well as epigraphy, numismatics, and literary sources, archaeologists determine forms and phasing of individual buildings, such as Pompey's Theatre-Portico Complex or the Forum Iulium, and also function, as with the concrete structure between the Tiber and the Aventine once thought to be the Porticus Aemilia, and recently re-identified (albeit controversially) as a ship-shed or *navalia*.[6] Architectural historians, probing the poetics of form, explore experiences of buildings, and cultural understandings of those experiences (as with the late second-century BC phase of the Sanctuary of Magna Mater).[7] Their analyses of political, social, and imperialistic factors approach the evolution of Rome and its buildings in diverse ways: by city region, or as reflections of a Republic failing, or as precocious precursors to grand projects of Imperial times.[8] Space is investigated as public, private, or both.[9] Sponsorship, too, is at issue: unlike later emperors, Republicans could not commission at will, but only as elected magistrates.[10] Implicit in some of these approaches is the notion of architecture's agency, an understanding that buildings were a contributing force in the Republic's evolution. Vast monuments of the Late Republic, for instance, gave sponsors presence, and with it, dangerous authority.[11] Also implicit is the notion of material agency: just as the development of concrete around the mid-second century BC freed architects to dream beyond the confines of post and lintel construction (the sweeping curves of the *navalia*'s vaults, the yawning arches of the Capitoline Via Tecta, the rounded *cavea* of Pompey's Theatre, and the apse of the crowning Temple of Venus Victrix), so it neutralized long-standing constraints on sponsoring magistrates — time and money — enabling a man like Pompey to build on a scale infeasible for earlier magistrates, and intimating that he operated outside of existing norms.[12]

More could be done on agency: for instance, concrete lent itself to revetment, and in this much fed a burgeoning interest in marble and coloured stone from beyond Rome and Italy; it may have helped to move coloured stones and the *luxuria* they signified out of residential architecture into the public realm, blurring lines between state and individual.[13] Investigations could also expand into broader considerations of the Late Republican object-scape.[14] Exceptionality in architecture — Pompey's astonishing self-supporting theatre, the fantasy theatres of Marcus Scribonius Curio, the Saepta Iulia's mile-long porticoes — sustained a climate of exceptionalism in politics, matching and reifying the extraordinary commands that allowed Pompey and Julius Caesar to circumvent regulations on magistracies. And if innovative forms and materials, together, could challenge the limits of the known, as Miguel John Versluys puts it, and introduce novel questions, perspectives, even practices, then sweeping change in what had been relatively conservative standards in building typology, form, material, and sponsorship, might have had consequences of its own: the very change that thrilled some may for others have been destabilizing, instilling

---

[6] For the Theatre-Complex of Pompey, see most recently Packer 2013. On the Forum Iulium, see Delfino 2014; Kindberg Jacobsen and Raja 2018. On the *navalia*, see Cozza and Tucci 2006; Tucci 2012 contra Arata and Felice 2011.

[7] MacDonald 1982; Pensabene and D'Alessio 2006.

[8] Coarelli 1983; 1985; 1988; 1997; 2012; 2014; Torelli 2006; 2007.

[9] Russell 2016.

[10] Davies 2017a. Even Steinby 2012, who argues that magistrates built at the Senate's pleasure, acknowledges change in the first century BC, when the Senate was transformed from the principal decision maker to a body that merely granted its consent.

[11] On Republican architecture and agency, see Davies (forthcoming).

---

[12] Davies 2017a; 2017b. On concrete's dating, see Mogetta 2021. Also MacDonald 1982; Van Oyen 2017 (with a different dating for concrete).

[13] On the ancient discourse on marble and *luxuria*, see Carey 2003, 91–92.

[14] Hodder 1979; 1982; Gosden 2005; Versluys 2017.

fear and a sense of loss of control. Such, scholars contend, was the case in Revolutionary Paris, where a fast-changing cityscape provided a measure of freedom but also insecurity, underscoring the inevitability of change itself. In the face of rapid globalization in the 1960s, destabilization of this kind provoked varied responses; instincts for re-tribalization, nostalgia, escapism, spiritual return, a search for 'roots' — and acceptance of a more surveyed environment, of precisely the kind that would develop in the age of Augustus. Much, indeed, has been written recently on the link between fear of change and tolerance of authority from extraordinary sources.[15]

This essay forms a tangent to such investigations. Borrowing from studies of embodied cognition, which acknowledge that much of what and how people think is shaped by inhabiting a human body, it explores, first, a perceptible increase in scale in Late Republican temples, from the perspective of what is sometimes described as the sixth sense — body awareness, or proprioception — while also inserting it into a broader cultural continuum. And second, taking a cue from the sensory turn, it investigates a heightened manipulation of sensory stimulation by the political elite, the complex build-up, as it will turn out, to the exploitation of spectacle entertainments by emperors of later years to gain the people's acquiescence.[16]

Beyond Human Scale: Radical Re-dimensioning

During the Late Republic, public architecture in Rome was radically re-dimensioned. Such is the amplification of scale, in fact, that many buildings erected in the decades before Caesar's assassination in 44 BC have more in common, in terms of size, with those erected under an Imperial government than with their Republican antecedents. This is evident in monuments such as the *navalia* or the so-called *tabularium* (the concrete *substructio* or substructure set into the saddle between the Capitoline and the Arx in 78 BC), but it is also true of a type of building (the most common type) that tends to be treated as a monolithic category: temples. Beginning with the Temple of Concordia in 121 BC, some were sufficiently grander than temples of previous decades that the shift begs explanation; and while that shift is often associated with the development of concrete, concrete

may explain what made larger scale suddenly possible, but fails to elucidate what that scale signified.

Studies in cognitive psychology show that, on the whole, humans are aware of monumentality, measured proprioceptively (or in relation to an innate sense of the scale of the body, mediated by proprioceptors, mechanosensory neurons in muscles, tendons, and joints). These studies also show that powerfully, subconsciously, monumentality signifies authority: as Sarah Goldhagen puts it, substance means weight; grand spaces engender awe.[17] In prehistoric cultures, Richard Bradley and others note that formative periods are often characterized by phases of monumentalization, with public buildings serving as metaphors for patterns of social behaviour; and monumentalization was also part of the process by which ancient institutions acquired and maintained power.[18] Throughout history, in fact, resources being available, governments of diverse cultures have erected — or, like Albert Speer on behalf of Adolph Hitler during the Third Reich, have aspired to erect — imposing buildings in hopes of effecting lasting power.[19]

And yet to this kind of subconscious response can be added a layer of cultural freighting. As Joy Monice Malnar and Frank Vodvarka put it, 'it is sensation–mediated by experience and culture–that shapes our response to spaces.'[20] In Greece, for instance, Edmund Thomas argues that from the fourth century BC, royal patrons deployed grand scale not only as an expression of power, but also to manifest moral values of 'magnificence' and 'greatness of spirit'.[21] In Late Republican Rome, monumental scale was not only innately authoritative, but encoded with a particular brand of authority.

In the age of the Gracchi (133–121 BC), there were, give or take, about seventy temples in the city. Of these, the largest, a mere handful, dated back to the earliest Republic, a couple more to the Regal period. The grandest, the Capitoline Temple of Jupiter Optimus Maximus, built over the course of the sixth century and dedicated as the first temple of the Republic, probably measured an astounding 54 by 74 m (Fig. 2.1, top row); less massive, the Temple of Castor and Pollux in the forum, of c. 496 BC, was nevertheless approximately 27.50 m wide on a podium roughly 5 m high; the nearby

---

15 Ellin 1997.

16 Pallasmaa 2012. On the emperors and the *ludi*, see e.g. Veyne 1976; Toner 2014, 16.

---

17 Goldhagen 2017, 55, 76, 113–14.

18 Bradley 2001; Thomas 2008, 5.

19 Goldhagen 2017, 76, 124.

20 Malnar and Vodvarka 2004, 59.

21 Thomas 2008, 20.

2. SENSING CHANGE: LATE REPUBLICAN ARCHITECTURE IN ROME

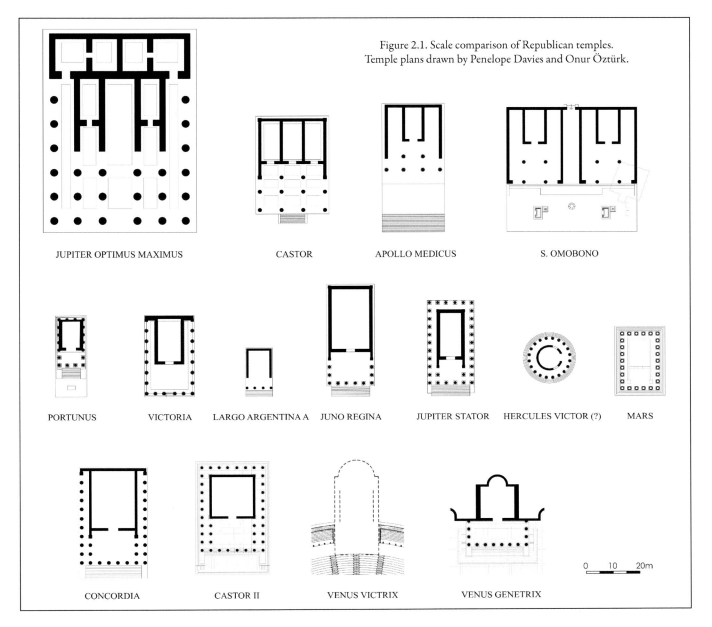

Figure 2.1. Scale comparison of Republican temples. Temple plans drawn by Penelope Davies and Onur Öztürk.

Temple of Saturn was similarly scaled. The Temple of Apollo Medicus of c. 431 BC, on the edge of the Forum Boarium, and twin temples at S. Omobono (mid-fifth century BC, perhaps) sit at the small end of this range, at roughly 21.45 and 20.5 m wide, respectively.[22] Set in the principal religious, political, or commercial zones, these early, monumental temples were typically vowed and dedicated by patrician dictators in the context of civic and military crises, and as well as housing cult statues, they served state functions: meetings of the Senate or the consuls (the Temples of Jupiter Optimus Maximus, Apollo, and Castor and Pollux) and the state treasury (the Temple of Saturn).[23]

The great majority of temples in the late second-century cityscape, though, were built after the end of the fourth century BC (Fig. 2.1, middle row). Archaeological evidence survives only for a sample of them. However, they seem to have been consistently smaller, typically measuring only 10 to 20 m across the façade: thus, the Temple of Portunus (late fourth/early third century BC, roughly 11 by 20 m), Temple A at Largo Argentina

---

[22] For bibliography and measurements, see Hopkins 2016; Davies 2017a. Pre-Augustan dimensions of the Temple of Bellona of c. 296 BC (at the cusp of change) are unknown, but the temple may have been of grand scale; sources record meetings of the Senate in its cella.

[23] Davies 2017a.

(*c.* 241 BC, approximately 9.50 by 16 m), and so on. The shift in scale from earlier temples probably corresponds to a move from wooden to stone entablatures, which, requiring narrower intercolumniations, perhaps, by extension, encouraged smaller overall dimensions.[24] But there was also functional change. Vowed and dedicated by (usually) consuls in the context of battle, many of them on the triumphal route, these were votive buildings; their principal role, besides housing a cult statue, was to serve as monuments to individuals and families of the expanded *nobilitas*, once wealthy plebeians had gained access to patrician privilege.[25]

By the second half of the second century BC, there were two types of temples in the cityscape, distinct in terms of date, materials, sponsorship, function, and, most perceptibly, size. The conservative consul Lucius Opimius inserted the Temple of Concordia into this cityscape to celebrate the *optimates*' violent suppression of the 'populist' Gracchans (Fig. 2.1, bottom row). The first temple sited in the forum since Archaic times, it measured an astonishing 30 by 40.80 m at the base of a 4 m high podium, and proximity to a diminutive shrine to Concordia set up as a plebeian protest by Gnaeus Flavius, aedile in 304 BC, further exaggerated these dimensions.[26] Sensed bodily, scale was no doubt deployed to impress; but so decisive was the break with nearly two centuries of built tradition, and so clearly did this new scale evoke the scale of Archaic temples (two of them standing nearby), that it was also probably encoded to oppress: to evoke the authority of the early state — a state, that is, before, as *optimates* probably saw it, plebeian access to patrician privilege opened the door to the populist tactics the Gracchi deployed. As if to reify the strategy, within five years, Lucius Caecilius Metellus Delmaticus, or his brother Lucius Caecilius Metellus Diadematus, both figureheads of the Senate's conservative faction, sponsored an aggressive, systemic re-conception of the Archaic Temple of Castor across the forum, in travertine with a pycnostyle arrangement of Corinthian columns, to harmonize with the Temple of Concordia (Fig. 2.2).[27] With these temples, one newly founded, the other restored, scale reasserted conservative authority and characterized it as synonymous with the state's 'proper' functioning; the *optimates* claimed the

sanction of the Archaic state, the *mos maiorum*, and cast themselves as defenders of this state in its purest form.

In short order, two more temples were conceived on a different kind of monumental scale, achieved by engulfing them in large hilltop sanctuaries. After a fire in 111 BC, another Caecilius Metellus (Gaius Caecilius Metellus Caprarius, consul in 113 BC and triumphator in 111 BC, or Quintus Caecilius Metellus Numidicus, consul of 109 BC) undertook a thorough restoration of the Temple of Magna Mater on the south-west corner of the Palatine, with vast concrete surroundings (Figs 2.4 and 2.5);[28] and on the saddle between the *area Capitolina* and the Arx, Quintus Lutatius Catulus, a Sullan (conservative) partisan, erected the huge *substructio* to support a temple (to Juno Moneta, maybe), or even three temples (Figs 2.6 and 2.7).[29] On Rome's most hallowed hills, scale buttressed and reasserted a conservative ideal of state authority.

This, in turn, was the backdrop for Pompey and Caesar. Begun around 61 BC, dedicated in 55 BC, Pompey's Theatre-Portico Complex surpassed all existing buildings in footprint and height (approximately 33.950 m^2, and about 45 m high, the altitude of the Arx).[30] Atop this man-made hill, the Temple of Venus Victrix loomed above viewers on the ground outside or seated in the *cavea*. Under construction from 54 BC, dedicated in 46 BC, Caesar's Temple of Venus Genetrix kept pace, at approximately 30 m across the front.[31] In isolation, these dimensions clearly — but also merely — impressed the proprioceptive sense and thereby exerted authority. And yet, set against the scale continuum outlined above, they did something more: though both men were populists in their own way, Pompey and Caesar appropriated a language of scale tightly associated with conservative senatorial authority. This implied conservative sanction for what was, in fact, a very different kind of authority, based not in Archaic tradition but in precariously granted extraordinary mandates that encouraged individualism — and the very autocracy with which great size would soon be equated.

A proprioceptive sense of architecture's scale, then, may have helped to mischaracterize Pompey's and Caesar's authority as traditionally Republican: patrons and observers alike identified excessively large scale not

---

[24] On the introduction of stone entablatures, see Davies 2012.

[25] Davies 2017a; Padilla Peralta 2020, 31–78.

[26] Levick 1978; *LTUR* I, 316–20, s.v. Concordia, Aedes (A. M. Ferroni); Davies 2017a, 155–59.

[27] Nielsen and Poulsen 1992; Davies 2017a, 160–61.

[28] Pensabene and D'Alessio 2006; Davies 2017a, 161–65.

[29] Tucci 2005; 2014; Coarelli 2010; Davies 2017a, 192–93 and 196–99.

[30] Packer 2013; Davies 2017a, 212–20 and 229–34.

[31] Liverani 2008, 48; Davies 2017a, 247–52.

2. SENSING CHANGE: LATE REPUBLICAN ARCHITECTURE IN ROME

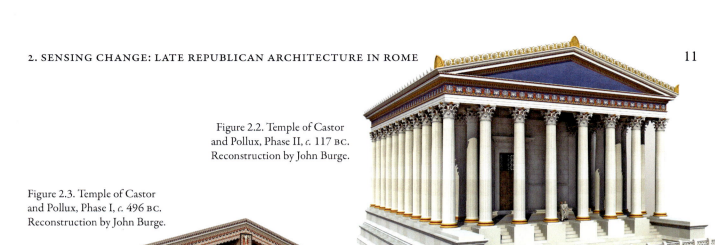

Figure 2.2. Temple of Castor and Pollux, Phase II, *c.* 117 BC. Reconstruction by John Burge.

Figure 2.3. Temple of Castor and Pollux, Phase I, *c.* 496 BC. Reconstruction by John Burge.

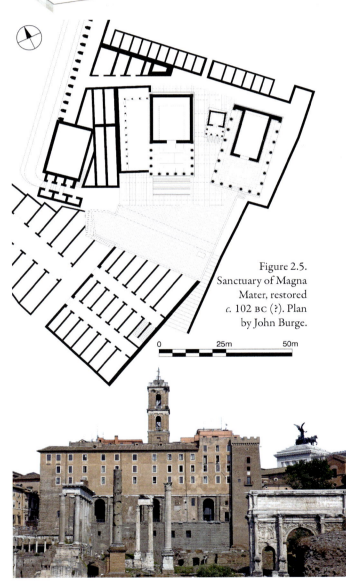

Figure 2.5. Sanctuary of Magna Mater, restored *c.* 102 BC (?). Plan by John Burge.

Figure 2.4. Sanctuary of Magna Mater, restored *c.* 102 BC (?). Reconstruction by John Burge.

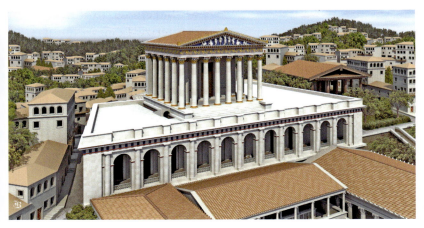

Figure 2.6. *Substructio* on the Capitoline saddle, 78 BC, actual state. Photo: Penelope Davies.

Figure 2.7 (left). *Substructio* and temples on the Capitoline saddle, 78 BC. Hypothetical reconstruction by John Burge.

just with a blanket authority, but with a particular type of authority originating in the Archaic period and patrician domination, and later claimed by senatorial conservatives. They need not have recognized this connection consciously or processed it logically; perhaps it is more realistic to suppose that for many, it worked on an unconscious and associative level. But when revived in the late second century and following, it is yet one more way, one among many, in which architecture played powerfully into the political struggles of the Late Republic.

A Fullness of Senses

Sensory Benefaction

Modern imaginings of ancient Rome have long privileged the sense of sight for reasons reaching back through time to Aristotle. Surviving evidence, too, allows readier reconstructions of the city's appearance than of its sound, smell, feel, or taste.[32] This poorly reflects ancient perceptions of the world. The sensory turns of recent years emphasize the synaesthetic nature of ancient perception instead, the senses neither sharply defined nor separate, but co-mingled — mutual stimulants that made for a richly textured experience of the world; colour, for instance, was not only seen, but felt, tasted, and smelt.[33] Recent evocations of this complex sensorium furnish a fuller impression of Rome and its diverse regions and expose the role of the senses in helping people navigate the city.[34] But Romans were more than simply passive reactors to random sensory stimuli: they could also be savvy manipulators of sensory experience, as the rest of this paper explores.

Ancient Mediterranean cities were not the constantly cleansed, odourless utopias of Enlightenment ideals. Rome, like other cities, was a place of intense and evolving sensation, contained and stimulated by the built environment.[35] From early days, public spaces were enlivened by the painted fictile ornaments of temples, and their varied building textures — wood, tuff, terracotta, and stucco (Fig. 2.3). On occasion, the sounds and scents of ritual and entertainment wafted through the air with a divine caress: coals of incense doused with wine, scented flowers, smoke and burning flesh.[36] The *vici* were likely different. Long before the riot of sensory titillation in Imperial times, conjured by Juvenal and Martial, the *vici* were probably drearier than public spaces and more challenging to the senses. The sweet aromas of bakeries, taverns, and street vendors' carts probably struggled to prevail over other pungent odours of quotidian life: garbage, unceremoniously dumped, clogged sewers, excrement, animal carcasses, bodies of the poor; the tang of industries — tile factories, potteries, tanneries, and fullers; smoke and ash and the smell of human flesh from extra-urban funerary pyres, inhaled onto the tongue.[37] Uncontrolled, temperatures rose and fell with the seasons, chilling the bones with cold and damp or coating the skin with a clammy veil of salty sweat. Noise came from all directions: an endless echo of construction and industry, wagons and draft animals, vendors peddling wares, heated arguments, casual conversation, children at play.[38] In the narrow streets, a dearth of personal space meant the constant touch of strangers, worsening as the population grew — not the healing touch of the holy man, but the coarsening touch of the ordinary.[39] Unhindered, noise and smell penetrated into dark, cramped living quarters through glass-less windows; crowded together after long hours of labour, bodies grew rank, since bathing, a privilege of the better off, was rare.[40] Indeed, exposure to, and an ability to control, a ceaseless stream of unsolicited sensation depended on social status. The moneyed few kept crowds at bay, moving through the city in carriages and litters holding perfumed cloth to their noses or retreating into private residences in Rome or in the country.[41] For most, home offered little respite from habitual sensory chaos. As

---

[32] Howes 2006; Hamilakis 2013.

[33] Bradley 2014; Butler and Purves 2014; Toner 2014, 1–4; also Zardini 2006, 301.

[34] e.g. Koloski-Ostrow 2015; Laurence 2017. On the ancient senses, see Butler and Purves 2014; Bradley 2015a; 2015b; Purves 2018; Rudolph 2018; Butler and Nooter 2019.

[35] Toner 2014; also Zardini 2006, 21.

---

[36] Toner 2014, 8; also Nuño and others 2021; and Clements 2015 on smell and the divine in the Greek world.

[37] Aldrete 2014, 46–53, who estimates 1500 bodies of the poor annually, and 90–150 corpses a day; also 350,000 gallons of human urine and 100,000 pounds of faeces a day; Toner 2014, 6; Bradley 2015b; Koloski-Ostrow 2015; Morley 2015.

[38] Aldrete 2014, 53–55; Laurence 2017, 14–21. On sound and built space in the Late Republic: Holter, Muth, and Schwesinger 2019.

[39] On touch, see Toner 2014, 10; Lennon 2018.

[40] Bradley 2015b; Zardini 2006, 202: though there was no glass in windows until the first century AD, shutters may have muffled some sound.

[41] Juv. III.239–48; Aldrete 2014, 52, 61; Toner 2014, 6–7, 11; Laurence 2017, 17.

Jerry Toner puts it, the senses helped establish and maintain boundaries between social groups.[42]

For society at all levels, the most positive invigorating sensory experiences probably came during religious festivals and triumphs, and these experiences intensified on the heels of conquest. According to the Roman historian Florus, the triumph of Manius Curius Dentatus in 275 BC was a game-changer:

> Ante hunc diem nihil praeter pecora Vulscorum, greges Sabinorum, carpenta Gallorum, fracta Samnitium arma vidisses: tum si captivos aspiceres, Molossi, Thessali, Macedones, Bruttius, Apulus atque Lucanus; si pompam, aurum, purpura, signa tabulae Tarentinaeque deliciae. Sed nihil libentius populus Romanus aspexit quam illas, quam timuerat cum turribus suis beluas, quae non sine sensu captivitatis summissis cervicibus victors equos sequebantur.

> (Up to that time the only spoils you could have seen were the cattle of the Volscians, the flocks of the Sabines, the wagons of the Gauls, the broken arms of the Samnites; now if you looked at captives, they were Molossians, Thessalians, Macedonians, Bruttians, Apulians and Lucanians; if you looked upon the procession, you saw gold, purple, statues, pictures and all the luxury of Tarentum. But upon nothing did the Roman people look with greater pleasure than upon those huge beasts, which they had feared so much.)[43]

So too was the Second Punic War, when scenic games abounded to placate a war-worn people as much as the gods. And as expansion spread into the broader Mediterranean in the first half of the second century BC, the novel sights, sounds, and smells of captive people and animals were matched by the rich new textures of looted ivory tusks, luxury furniture, glistening gems, tapestries in vivid hues, enticing aromas of foreign spices, and titillating tastes conjured by captured cooks.[44] With the introduction of such luxuries, the divide between the haves and the have-nots of sensory delight widened to a chasm. For the wealthy, pillaged luxuries, sold at auction, became available for private indulgence in homes that grew more lavish by the decade, alongside a growing abundance of imported goods (evoking accusations of *luxuria* and immorality);[45] but for most, public festivals, endowed by magistrates acting for the state, afforded the greatest sensory delights, temporary relief from at best a neutral, at worst a negative daily sensorium. The gift of positive sensory experience — which might be termed sensory benefaction — became a useful means of social control by the political elite, and for individuals within that group, sensory benefaction became a compelling means of self-advancement. As early as Marcus Claudius Marcellus, who in his ovation of 211 BC, during the Second Punic War, introduced the Roman people to the haptic delights of Greek sculpture, elite suspicion characterized individuals who furnished the people with extreme sensory delights — sensational delights — as demagogues.[46]

Recognizing an appetite for positive sensory stimulation, magistrates integrated sensory benefaction into the more permanent medium of architecture. Experienced proprioceptively, forms multiplied: the welcoming curves of arches, vaults, and circular temples. Decorative novelties — paintings and sculpture — intrigued the eye and body.[47] New materials — marble, gilt — invited the hand's caress, the tongue's imagined tasting, while aqueducts brought cool water to dance in the mouth and quench the thirst.[48] Amplified sound charmed the ear — bronze *dolia* in Mummius's Temple of Luna, pillaged from the theatre in Corinth in 146 BC.[49] Since only magistrates could commission public architecture, these sensory benefactions sustained social hierarchies. Yet such is architecture's power over the senses, such was the elite's collective suspicion of individuals who exploited it, and such, apparently, was the popular appreciation of sen-

---

[42] Toner 2014, 4–8; also Aldrete 2014, 58–63.

[43] Flor., *Epit.* I.13.26–7, translation by Forster; also I.13.18.6; Plut., *Pyrrh.* xv.1; Zon. VIII.2.7; Sen., *Ep.* XIII; Plin., *HN.* VIII.16–17.

[44] Ivory: Liv. XXXVII.59 (Cornelius Asiaticus, 189 BC). Furniture: Plin., *HN.* XXXIV.14; Liv. XXXIX.6.3–7.2 (Manlius Vulso, 186 BC). Tapestries: Liv. XLV.35.3, 40.1–5, 42.12; Pol. XXXVI.5.9; Plut., *Aem.* XXXII (Aemilius Paullus's triumph of 168 BC). See Pape 1975; Pietilä-Castrén 1982, 134–36; Dauster 2003; Östenberg 2009.

[45] Toner 2014, 8.

[46] Plut., *Marc.* XXI.1–5; Pape 1975, 95; Gros 1979, 103–05.

[47] e.g. the platform on the east side of the Palatine associated with the Temple of Fortuna Respiciens (Ferrea 2002); the *navalia* (Cozza and Tucci 2006); the Round Temple by the Tiber, perhaps Lucius Mummius's Temple of Hercules Victor (Rakob and Heilmeyer 1973, 19–21, 23 (who date it to *c.* 100–90 BC); Ziółkowski 1988, 315–16; Stamper 2005, 72). Paintings: Coarelli 1976; La Rocca 1984. Sculpture: Pensabene and d'Alessio 2006, 32.

[48] Materials: Plin., *HN.* XXXIII.57, XXXVI.185; Vell. Pat. I.11.2–5; Jackson and Marra 2006; Aqua Marcia: Frontin., *Aq.* II.7; Cornell 2014, 2 947, F12; Hodge 1992; Evans 1994.

[49] *Dolia*: Pape 1975, 45; Pietilä-Castrén 1991, 103–05; Lippolis 2004, 40; Cadario 2014, 85–86. Liv. XLVIII; App., *B Civ.* I.28.12; Val. Max. II.4.2; Aug., *Civ.* I.32; Oros. IV.21.4; Vell. Pat. I.15.2. On stone theatres and acoustics, see Vitr., *De arch.* v.5.7.

sory benefaction, that it also demanded control. When the censors of 154 BC let a contract for Rome's first stone theatre on the south-west slope of the Palatine, a promise of well-honed acoustics and year-round visual delectation, Publius Cornelius Scipio Nasica persuaded the Senate to demolish it. Assessments of his rationale focus on the platform it would have offered the censors, to frame their status before the seated public as monarchs and *strategoi* did in Greek theatres, and on fears that the comfort of seats and efficient acoustics might encourage Romans to assemble of their own volition and debate — and thus exploit sensory architecture to challenge the very social hierarchies that earlier forms of audience segregation had aimed to enforce.[50]

Late Republican Architecture and Sensory Benefaction

Such was the backdrop to the Late Republic when the intersection of architecture and sensory experience tightened, and these fledgling issues — social control, 'demagogic' behaviour, and popular usurpation of sensory benefaction — reached maturation. For senatorial conservatives, the goal at first seems to have been less to keep their own in check than to assert a collective monopoly over sensory benefaction to maintain social control. This is apparent at the Sanctuary of Magna Mater, as restored in the years after the suppression of the Gracchans. Exceptionally among Roman cults, that of Magna Mater, a favourite with the non-elite, stood at the far edge of elite self-identity: though integrated into state religion and heavily Romanized, the goddess's foreign origins, Cicero insists, were never forgotten, and modelled on Adonis, her priests, the self-castrated *Galli*, were the very antithesis of Roman manhood.[51] Permeated with otherness, rituals in her honour were a riotous assault on the senses. Metroac festivals witnessed public grief and weeping, self-flagellation, even self-castration, along with delirious displays of exhilaration and ecstasy; and during the Megalesia, *Galli* paraded in robes of luscious yellow, to the sound of tympana, cymbals, flutes, and horns, filling the air to a foreign

Phrygian meter. Visually arresting in their crested helmets, *Corybantes* leapt and reeled in their dance, shaking their heads, clashing their armour loudly; crowds of adherents scattered the path with sweet-smelling roses.[52] This multi-sensorium transformed the hallowed Palatine into the people's realm, the gift not of the political elite but of the very epitome of the non-Roman. This ritual protest called for containment, which, in some measure, architecture could provide. A tunnel-like Via Tecta or covered road built into the vast concrete platform in front of the temple (Figs 2.4 and 2.5)[53] ensured that as the procession from the Circus Maximus neared the climax of its journey, it was cast into sudden darkness, cool and dank, removed from visual and aural perception at the most perceptible spot on its path, its explosive energy stilled. As a counterpoint, moreover, just a few decades later, in the wake of civil war and Sulla's brutal dictatorship, an analogous structure showcased the ideals of senatorial conservatives. Running through the Capitoline substructure, a second Via Tecta presented huge arches toward the forum (Figs 2.6, 2.7, and 2.8), and in a multisensory, state-endowed performance with roots in a long tradition, framed state officials as they performed 'proper' social hierarchy: pontiffs and augurs processing in regalia between functions at the Arx and the Capitol, and triumphal processions on the final leg of their journey, with finely clad officiants, dancers, flautists, actors, torch- and incense-bearers, sacrificial animals, the Senate, and the army.[54]

If, during the last decade of the second century and first half of the first, sensory benefaction remained a prerogative of the political elite as a body, deployed to maintain status and authority over those with fewer resources for private luxury, within that body, competitive stimulation began a steady climb. The most obvious

---

[50] Von Hesberg 1999; Frézouls 1983, 195–97; Sordi 1988, 327–41; Gruen 1992, 205–22; Forsythe 1994; Gros 1994, 293–94; Dauster 2003, 70; Wallace-Hadrill 2008, 160–69; Davies 2017a, 141–43.

[51] Dion. Hal., *Ant. Rom.* II.19.3–5 (after 23); Cic., *Har. resp.* XXI–XXII; Ov., *Fast.* IV; also Pol., *Hist.* XXI.37.4–6; Serv., *Georg.* II. 394; Roller 1999, 283; Bremmer 2005, 33–41; Latham 2007, 187–88. Obs. 44a.

[52] Lucr. II. 601–43; Dion. Hal., *Ant. Rom.* II.19.2–5; Gell., *NA* II.24.2; *CIL* I.1, 234; Cic., *de senec.* XIII.45; Liv. XXXVII.9.9, 18.9–10; Diod. Sic. XXXVI.13; Val. Max. VII.7.6; also Pol., *Hist.* XXI.37.4–6; Ov., *Fast.* IV. Cumont 1911, 56–57; Graillot 1912; Morgan 1973, 235–36; Roller 1999, 283; Pensabene and D'Alessio 2006, 46–47; Toner 2014, 8; Latham 2016, 165–68. Takács 1996, 374, believes the cult was only orgiastic in Pessinus. Nauta 2005, 110, argues that the cult's orgiastic aspects were not on public display in the festival processions in Rome.

[53] Pensabene and D'Alessio 2006; Davies 2017a, 162–65. On ritual protest, see Low 2000, 184.

[54] Delbrück 1907–1912; Tucci 2005; Davies 2017a, 196–98. For processions and triumphs, see Versnel 1970; Brilliant 1999; Beacham 1999, 40–43; Beard 2009; Bastien 2007; La Rocca 2008; Latham 2016.

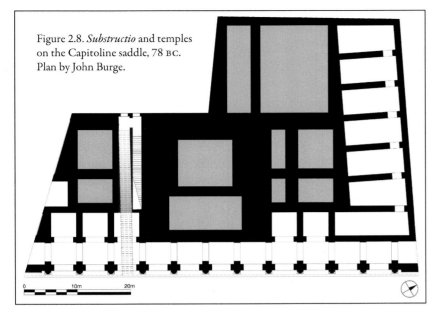

Figure 2.8. *Substructio* and temples on the Capitoline saddle, 78 BC. Plan by John Burge.

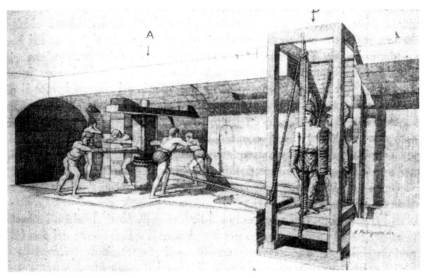

Figure 2.9. Galleries under the forum pavement, 78–74 BC (?). Reconstruction from Carettoni 1956–1958, fig. 13.

outlets were state entertainments and privately endowed gladiatorial games, which offered more than simply visual delights. With animal and human combat came the vivid red smell and iron taste of blood, and pain or triumph experienced empathetically. Animals, from further and further afield and in astounding numbers, dizzied the crowds with their visual, aural, and olfactory diversity: canine hunts and fights with one hundred Libyan lions in Sulla's games of 98 BC paled in comparison with Marcus Aemilius Scaurus's games only fifty years later, featuring 150 Syrian leopards and panthers, five crocodiles in a custom-built pool, Rome's first hippopotamus, and a gigantic set of bones ascribed to Cetus, the sea-monster of Andromeda's myth.[55] For this sensory exuberance, architecture became a more obvious and vital framework to contain animals and audiences alike. Special effects sky-rocketed, and venues were fitted out with materials of escalating haptic appeal and value. The first of their kind in Rome, columns of cool grey-blue Hymettian marble probably furnished a temporary theatre during Lucius Licinius Crassus's aedileship between 105 and 103 BC.[56] For respite from driving rain or searing sun on the skin, by the 70s audiences were provided with awnings of cotton or fine linen;[57] stages were sheathed with creamy ivory, glittering silver, lustrous gold, and outfitted with silver props.[58] Artworks enriched the people's sensory wealth — as when Gaius Claudius Pulcher borrowed a Praxitelean sculpture of Eros from his friend Heius in Messana to embellish the forum for aedilician games in 99 BC, and Aemilius Scaurus bought all the publicly owned paintings of Sikyon as a gift for Rome.[59] Art was even deployed to titillate the senses with trickery: Aemilius Scaurus commissioned a *scaena* with such masterful *trompe l'oeil* paintings of architecture that crows flew into the roof tiles.[60]

By the 50s BC, the decade of Pompey's Complex, the marriage of architectural and sensory benefaction was fully realized,

---

[55] Sulla's games: Plut., *Sull.* v.1; Plin., *HN* VIII.53; Sen., *Dial.* x.13.6; Keaveney 2005, 28–30. Aemilius Scaurus's games: Plin., *HN* XXXV.127; Medri 1997, 85.

[56] Plin., *HN* XXXVI.5–8, mentions them immediately after describing the columns Aemilius Scaurus moved from his theatre to his Palatine house in 58 BC. Klar 2006, 172, 182 n. 41.

[57] Lutatius Catulus: Val. Max. II.4.6; Amm. Marc. XIV.6.25; Plin., *HN* XIX.23. Liv. XCVIII places the dedication in 69. Lentulus Spinther: Val. Max. II.4.6.

[58] Ivory: Lutatius Catulus: Val. Max. II.4.6; Amm. Marc. XIV.6.25; Plin., *HN* XIX.23. Liv. XCVIII. Silver: C. Antonius (Hybrida?), consul in 63 BC. Gold: Petreius, perhaps the praetor of 64 BC. Silver props: Publius Lentulus Spinther, aedile in 63 BC. Val. Max. II.4.6; Beacham 1999, 13.

[59] Plin., *HN* XXXV.127; Medri 1997, 85.

[60] Cic., *Verr.* II.4.3; Plin., *HN* XXXV.23; Pape 1975, 49–51, 198.

Figure 2.10. Theatres of M. Scribonius Curio, 53 BC. Hypothetical reconstruction by Onur Öztürk.

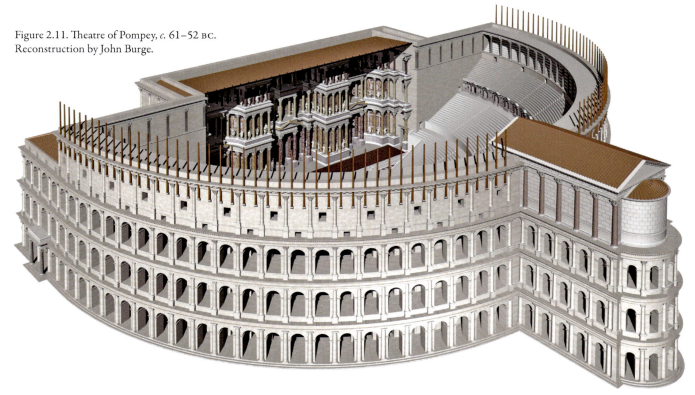

Figure 2.11. Theatre of Pompey, c. 61–52 BC. Reconstruction by John Burge.

and the competition was on to explode this exuberance into mind-blowing hyperbole. For Pliny, two structures stood out. Aemilius Scaurus's theatre of 58 BC, 'the greatest of all the works ever made by man', was a marvel of material and visual texture: the *scaena*'s lowest level was marble, a second glass, and a third gilded wood. There were scene paintings, 360 columns, three thousand bronze statues, and cloths of gold.[61] But it was left to Scribonius Curio's ingenuity in 53 BC to offer a fully haptic experience during games for his late father (Fig. 2.10):

Theatra iuxta duo fecit amplissima ligno, cardinum singulorum versatili suspensa libramento, in quibus utrisque antemeridiano ludorum spectaculo edito inter sese aversis, ne invicem obstreperent scaenae, repente circumactis — ut constat, post primos dies etiam sedentibus aliquis —, cornibus in se coeuntibus faciebat ampitheatrum gladiatorumque proelia edebat, ipsum magis auctoritatum populum Romanum circumferens.

(He built close to each other two very large wooden theatres, each poised and balanced on a revolving pivot. During the forenoon, a performance of a play was given in both of them and they faced in opposite directions so that the two casts should not drown each other's words. Then all of a sudden the theatres revolved (and it is agreed that after the first few days they did so with some of the spectators actually remaining in their seats), their corners

---

[61] Plin., *HN* XXXVI.5–6, 50, 114–15, 189, translation by Rackham. Cic., *Sest.* CXVI; Medri 1997, 100. The estimated capacity of its wooden *cavea* is eighty thousand.

met, and thus Curio provided an amphitheatre in which he produced fights between gladiators, though they were less at risk than the Roman people itself as it was whirled around by Curio.)[62]

Combining the spectacles of theatre and amphitheatre, Curio added the whole-body experience of riding his contraption as it moved. The draw was irresistible: as Pliny declares, 'the entire Roman people' flocked to the experience. To him, Curio's political motive was evident:

> et per hoc quaeritur tribuniciis contionibus gratia, ut pensiles tribus quatiat, in rostris quid non ausurus apud eos, quibus hoc persuaserit!

> (To win favour for the speeches [he] would make as a tribune, so he might continue to agitate the swaying voters, since on the speakers' platform he would shrink from nothing in addressing men whom he had persuaded to submit to such treatment.)[63]

The Final Showdown: Pompey and Caesar

Pompey's Theatre Complex, a self-supporting miracle of concrete engineering, complete with the city's first public garden in a vast portico, was an orgy of sensory exuberance. Within the vast *cavea*, with seating for forty thousand (Figs 2.11 and 2.12), as entertainments fed the eye and ear, water flowed in channels to sooth the skin from the summer heat.[64] A multitude of sculptures peopled the complex, a visual and tactile delight: Hercules twice, Apollo and the Muses, Victoria, a pair of Pans, fourteen Nations by Coponius, and a grand collection of 'marvels'; antique paintings and Attalid tapestries added to the richness.[65] The portico proffered plane trees, favoured for their shade, and probably plundered trees from Pompey's conquests,[66] while a fountain flowed from a sculpture of a drunken satyr: trickling water made music with the birdsong and the rustling leaves. In an aural haven from the city's din, in the garden's broken

spaces, voices could muffle, privacy was conceivable.[67] Cooled by the water and the shade, air settled softly on the skin, fresh from the trees' filtration, sweet with the scent of vegetation — like perfumed balsam from Judean royal gardens, a luxury of the few made public.[68] Texture abounded, titillating the touch through visual perception: the plane trees' dappled bark, leaves of every form and hue, light and shadow dancing on the breeze; the tapestries' golden thread, lifting the light as they swayed. A veritable banquet for the senses, in a paradise world.

This was the grand stage for opening ceremonies that were legend even before the fact; to quote Cicero:

> Instant post hominum memoriam apparatissimi magnificentissimique ludi, quales non modo numquam fuerunt, sed ne quo modo fieri quidem posthac possint possum ullo pacto suspicari.

> (The most carefully prepared and magnificent games within the memory of man are just at hand, games such as not only never have been exhibited, but such that we cannot form a conception how it will be possible for any like them ever to be exhibited for the future.)[69]

The city was bursting with sensory plenty: musical and gymnastic contests, a horse race and five days of wild beast hunts in the Circus, rare animals, some imported for the first time, others in record numbers: 500–600 lions, 410 leopards, and Rome's first rhinoceros; rare monkeys, lynx, vicious Gallic wolves, and, 'a most terrifying spectacle', a hunt with eighteen elephants. *Ludi scaenici* featured all the tongues of the *vici* — Latin, Greek, and Oscan — and inside the Theatre, props delighted the eye and ear: 'a train of 600 mules, [...] 3000 bowls, [... and] brightly-coloured infantry and cavalry armour' (sescenti muli [...] creterrarum tria milia, [...] armatura varia peditatus et equitatus).[70]

In Cicero's view, Pompey's games in 55 BC were 'most splendid', but not to his taste: Pompey had pitched them brazenly to the crowds.[71] The same could be said of the complex as a whole, which offered the people the sensory pleasures of the wealthy on a grander scale than ever before. If it exalted the sponsor to perilous heights for a

---

[62] Plin., *HN* XXXVI.117–18, adapted from Leonard H. G. Greenwood's translation; Sear 2006, 56.

[63] Plin., *HN* XXXVI.120, translation Leonard H. G. Greenwood.

[64] Val. Max., II.4.6; also Mart., *Epig.* VI.9.

[65] Coarelli 1972; Kuttner 1999; Davies 2017a, 229–34, with bibliography.

[66] Mart., *Epig.* II.14.19; Prop., II.32.12–16. Grimal 1943, 175, suggests laurel and myrtle on analogy with gardens at Croton. Also Gleason 1990; 1994. On trees in the triumph: Plin., *HN* XII.20, 111, XXV.5–8, XXXIII.151, XXXVII.11; App., *Mith.* CXVI; Miles 2008, 233; Östenberg 2009, 188.

---

[67] On the peaceful impact of fountains in urban environments, and the potential for privacy: Garza and others 2016; Holter, Muth, and Schwesinger 2019, 45.

[68] Plin., *HN* XII.111.

[69] Cic., *Pis.* 65, translation by Charles Duke Yonge.

[70] Cic., *Fam.* VII.1.3; also Cass. Dio XXXIX.38.2–5; Plut., *Pompon* LII.5; Plin., *HN* VII.158.

[71] Cic., *Fam.* VII.1.3.

Figure 2.12. Theatre-Portico Complex of Pompey, c. 61–52 BC. Reconstruction by John Burge and James E. Packer.

Figure 2.13. Circus Maximus, actual state. Photo: Penelope Davies.

Figure 2.14. Forum Iulium, begun c. 54 BC, actual state. Photo: Penelope Davies.

Republic, there were other risks, too, already recognized, perhaps, in 154 BC. For audience members, a heightening of the senses in response to these stimuli must have amplified a feeling of embodiment, presence, and self-awareness. At the same time, studies in social psychology indicate a surge in group identity in crowds, intensified, Garrett Fagan notes, when members of the crowd assembled in subgroups of like social background, as they did for Roman games; this engenders a sense of empowerment, seen, for instance, in English football stadia, and the Pompeii amphitheatre in AD 59[72] — and in Late Republican Rome. Audience participation in temporary theatres (as in public meetings or *contiones*) was at an all-time high, as the *plebs* spoke out more and more boldly from the *cavea*, turning the theatre's acoustics to its own advantage. If mobilized, a heightened sense of presence together with an emboldened group identity risked destabilizing social hierarchies, and populists like Publius Clodius, aedile in 57 BC, did exactly that, seizing opportunities to incite unrest, provoking food riots at the *ludi Apollinares* to protest Cicero's recall from exile, and using his *ludi Megalenses* to stage class warfare.[73] But the people had a momentum of their own: when the Senate announced Cicero's recall at the *Floralia* of the same year, the crowd roared its approval, applauded the games' sponsor Marcus Lentulus Spinther, and all but lynched Clodius.[74] And as the inauguration of Pompey's Theatre approached, Cicero acknowledged the crowd's potential, taunting Piso,

> Da te populo, committe ludis. Sibilum metuis? Vbi sunt vestrae scholae? Ne acclametur times? [...] Manus tibi ne adferantur?

> (Trust yourself to the people, venture on attending these games. Are you afraid of hisses? [...] Are you afraid that there will be no acclamations raised in your honour? You are afraid that violent hands may be laid on you.)[75]

Until Pompey's Theatre Complex, the risks of demagoguery and popular uprising were kept in check by making entertainment structures ephemeral, analogous to the temporary nature of a magistrate's term; hence the demolition of the theatre of 154 BC. So this was Pompey's

bold transgression: Rome's first permanent theatre, promising entertainment all through the year, year upon year — a dangerous analogy, in turn, for an autocrat's dreams. More than that, since — despite its permanence — each phase of entertainment was ephemeral, Pompey's genius was to append Rome's first public garden for year-round sustenance to the senses (Fig. 2.12), where, like the drunken satyr, a visitor's thirst for sensory pleasure could be endlessly glutted. Gratification followed: the gift of a statue for his Curia, and a third consulship in 52 BC.[76] But with gratification for Pompey, also greater awareness of yawning inequities between the classes. Violence, unabated.[77]

Caesar's response came in stages. With his quadruple triumph over Gaul, Egypt, Pontus, and Numidia in 46 BC came an orgy of ephemeral delights, augmented by games for his late daughter Julia and the inauguration of his forum (which, in Cassius Dio's eyes, surpassed all previous games in splendour and expense).[78] Musical and theatrical performances, in all the districts and languages of the city, fed the ear and eye; gladiatorial combats were innumerable and varied; in equestrian displays, young noblemen showed off their dexterity; four hundred lions were corralled in the city, and the first giraffe, probably from Egypt. The nose and the palate were sated: the sweet smell of sacrifice, and banquets for days on end, twenty thousand couches at a sitting (and again after Caesar's Spanish triumph in 45 BC, when he catered for two separate banquets, for fear of underproviding).[79] Newly built architecture, temporary and permanent, formed the striking setting for this munificence. He repaved the forum (so it is thought) using travertine, smooth underfoot, a complex, creamy hue — permanent yet porous, hard yet pocked with holes; through hatches, gladiators or small animals appeared as if magically, raised into the piazza in elevators for riveting reversals in the action (Fig. 2.9).[80] Awnings of lustrous silk, draped from

---

[72] Fagan 2011, 80–124.

[73] Cic., *Mil.* XXXVIII; Cic., *Har. resp.* XXII; Frézouls 1983, 204–05; Tatum 1999, 182–83, 211–12; Seager 2002, 97. On *contiones*, see Millar 1998; Mouritsen 2001; Morstein-Marx 2004.

[74] Cic., *Att.* II.19; Cic., *Sest.* CXVI–CXXIII; Cic., *Planc.* LXXVIII; Frézouls 1983, 204–05; Tatum 1999, 181.

[75] Cic., *Pis.* LXV, translation by Charles Duke Yonge.

[76] Plut., *Brut.* XIV; Cic., *Div.* II.23; Suet., *Aug.* XXXI; Johansen 1973; Sapelli 1990; Coarelli 1996, 378–79; 1997, 574–75; *LTUR* IV, 367, s.v. Statua: Cn. Pompeius (E. Papi).

[77] See Nippel 1995; Lintott 1999; Davies 2019.

[78] Suet., *Caes.* XXVI.2; Liv., *Per.* CVI; Plut., *Caes.* XXIII.5, LV.4; Pomp. Trog. LIII.4; Cass. Dio XXXIX.64, XLIII.22.2–23; Weinstock 1971, 88–90.

[79] Suet., *Iul.* XXXVIII.2.39; Plut., *Caes.* LV.4; Vell. Pat. II.56.2; Liv., *Per.* CXVI; Weinstock 1971, 198; Meier 1982, 461–62.

[80] Carettoni 1956–1958; Giuliani and Verduchi 1987, 53–61; Wiseman 1990; *LTUR* III, 343–45 s.v. Forum Romanum (lastricati) (D. Palombi). Filippi 2013, 166 and 168, identifies Cotta's pavement as a peperino layer and the travertine pavement as Caesarian. On

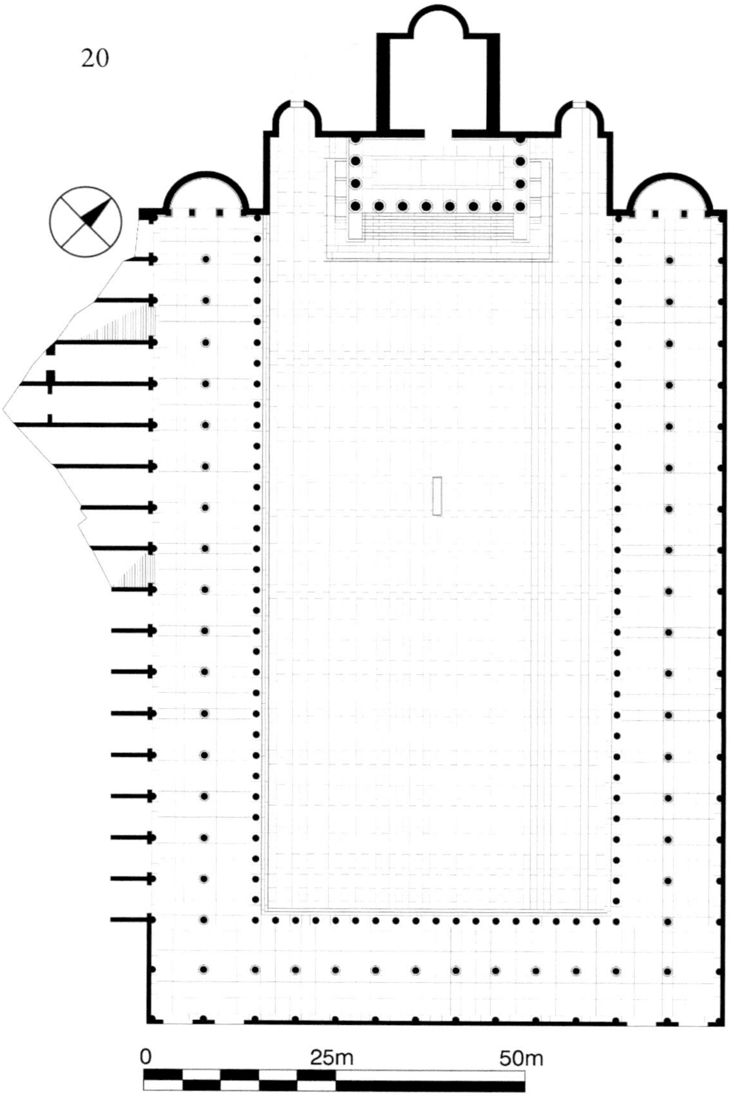

Figure 2.15. Forum Iulium, begun *c.* 54 BC.
Plan of initial phase by John Burge.

umentalized into its canonical shape (Fig. 2.13).[82] And in Rome's first artificial lake, fleets from Tyre and Egypt clashed in a mock sea battle, roiling the glittering waves, splashing those nearby.[83] In Velleius Paterculus's words, Caesar entertained the city 'to repletion' (*replevit*).[84] If all of Rome attended Curio's games, 'such a throng flocked to all these shows from every quarter', according to Suetonius, 'that many strangers had to lodge in tents pitched in streets or along the roads, and the press was often such that many were crushed to death' (ad quae omnia spectacula tantum undique confluxit hominum, ut plerique advenae aut inter vicos aut inter vias tabernaculis positis manerent, ac saepe prae turba elisi exanimatique sint plurimi et in his duo senatores).[85] In terms of ephemeral delights, Pompey was outdone.

After the final banquet, Caesar returned to the Domus Publica on foot, with a vast escort of bustling crowds and lumbering elephants bearing torches. On his way, he donned slippers and garlands of aromatic flowers to inaugurate a more permanent response to Pompey's Complex, the Forum Iulium, begun in 54 BC and designed, according to Appian, as a place for the transaction of public business, similar to the public squares of the Persians, where people assemble to seek justice or to learn the laws (Figs 2.14, 2.15, and 2.16).[86] What was unveiled, a monument so staggering that Pliny compared it to the pyramids of Egypt, would counter and diffuse his late rival's architectural exuberance, so Appian states, as a forum for the Roman people, not for buying and selling, but a meeting with a soberer form of sensuous magnificence: a massive deployment of translucent marble, newly imported from Carrara.[87] This luscious, cool fabric struck a single note of pure radiance, a foil for the barrage of sensations of Pompey's Theatre and Portico. Water pooled in shallow fountains, conditioning the air, but artworks were few, forcing the senses

Caesar's Sacra Via residence all the way to the Temple of Jupiter, were 'a sight, it is said, more wonderful even than the show of gladiators which he exhibited' (quod munere ipso gladiatorio mirabilius visum tradunt);[81] for three days of athletic contests, a temporary stadium was erected on the Campus Martius, and for five days of wild beast hunts, 'a kind of hunting-theatre of wood', to quote Cassius Dio, 'which was called an amphitheatre from the fact that it had seats all around without any stage.' For a battle pitching two armies of five hundred foot soldiers, twenty elephants, and thirty horsemen a side against each other, the Circus Maximus was fully mon-

---

travertine, see Goldhagen 2017, 159.

81 Plin., *HN* XIX.23, translation John Bostock; Cass. Dio XLIII.24.2.

82 Cass. Dio XLIII. 22–23; Suet., *Iul.* XXXIX; Dion. Hal., *Ant. Rom.* III.68.1–4; App., *B Civ.* II.102; Plin., *HN* VIII.53; App., *B Civ.* II.102. Weinstock 1971, 88, 92; Meier 1982, 444; Humphrey 1986, 73–77; Favro 1996, 62, 67; Liverani 2008, 49; Marcattili 2009.

83 Suet., *Iul.* XXXIX; Cass. Dio XLIII.23; App., *B Civ.* II.102; Vell Pat. II.56; Coleman 1993, 50; Coarelli 1997, 584–85; *LTUR* III, 338, s.v. Naumachia Caesaris (A. M. Liberati).

84 Vell. Pat. II.56, translation by Frederick W. Shipley.

85 Suet., *Iul.* XXXIX.4, translation by John C. Rolfe.

86 App., *B Civ.* II.102, translation by Charles H. Oldfather. Forum: Amici 1991; Delfino 2008, 52–54; 2014; Pinna Caboni 2008, 57.

87 Plin., *HN* XXXVI.103; App., *B Civ.* II.102, translation by Charles H. Oldfather.

2. SENSING CHANGE: LATE REPUBLICAN ARCHITECTURE IN ROME

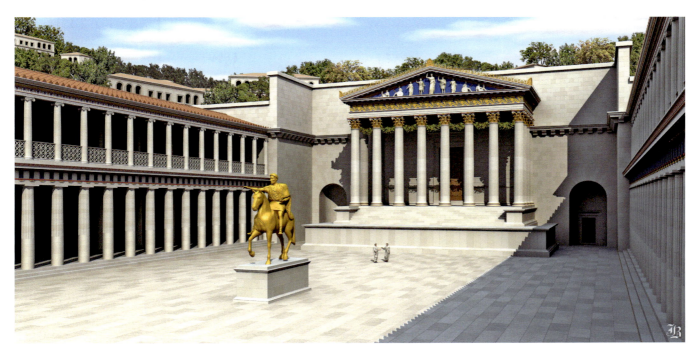

Figure 2.16. Forum Iulium, begun *c.* 54 BC. Reconstruction by John Burge.

to focus.[88] The forum's open spaces discouraged quiet meandering, intimate gathering, and private agendas; illuminated by the marble's reflectivity, the spaces may have felt surveyed.[89] High walls shut out noise from surrounding streets; sound generated inside, contained and amplified, bounced sharply, unimpeded, off solid marble walls and columns, and moved hauntingly through the portico spaces.[90] Addressing crowds from the high tribunal fronting the Temple of Venus Genetrix, Caesar could hope to be heard, the acoustics honed for his advancement not through distractions from life but through the business of life: law, justice, and elections.[91]

In the nearly two years that followed, Caesar pursued a more far-reaching strategy as a dictator, focused not on a single microcosmic multisensorial wonderland, like Pompey's Complex, but across Rome writ large; and rather than offering a heady explosion of sensory delights to disguise the challenges of city living, to seduce the crowds towards an amplification of his own status he eased discontents by normalizing and institutionalizing a higher standard of living for a greater number of people; he rendered to the *plebs* some of the luxuries previously reserved for the elite, narrowing the gap between the haves and the have-nots. On the east slope of the Arx and near the Circus Flaminius, two new theatres would complement Greek and Latin libraries, where the public could enjoy the edifying sound of literary recitals, inside cool, insulated walls.[92] And at this time, too, another radical change of tack: he drafted legislation to remove, or at least mitigate, obstacles to pleasing sensory experience for the crowd. Thus, as well as coating public places with a satin skin of marble, in his *lex Iulia Municipalis* he provided for the maintenance of surfaces that detracted from Rome's salubriousness, requiring aediles to tend to public streets and to charge property owners with the repair and dryness of streets fronting their land; underfoot, the city was to feel cared for. As well as managing desirable sound, he controlled undesirable noise by banning wagons from the city and residential parts of the suburbs from sunrise until the tenth hour, with certain

---

[88] In the temple: the cult statue; perhaps a statue of Cleopatra; and paintings by Timomachus. On axis with the temple: a bronze statue of Alexander on Bucephalus by Lysippus, reworked as a portrait of Caesar. Plin., *HN* VIII.154–45; Stat., *Silv.* 1.1.84–90; Suet., *Caes.* LXI; Cass. Dio XXXVII.54.2; Weinstock 1971, 86–87; Westall 1996, 88; Delfino 2008, 53; Zanker 2008, 74. Among honours Caesar accepted was a cuirassed statue in the Forum Iulium: Plin., *HN* XXXIV.18.

[89] On 'interdictory spaces', see Flusty 1997.

[90] On marble and acoustics, see Aldrete 2014, 55.

[91] See aural simulation models for the similarly designed Temple of Castor in Holter, Muth, and Schwesinger 2019.

[92] Suet., *Iul.* XLIV; Dix 1994, 286–87; Sear 2006, 62; Miles 2008, 238. Coarelli 1997, 586–88, argues for one theatre on the site of the Theatre of Marcellus. Sen., *Controv.* IV. pref. 2, attributes the invention of author recitals to Gaius Asinius Pollio.

exemptions; ox- and donkey-wagons and dung collectors who had entered by night could also leave by day, to remove malodorous refuse from the city as efficiently as possible.[93] Quieter, streets would also be less crowded, so those without litters or carriages felt less of the intrusive touch of strangers. At liberty to move more freely in the streets, they could occupy space bodily, reclaim their city.[94] And to quell agitation born of harsh living conditions, low-end rents were remitted for all of 46 BC; public lands were auctioned, the pomerium extended, and a plan mooted to canalize the Tiber to expand the Campus Martius for housing.[95]

[93] *Tabula Heracleensis* 7–21; Johnson, Coleman-Norton, and Bourne 1961, 93–97; Robinson 1992, 17; Favro 1996, 75–76. Crawford 1996, 355–62; Gardner 2009, 64; Zardini 2006, 214: The ground defines the surface of cities and makes a decisive contribution to their character. Also Classen 2006, 296–97, on nineteenth-century European arguments on the public nature of city cleanliness (e.g. English sanitary reformer Edwin Chadwick's view that cleaning up Paris under Napoleon III would mitigate social unrest).

[94] Zardini 2006, 255, citing Walter Benjamin (1927–1940) on streets as the 'dwelling place of the collective'.

[95] Cass. Dio XLII.50, XLIII 47.4; Cic., *Off.* II.83–84; Cic., *Att.* XIII.20, 33a, 35; Suet., *Iul.* XXXVIII.2, 44; Plut., *Quint.* III.7; Plut., *Caes.* LVIII; Le Gall 1953, 130–33; Meier 1982, 418; Lagunes 2004, 117–29; Aldrete 2014, 182–84; Donati 2008, 39; Liverani 2008, 49–50.

Conclusion

Reading Late Republican architecture through the lens of embodiment leads to subtle shifts in perspective. Consciously or subconsciously, sponsors seem to have recognized the power of embodied space, and used it, variously, for group- and self-advancement and to establish and maintain social hierarchies. Alert to this architectural language, the people responded; they played their part in occupying built structures to destabilize society. In the end, the Republic crumbled in a battle between strategies. Pompey, building on a long tradition, offered sensory overload to distract from the sensory trials of unprivileged urban living, even prevailing over the restrictive transience of festivals by means of a permanent entertainment structure and a public garden. Caesar coupled temporary munificence with short- and long-term plans to reduce those sensory trials and reduce agitation. Yet narrowing the chasm between the haves and the have-nots also challenged elite ideals of social hierarchy; not surprisingly, perhaps, Caesar did not live to see the outcome of his plans. It is hard to see where they might have led, if not combined, as they were, with the controlling effects of the most luxurious, permanent sensory benefaction to date — Agrippa's public baths — *and* a level of surveillance, anticipated with Caesar, that edged with Augustus toward totalitarianism.

Works Cited

Aldrete, G. S. 2014. 'Urban Sensations: Opulence and Ordure', in J. Toner (ed.), *A Cultural History of the Senses in Antiquity* (London: Bloomsbury), pp. 45–68.

Amici, C. M. 1991. *Il Foro di Cesare* (Florence: Olschki).

Arata, F. P. 2010. 'Osservazioni sulla topografia sacra dell'Arx Capitolina', *Mélanges de l'Ecole française de Rome: antiquité*, 122: 117–46.

Arata, F. P. and E. Felice. 2011. 'Porticus Aemilia, navalia o horrea? Ancora sui frammenti 23 e 24 b-d della Forma Urbis', *Archeologia classica*, 62: 127–53.

Banducci, L. M. 2018. 'Tastes of Roman Italy: Early Roman Expansion and Taste Articulation', in K. C. Rudolph (ed.), *Taste and the Ancient Senses* (New York: Routledge), pp. 120–37.

Bastien, J.-L. 2007. *Le triomphe romain et son utilisation politique à Rome aux trois derniers siècles de la république* (Rome: École française de Rome).

Beacham, R. C. 1999. *Spectacle Entertainments of Early Imperial Rome* (New Haven: Yale University Press).

Beard, M. 2009. *The Roman Triumph* (Cambridge, MA: Harvard University Press).

Bradley, M. 2014. 'Colour as Synaesthetic Experience in Antiquity', in S. Butler and A. C. Purves (eds), *Synaesthesia and the Ancient Senses* (London: Routledge), pp. 127–40.

—— 2015a. 'Foul Bodies in Ancient Rome', in M. Bradley (ed.), *Smell and the Ancient Senses* (London: Routledge), pp. 133–45.

—— (ed.). 2015b. *Smell and the Ancient Senses* (London: Routledge).

Bradley, R. 2001. 'The Birth of Architecture', in W. G. Runciman (ed.), *The Origins of Human Social Institutions* (Oxford: Oxford University Press), pp. 69–92.

Bremmer, J. N. 2005. 'Attis: A Greek God in Anatolian Pessinous and Catullan Rome', in R. R. Nauta and A. Harder (eds), *Catullus' Poem on Attis: Text and Contexts* (Leiden: Brill), pp. 25–64.

Brilliant, R. 1999. '"Let the Trumpets Roar!" The Roman Triumph', in B. Bergmann and C. Kondoleon (eds), *The Art of Ancient Spectacle* (New Haven: Yale University Press), pp. 221–30.

Butler, S. and S. Nooter. 2019. *Sound and the Ancient Senses* (London: Routledge).

Butler, S. and A. C. Purves. 2014. *The Senses in Antiquity: Synaesthesia and the Ancient Senses* (London: Routledge).

Cadario, M. 2014. 'Preparing for Triumph. *Graecae artes* as Roman Booty in L. Mummius' Campaign (146 BC)', in C. H. Lange and F. J. Vervaet (eds), *The Roman Republican Triumph: Beyond the Spectacle* (Rome: Quasar), pp. 83–101.

Carettoni, G. 1956–1958. 'Le gallerie ipogee del Foro Romano e i ludi gladiatori forensi', *Bullettino della Commissione archeologica comunale di Roma*, 76: 23–44.

Carey, S. 2003. *Pliny's Catalogue of Culture: Art and Empire in the Natural History* (Oxford: Oxford University Press).

Classen, C. 2006. 'The Deodorized City: Battling Urban Stench in the Nineteenth Century', in M. Zardini (ed.), *Sense of the City: An Alternate Approach to Urbanism* (Baden: Lars Müller), pp. 292–99.

Clements, A. 2015. 'Divine Scents and Presence', in M. Bradley (ed.), *Smell and the Ancient Senses* (London: Routledge), pp. 46–59.

Coarelli, F. 1972. 'Il complesso Pompeiano del Campo Marzio e la sua decorazione scultorea', *Rendiconti della Pontificia Accademia di Archeologia*, 44: 99–122.

—— 1976. 'Cinque frammenti di una tomba dipinta dall'Esquilino', in *Affreschi romani dalle raccolte dell'Antiquarium Comunale* (Rome: Assessorato antichità, belle arti e problemi della cultura), pp. 22–28.

—— 1983. *Il Foro Romano: periodo arcaico* (Rome: Quasar).

—— 1985. *Il Foro Romano: periodo repubblicano e augusteo* (Rome: Quasar).

—— 1988. *Il Foro Boario: dalle origini alla fine della Repubblica* (Rome: Quasar).

—— 1996. *Revixit ars: arte e ideologia a Roma; dai modelli ellenistici alla tradizione repubblicana* (Rome: Quasar).

—— 1997. *Il Campo Marzio: dalle origini alla fine della repubblica* (Rome: Quasar).

—— 2010. 'Substructio et tabularium', *Papers of the British School at Rome*, 78: 107–32.

—— 2012. *Palatium: il Palatino dalle origini all'impero* (Rome: Quasar).

—— 2014. *Collis: il Quirinale e il Viminale nell'antichità* (Rome: Quasar).

Coleman, K. M. 1993. 'Launching into History: Aquatic Displays in the Early Empire', *Journal of Roman Studies*, 83: 48–74.

Cornell, T. J. 2014. *The Fragments of the Roman Historians* (Oxford: Oxford University Press).

Cozza, L. and P. L. Tucci. 2006. 'Navalia', *Archeologia classica*, 57: 175–202.

Crawford, M. 1996. *Roman Statutes* (London: Institute of Classical Studies).

Cumont, F. 1911. *The Oriental Religions in Roman Paganism* (New York: Dover).

Dauster, M. 2003. 'Roman Republican Sumptuary Legislation, 182–102', in C. Deroux (ed.), *Studies in Latin Literature and Roman History* (Brussels: Latomus), pp. 65–93.

Davies, P. J. E. 2012. 'On the Introduction of Stone Architraves in Republican Temples in Rome', in M. L. Thomas and G. E. Meyers (eds), *Monumentality in Etruscan and Early Roman Architecture: Ideology and Innovation* (Austin: University of Texas Press), pp. 139–65.

—— 2017a. *Architecture and Politics in Republican Rome* (Cambridge: Cambridge University Press).

—— 2017b. 'A Republican Dilemma: City or State? Or, the Concrete Revolution Revisited', *Papers of the British School at Rome*, 85: 71–107.

—— 2019. 'Vandalism and Resistance in Republican Rome', *Journal of the Society of Architectural Historians*, 78: 6–24.

—— (forthcoming). 'On Architecture's Agency in Fourth Century Rome', in S. Bernard, L. Mignone, and D. E. Padilla (eds), *Republican Rome in the Long Fourth Century*.

Delbrück, R. 1907–1912. *Hellenistische Bauten in Latium* (Strasbourg: Trübner).

Delfino, A. 2008. 'Il Foro di Cesare nella fase cesariana e augustea', in C. Balsamo (ed.), *Giulio Cesare: l'uomo, le imprese, il mito* (Milan: Silvana), pp. 52–54.

—— 2014. *Forum Iulium: l'area del Foro di Cesare alla luce delle campagne di scavo 2005–2008; le fasi arcaica, repubblicana e cesariano-augustea*, British Archaeological Reports, International Series, 2607 (Oxford: Archaeopress).

Dix, T. K. 1994. '"Public Libraries" in Ancient Rome: Ideology and Reality', *Libraries and Culture*, 29: 282–96.

Donati, A. 2008. 'Cesare e il diritto', in C. Balsamo (ed.), *Giulio Cesare: l'uomo, le imprese, il mito* (Milan: Silvana), pp. 38–41.

Ellin, N. 1997. 'Shelter from the Storm or Form Follows Fear and Vice Versa', in N. Ellin (ed.), *Architecture of Fear* (Princeton: Princeton Architectural Press), pp. 13–45.

Evans, H. B. 1994. *Water Distribution in Ancient Rome: The Evidence of Frontinus* (Ann Arbor: University of Michigan Press).

Fagan, G. G. 2011. *The Lure of the Arena: Social Psychology and the Crowd at the Roman Games* (Cambridge: Cambridge University Press).

Favro, D. 1996. *The Urban Image of Augustan Rome* (Cambridge: Cambridge University Press).

Ferrea, L. 2002. *Gli dei di terracotta: la ricomposizione del frontone da via di San Gregorio* (Milan: Electa).

Filippi, D. 2013. 'Regione VIII. Forum Romanum Magnum', in A. Carandini and P. Carafa (eds), *Atlante di Roma Antica*, I: *Biografia e ritratti della città* (Milan: Electa), pp. 143–206.

Flusty, S. 1997. 'Building Paranoia', in N. Ellin (ed.), *Architecture of Fear* (Princeton: Princeton Architectural Press), pp. 47–59.

Forsythe, G. 1994. 'Review of Erich S. Gruen, *Culture and National Identity in Republican Rome*. Ithaca: Cornell University Press, 1992', *Bryn Mawr Classical Review*, 11 February 1994.

Frézouls, E. 1983. 'La construction du *theatrum lapideum* et son contexte politique', in H. Zehnacker (ed.), *Théâtre et spectacles dans l'antiquité* (Leiden: Brill), pp. 193–214.

Gagliardo, M. C. and J. E. Packer. 2006. 'A New Look at Pompey's Theater: History, Documentation, and Recent Excavation', *American Journal of Archaeology*, 110: 93–122.

Gardner, J. F. 2009. 'The Dictator', in M. Griffin (ed.), *A Companion to Julius Caesar* (Chichester: Wiley-Blackwell), pp. 57–71.

Garza, F. J. E. and others. 2016. 'Fountains as Sound Elements in the Design of Urban Public Walks Soundscapes', in F. Miyara and others (eds), *22nd International Congress on Acoustics ICA 2016: Proceedings* (Gonnet: Asociación de acústicos argentinos), pp. 1–10.

Giuliani, C. F. and P. Verduchi. 1987. *L'area centrale del Foro Romano* (Florence: Olschki).

Gleason, K. L. 1990. 'The Garden Portico of Pompey the Great: An Ancient Public Park Preserved in the Layers of Rome', *Expedition*, 32: 4–13.

—— 1994. 'Porticus Pompeiana: A New Perspective on the First Public Park of Ancient Rome', *Journal of Garden History*, 14: 13–27.

Goldhagen, S. 2017. *Welcome to your World: How the Built Environment Shapes our Lives* (New York: Harper).

Gosden, C. 2005. 'What Do Objects Want?', *Journal of Archaeological Method and Theory*, 12: 193–211.

Graillot, H. 1912. *Le culte de Cybèle, mère des dieux, à Rome et dans l'Empire romain* (Paris: Fontemoing et Cie).

Grimal, P. 1943. *Les jardins romains à la fin de la république et aux deux premiers siècles de l'empire; essai sur le naturalisme romain* (Paris: De Boccard).

Gros, P. 1979. 'Les statues de Syracuse et les "dieux" de Tarente (la classe politique romaine devant l'art grec à la fin du IIIᵉ siècle avant J.-C.)', *Revue de l'étude latine*, 57: 85–114.

—— 1994. 'Le schéma vitruvien du théâtre latin et sa signification dans le système normatif du de architectura', *Revue archéologique*, 1994.1: 57–80.

Gruen, E. S. 1992. *Culture and National Identity in Republican Rome* (Ithaca: Cornell University Press).

Hamilakis, Y. 2013. *Archaeology and the Senses: Human Experience, Memory and Affect* (Cambridge: Cambridge University Press).

Hesberg, H. von. 1999. 'The King on Stage', in B. Bergmann and C. Kondoleon (eds), *The Art of Ancient Spectacle* (New Haven: Yale University Press), pp. 65–75.

Hodder, I. 1979. 'Economic and Social Stress and Material Culture Patterning', *American Antiquity*, 44: 446–54.

—— 1982. *Symbols in Action* (Cambridge: Cambridge University Press).

Hodge, T. 1992. *Roman Aqueducts and Water Supply* (London: Duckworth).

Holter, E., S. Muth, and S. Schwesinger. 2019. 'Sounding out Public Space in Late Republican Rome', in S. Butler and S. Nooter (eds), *Sound and the Ancient Senses* (London: Routledge), pp. 44–60.

Hopkins, J. N. 2016. *The Genesis of Roman Architecture* (New Haven: Yale University Press).

Howes, D. 2006. 'Architecture of the Senses', in M. Zardini (ed.), *Sense of the City: An Alternate Approach to Urbanism* (Baden: Lars Müller), pp. 322–31.

Humphrey, J. H. 1986. *Roman Circuses: Arenas for Chariot Racing* (London: Batsford).

Jackson, M. and F. Marra. 2006. 'Roman Stone Masonry: Volcanic Foundations of the Ancient City', *American Journal of Archaeology*, 110: 403–36.

Johansen, F. 1973. 'Antike portraetter af Gnaeus Pompeius Magnus', *Meddelelser fra Ny Carlsberg Glyptotek*, 30: 89–115.

Johnson, A. C., C. Coleman-Norton, and P. R. Bourne. 1961. *Ancient Roman Statutes* (Austin: University of Texas Press).

Keaveney, A. P. 2005. *Sulla: The Last Republican*, 2nd edn (London: Routledge).

Kindberg Jacobsen, J. and R. Raja. 2018. 'A High-Definition Approach to the Forum of Caesar in Rome: Urban Archaeology on a Living City', in R. Raja and S. Sindbæk (eds), *Urban Network Evolutions: Towards a High-Definition Archaeology* (Aarhus: Aarhus University Press), pp. 21–26.

Klar, L. 2006. 'The Origins of the Roman *scaenae frons* and the Architecture of Triumphal Games in the Second Century B.C.', in S. Dillon and K. E. Welch (eds), *Representations of War in Ancient Rome* (Cambridge: Cambridge University Press), pp. 162–83.

Koloski-Ostrow, A. O. 2015. 'Roman Urban Smells: The Archaeological Evidence', in M. Bradley (ed.), *Smell and the Ancient Senses* (London: Routledge), pp. 90–109.

Kuttner, A. L. 1999. 'Culture and History at Pompey's Museum', *Transactions of the American Philological Association*, 129: 343–73.

La Rocca, E. 1984. 'Fabio o Fannio: l'affresco medio-repubblicano dell'Esquilino come riflesso dell'arte rappresentativa e come espressione di mobilità sociale', *Dialoghi di archeologia*, 2: 31–53.

—— 2008. 'La processione trionfale come spettacolo per il popolo romano: trionfi antichi, spettacoli moderni', in E. La Rocca and S. Tortorella (eds), *Trionfi romani* (Milan: Electa), pp. 34–55.

Lagunes, M. M. S. 2004. *Il Tevere e Roma: storia di una simbiosi* (Rome: Gangemi).

Latham, J. A. 2007. 'The Ritual Construction of Rome: Procession, Subjectivities, and the City from the Late Republic to Late Antiquity' (unpublished doctoral dissertation, Santa Barbara, University of California, Santa Barbara).

—— 2016. *Performance, Memory, and Processions in Ancient Rome: The Pompa Circensis from the Late Republic to Late Antiquity* (Cambridge: Cambridge University Press).

Laurence, R. 2017. 'The Sound of the City: From Noise to Silence in Ancient Rome', in E. Betts (ed.), *Senses of the Empire: Multisensory Approaches to Roman Culture* (Abingdon: Routledge), pp. 13–22.

Le Gall, J. 1953. *Le Tibre: fleuve de Rome dans l'antiquité* (Paris: Presses universitaires de France).

Lennon, J. 2018. 'Contaminating Touch in the Roman World', in A. C. Purves (ed.), *Touch and the Ancient Senses* (London: Routledge), pp. 121–33.

Levick, B. 1978. 'Concordia at Rome', in R. A. G. Carson and C. M. Kraay (eds), *Scripta nummaria romana: Essays Presented to Humphrey Sutherland* (London: Spink), pp. 217–33.

Lintott, A. W. 1999. *Violence in Republican Rome* (Oxford: Oxford University Press).

Lippolis, E. 2004. 'Triumphata Corintho: la preda bellica e i doni di Lucio Mummio Achaico', *Archeologia classica*, 55: 25–82.

Liverani, P. 2008. 'Cesare urbanista: l'uomo, le imprese, il mito', in C. Balsamo (ed.), *Giulio Cesare: l'uomo, le imprese, il mito* (Milan: Silvana), pp. 42–59.

Low, S. 2000. *On the Plaza: The Politics of Public Space and Culture* (Austin: University of Texas Press).

LTUR = Eva Margareta Steinby (ed.). 1993–2000. *Lexicon topographicum urbis Romae*, 6 vols (Rome: Quasar).

MacDonald, W. L. 1982. *The Architecture of the Roman Empire*, I: *An Introductory Study* (New Haven: Yale University Press).

Malnar, J. M. and F. Vodvarka. 2004. *Sensory Design* (Minneapolis: University of Minnesota Press).

Marcattili, F. 2009. *Circo Massimo: architetture, funzioni, culti, ideologia* (Rome: L'Erma di Bretschneider).

Medri, M. 1997. 'Fonti letterarie e fonti archeologiche: un confronto possibile su M. Emilio Scauro il Giovane, la sua *domus "magnifica"* e il *teatrum "opus maximum omnium"*', *Mélanges de l'École française de Rome: antiquité*, 109: 83–110.

Meier, C. 1982. *Caesar: A Biography* (London: Fontana).

Miles, M. M. 2008. *Art as Plunder: The Ancient Origins of Debate about Cultural Property* (Cambridge: Cambridge University Press).

Millar, F. 1998. *The Crowd in Rome in the Late Republic* (Ann Arbor: University of Michigan Press).

Mogetta, M. 2021. *The Origins of Concrete Construction in Roman Architecture: Technology and Society in Republican Italy* (Cambridge: Cambridge University Press).

Monterroso Checa, A. 2006. 'Theatrum Pompei', *Romula*, 5: 27–58.

Morgan, G. 1973. 'Villa Publica and Magna Mater: Two Notes on Manubial Building at the Close of the Second Century B.C.', *Klio*, 55: 214–45.

Morley, N. 2015. 'Urban Smells and Roman Noses', in M. Bradley (ed.), *Smell and the Ancient Senses* (London: Routledge), pp. 110–19.

Morstein-Marx, R. 2004. *Mass Oratory and Political Power in the Late Roman Republic* (Cambridge: Cambridge University Press).

Mouritsen, H. 2001. *Plebs and Politics in the Late Roman Republic* (Cambridge: Cambridge University Press).

Nauta, R. R. 2005. 'Catullus 63 in a Roman Context', in R. R. Nauta and A. Harder (eds), *Catullus' Poem on Attis: Text and Contexts* (Leiden: Brill), pp. 87–119.

Nielsen, I. and B. Poulsen. 1992. *The Temple of Castor and Pollux*, I: *The Pre-Augustan Temple Phases with Related Decorative Elements* (Rome: De Luca).

Nippel, W. 1995. *Public Order in Ancient Rome* (Cambridge: Cambridge University Press).

Nuño, A. A., J. A. Ezquerra, and G. Woolf. 2021. *Sensorium: The Senses in Roman Polytheism* (Leiden: Brill).

Östenberg, I. 2009. *Staging the World: Spoils, Captives, and Representations in the Roman Triumphal Procession* (Oxford: Oxford University Press).

Packer, J. E. 2013. 'The Theater of Pompey: The Archaeological Evidence, the Architecture, and the Destruction', *Acta ad archaeologiam et artium historiam pertinentia*, 27: 9–39.

Packer, J. E., J. Burge, and M. C. Gagliardo. 2007. 'Looking Again at Pompey's Theater: The 2005 Excavation Season', *American Journal of Archaeology*, 111: 505–22.

Padilla Peralta, D. 2020. *Divine Institutions: Religions and Community in the Middle Roman Republic* (Princeton: Princeton University Press).

Pallasmaa, J. 2012. *The Eyes of the Skin: Architecture and the Senses* (Chichester: Wiley).

Pape, M. 1975. 'Griechische Kunstwerke aus Kriegsbeute und ihre öffentliche Aufstellung in Rom: Von der Eroberung von Syrakus bis in augusteische Zeit' (unpublished doctoral dissertation, University of Hamburg).

Pensabene, P. and A. D'Alessio. 2006. 'L'immaginario urbano: spazio sacro sul Palatino tardo-repubblicano', in L. Haselberger and J. Humphrey (eds), *Imaging Ancient Rome: Documentation, Visualization, Imagination; Proceedings of the Third Williams Symposium on Classical Architecture* (Portsmouth, RI: Journal of Roman Archaeology), pp. 30–50.

Pietilä-Castrén, L. 1982. 'New Men and the Greek War Booty in the 2nd Century BC', *Arctos*, 16: 121–43.

—— 1991. 'L. Mummius' Contributions to the Agonistic Life', *Arctos*, 15: 103–05.

Pinna Caboni, B. 2008. 'Il foro di Cesare: aspetti della decorazione architettonica', in C. Balsamo (ed.), *Giulio Cesare: l'uomo, le imprese, il mito* (Milan: Silvana), pp. 57–59.

Purves, A. C. 2018. *Touch and the Ancient Senses* (London: Routledge).

Rakob, F. and E. D. Heilmeyer. 1973. *Der Rundtempel am Tiber in Rom* (Mainz: von Zabern).

Robinson, O. F. 1992. *Ancient Rome: City Planning and Administration* (London: Routledge).

Roller, L. E. 1999. *In Search of God the Mother: The Cult of Anatolian Cybele* (Berkeley: University of California Press).

Rudolph, K. C. 2018. *Taste and the Ancient Senses* (New York: Routledge).

Russell, A. 2016. *The Politics of Public Space in Republican Rome* (Cambridge: Cambridge University Press).

Sapelli, M. 1990. 'Palazzo Spada: restauro della statua di Pompeo', *Bollettino d'arte*, 5–6: 180–85.

Seager, R. 2002. *Pompey the Great: A Political Biography* (Oxford: Blackwell).

Sear, F. B. 2006. *Roman Theatres: An Architectural Study* (Oxford: Oxford University Press).

Sordi, M. 1988. 'La decadenza della Repubblica e il teatro del 154 a.C.', *Invigilata Iucernis*, 10: 327–41.

Stamper, J. W. 2005. *The Architecture of Roman Temples: The Republic to the Middle Empire* (Cambridge: Cambridge University Press).

Steinby, E. M. 2012. *Edilizia pubblica e potere politico nella Roma repubblicana* (Rome: Jaca).

Takács, S. A. 1996. 'Magna Deum Mater Idaea, Cybele, and Catullus' *Attis*', in E. Lane (ed.), *Cybele, Attis, and Related Cults: Essays in Memory of M. J. Vermaseren* (Leiden: Brill), pp. 367–86.

Tatum, W. J. 1999. *The Patrician Tribune: Publius Clodius Pulcher* (Chapel Hill: University of North Carolina Press).

Thomas, E. 2008. *Monumentality and the Roman Empire: Architecture in the Antonine Age* (Oxford: Oxford University Press).

Thompson, E. 2006. 'Noise and Noise Abatement in the Modern City', in M. Zardini (ed.), *Sense of the City: An Alternate Approach to Urbanism* (Baden: Lars Müller), pp. 190–99.

Toner, J. 2014. 'Introduction: Sensing the Ancient Past', in J. Toner (ed.), *A Cultural History of the Senses in Antiquity* (London: Bloomsbury), pp. 1–21.

Torelli, M. 2006. 'The Topography and Archaeology of Republican Rome', in N. Rosenstein and R. Morstein-Marx (eds), *A Companion to the Roman Republic* (Oxford: Blackwell), pp. 81–101.

—— 2007. 'L'urbanistica di Roma regia e repubblicana: la città medio-repubblicana', in P. Gros and M. Torelli (eds), *Storia dell'urbanistica: il mondo romano* (Rome: Laterza), pp. 81–157.

Tucci, P. L. 2005. '"Where High Moneta Leads her Steps Sublime." The "Tabularium" and the Temple of Juno Moneta', *Journal of Roman Archaeology*, 18: 6–33.

—— 2012. 'La controversa storia della porticus Aemilia', *Archeologia classica*, 63: 575–91.

—— 2014. 'A New Look at the Tabularium and the Capitoline Hill', *Rendiconti della Pontificia Accademia Romana di Archeologia*, 86: 43–124.

Van Oyen, A. 2017. 'Finding the Material in "Material Culture"', in A. Van Oyen and M. Pitts (eds), *Materializing Roman Histories* (Oxford: Oxbow), pp. 133–52.

Versluys, M. J. 2017. 'Discussion. Object-scapes: Towards a Material Constitution of Romanness?', in A. Van Oyen and M. Pitts (eds), *Materializing Roman Histories* (Oxford: Oxbow), pp. 91–200.

Versnel, H. S. 1970. *Triumphus: An Inquiry into the Origin, Development and Meaning of the Roman Triumph* (Leiden: Brill).

Veyne, P. 1976. *Le pain et le cirque* (Paris: Du Seuil).

Wallace-Hadrill, A. 2008. *Rome's Cultural Revolution* (Cambridge: Cambridge University Press).

Weinstock, S. 1971. *Divus Julius* (Oxford: Clarendon).

Westall, R. 1996. 'The Forum Iulium as Representation of Imperator Caesar', *Mitteilungen des Deutschen Archäologischen Instituts: Römische Abteilung*, 103: 83–118.

Wiseman, T. P. 1990. 'The Central Area of the Roman Forum', *Journal of Roman Archaeology*, 3: 245–47.

Zanker, P. 2008. 'Le irritanti statue di Cesare e i suoi ritratti contraddittori', in C. Balsamo (ed.), *Giulio Cesare: l'uomo, le imprese, il mito* (Milan: Silvana), pp. 72–79.

Zardini, M. 2006. *Sense of the City: An Alternate Approach to Urbanism* (Baden: Lars Müller).

Ziółkowski, A. 1988. 'Mummius' Temple of Hercules Victor and the Round Temple on the Tiber', *Phoenix*, 42: 309–33.

3. FIND A LOVER IN AUGUSTAN ROME: HOW OVID'S *ARS AMATORIA* BECAME A CRITICISM OF AUGUSTUS'S MORAL POLITICS

Eric M. Moormann

Radboud Institute for Culture and History, Nijmegen
(eric.moormann@ru.nl)

Tot tibi tamque dabit formosas Roma puellas
(Rome will give you so many girls and such beautiful ones)[1]
In memoriam Marc van der Poel

Introduction[*]

The second half of the first century BC was a crucial period for the urban development of Rome. From a relatively provincial town, the *urbs* increasingly acquired splendour and prestige in which interventions by some political rivals in the ongoing conflicts played a crucial part: Pompey and Caesar, to mention a couple of them only, were responsible for huge complexes like the Theatre of Pompey and the Forum of Caesar. Their projects were to be continued and enhanced under Augustus, who at the end of this century could boast of having transformed Rome into a shiny marble town.[2] In this contribution, it is at this moment we step in and look at the great works completed, partly new, partly enlargements of existing complexes, so that we can tie in with the main protagonist of this book, Caesar, in the way of a fulfilment of his ambitions by his adoptive son Octavian or Caesar Augustus.

In the summer of 2 BC, great festivities took place in Rome. The Temple of Mars Ultor in the Forum Augustum was inaugurated after a long building process, and because of the elevation of Gaius and Lucius to the envisaged successors of Augustus, mock battles with ships were organized in the Gardens of Caesar located in Trans Tiberim (modern Trastevere), in a specially made artificial lake. Ovid uses this very day — 12 May or 1 August — in his *Ars amatoria* as a backdrop and starting point for his (or his narrator's) considerations on the play of love: it is in Rome where you can find the most

and finest girls on earth (cf. motto).[3] Just as in Ovid's *Tristia*, the topography of the city of Rome plays an essential role in the introduction of the *Ars amatoria*'s theme. It forms part of the *inuentio*:[4] the voice of the narrator which represents the authority in the didactic poem — of which the *Ars* is a specimen. The narrator virtually leads a young man during his walk through the town and points out the locations where the love-seeking person has the best chances of encountering a girl.[5] In 135 verses, all kinds of places are being addressed, and the imaginary trip ends at the complex built to accommodate *naumachiae* in Caesar's gardens. In book III, a number of these spots will return in a brief form as the locations where a girl might meet a boy or young man (Fig. 3.1).[6]

---

[*] This article is based on a Dutch paper from a few years ago, see Moormann 2014. In that stage, the peer reviewers and editors of the periodical Lampas as well as Diederik Burgersdijk and David Rijser provided me with precious suggestions. This new version profited from fine suggestions by John Clarke, Lien Foubert, Christina Häuber, Christopher Hallett, Mark Heerink, Paolo Liverani, Rubina Raja, Stijn Timmermans, and the anonymous referees.

[1] Ov., *Ars am.* I.55. All translations are by the author, unless stated otherwise.

[2] e.g. Suet., *Aug.* XXIX.2. See n. 17.

[3] I cite the OCT edition of Kenney 1961. For book I, there are a few commentaries, see Hollis 1977; Pianezzola 1991; Dimundo 2003. For a modern American translation with brief notes, see Hejduk 2014. However, they do not dedicate much attention to the topographical and archaeological details. See also the collection of studies in Gibson, Green, and Sharrock 2006. For the topography of Rome, see the indispensable *Lexicon topographicum urbis Romae* (*LTUR*) and Carandini and Carafa 2017. For Rome under Augustus, see Favro 1996; Haselberger 2002. For Ovid and Augustus, see Barchiesi 1994; Pandey 2018, 170–84.

[4] For the *inuentio*, see Dimundo 2003, 14. At the beginning of the Ov., *Tr.* 1.1.1–16, the book walks through the town, looking for the house of the *princeps*. It wants to deliver itself here to convey the author's complaint. In the Ov., *Fast.*, the calendar festivities are related with spots in town cf. Green 2004. Further 'topographical' poets in the *aurea aetas* of Augustus, but some decades earlier, are Virgil and Propertius. A good introduction to these poetical evocations is Barchiesi 2005. See for the association poets make with monuments Boyle 2003. On moving around the city, see Jenkyns 2013, 143–91.

[5] Ov., *Ars am.* 1.41–76. On the didactic elements: Dimundo 2003, 7–10. The title itself — *Ars* as Handbook or Technique — is an allusion to this genre, see Dimundo 2003, 7.

[6] Ov., *Ars am.* III.387–94: the Portico of Pompey, the Temple of Apollo Palatinus, the Temple of Isis, the three theatres, the

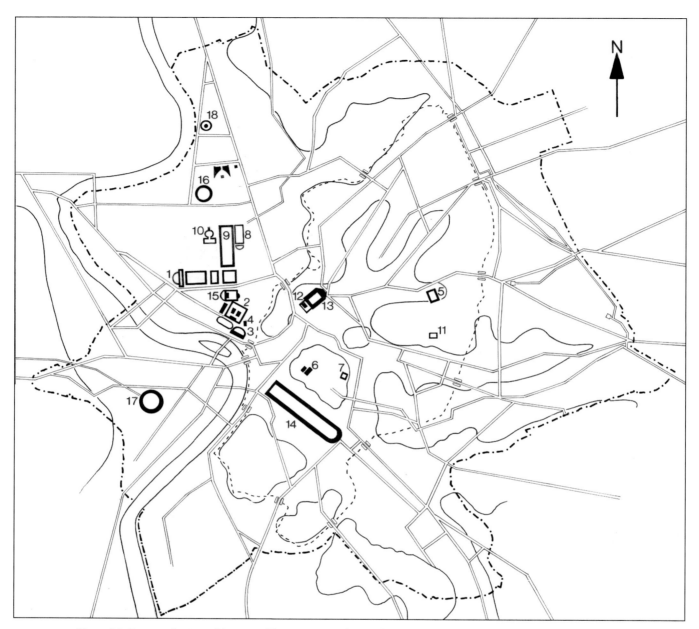

Figure 3.1. Rome at the time of Augustus. The monuments discussed in Ov., *Ars am.* 1.67–176 and some more complexes: 1) Theatre and Porticus of Pompey; 2) Porticus of Octavia; 3) Theatre of Marcellus; 4) Temple of Apollo Sosianus; 5) Porticus of Livia; 6) Temple of Apollo Actiacus and House of Augustus; 7) Adonaea under later Temple of Elagabal; 8) Iseum Campense; 9) Saepta Iulia; 10) Pantheon of Agrippa; 11) Iseum Metellinum; 12) Forum Iulium; 13) Forum Augustum; 14) Circus Maximus; 15) Theatre of Balbus; 16) Amphitheatre of Statilius Taurus (location uncertain) and Horologium Augusti; 17) Naumachia of Augustus; 18) Mausoleum of Augustus. Figure: René Reijnen, Radboud University.

On the basis of the frivolous contents, *Ars amatoria* has been considered a critical, somewhat cryptic attack on the emperor and his laws regarding marriage and adultery. This concern for family politics would be based on his attention to the growth of the population after the decades-long exhaustion due to wars and other disasters.[7] The *Ars amatoria* might have been among the reasons or even the main reason for Ovid's exile in

---

amphitheatre, and the Circus Maximus. The *triumphus* described in Ov., *Ars am.* 1.177–228 has something of a topographical character as well, but it is less relevant for my argument.

[7] Gurval 1998, 133 counts Ovid, Propertius, and Tibullus as opponents of Augustus. On Ovid's 'political' poetry and its implications, see Davis 2006, 9–22. Rather explicit is the political reading of Pianezzola 1991, 21.

AD 8 to Tomis at the Black Sea — despite the time gap of almost eight or even nine years.[8] Various scholars do not acknowledge hints at opposition.[9] Others are aware of Ovid's subversion, so that a German trio composed of a classical archaeologist, classicist, and ancient historian — Ralf von den Hoff, Wilfried Stroh, and Martin Zimmermann — characterize Ovid as 'ein erster Dichter der Opposition' and consider the *Ars amatoria* as one of the main causes of the emperor's irritation.[10] Apparently, the emperor had gradually lost his patience with Ovid's witty, but in many ways problematic, verses and made his decision much later than one would expect.[11] The era of peace, established supposedly by Augustus himself, had to enhance the growth and flourishing of the family as the basis of Roman society, and in this moral policy, Ovid's *Art of Love* was out of place.

The locales of the lover's search within many splendid monuments in Augustan Rome have played a secondary role in the discussion of the presence or absence of political opposition. In studies related to the *Ars amatoria* some attention has been paid to these locations. However, they have received less attention than they deserve, and they have not been taken into account as elements of opposition to Augustus's policies encouraging chastity and increasing the birth rate.[12] This is why I want to discuss whether Ovid's selection of locations, so relevant for Augustan building politics, contains specific elements inappropriate for the lover's search and whether Ovid made those choices on purpose to protest the sexual and moral politics of his days.

To encounter as many nice girls as possible, Ovid singles out spots where masses of people come together, and women can move relatively freely. Conversely, the same is true for the girls who want to find a boy.[13] Most of these places were destined to accommodate large groups of people who spent their free time strolling among monumental architecture, works of art, and patches of green. In that respect, the selection is not necessarily politically subversive: the monuments chosen belong to Augustus's most important building activities, and Ovid's selection underlines their importance.[14] *Ars amatoria* is the first poetic description of an Augustan Rome completed after some twenty-five years of absolute reign and fervid construction activities. Ovid ties in with predecessors describing monuments in the *urbs* and completes a series of venerable poetic examples from Catullus and Horace onwards.[15] He returns to the theme in the *Tristia*. So, we cannot but agree wholeheartedly with Richard Jenkyns, who, in his fine book on imaginative descriptions and evocations of Rome, sees the *Ars amatoria* and the *Fasti* as celebrations of the city.[16]

The description suggests a real walk through Rome, just in the buzzing festivities of 2 BC, as sketched above, but it may at the same time be a fine appraisal of monuments to be visited during different strolls. Nevertheless, Ovid's imaginary walk is not a mere panegyric. Ovid transgresses the domain of appropriateness by singling out Augustan buildings and places, which consciously and deliberately may have stimulated the poet to stealthily write down subversive intentions against Augustus's moral politics. Monuments erected under his predecessors Pompey and Caesar and now featured in the *Ars amatoria* became Augustan edifices thanks to completion and restoration programmes. All complexes singled out by Ovid can be connected with the booming business of the public and private investments of the Early Roman Empire, which radically changed the townscape and constitute a final summa of these fervid construction activities, culminating in the Forum Augustum inaugurated

---

8 He recalls two faults in Ov., *Tr.* II.207–08, which is quoted below. The *carmen* would be the *Ars amatoria*, an *error* involving some affair with Iulia Minor or a conspiracy. See i.e. Boyle 2003, 46–48, 251; Leitner 2005; Ingleheart 2010, 103–09, 121–31; Häuber 2017, 722 references to the *Fasti* as a possible reason. On an exile in AD 9, see Hutchinson 2017.

9 Dimundo 2003, 28; Jenkyns 2013, 107 and 328.

10 Janka 2014 contra Dimundo 2003; von den Hoff, Stroh, and Zimmermann 2014, 209–13, 247–50 (with lengthy bibliography at 324–30). See also Stroh 1979; Davis 2006; Gibson 2009. For a survey of the various motifs, see Leitner 2005.

11 It might be a reference to Augustus's diminished *patientia* or *clementia*. See Sen., *Ben.* VI.32.1–2: when he had to deal with Julia Minor's alleged debaucheries, Augustus could not master his anger (*parum potens irae*) and longed for the time he had Agrippa and Maecenas at his side.

12 See Janka 2014, 22. The study of the monuments still 'unterbleibt' in Dimundo 2003 and other works. Indeed, monuments play no or a minor role in the long section on these verses (Dimundo 2003, 59–94).

13 As described in Ov., *Ars am.* III.387–94.

14 Contra Boyle 2003, 176–77, who argues that the discussed spots did not belong to the Augustan building programme. As we will see, even those monuments that are older (Porticus of Pompey and Forum of Caesar) or related to other persons (Porticus of Livia and Porticus of Octavia), were remade or completed under Augustus.

15 See the fine volume edited by Östenberg, Malmberg, and Björnebye 2015, containing various contributions on literary walks, but not on that in the *Ars amatoria* studied in this paper.

16 Jenkyns 2013, 107 and 328.

on the very day of the imaginary walk.[17] Ovid's Rome is a purely Augustan Rome, without many references to its historical links to the founders who played such an important role in Augustus's remake of the capital of his empire. These buildings transformed the town into a Late Hellenistic luxurious metropolis, accommodating a refined lifestyle. However, in his city appropriation,[18] the poet has turned Rome into an erotic playground — surely not the function Augustus had envisaged as a proper interpretation of his building policy.

Ovid presents a systematic treatment of various categories of public buildings that improve the living conditions in town. In the first place, he deals with three porticoes: Porticus of Pompey, Porticus of Octavia, and Porticus of Livia. They constitute courtyards surrounded by four colonnades, which contained shrines, gardens, and assembly halls.[19] The porticoes themselves accommodated works of art and served as walking galleries. Since they were closed off, they facilitated the stroll, which became a focused action within these precincts.[20] Secondly, Ovid presents a few temples and gathering places of three foreign cults, followed by fora, theatres, the Circus Maximus, and, finally, Augustus's *naumachia* in the artificial pond in Trans Tiberim.[21] Many of these monuments are provided with porticoes as well, and, for that reason, they include important elements characterizing the first category of the explicitly labelled *porticus*.

The genre of the didactic poem obliged Ovid to classify his locations systematically,[22] while, at the same time, his narrator feels free to create a topographical mess. By virtue of this order of monuments and locations, a logical walking route has lost relevance, and the lover has to crisscross through the town, assuming a one-day walk. Yet the area in question remains restricted to a few of the fourteen Augustan *regiones* in the centre of town, most of them being each other's neighbours: III (Oppius), VIII (fora), IX (Campus Martius), X (Palatine), and XIV (Trans Tiberim).[23] Our love seeker is a flâneur, not desiring to follow a systematic order but loving the freedom of this randomness.[24] This created chaos has a corresponding predecessor in the itineraries of Aeneas's walk with Evander through the proto-urban settlement of Rome, painted by Virgil, and a follow-up in the visit of Emperor Constantius to Rome in AD 357, as described by the contemporary historian Ammianus Marcellinus. However, here the order might have reflected the importance of the buildings and strengthened the rhetorical effect the list should create.[25] Many more Latin authors evoked the art of walking and moving around the ancient and modern buildings of the expanding centre of Rome.[26]

The numerous conjunctions (many times *nec* followed by a negative verb like *uitetur*, v. 1.71, *praetereat*, v. 1.75, *fuge*, v. 1.77, *fugiat*, v. 1.135) give the impression that the narrator is afraid to skip some relevant monument and rapidly provides a reference with this kind of 'oh, yes'. His restless movement suggests that he is breathless due to his excitement or enthusiasm. As something hastily put together, we experience this summation by suggestions like 'don't forget' and 'you also should'. Interjections of this kind are typical for the didactic poem. It is no problem that the walk cannot be experienced as a realistic tour. Highlighting well-chosen monuments is Ovid's main concern and not the (unpractical) promenade through Rome.

In what follows, we make a tour of the monuments mentioned or briefly described by Ovid and provide them with a brief topographical and archaeological commentary, especially asking whether there are hints

---

[17] For this new Rome as *urbs ornata* after Suet., *Aug.* XXVIII.3, see Haselberger 2002, 20–23; Boyle 2003, 35–41.

[18] There are many more appropriations of Rome, e.g. those worked out in Östenberg, Malmberg, and Bjørnebye 2015. A predecessor of such a description is Horace's evocation of Rome a couple of decades before, during the fervid changes due to Augustus's building programme, see Corbeill 2015; O'Sullivan 2015, 116–17. For Augustan evocations, see O'Sullivan 2015.

[19] For this type of buildings, see Gros 1996, 95–120; Jenkyns 2013, 95–98; Gros 2020. In relation to Ovid, see Boyle 2003, 176–77; Ingleheart 2010, 250. The thirty-eight porticoes in Rome are discussed in *LTUR* IV, 116–53. Ov., *Ars am.* III.383–66 includes five porticoes cf. Jenkyns 2013, 104–05.

[20] Grimal 1969, 171–88 elaborates on the concept of 'promenades' in porticoes. For art collections in Rome, see Rutledge 2012; Gahtan and Pegazzano 2015.

[21] Regarding these types of buildings, see Gros 1996.

[22] For the Ov., *Ars am.* as a didactic poem, see Hollis 1977, xvii–xix; Volk 2002; Dimundo 2003, 13–23; Davis 2006, 3.

[23] See the map in *LTUR* IV, 518–19. On the regions, D. Palombi, *LTUR* IV, 197–204 s.v. Regiones quatuordecim topografia.

[24] Cf. Zanker 2000, 216–19.

[25] Verg., *Aen.* VIII.306–69; Amm. Marc. XVI.10. Simpson 1987, 247 describes the order of Ovid's topographical items as a modern bus ride. Liverani 2007, 172–80 sees Ammianus's passage as a specimen of rhetoric in which the monuments are mere recordings of Rome's splendour.

[26] See Jenkyns 2013, 143–91 on movement in the city. A fine imaginary stroll through Augustan Rome is found in Favro 1996; cf. O'Sullivan 2015. See also Östenberg, Malmberg, and Bjørnebye 2015; Rutledge 2012.

Monuments of Love in Ovid's Ars amatoria I

The monuments where the lover should go receive succinct but explicit descriptions in the lines 67–176: three porticoes, two fora, two theatres, the Circus Maximus and/or an amphitheatre, and, finally, the complex of the *naumachia* of Caesar. Some more monuments are hiding under less concrete descriptions, such as the Theatre of Marcellus, the meeting places of the worshippers of Adonis, the God of Israel, and Isis.

Porticus of Pompey or Porticus Pompeianae

> tu modo Pompeia lentus spatiare sub umbra,
> cum sol Herculei terga leonis adit,
>
> (You may just walk in Pompey's shade,
> when the sun reaches the back of Hercules' lion,)[27]

Together with the Theatre of Pompey, the Portico of Pompey formed the largest complex in the Campus Martius during the late first century BC. Inaugurated by the *generalissimo* in 55 BC, Augustus turned the complex of his adoptive father's opponent into an Augustan complex.[28] The ample space of 180 by 135 m served as a reception area *post scaenam* during the intervals of entertainment and functioned in daily life as a walking ground or city park for the idle citizens. Connected with its eastern porticus, there was a meeting room for the Senate, the Curia of Pompey.[29] Here, on 15 March of 44 BC, Caesar was murdered at the feet of a statue of Pompey.[30]

Immediately after the inauguration of the complex, Catullus defined it as a locus to find girls; he suspects that his friend Camerius may have taken advantage of it for this purpose:

> 'aufertis' sic usque flagitabam
> 'Camerium mihi, pessimae puellae?'
> 'en', inquit quaedam, sinum reducens,
> 'en hic in roseis latet papillis!'
>
> (I kept demanding, 'Are you keeping
> Camerius from me, you bad girls?'
> Baring her breast, one of them answered,
> 'Look, he's hiding between my rosy breasts!')[31]

The colonnades contained Greek panel paintings, such as representations of Cadmus, his sister Europa, and Pompey's great role model, Alexander the Great. Cicero's friend Titus Pomponius Atticus has been associated with the acquisition of works of art for Pompey's magnificent edifice, and in this matter, he would advise the young Augustus as well.[32] Recent research by Spanish scholars has made clear that Augustus closed this Curia and transformed it into a 'memoria de la labor de *Divus Iulius*'. In this way, it became a *piaculum*, an offer to repair the holy law. This happened at the end of the first century BC, so that in Ovid's days, the spot may still have been an extraordinary holy and respectable place.[33]

The central open area surrounded by the colonnades was shaded by planes,[34] just as the *post scaenam* of the large theatre of Pompeii, which contained flower beds and grass lawns embellished by statues — and nowadays forms the best parallel thanks to its fine preservation.[35] The collection included: the nine Muses (now in various collections), a Sappho made by Silanion, stemming from Verres's booty, and a sleeping satyr.[36] These figures

---

27 Ov., *Ars am.* 1.67–68.

28 *R. Gest. div. Aug.* XX. For the Theatre of Pompey, see Denard 2002; Gagliardo and Packer 2006. See also P. Gros, *LTUR* V, 35–38 s.v. Theatrum Pompei; Tosi and Baccelle 2003, 22–24. On Pompey and the Campus Martius, see Coarelli 1997, 539–80. For the Porticus, see Gleason 1990; 1994; F. Coarelli, *LTUR* I, 334–35 s.v. Curia Pompei, Pompeiana; P. Gros, *LTUR* IV, 148–89 s.v. Porticus Pompei; P. Sabbatini Tumolesi, *LTUR* IV, 149–50 s.v. Porticus Pompei (specifically on the murder of Caesar); Haselberger 2002, 207; Carandini and Carafa 2017, tab. 220–21; Monterroso Checa 2020, 35; Davis (in this volume), 17–19.

29 Sauron 1994, 255–58, pl. XX; Tosi and Baccelle 2003, 755–61; Beard 2007, 27, fig. 6.

30 Cic., *Div.* II.23; Plut., *Caes.* LXVI.1; Suet., *Aug.* XXXI.5. The

colossal nude portrait of Pompey, now exposed in Palazzo Spada not far from the porticus, has sometimes been related to the decoration of this room, but it is a later work of art. See Maderna 1988, 217–18; Papini 2000, 148–49, cat. 5; Hallett 2005, 156 nn. 68 and 337, appendix F.

31 Cat. 55.9–12. Translation taken from O'Sullivan 2015, 115. He gives a fine analysis of Catullus's walk.

32 Cic., *Att.* IV.9.1. See Hallett 2018a, 185.

33 The spot of the murder would be next to the latrines nowadays visible in the excavations on Largo Argentina, at the side of Teatro Argentina. See Monterroso Checa and others 2017, 62–65, 69, and 74, figs 17–19.

34 Prop. II.32.12–13.

35 See Poehler 2016 for recent research in this area and an overview of previous explorations.

36 Sauron 1994, 259–65; Kuttner 1999; Monterroso Checa

transformed the garden into an Arcadian landscape. One more sculptural ensemble represented images of the fourteen nations subdued by Pompey and carved by Coponius, as we know from Pliny the Elder.[37] He describes two peculiar statues, which were made deliberately for this spot:

> Pompeius Magnus in ornamentis labora mirabiles fama posuit effigies ob id diligentius magnorum artificum ingeniis laboratas, inter quas legitur Eutychis a uiginti liberis rogo inlata Trallibus enixa XXX partus, Alcippe elephantum, quamquam id inter ostenta est, namque et serpentem peperit inter initia Marsici belli ancilla et multiformes pluribus modis inter monstra partus eduntur.

> (Among the decorations of his theatre, Pompey the Great located remarkable images, rendered on purpose very meticulously by artists of the highest reputation. Among others one reads about Eutychis, a woman who was cremated at Tralleis by twenty (of her) children — she had given birth thirty times — and about Alcippe who gave birth to an elephant, although that must be regarded as a prodigy, for, at the beginning of the Marsian War a slave gave birth to a snake, and, among the auspices births of all kinds and sorts are mentioned.)[38]

Pliny's description forms part of a discussion of wonderful births and miscarriages. The bizarre statuary groups are also mentioned by Tatianus in his Christian apologetic treatise *Oratio ad Graecos*,[39] where most of these female figures are characterized as prostitutes. In the eyes of a moralist, this is a reason to judge Greek art as pernicious.

Based on these data, Filippo Coarelli has reconstructed three sets of seven statues (we may think of the genre of *hebdomades* in canon building of literature by Varro): seven Greek female poets, seven famous hetaerae, and seven women who had given birth to monsters. Mary Beard dismisses this reconstruction as nonsense in her *The Roman Triumph*, as she does with an interpretation of Gilles Sauron, but she fails to offer an alternative explanation.[40] The French scholar acknowledges Varro

as the designer of this complicated ensemble of statues, for which he has developed a rather far-fetched interpretation.[41]

Ann Kuttner reads Tatianus's phrases as a reaction against erotic poetry in which the Portico of Pompey played a role. She mentions the first literary evocation, immediately in 55, which is Catullus's *Carmen* 55 quoted above, and gives other cases up to Martial.[42] Jane DeRose Evans places Tatianus's invectives in the perspective of his Christian apologetics and dismisses his venom against these 'whores' by analysing the names of these persons more precisely. She recognizes numbers of nine women rather than seven, first the nine mythical and nine modern Muses, the latter being the canonical poetesses beginning with Sappho.[43] Other groups include the nine protagonists of the New Comedy and, as their counterparts, the nine tragic heroines. Images of this genre of groups existed as early as the Late Classical and Hellenistic eras and would perfectly grace this artistic environment. Even if many uncertainties hamper all proposals, Evans's reading seems the most attractive proposal, thanks to its thematic correspondence with the literary and theatrical context of Pompey's Theatre and Porticus.

The Dionysiac theme expressed by the theatre figures and the idyllic landscape appears to have dominated this setting, which is nothing but logical in the theatre's ambience and suits the play of love. Although he does not say it explicitly, Ovid may have made his own connection between the unnatural births and Augustus's concept of the family. And what is more: in correspondence with the monstrous births, had Augustus's mother Atia not been conquered by Apollo in the shape of a snake?[44] This story was known at that time and belonged to a series of other snake conceptions that happened to

---

2020, 36–38. See Miles 2008, 231–37 on Pompey's acquisition of numerous works of art, esp. 235–27 on the Sappho by Silanion.

[37] Plin., *HN*. XXXVI.41. See Monterroso 2008. He locates the statues in the portico at the upper side of the theatre's *cavea*. Cf. Carey 2006, 62–63, 86, and 98 on the propagandistic power. She demonstrates that Pliny sees them as *mirabilia*.

[38] Plin., *HN*. VII.3.

[39] Tatianus, *Oratio ad Graecos* XXXIII.

[40] Coarelli 1971–1972; Beard 2007, 24–25 and 342 n. 50. Beard doubts whether all works mentioned by Tatianus really stood

in the Portico of Pompey. If she is right, the interpretations of Coarelli and other scholars are no longer relevant.

[41] Sauron 1994, 272–80. His extremely learned book has an associative character and connects many heterogeneous sources while trying to provide arguments in favour of his hypotheses, which, as such, are not demonstrable. Sauron's reading was taken over by Gros 1996, 99–100 and Coarelli 1997, 575–76. Kuttner 1999, 344 n. 4 characterizes his discussion as 'dense and speculative', an opinion I cannot underline enough.

[42] Kuttner 1999, 352–53.

[43] DeRose Evans 2009. For these female poets, see De Vos 2012.

[44] Suet., *Aug.* XCIV.4 and Cass. Dio XLV.1.2–3. On this story most extensively Lorsch 1997. Admittedly, Ovid does not refer to it, either here or in other works.

mothers of famous men.[45] Subversion typifies the sexual activities, and one more macabre association of Pompey's Porticus was *locus sceleratus*, the place soiled by Caesar's blood. Augustus had the Curia changed into a place of memory of Caesar. In sum, the place was full of *gravitas* connected with the serious side of Augustan policy.

Porticus Octaviae and Theatre of Marcellus

> aut ubi muneribus nati sua munera mater
> addidit, externo marmore diues opus;
>
> (or where the mother added her treasures to the treasures of her son, a building rich in foreign marble;)[46]

Ovid hints at two joining monuments of Augustan euergetism, *munera*, in the southern Campus Martius, not far from the Theatre of Pompey: the Porticus Octaviae founded by Augustus's sister, mother of Marcellus, and (less markedly mentioned) the Theatre of Marcellus.[47] In the medieval ghetto, the entrance of the porticus remained preserved thanks to restorations under Septimius Severus (inscription on the architrave) and its subsequent adaptation as the front porch of the church Sant'Angelo in Pescheria. Augustus's sister Octavia devoted the Latin and Greek libraries inside the complex to the memory of Marcus Claudius Marcellus, who had died as early as 23 BC at the tender age of twenty-one. Octavia completed the edifice, which had been partly built under Augustus (or by Marcellus under the name of Augustus) from 27 BC onwards. The new colonnades surrounded two older temples dedicated to Jupiter Stator and Juno Regina and included a meeting place for the Senate, Curia Octaviae. Their restoration took place at the same time as the new elements were constructed. This complex would have had the aspect of an art gallery, just as the Porticus of Pompey. Pliny lists statues of Phidias, Praxiteles, Lysippus (his bronze *Turma Alexandri*, a group of horse riders commanded by Alexander the Great and allegedly coming from Dion),[48] and various panel paintings. We cannot determine a specific iconographic programme of these pieces; their value was based on the signatures of famous Greek artists who had made these noble works of art.[49]

As in a few other cases, Ovid recalls the use of precious material, here elements of imported marble (*externo marmore*). The insertion of stone types in monuments from various parts of the Roman Empire increased notably under Augustus.[50] The floor of the Forum Augustum, for instance, was covered with marbles from the entire Roman Empire, symbolizing the subjection of the remote countries and the unity of the empire.

This Porticus Octaviae constituted a monument in memory of Marcellus, Augustus's beloved nephew, while simultaneously serving as a symbol of Augustus's imperium. The high-culture atmosphere corresponded with the high esteem of the emperor for the prematurely deceased genius who had been singled out as the future successor. Now, at the moment chosen by Ovid for his protagonist's walk in Marcellus's *lieu de mémoire*, the poet finally presented his successor: Gaius and Lucius were the candidates. The complex acquired an honourable place in town, in correspondence with its function as place of memory. Allusions to frivolous encounters, therefore, would be out of place and in this respect, Ovid would have made a faux pas in the eyes of the sovereign.

A still more impressive monument recording Marcellus is the theatre named after him. It was built by Augustus and inaugurated in 17 BC during the *Ludi saeculares*. It has for the greater part been preserved in the medieval Castello Savelli.[51] Ovid briefly hints at this monument as *muneribus nati*. It is striking that both the Theatres of Pompey and Marcellus are not mentioned by their names and do not figure as loci for our love hunter. Nevertheless, they are rather significant markers in the landscape of Campus Martius connected with personalities of high prestige. If we consider the specific moment of action, we may assume that no spectacles were taking

---

[45] Lorsch 1997, 798.

[46] Ov., *Ars am.* 1.69–70.

[47] Hollis 1977, 45 refers to the Theatre of Marcellus; Dimundo 2003, 61 mention the Porticus Octaviae. For the portico, see A. Viscogliosi, *LTUR* IV, 141–45 s.v. Porticus Octaviae; Carandini and Carafa 2017, tab. 223. Not to be confounded with the Porticus Octavia erected in 167–163 BC. A. Viscogliosi, *LTUR* IV, 139–41 s.v. Porticus Octavia; Haselberger 2002, 206. On the works of art, see Celani 1998, 151–61.

[48] Vell. Pat. 1.13.4; Plin., *HN* XXXIV.64. A Late Hellenistic group found in the Sanctuary of Juno Sospita at Lavinium might

provide a good impression of this Lysippean masterpiece. For references to Turma Alexandri, see Coarelli 1981, 250, 254–55, 258–59, and 283; Moreno 1981, 185–88.

[49] Carey 2006, 79–80, 86, and 98. On the significant presence of originals as evidenced by inscriptions, see Keesling 2018.

[50] It is told by Asconius, *In Pisonem et Pro Scauro* XLV that Augustus placed four marble columns in the Theatre of Marcellus, stemming from the house of Scaurus, which Ovid might refer to. In that case *externo marmore* may also be an allusion to that feature.

[51] P. Ciancio Rossetto, *LTUR* V, 31–35 s.v. Theatrum Marcelli; Ciancio Rossetto and Pisani Sartorio 2017.

place in them on this particular day when the young man passes by them on his itinerary of love.

Porticus of Livia

> nec tibi uitetur quae priscis sparsa tabellis
> porticus auctoris Liuia nomen habet,
>
> (and don't avoid the portico covered with old paintings which bears the name of its patron, Livia,)[52]

Now we have to make one of the announced illogical detours to the somewhat distant Porticus of Livia on the Oppian Hill where Nero's later Golden House and the Baths of Trajan were located.[53] This building is the perfect symbol of austerity in the Augustan era. Before its construction, the house of Vedius Pollio (contemporary of Caesar and former friend of Augustus) was torn down. It had been willed to Augustus by Vedius before his death in 15 BC, but it bore a bad reputation due to its immeasurable luxury.[54] The Porticus of Livia was an instrument to finalize its *damnatio memoriae*. The reference to its *auctor* might be a pun on Augustus's name. Ovid would write about it in *Fasti* under 11 June:

> [...] ubi Livia nunc est
> porticus, immensae tecta fuere domus:
> urbis opus domus una fuit spatiumque tenebat,
> quo breuius muris oppida multa tenent.
> haec aequata solo est, nullo sub crimine regni,
> sed quia luxuria uisa nocere sua.
>
> (where now is Livia's portico, were the roofs of a gigantic house: one house comprised the mass of a city and occupied the space which many towns could not encompass with their walls. This was razed to the ground, not for high treason, but because it has seemed to be noxious by its luxury.)[55]

The complex was full of works of art, including venerable old paintings, and there was a garden, but unfortunately, Ovid tells us nothing about these features. The porticus probably had a temple dedicated to Concordia, a symbol of the bond between Livia and Augustus. According to Ovid, the Porticus of Livia was clear proof of their happy marriage:[56]

> te quoque magnifica, Concordia, dedicat aede
> Liuia, quam caro praestitit ipsa uiro.
>
> (Livia honours you also with a magnificent temple, Concordia, which she personally donated to her beloved husband.)[57]

There, the empress was represented in a divine effigy of Ceres, who bestows bounty and, at the same time, is a symbol of chastity. This image was no attempt at divinization in life but only underlined that Livia possessed the same qualities as the goddess, whereas Concordia was the 'guardian of family and conjugal life'.[58] Alessandro Barchiesi interprets Ovid's recommendation of this place in the *Ars amatoria* as an 'indelicatezza' and notes the strong contrast between it and the delicate description in the *Fasti* just quoted.[59] We should see Ovid's amorous allusion in the *Ars amatoria* to this place, full of symbolic messages and expressing the notion of the unity of man and woman in their marriage, as a violation of the rules Augustus had instituted some twenty years before, prescribing severe moral conduct regarding marriage and family politics and condemning adultery and prostitution.[60] A further point of consideration is the suggestion of Augustan modesty. By using his inherited real estate, Augustus's *munificentia* could be seen as a grand act: he gave away both the luxurious house and the grounds on which it was built as public property to the citizens of Rome.

Temple of Apollo Palatinus

> quaque parare necem miseris patruelibus ausae
> Belides et stricto stat ferus ense pater;
>
> (nor the place where the Belides dared to kill their poor cousins and their ferocious father stood with a drawn sword;)[61]

---

[52] Ov., *Ars am.* I.71–72.

[53] C. Panella, *LTUR* IV, 127–29 s.v. Porticus Liviae; Neumeister 2010, 53–57; Haselberger 2002, 204; Boyle 2003, 244–47; Carandini and Carafa 2017, tab. 118–19.

[54] Cass. Dio LIV.23.1–6. Flory 1984; C. Panella, *LTUR* II, 211–12 s.v. Domus: P. Vedius Pollio; Green 2004, 228. See the testimonies collected in Frazer 1929, 304–05: the monument served as an instrument of *damnatio memoriae* of Vedius. So not for a much higher accusation, viz. high treason or *perduellio*.

[55] Ov., *Fast.* VI. 639–44.

[56] Green 2004, 227–28.

[57] Ov., *Fast.* VI. 637–38.

[58] Flory 1984, 312 and 317; Neumeister 2010, 55–56.

[59] Barchiesi 1994, 81.

[60] *Lex Iulia de maritandis ordinibus* of *c.* 18 BC. and the probably contemporary *Lex Iulia de adulteriis coercendis*. On these laws, see most extensively McGinn 1993, 70–104 and 140–215. Cf. Hollis 1971, 37; Davis 2006, 33–34, 139 nn. 75–76 and 85. Davis 2006, 86–95 discusses Ovid's disclaimers of inciting adultery.

[61] Ov., *Ars am.* I.73–74.

Again we come to a portico, this one fencing off the holy precinct of the Temple of Apollo Palatinus, which belonged to Augustus's formidable complex of house-cum-shrine, full of works of art.[62] The Belides are the grandchildren of Belus, better known as the Danaids, who, on command of Danaus (*ferus ... pater*), killed their cousins and newly married husbands, sons of Aegyptus, on the wedding night. Fifty statues were exhibited in the colonnades: forty-nine girls, who committed the murder (only Hypermnestra refused), and their father Danaus. They have been recognized in herms of red or black marble, representing young women with complete torsos. The angle of their gesticulating arms could be associated with carrying water containers (with holes), which was their eternal punishment. The black marble is a reference to sunburnt Egypt, the country where the slaughter took place. Even if the statues were small and had an ornamental function, they may still have conveyed this message. We may compare them to the almost contemporary caryatids in the Forum Augustum, symbolizing defeated nations.[63] Ovid mentions the place in *Amores*; his protagonist found a nice girl among the Danaids but refrained from further actions due to the moral implications.[64]

The motif is provocative for various reasons. Of course, the Danaids are punished for their gruesome action and form a negative example of the bond of marriage propagated by Augustus, as made evident in the just mentioned Porticus of Livia; Ovid's narrative order may have arisen with this association in mind. What is more, Augustus re-establishes order by showing this example and makes a 'heavenly home on the Palatine a hell for dissenting subjects'.[65] At the same time, we recognize the following comparandum: the Danaids are the citizens of the Roman Empire who have suffered from an audacious opponent (Mark Antony) or a malicious power (Egypt), ruled by a foreign dynast (Cleopatra). This conflict was a civil war comparable to the conflict between Aegyptus and Danaus, who are brothers and sons of Belus.[66] The citizens suffer from the past, and the legend conveys a myth's translation from east to west or from south to north. Whilst the Danaids provide a great example, this is also true for another gruesome myth represented in the Temple of Apollo: the slaughter of Niobe's offspring. Her children were immortalized on ivory reliefs on the temple's doors, as we know from Propertius's *Elegiae*.[67] Having a large progeny can have serious consequences. Especially if one displays *superbia*, as Niobe does in a confrontation with Apollo's mother, Latona.[68] In and around the Temple of Apollo, we observe marital morality as a central leitmotif. Flirtations in such a sacred realm are entirely out of place.

A final aspect of offence might be the fact that temple buildings had become a mere imperial activity so that the link between erotic strolls and holy shrines touches upon the persona of the emperor and his family. In *Tristia*, the poet returns to this locale and remembers various erotic adventures connected with the gods venerated in the described shrines.[69] Among them feature places for the following foreign cults.

---

[62] P. Gros, *LTUR* I, 54–57 s.v. Apollo Palatinus; Haselberger 2002, 46–47; Boyle 2003, 222–25; Zink and Piening 2009; Rutledge 2012, 237–50; Carandini and Carafa 2017, tab. 70–72; Pandey 2018, 83–141; Kaderka 2018, 237–39 and 243–53.

[63] For the reconstruction of the Portico of the Danaids, see Quenemoen 2006. On the herms most recently, see Häuber 2014, 573–74 (n. 23: contra their belonging to the portico's programme); Hallett 2018a, 184–85, fig. 16.3; Kaderka 2018, 245. On the herms of the Forum Augustum, see Spannagel 1999, 286–87; Goldbeck 2015. One might think of a peculiar parallel, the image of the Danaids on the illustrious shoulder belt of Pallas (Verg., *Aen.* x.497–99). After Turnus killed him (and signed his own death sentence by taking over the belt with the *nefas* image), he wore the belt during the fatal duel with Aeneas, who was ignited by anger after seeing the belt on Turnus's shoulders. Pandey 2018, 111–14 and Barchiesi 2019, 422 see a link between this and the portico.

[64] Ov., *Am.* II.2.3–8. See Pandey 2018, 114–17: The stroll took place a couple of years after the introduction of the *Leges Iuliae* of 18 BC (see n. 60). See also n. 65.

[65] Pandey 2018, 169. Further, similar associations at 85, 89–96 on masculinity, 116–17.

[66] Boyle 2003, 223, following Galinsky 1996, 220–21; Dimundo 2003, 62. Celani 1998, 187–92 is vague, only referring to the contrast between East (Mark Antony) and West (Octavian). In Ov., *Am.* II.2.3–4 the lover describes this portico as the place he saw his new flame. This is an innocent moment since they have not been in contact, for he asks for help from the eunuch Bagoas to get in touch with her. Cf. Edwards 1996, 24.

[67] Prop. II.31.

[68] There were other works of art, e.g the Heifer of Myron known from numerous epigrams thanks to its realism. Propertius mentions the animal in the mentioned poem on four animals that seem alive. Ovid recalls the statue in Ov., *Ponto.* IV.1.34. In the time of Vespasian, the statue was exposed in the Templum Pacis, in a kind of museum. For all these Greek works of art, see Celani 1998, 91–102; Tucci 2017; Moormann 2022, 141–47. Concerning the motif of the Niobids, we may recall that one of the pediments of the contemporary Temple of Apollo Sosianus next to the Portico of Octavia and the Theatre of Marcellus contained a Greek sculpture group of the Niobids, see Celani 1998, 102–05; Kaderka 2018.

[69] Ov., *Tr.* II.287–300. See Ingleheart 2010, 251–59.

Adonis, the Jews, and Isis

> nec te praetereat Veneri ploratus Adonis,
> cultaque Iudaeo septima sacra Syro,
> nec fuge linigerae Memphitica templa iuuencae
> (multas illa facit, quod fuit ipsa Ioui).
>
> (and let not escape you Adonis wept by Venus, nor the seventh-day cult sacred to the Syrian Jew, and don't flee the Memphis temple of the linen-dressed heifer (she changes many girls into what she herself was for Jupiter).)[70]

This brief record of foreign cults in Rome — Adonis, Isis, and the Jews — differs at first sight from Ovid's references to specific places, but we may assume that he here also makes allusions to sacral buildings with accommodations where many people, especially women, could come together. Ovid probably asks his seeking man implicitly to focus on the monuments themselves and the significance both Augustus and Ovid attribute to them. The three gods come from the same area in the Near East and could be seen as neighbours: Adonis came from Phoenicia, the God of Israel lived nearby, and Isis had her origin in Egypt.

We do not have independent evidence of a synagogue in Rome dating to this era, although there were Jewish communities in Rome from the second century BC onwards. Katherine Welch suggests that the synagogue in the Subura could date back to the time of Caesar.[71] Thanks to its location and connection with Augustus's adoptive father, it would constitute a likely candidate. However, apart from some written mentions, we do not know much about other (mostly later) synagogues.[72] We cannot assume that the prayer accommodations had the form of the Roman temple squares, whether or not surrounded by a portico; they may have been closed-off rooms like the Late Antique synagogues in Dura-Europos and Ostia. It strikes us that Ovid lets the young man search here for beautiful girls since men and women were kept separate during Jewish ceremonies. In that respect, they would match Augustan standards of behaviour and so do not fit with Ovid's amorous city walk.[73]

Adonis was a mythical lover, praised for his beauty and brought to life again by Venus, as Ovid amply described in his *Metamorphoses*.[74] His cult place was the Adonaea, a garden complex with potted plants on the Palatine and associated with the Domus Augustana. In their first phase, these gardens are dated to the Flavian period. Archaeologists from the French School of Rome have explored traces under the Temple of Elagabal in the Vigna Barberini. Ovid could not have alluded to those gardens unless there existed an unknown earlier version, in which case its mention after the Portico of the Danaids provides a topographical clue. Pierre Grimal has suggested the location of an Adoneum in the Campus Martius, which has not been met with approval.[75] In all cases, we are struck by the fact that we are dealing with a garden, the *locus amoenus* of Venus and Adonis. The plants represent the second and eternal stage of their love. The Garden of Adonis can be seen as a pendant of the Portico of Pompey, full of hints at lovers. The Flavian complex bears a resemblance to a portico precinct, ideally matching Ovid's typology of buildings.[76]

When we look at Isis, Ovid can have thought of two sanctuaries. Firstly, the Iseum Campense in the Campus Martius, probably founded between 20 and 10 BC, although, if we give credit to a reference in Cassius Dio's *History*,[77] it has been argued that Octavian started it, together with his two triumviri, as early as 43 BC. If we accept this later date, Augustus illustrated his successes in the land of the Nile using this monument, a message taken up by his Flavian successors when they constructed the huge Iseum in the area of the Santa Maria sopra Minerva.[78] A second candidate would be the Iseum Metellinum on the Oppian, not far from the Porticus Liviae, if its foundation to the *gens Metella* dating to around 70 BC is accurate. However, since recent scholarship has problems identifying the Iseum with the

---

[70] Ov., *Ars. am.* I.75–78.

[71] K. Welch, *LTUR* IV, 379–83, esp. 382. There might have existed a 'client-patron bond between Jews and the Iulii Caesares forged at a neighbourhood level in the Subura'. Less sure G. De Spirito, *LTUR* IV, 392 s.v. Synagogae, S. Σιβουρησίων/ Σιβουρήσων.

[72] G. De Spirito, *LTUR* IV, 389–93 s.v. Synagogae; Haselberger 2002, 237–38.

[73] Simpson 1987. For festivals, see Boyle 2003, 177.

[74] Ov., *Met.* X.519–739.

[75] Grimal 1969, 184–88. See M. Royo, *LTUR* I, 14–16 s.v. Adonaea.

[76] The different interpretations have been clearly summarized by M. Royo, *LTUR* I, 14–16 s.v. Adonaea. For the tradition of Adonis gardens on the Palatine, see Villedieu 2001. Simpson 1987 also suggests the Palatine, but admits that there are few indications regarding this period.

[77] Cass. Dio XLVII.15.4.

[78] F. Coarelli, *LTUR* IV, 107–09 s.v. Iseum et Serapeum in Campo Martio; Isis Campensis; Lembke 1994, 65–67 Augustan phase; 74–77. For Augustan activities in the Campus Martius, see Haselberger 2002, 152; Versluys, Bülow Clausen, and Capriotti Vittozzi 2018, 29–40, 71–72.

remains in Via Pasquale Villari, this candidate should be left out.[79]

It has been argued that Isis would have been a persona non grata in the first decades of the reign of Augustus, which might only have been true for cult practice inside the pomerium. She would have gained a bad reputation as the symbol of Egypt as the land of Cleopatra and Mark Antony, but this hypothesis seems contradicted by the numerous references to the goddess in Augustan art. Isis has not been deemed *damnatio memoriae* at any point. On the contrary, she had many manifestations in the Temple of Apollo Palatinus, the previous so-called *studiolo* of the House of Augustus, and the House of Livia.[80]

The expression 'linigerae iuuencae' in line 77 refers to a wonderful metamorphosis: Jupiter turned his lover Io into a heifer, who regained her human form to give birth to Epaphus.[81] This happened under Isis's approving gaze, who, in this way, validated the relationship between Io and Jupiter. Thus, we get a further link to the lover's itinerary that is the portico of the Belides described before, in which Egypt plays a role as well. The topic connects the monument with the statues of the wondrous births in the Porticus of Pompey.

Again, we observe formal correspondences with previously presented buildings, gardens, and porticoes. The Isea had water basins and green spaces, so even if they may not yet have the grand appearance of the Flavian Iseum Campense,[82] our still lonely lover may have found good hunting grounds here.

---

79 M. De Vos, *LTUR* III, 110–12 s.v. Iseum Metellinum Reg. III; Haselberger 2002, 149–52; Häuber 2014, 51–94, esp. 53–55 for the refutation.

80 De Vos 1980, 74. Likewise, the adornment of the temple complex included references to Isis, see Boyle 2003, 223–24; Davis 2006, 31; contra Gurval 1995, 124. For the terracotta sima with Isis and sphinxes and the terracotta antefixes with the head of Bes and an elephant, see Strazzulla 1990, 81–92. Thanks to these decorative elements, the hypothesis of Augustus's aversion to the cult of Isis should be mistrusted. Lembke 1994, 66, 76, and 87 mentions the House of Augustus and related buildings, but dates them too late, viz. the 20s BC. That is why her rejection of the cult of Isis in the time of Augustus looks forced. On Isis and Augustan art, see van Aerde 2019. On the terracottas as a set and their significance, see Hallett 2018a. For the House of Augustus as that of a very young Octavian, see most recently Lipps 2018.

81 Io as a heifer and guarded by Argus was the central depiction in one of the main rooms of the House of Livia, next door to the Temple of Apollo. Io's arrival in Egypt in the presence of Isis would be a theme of the *ekklasterion* paintings in the Temple of Isis in Pompeii. Ingleheart 2010, 256–57 gives many more references to Isis and Io in Ovid's work.

82 J.-C. Grenier, *LTUR* III, 358–59 s.v. Obelisci, Iseum

Forum Iulium

> et fora conueniunt (quis credere possit?) amori,
> flammaque in arguto saepe reperta foro.
> subdita qua Veneris facto de marmore templo
> Appias expressis aera pulsat aquis,
> illo saepe loco capitur consultus Amori,
> quique aliis cauit, non cauet ipse sibi;
> illo saepe loco desunt sua uerba diserto,
> resque nouae ueniunt, causaque agenda sua est.
> hunc Venus e templis, quae sunt confinia, ridet;
> qui modo patronus, nunc cupit esse cliens.
>
> (Likewise the forums are conducive to love — who could believe it! and flame often blazes up in the noisy forum. Placed at the foot of the marble temple of Venus Appias hits the air with water jets; at this place a lawyer is often entrapped by Amor and while still pleading for others, he lets down his own guard; often that's where the orator is at a loss for words, and he has to plead an unprecedented case *pro se*. Venus laughs at him from her adjacent temple; he was just a patron, now wants to be the client.)[83]

One may ask whether people were allowed to flirt in a forum (*fora* in line 79 defines the class of monuments). In the Forum of Caesar, people, who are not fully engaged with their work, would disturb the juridical practice, and lawyers cannot defend themselves against Amor.[84] Ovid dedicates many lines to this risky commotion. One association could be the adjacent Subura, where prostitutes came down, whereas it was also the area where Caesar's family had held its residence.[85] He refers to a Temple of Venus two times, which, next to the law offices, links the event with the Forum of Caesar.[86] This forum was voted by Caesar in 54 and inaugurated in 46 BC and had, as

---

Campense; Versluys, Bülow Clausen, and Capriotti Vittozzi 2018. A third obelisk, the Obelisco Dogali, stands next to the Baths of Diocletianus, see Versluys, Bülow Clausen, and Capriotti Vittozzi 2018, 333–49. The fourth is in the Boboli Gardens in Florence, see Capecchi 2003. For the Egyptian and Egyptianizing statues in the Capitoline Museums, see Ensoli Vittozzi 1990.

83 Ov., *Ars am.* I.79–88.

84 Neumeister 2010, 95–97 sees lawyers as incapable of defending their own case without relying on jurisprudence. This might incapacitate them, despite the presence of Venus.

85 For its topography, see K. Welch, *LTUR* IV, 379–83; Emmerson 2020, 106–07. However, we should take into account that Caesar was born in this area (Suet., *Iul.* XLVI).

86 Amici 1991; C. Morselli, *LTUR* II, 299–306 s.v. Forum Iulium; P. Gros, *LTUR* II, 306–07 s.v. Forum Iulium, Venus Genetrix, aedes; Neumeister 2010, 94–98; Westall 1996; Haselberger 2002, 134–35; Boyle 2003, 202–05; Rutledge 2012, 226–35; Delfino 2014; Carandini and Carafa 2017, tab. 28–29.

its focus, the Temple of Venus Genetrix commemorating the Battle of Pharsalus in 48 BC. Its completion and the official opening took place in 29 BC, for which reason we can consider it in the age of Ovid, an almost completely Augustan monument, whereas the vestiges we see nowadays are mostly Trajanic.[87] The surrounding accommodations, behind the precinct's portico, served as offices for lawyers and politicians. Caesar planned to include the new Curia Senatus, but this edifice would only be completed under Augustus, located at the western side of the Argiletum. Formally, the forum has a feature in common with the previously treated monuments, viz. its portico around piazza and temple.

Caesar's forum contained many artworks, and its building materials were precious as well.[88] The visitor's eye met with an impressive statue in the centre of the piazza representing Caesar in military attire on horseback. If we may believe Statius,[89] this equestrian statue of Caesar had initially been an equestrian portrait of Alexander the Great by Lysippus. Alexander's head had been replaced with Caesar's.[90] There is a similar reworking of a bronze statue of Domitian that was changed into a Nerva from the Augusteum in Misenum (now in the Castello di Bacoli). Next to it stood a portrait of his favourite horse,[91] although it has been suggested that this was the same statue as the equestrian portrait. Finally, there was a cuirassed statue, a *statua loricata*.[92] It is evident that Caesar wanted to present himself as a great military leader.[93]

One of the masterpieces was the Fountain of the Appiads (here sg. *Appias*; plur. *Appiades*)[94] — child or children/nymphs of Appius — made by the contemporary artist Stephanus.[95] The Appius mentioned was Appius Claudius Caecus, who, as a censor, started the construction of the Aqua Appia and the Via Appia. Because this aqueduct did not provide this part of Rome with water (the Aqua Marcia did this), the fountain served as a symbol of the bounty given by water in general.[96] The statue in question may have come from the property of the aforementioned Vedius Pollio. Its translation could serve as one more Augustan example of annihilating private luxury and transferring *bonum priuatum* into *bonum commune* set up in public space.[97] We do not know what the fountain looked like, because we lack coin images. Paul Zanker characterized this ensemble as 'ein heiterer Ort'.[98]

The temple sheltered the cult statue from the hand of Arcesilaus.[99] The cult statue is lost, but it looked like the Aphrodite by Callimachus, if we depend on the coin images: a slim female figure dressed in a wet-look chiton that left bare one of the breasts. Arcesilaus's Venus was more chaste in that she had both breasts covered. The cella housed many more artworks such as panel paintings by Timomachus featuring Medea before the infanticide, the Suicide of Ajax, the Venus Anadyomene by Apelles, and a golden statue of Cleopatra dedicated by Caesar.[100] Finally, Augustus installed a portrait of his adoptive father briefly after the assassination. The Cleopatra statue, which, according to Richard Westall, would have been dedicated by Augustus in 29 BC, has raised some discussion. In this context, she would not feature as the lover of the deceased Caesar, but as the queen defeated by Caesar's successor and adoptive son. This suggestion is difficult to believe, as Augustus would have had little interest in

---

87 *R. Gest. div. Aug.* IV.20.3; Cass. Dio XLV.6.4. Kindberg and Raja 2018 provides information on a current Danish-Italian research programme on this forum, the Caesar's Forum Project. See also Delfino 2014; Egelund 2018; Davis (in this volume), 20–21; Di Siena and others (in this volume); Hass and Raja (in this volume).

88 Westall 1996, 87 expresses doubts on the reliability of Ovid's mentioning of the marble temple for reasons unclear to me. The poet stresses the wealth of the temple in what follows.

89 Stat., *Silv.* I.1.84–85.

90 See C. Morselli, *LTUR* II, 300; Hallett 2018b, 279–80, 281–82 n. 37.

91 Suet., *Iul.* LXI; Plin., *HN.* VIII.155.

92 Plin., *HN.* XXXIV.18.

93 Zanker 2009, 290–92.

94 Ov., *Ars am.* III.452.

95 Plin., *HN.* XXXVI.33.

96 This work of art also features in Ov., *Ars am.* III.452 and Ov., *Rem. am.* 659–60. In the first passage, the Appiads and Venus cast an undisturbed glance at a riot.

97 Hollis 1977, 49 suggests that it was a second copy. Coarelli (*LTUR* I, 59–60 s.v. Appiades; *LTUR* I, 133–35 s.v. Atrium Libertatis) localizes the statue group in the adjacent *Atrium Libertatis*, where many works collected by Vedius Pollio were exposed, on the basis of the list including the Appiads in Plin., *HN.* XXXVI.33. So do P. Gros *LTUR* II, 307 s.v. Forum Iulium: Venus Genetrix, aedes; Celani 1998, 206–07; Boyle 2003, 203, but the text does not permit such a conclusion. On the collection of Vedius Pollio, see Celani 1998, 115–22; Miles 2008, 238–40. On house destructions as a political action, see Foubert 2010, 76–78.

98 Zanker 2000, 213, relying on Ovid (the passage is not specified here, but it can be nothing but our text).

99 Plin., *HN.* XXXV.156.

100 App., *B Civ.* II.15.102. Westall 1996, 93–98 sees them as references to Caesar's rival Pompey. On the statue, see Westall 1996, 109–10; Zanker 2009, 292; Rutledge 2012, 228–29.

3. FIND A LOVER IN AUGUSTAN ROME

placing a precious portrait of his former enemy in this conspicuous position.[101]

Venus Genetrix does not represent the goddess of love: she symbolizes the founding mother of Rome, an association propagated by Sulla and fostered by Caesar and Augustus. If we take into account the juridical function of the forum and the display of Augustus's venerable roots and Venus's specific role, we may conclude that love seeking was not appropriate in this context.

Theatres and the Circus Maximus

> sed tu praecipue curuis uenare theatris:
> haec loca sunt uoto fertiliora tuo.
> illic inuenies quod ames, quod ludere possis,
> quodque semel tangas, quodque tenere uelis.
> ut redit itque frequens longum formica per agmen,
> granifero solitum cum uehit ore cibum,
> aut ut apes saltusque suos et olentia nactae
> pascua per flores et thyma summa uolant,
> sic ruit ad celebres cultissima femina ludos;
> copia iudicium saepe morata meum est.
> spectatum ueniunt, ueniunt spectentur ut ipsae:
> ille locus casti damna pudoris habet.

(But hunt especially in the curved theatres: these places are more fertile than you might hope. There you'll find what you may love, what you may play with, and what you may touch one time and want to keep. As many ants are going and coming in a long row, while they carry their usual food with their grain-bearing mouths, or as bees reach their woods and fragrant meadows and fly from flower to flower and the tips of thyme, so, the most cultured women rush to the famous plays: their multitude has often disturbed my judgment. They come to look, they come to be seen in person: that place has occasioned the loss of chaste modesty.)[102]

As before with *fora*, the plural *theatris* defines a category of buildings. Apart from the barely mentioned Theatres of Pompey and Marcellus, Rome got one more theatre under Augustus: the Theatre of Balbus.[103] With Ovid, we see public games in one of these theatres or an amphitheatre.[104] With the lengthy narration of the Rape of the Sabine Women in lines 101–34, Ovid leads the reader

to the Circus Maximus. The rape took place in the Vallis Murcia, located between Titus Tatius's Aventine and Romulus's Palatine, consequently the later Circus Maximus.[105]

The story of the Sabine Virgins bears an etiological character, marking the *synoikismos* of the inhabitants of the Palatine with the Sabines residing on the Aventine, which would strengthen the power of the still nascent state of Rome. There lies a certain spiciness in the very nature of the rape, not being consonant with Augustus's propagation of fine mores, although it obtained a stamp of approval as being an important event of the first king, Romulus, to expand his reign.[106] The episode was explained positively thanks to the fact that the mothers of the Sabine girls forgave the Roman men around Romulus and got the right of marriage. The abduction caused fertile and stable marriages, which would expand the Roman population in good prosperity. Keeping this in mind, the story became acceptable in Augustan ideology.

Another important point is that the separation of men and women in Ovid's version of the story is an excellent example of anachronism, as is the primitive representation of the complex. This rustic condition of early pre-urban Rome has been evoked other times; think of the aforementioned walk made by Aeneas and Evander in the still rough 'Land of Saturn'. The valley between Aventine and Palatine was crucial in other aspects, thanks to the cult of the fertility deities Ops and Consus. Moreover, Aeneas and Romulus were forebears of and examples to the emperor who gave them much space in public imagery.[107]

The foundation of the Circus Maximus was attributed to Tarquinius Priscus or his son Tarquinius Superbus.[108] In 46 BC, the venue got its definitive shape under Caesar, with the long barrier, *spina*, in the middle of the arena and fixed tribunes for 150,000 spectators. In 33 BC, Agrippa had a statue depicting seven dolphins

---

101 Westall 1996, 107. He refers to Cass. Dio LI.22.3, but Dio only reports the statue in connection with Augustus's triumph.

102 Ov., *Ars am.* I.89–100.

103 Tosi and Baccelle 2003, 24–27; Haselberger 2002, 241–42; Boyle 2003, 260–61.

104 On the meaning of 'spectacles in Rome's theatres', see Ingleheart 2010, 247.

105 F. Coarelli, *LTUR* III, 289–90 s.v. Murcia. On this passus at length Dimundo 2003, 69–82. In Ov., *Tr.* II.283–84, the Circus has become a 'venue of vice', see Ingleheart 2010, 248–50.

106 Davis 2006, 102–05 acknowledges subversive tendencies in this passage. For less anti-Augustan interpretations, see Heldmann 2001, 374–87; Dimundo 2003, 18–19 and 69–82.

107 See Dardenay 2010; 2012. For the impact within Imperial politics, see Hekster 2015, 240–50 and 261–66.

108 P. Ciancio Rossetto, *LTUR* I, 272–77 s.v. Circus Maximus. See also Golvin 1988, 63–64; Neumeister 2010, 225–41; Tosi and Baccelle 2003, 30–32; Zanovello 2003, 846–64; Haselberger 2002, 87–89; Boyle 2003, 199–202 and 260–61.

mounted on the *spina* and in 10 BC, Augustus added the obelisk from Heliopolis (which now graces Piazza del Popolo).[109] This needle and the Horologium Augusti in the northern Campus Martius commemorated the conquest of Egypt. So, it seems that our lover visits the third monument connected with Augustus's victory over Mark Antony and Cleopatra, after the Forum Iulium and the Temple of Apollo Palatinus.

There is no need here to dwell on the story of the Sabines in *Ars amatoria*, after which follows an extensive presentation of approaching strategies when diving into the crowd gathered in the Circus (v. 135–70). The following verses explain how to conquer a girl:

> Nec te nobilium fugiat certamen equorum:
> multa capax populi commoda Circus habet.
> nil opus est digitis per quos arcana loquaris,
> nec tibi per nutus accipienda nota est;
> proximus a domina nullo prohibente sedeto.
> iunge tuum lateri qua potes usque latus.

> (The Circus, full of people, has many facilities. Don't miss the race of the noble horses: the Circus, with space for many people, offers many opportunities. You don't have to speak in sign language and you shouldn't either call attention by nodding; go and simply sit next to your lady; no one forbids it. Let your flank nestle as near as possible next to her.)[110]

It was an essential advantage for the young man that the Circus had a free seating system (and not yet the separated sections it would get in the subsequent era — just like other public spectacle venues). So here, as well as in the *Amores*, Ovid can expand freely on possibilities to find a girl. He clearly does not send a negative message.[111]

Gladiatorial Games in the Saepta Iulia

> hos aditus Circusque nouo praebebit amori,
> sparsaque sollicito tristis harena foro.
> illa saepe puer Veneris pugnauit harena,
> et, qui spectauit uulnera, uulnus habet.

dum loquitur, tangitque manum, poscitque libellum,
et quaerit posito pignore, uincat uter,
saucius ingemuit telumque uolatile sensit
et pars spectati muneris ipse fuit.

(The Circus provides these entries to the new love, Just as the sad sand thrown over the troubled forum. Often the son of Venus has battled in that arena And he who has looked at wounds, has himself a wound. While speaking and touching her hand and getting a programme and trying a bet on who will win, he has moaned, wounded, and felt the flying missile and he himself has become part of the spectacle.)[112]

With the last line referring to the Circus (v. 163) Ovid makes a bridge to the Forum Romanum (in singular, hence a specific place; cf. supra on the Forum Iulium). Here gladiatorial games were organized for centuries (v. 170: *munus*) until permanent amphitheatres would be constructed. The Circus Maximus also accommodated these games, but the specific change suggests that Ovid takes the male lover from the Circus to a new location. The battles themselves are only hinted at in these verses: the effect of Amor's arrows is equal to the wounds incurred by the gladiators and cannot be avoided.

While Pompeii and other towns in Italy got their permanent amphitheatres in the second quarter of the first century BC, it happened relatively late in Rome, probably due to local traditions of *munera*. In 30–29 BC, Statilius Taurus founded an amphitheatre partly in stone in the southern Campus Martius, next to the Circus Flaminius in the later ghetto (Monte de' Cenci), as has been argued most recently by Welch. Despite its importance, and due to the limited capacity and dimensions, it was not large enough for the grand festivities of 2 BC.[113] Filippo Coarelli has argued that Ovid refers to the Forum Romanum, still remembering the games of some years before. That would imply that no games were held in 2 BC.[114] This is not very likely, for this sort of manifestation was indispensable during great festivities. My doubt is strengthened by a brief remark made by Velleius Paterculus, who clearly mentions *munera*, a *naumachia*, and *spectacula*.[115] Cassius Dio mentions the

---

[109] J.-C. Grenier, *LTUR* III, 355–56, s.v. Obeliscus Augusti, Circus Maximus; Haselberger 2002, 182–83. Originally voted by Sethi I (1294–1279) and his successor Ramses II (1279–1213). Constantine added the obelisk of Tutmoses III (1279–1425), now in Piazza San Giovanni J.-C. Grenier, *LTUR* III, 356–57, s.v. Obeliscus Constantii, Circus Maximus.

[110] Ov., *Ars am.* I.135–40.

[111] Neumeister 2010, 227–31 gives a fine combined reading of our passage and Ov., *Am.* III.2.

[112] Ov., *Ars am.* I.163–70.

[113] Golvin 1988, 52–53; A. Viscogliosi, *LTUR* I, 36–37 s.v. Amphitheatrum Statilii Tauri; Haselberger 2002, 44–45; Tosi and Baccelle 2003, 12; Welch 2007, 108–27. See also Häuber 2017, 328–37; Hallett 2018a, 194–95.

[114] Coarelli 1992, 225; Boyle 2003, 182 keeps the options vague.

[115] Vell. Pat. II.100.2 mentions them in the context of the sex

Saepta Iulia as the locus of large games in 7 BC and in connection with the celebrations of 2 BC.[116] The Saepta might be a plausible candidate to host the games because they could accommodate large masses of people thanks to their dimensions (310 by 120 m) and the presence of a portico over the entire length.[117] Augustus could have been commemorating his great companion and supporter Agrippa, the father of Lucius and Gaius, who had died ten years before. Agrippa had restructured the Saepta in 26 BC, and erected nearby the Pantheon as well as his public Baths. An ideological aspect, which might link with our topic, is that Augustus restructured the *munera* so that the emperor unofficially acquired the monopoly to organize them by limiting the possibilities of private patrons from the senatorial elite. By doing so, he expressed his power towards the political elite in this respect as well.[118]

Naumachia of Augustus

> quid, modo cum belli naualis imagine Caesar
> Persidas induxit Cecropiasque rates?
> nempe ab utroque mari iuuenes, ab utroque puellae
> uenere, atque ingens orbis in Vrbe fuit.
> quis non inuenit turba, quod amaret, in illa?
> eheu, quam multos aduena torsit amor!

> (And what was there now when the emperor, with the image of a sea battle introduced Persian and Greek ships? For from both seas have come young men and girls and the large world was in the City. Who did not find in that multitude something to love? Oh, how many were vexed by a foreign love!)[119]

Here not the mock sea battle itself is meant, but the pond to accommodate a *naumachia* installed by Augustus in 2 BC in or near the Horti Caesaris. This would be a basin of 600 by 400 m with an islet in its centre and located in Trans Tiberim (in the area of the church of San Cosimato).[120] The islet was embellished with statues of Gaius and Lucius. The event showed the Battle of Salamis. The 'Cecropides' are the descendants of the Athenian mythical king Cecrops, the Athenians. It has the significance of a re-enactment of the Battle of Actium. Spannagel hints at a connection with the conflict with the Parthians, to which the Temple of Mars Ultor in the Forum Augustum is the most important reference. However, in that conflict, water was no factor of relevance. Otherwise, Spannagel's other parallel, the *naumachia* that Caesar organized at the inauguration of his forum, was not connected with any sea battle at all.[121] So, we cannot but conclude that mock battles took place two times to illustrate the inauguration of a forum.

The pond was specifically dug for this *naumachia*, and the water was imported from the Aqua Alsietina.[122] According to Cassius Dio, Gaius and Lucius took the initiative,[123] although Augustus suggested that he did so in *Res gestae*.[124] They also organized the gladiatorial games, so we can ask whether Ovid speaks about both events at the same time.

Spannagel has argued that Ovid 'diskreditiert' the *naumachia* and the subsequently described triumphs as ideal places to find a lover on the basis of *Ars amatoria*.[125] Apparently, the young man has to explain to the girl all things to be seen,[126] but I fail to recognize this in this passage. Ovid instructs the aspiring lover: it does not matter what you say, only that you keep the conversation going.

---

scandal of Augustus's daughter Julia in 2 BC.

[116] Cass. Dio LV.10. N. Purcell, *LTUR* II, 331–32 s.v. Forum Romanum (the Republican period) on games starting in the late fourth century BC on the Forum Romanum. N. Purcell, 338 s.v. Forum Romanum (the Imperial period) suggests a definite end of these games after a fire in 9 BC. Cf. Golvin 1988, 56–58: no games on the Forum after 7 BC, viz. after the restoration due to a fire. For the games in the public realm until the end of the Republic, Golvin 1988, 15–44.

[117] Golvin 1988, 53, 59; E. Gatti, *LTUR* IV, 228–29, s.v. Saepta Iulia; Coarelli 1997, 153–63; Haselberger 2002, 219; Häuber 2017, 124–26, 218–41; Poggio 2018, 194–97. Coarelli estimates the length of the portico to 740 m and refers to 55,000 voting people for the election of the *comitia tributa* in this complex. Dimundo 2003, 90 suggests the Forum Romanum as the place of action.

[118] For this reorganization, see Slater 1996, 79–81.

[119] Ov., *Ars am.* I.171–76.

[120] Golvin 1988, 59–60; A. M. Liberati, *LTUR* III, 337, s.v. Naumachia Augusti; Haselberger 2002, 179; Tosi and Baccelle 2003, 817–21; Berlan-Bajard 2006, 39, 162–78, 323–41, 407–09. Augustus mentions it in *R. Gest. div. Aug.* XXIII. See also Davis 2006, 95–98. For a good overview of the area, see Emmerson 2020, 215–15.

[121] Spannagel 1999, 27–28. For the *naumachia* of Caesar, see A. M. Liberati, *LTUR* III, 338, s.v. Naumachia Caesaris; Tosi and Baccelle 2003, 816–17; Berlan-Bajard 2006, 153–62, 326–30, 401–16. This *naumachia*, constructed in 46 BC should be sought in the Campus Martius and differs from that of Augustus.

[122] Suet., *Aug.* XLIII.

[123] Cass. Dio. LV.10.6–8.

[124] Cf. Suet., *Aug.* XLIII.

[125] Ov., *Ars am.* I.213–28.

[126] Spannagel 1999, 27 n. 88.

In what follows, the poet turns to 'moving' events, such as the triumphal procession (v. 177–28) and the banquet (v. 229–59), as opportunities to meet girls. Hereafter, book I continues with the things a conqueror should do with his conquered.

Conclusion

According to some scholars, Ovid concludes in *Tristia* that his *Ars amatoria* caused him his exile (cf. n. 7):

> Perdiderint cum me duo crimina: carmen et error,
> Alterius facti culpa silenda mihi.
>
> (Now that two crimes, poem and error, have ruined me, I should keep silence on the blame of the other fact.)[127]

However, at the same time, he tries to downplay the problem:

> denique composui teneros non solus amores:
> composito poenas solus amore dedi.
>
> (After all I was not the only one to write sweet love songs: I alone have been punished with writing love songs.)[128]

Apparently, Ovid's *Ars amatoria* and *Amores* (his *teneros amores*) contained problematic strophes that condemned the poet to exile in AD 8 or 9. At the same time, his poems were some ten years old and could not be considered novelties in Roman literary circles; they could not be a new argument favouring expulsion.[129] Regarding the value of Ovid's statement, a debate has become inevitable. In *Tristia*, the poet tried to lessen the burden of evidence by calling the *Ars amatoria* a handbook for prostitutes,[130] which is at odds with the contents: the first two books are for men, and throughout the work, little attention is paid to *meretrices* at all.[131] Some scholars, such as Davis, consider these verses proof of Ovid's politically risky position. Davis detects the insulting force in the poet's stimulation of men and women to have free sexual intercourse in the sense of *adulterium* or *stuprum*, according to the *Lex Iulia*. Gibson recognizes a subversion of societal order by his 'constant flirtation with adultery'.[132]

Jenkyns suggests too narrow and private an involvement of the poet with the court.[133] In her study on 'reader response on a range of Augustan icons', Nandini Pandey argues that Ovid's mistake was Augustus's misreading of his texts and suggests a highly plausible mentality change among the poet's readership.[134] In her view, the erotic approach of these Augustan monuments diminishes the historical and political importance of Augustus's monumental reshaping of Rome.

When we take into account the monuments in Rome highlighted by Ovid,[135] I think that his selection corroborates the subversion hypothesis to a certain degree, as he seems to suggest personally in *Tristia*,[136] where various Augustan monuments reappear.[137] The monuments demonstrate Augustus's rebuilding of the old Regal and Republican city as a new *urbs Augusta*, dominated by his powerful constructions. In some cases (e.g. the Porticus Liviae, the Temple of Apollo, and the Forum of Caesar), the monuments show clear connections with aspects of the moral politics of Augustus or invite a viewer to recall other painful events in the past. Apart from a few cases (viz. the theatres), Ovid consciously selects the locations, which played a crucial role in Augustan politics, and never in the frivolous sense our poet ascribes to them. I do not immediately want to suggest that Ovid was banished (to an exile that would last almost ten years) for that very reason only, but he cannot have acquired a strong consent from the side of the emperor with this section of the *Ars amatoria*. Like his readers, he was happy with these lavish expressions of Augustan euergetism and could not but exemplify their qualities as places to meet lovers. This does not imply that the poet is critical about the building programme itself. He only adds witty extras to the austere and morally edifying qualities these monuments would convey. As a 'sincere Augustan', he belonged to the admiring citizens, and perhaps it was not his fault that Augustus would blame him for his catalogue of Augustan monuments.

A peculiarity, which is common to all places we have seen, is that they were crowded with panel paintings and

---

[127] Ov., *Tr.* II.207–08.

[128] Ov., *Tr.* II.361–62.

[129] Von Albrecht 1997, 789. On the *Tristia* passages, see Ingleheart 2010, 202–04 and 293–94.

[130] Ov., *Tr.* II.303–04.

[131] See Ingleheart 2010, 261–62.

[132] Davis 2006; Gibson 2009, 298. He brings out the contrast

between Ovid and Propertius, his predecessor. For this poetical ambient, see also von den Hoff, Stroh, and Zimmermann 2014, 143–59, 204–13.

[133] Jenkyns 2013, 107. We may think of the scandal, which was provoked by Augustus's daughter Julia and led to her exile in 2 BC.

[134] Pandey 2018, 22–26, 33, and 158–70.

[135] For discussions on this, see Boyle 2003; Volk 2010, 96–100.

[136] Ov., *Tr.*, II.279–300.

[137] See Ingleheart 2010, 246–300.

statues. The latter filled porticoes and piazzas and, in a certain sense, functioned as the inhabitants of the spaces. In that way, they communicated with the lover and his possible prospective lovers and fulfilled an essential role in what Paul Zanker has aptly called 'Bild-Räume', sets of images in relation with their setting.[138] As was suggested by Rubina Raja, the sculptural programmes conveyed 'the feeling of being surrounded by "living beings" — not just dead sculptures. And these would have given the impression of energetic movements and liveliness.'[139] The statues functioned as devices in playful hide-and-seek. Ovid had no opportunity to catalogue them in detail in his verses and limited himself to a few pieces, e.g. the Appiades fountain in the Forum Iulium, but the flâneur would appreciate this bounty of artworks.[140]

Ovid does not suggest the Forum Augustum itself as an ideal place of encounter. That clearly would have been a transgression of all norms. Pandey suggests that this silence might have to do with 'respecting its inimicality to the pursuit of Venus', being a map of Augustus's male power.[141] Or do we have to assume a more practical reason for its absence? This monument was the last grand jewel in Augustus's building crown and would become iconic within Augustan Rome. It was just inaugurated on the day of the virtual walk and might not have been open yet to the public, and so it was out of bounds for the young lovers when Ovid started the composition of his *Ars amatoria* in the same 2 BC.[142] He might even be suggesting that it was a new place for our explorations, which was about to be opened.

The precise date of the forum's inauguration — and, consequently, of our walk — is contested: 12 May or 1 August of the year 2 BC. By describing the temple under the fourth Ides of May, Ovid himself implies 12 May as that very day,[143] whereas Cassius Dio has 1 August.[144] It seems a futility, but it certainly has some sense in connection with the inception of the *Ars amatoria*, in which we find concrete performances mentioned. In his thorough study on the Forum Augustum, Spannagel discusses this aspect at length and concludes that, despite his slight preference for Ovid's May dating, no sound conclusion can be drawn. Hannah argues that the astrological constellation of those days advocates an inauguration in May. As for Hannah, Boyle, Davis, and others, Ovid's date seems based on his research for the *Fasti* and the Roman calendar. Moreover, as a possible eyewitness, he may have been more trustworthy than Dio (writing two hundred years later), even if his suggestion might be based on old sources that have not come down to us.[145] A point that might plead in favour of August is that Ovid refers to hot summer days by mentioning Leo and the date of the Rape of the Sabines, 18 August,[146] but even these references are not conclusive.[147]

The city of Rome had become a large construction site during the reign of Augustus, and this construction phase came to an end with the opening of the Forum Augustum. Monuments in travertine, brick, and marble substituted old edifices, often constructed in tuff, wood, and mud brick. Ovid focused on a series of these buildings as examples of the splendid new town that emerged thanks to Augustus's interventions and used them to criticize his sexual regulations in a quiet and witty way. The presentations of buildings form part of Ovid's mild criticism of Augustus's moral policy and, therefore, must be analysed in that view. Unfortunately, in the end, Ovid's text ends up being more secular and tenable than all those porticoes, courtyards, and columns. *Marmore perennius*, I would say.

---

[138] Zanker 2000.

[139] I owe the suggestion about the vividness of the area thanks to the statues in this formula to Rubina Raja (email from 19 May 2020).

[140] Zanker 2000, 220 speaks of an 'Assoziationsfülle'.

[141] Pandey 2018, 172. In a certain way Ovid would refer to it in his discussion of Gaius's triumph later in the *Ars amatoria*, see Pandey 2018, 178–83.

[142] In discussions on the section of the *Ars amatoria* studied in this contribution, this absence has not been noticed, let alone been seen as an omission by Ovid. The poet refers to it in Ov., *Tr.* II.295–96 (cf. Ingleheart 2010, 254–56). The literature on this monument is immense. See, among others, V. Kockel, *LTUR* III, 289–95 s.v. Forum Augustum; Spannagel 1999; Davis 2006, 39–48; Goldbeck 2015; Pandey 2018, 42–184.

[143] Ov., *Fast.* v.545–98.

[144] Cass. Dio. LX.5.3. Still important the lengthy comment in Frazer 1929, 61–72. He follows Cassius Dio's indication and the reference to games on 12 May.

[145] Spannagel 1999, 41–59 (with various proposals pro and contra both dates); Hannah 1997 does not mention the *Ars amatoria*. For 12 May, V. Kockel, *LTUR* III 289 s.v. Forum Augustum, with a reference to Ovid (in the text mistakenly 1 May); Boyle 2003, 205–06; Davis 2006, 40 and 141 n. 112. For 1 August, Berlan-Bajard 2006, 39.

[146] Ov., *Ars am.* I.67–68.

[147] Dimundo 2003, 72–73 on the *Consualia* celebrated on that day.

Works Cited

Aerde, M. van. 2019. *Egypt and the Augustan Cultural Revolution: An Interpretative Archaeological Overview*, BABESCH Supplementa, 38 (Leuven: Peeters).

Albrecht, M. von. 1997. *A History of Roman Literature: From Livius Andronicus to Boethius with Special Regard to its Influence on World Literature* (Leiden: Brill).

Amici, C. M. 1991. *Il Foro di Cesare* (Florence: Olschki).

Barchiesi, A. 1994. *Il poeta e il principe: Ovidio e il discorso augusteo* (Rome: Laterza).

—— 2005. 'Learned Eyes: Poets, Viewers, Image Makers', in K. Galinski (ed.), *The Cambridge Companion to the Age of Augustus* (Cambridge: Cambridge University Press), pp. 281–305.

—— 2019. 'Virgilian Narrative: Ecphrasis', in C. Martindale and F. Mac Góraín (eds), *Cambridge Companion to Virgil*, 2nd edn (Cambridge: Cambridge University Press), pp. 413–24.

Beard, M. 2007. *The Roman Triumph* (Cambridge, MA: Harvard University Press).

Berlan-Bajard, A. 2006. *Les spectacles aquatiques romains* (Rome: École française de Rome).

Boyle, A. J. 2003. *Ovid and the Monuments: A Poet's Rome*, Ramus Monographs, 4 (Bendigo: Aureal).

Capecchi, G. 2003. 'L'obelisco dell'anfiteatro', in L. Medri (ed.), *Il giardino di Boboli* (Siena: Banca Toscana), pp. 56–59.

Carandini, A. and P. Carafa. 2017. *The Atlas of Rome: Biography and Portraits of the City* (Princeton: Princeton University Press).

Carey, S. 2006. *Pliny's Catalogue of Culture: Art and Empire in the 'Natural History'* (Oxford: Oxford University Press).

Celani, A. 1998. *Opere d'arte greche nella Roma di Augusto*, Aucnus, 8 (Naples: Edizioni scientifiche italiane).

Ciancio Rossetto, P. and G. Pisani Sartorio. 2017. *Theatrum Marcelli*, Monumenti Romani, 10 (Rome: Istituto nazionale di studi romani).

Coarelli, F. 1971–1972. 'Il complesso pompeiano del Campo Marzio e la sua decorazione scultoreo', *Atti della Pontificia Accademia: rendiconti*, 44: 99–122.

—— 1981. 'Alessandro, i Licinii e Lanuvio', in *L'art décoratif à Rome à la fin de la république et au début du principat* (Rome: École française de Rome), pp. 229–84.

—— 1992. *Il foro romano*, II: *Periodo repubblicano e augusteo*, 2nd edn (Rome: Quasar).

—— 1997. *Il Campo Marzio: dalle origini alla fine della Repubblica* (Rome: Quasar).

Corbeill, A. 2015. '"A Shouting and Bustling on All Sides" (Hor. Sat. 1.9.77–8): Everyday Justice in the Streets of Republican Rome', in I. Östenberg, S. Malmberg, and J. Bjørnebye (eds), *The Moving City: Processions, Passages and Promenades* (London: Bloomsbury), pp. 89–98.

Dardenay, A. 2010. *Les mythes fondateurs de Rome* (Paris: Picard).

—— 2012. *Images des fondateurs: d'Énée à Romulus*, Scripta antiqua, 43 (Bordeaux: Ausonius).

Davis, P. J. 2006. *Ovid and Augustus: A Political Reading of Ovid's Erotic Poems* (London: Duckworth).

Delfino, A. 2014. *Forum Iulium: l'area del Foro di Cesare alla luce delle campagne di scavo 2005–2008; le fasi arcaica, repubblicana e cesariano-augustea*, British Archaeological Reports, International Series, 2607 (Oxford: Archaeopress).

Denard, H. 2002. 'Virtuality and Performativity: Recreating Rome's Theatre of Pompey', *A Journal of Performance and Art*, 24: 25–43.

DeRose Evans, J. 2009. 'Prostitutes in the Portico of Pompey? A Reconsideration', *Transactions of the American Philological Association*, 139: 123–45.

De Vos, M. 1980. *L'egittomania in pitture e mosaici romano-campani della prima età imperiale*, Études préliminaires aux religions orientales dans l'Empire romain, 84 (Leiden: Brill).

De Vos, M. J. 2012. 'Negen aardse Muzen. Gender en de receptie van dichteressen in het oude Griekenland en Rome' (unpublished doctoral thesis, Radboud University Nijmegen).

Dimundo, R. 2003. *Ovidio: lezioni d'amore: saggio di commento al I Libro dell'Ars amatoria*, Scrinia, 22 (Bari: Edipuglia).

Edwards, C. 1996. *Writing Rome: Textual Approaches to the City* (Cambridge: Cambridge University Press).

Egelund, L. 2018. 'A Space for Caesar: The Heart of Rome and Urban Development', in R. Raja and S. M. Sindbæk (eds), *Urban Network Evolutions: Towards a High-Definition Archaeology* (Aarhus: Aarhus University Press), pp. 45–50.

Emmerson, A. L. C. 2020. *Life and Death in the Roman Suburb* (Oxford: Oxford University Press).

Ensoli Vittozzi, S. 1990. *Musei Capitolini: la Collezione Egizia* (Milan: Silvana).

Favro, D. 1996. *The Urban Image of Augustan Rome* (Cambridge: Cambridge University Press).

Flory, M. B. 1984. 'Sic exempla parantur: Livia's Shrine to Concordia and the Porticus Liviae', *Historia: Zeitschrift für Alte Geschichte*, 33: 309–30.

Foubert, L. 2010. 'The Palatine Dwelling of the Mater Familias: Houses as Symbolic Space in the Julio-Claudian Period', *Klio*, 92: 65–82.

Frazer, J. G. 1929. *Publii Ovidii Nasonis Fastorum libri sex: The Fasti of Ovid* (London: Macmillan).

Gagliardo, M. C. and J. E. Packer. 2006. 'A New Look at Pompey's Theater: History, Documentation, and Recent Excavation', *American Journal of Archaeology*, 110: 93–122.

Gahtan, M. W. and D. Pegazzano. 2015. *Museum Archetypes and Collecting in the Ancient World*, Monumenta graeca et romana, 21 (Leiden: Brill).

Galinsky, K. 1996. *Augustan Culture: An Interpretive Introduction* (Princeton: Princeton University Press).

Gibson, R. 2009. 'The Success and Failure of Roman Love Elegy as an Instrument of Subversion: The Case of Propertius', in G. Urso (ed.), *Ordine e sovversione nel mondo greco e romano* (Pisa: ETS), pp. 279–99.

Gibson, R., S. Green, and S. Sharrock. 2006. *The Art of Love: Bimillennial Essays on Ovid's 'Ars amatoria' and 'Remedia amoris'* (Oxford: Oxford University Press).

Gleason, K. L. 1990. 'The Garden Portico of Pompey the Great', *Expedition*, 32.2: 4–13.

—— 1994. 'Porticus Pompeiana: A New Perspective on the First Public Park of Ancient Rome', *The Journal of Garden History*, 14.1: 13–27.

Goldbeck, V. 2015. *Fora augusta: Das Augustusforum und seine Rezeption im Westen des Imperium Romanum*, Ikonika, 5 (Regensburg: Schnell & Steiner).

Golvin, J.-C. 1988. *L'amphithéâtre romain* (Paris: De Boccard).

Green, S. J. 2004. 'Playing with Marble: The Monuments of the Caesars in Ovids "Fasti"', *The Classical Quarterly*, 54: 224–39.

Grimal, P. 1969. *Les jardins romains*, 2nd edn (Paris: Presses universitaires de France).

Gros, P. 1996. *L'architecture romaine: du début du IIIe siècle av. J.-C. à la fin du Haut-Empire*, I: *Les monuments publics* (Paris: Picard).

—— 2020. 'Le quadriportique derrière la scène: évolution monumentale et sémantique d'une annexe fonctionnelle', in S. F. Ramallo Asensio and E. Ruiz Valderas (eds), *La 'porticus post scaenam' en la arquitectura teatral romana* (Murcia: Universidad de Murcia), pp. 17–30.

Gurval, R. A. 1995. *Actium and Augustus* (Ann Arbor: Michigan University Press).

Hallett, C. 2005. *The Roman Nude: Heroic Portrait Statuary 200 BC-AD 300* (Oxford: Oxford University Press).

—— 2018a. 'Terracotta, Antiquarianism, and the "Archaic Revival" of Early Augustan Rome', in W. T. Wootton and others (eds), *Visual Histories of the Classical World: Essays in Honour of R. R. R. Smith* (Turnhout: Brepols), pp. 181–203.

—— 2018b. 'Afterword: The Function of Greek Artworks within Roman Visual Culture', in G. Adornato and others (eds), *Restaging Greek Artworks in Roman Times* (Milan: Edizioni universitarie di lettere economia diritto), pp. 276–87.

Hannah, R. 1997. 'The Temple of Mars Ultor and 12 May', *Römische Mitteilungen*, 104: 527–36.

Haselberger, L. 2002. *Mapping Augustan Rome*, Journal of Roman Archaeology Supplementary Series, 50 (Portsmouth, RI: Journal of Roman Archaeology).

Häuber, C. 2014. *The Eastern Part of the Mons Oppius in Rome: The Sanctuary of Isis et Serapis in Regio III, the Temples of Minerva Medica, Fortuna Virgo and Dea Syria, and the Horti of Maecenas* (Rome: L'Erma di Bretschneider).

—— 2017. *Augustus and the Campus Martius in Rome: The Emperor's Rôle as Pharaoh of Egypt and Julius Caesar's Calendar Reform, the Montecitorio Obelisk, the Meridian Line, the Ara Pacis, and the Mausoleum Augusti in Honour of Eugenio La Rocca on the Occasion of his 70th Birthday* (Munich: Hochschule München).

Hejduk, J. D. 2014. *The Offense of Love: 'Ars amatoria', 'Remedia amoris', and 'Tristia' 2* (Madison: University of Wisconsin Press).

Hekster, O. 2015. *Emperors and Ancestors: Roman Rulers and the Constraint of Tradition* (Oxford: Oxford University Press).

Heldmann, K. 2001. 'Dichtkunst oder Liebeskunst? Die mythologischen Erzählungen in Ovids Ars Amatoria', *Nachrichten der Akademie der Wissenschaften in Göttingen*, I: *Philologisch-Historische Klasse*, 5: 353–414.

Hoff, R. von den, W. Stroh, and M. Zimmermann. 2014. *Divus Augustus: Der erste römische Kaiser und seine Welt* (Munich: Beck).

Hollis, A. S. 1977. *Ovid: Ars amatoria; Book I* (Oxford: Oxford University Press).

Hutchinson, H. 2017. 'Some New and Old Light on the Reasons for Ovid's Exile', *Zeitschrift für Papyrologie und Epigraphik*, 203: 76–84.

Ingleheart, J. 2010. *A Commentary on Ovid, Tristia, Book 2* (Oxford: Oxford University Press).

Janka, M. 2014. 'Osalba Dimundo: Ovidio. Lezioni d'amore. Saggio di comment al I libro dell'Ars amatoria', *Gnomon*, 86: 19–27.

Jenkyns, R. 2013. *God, Space, and City in the Roman Imagination* (Oxford: Oxford University Press).

Kaderka, K. 2018. *Les décors tympanaux des temples de Rome* (Bordeaux: Ausonius).

Keesling, C. M. 2018. 'Epigraphy of Appropriation: Retrospective Signatures of Greek Sculptors in the Roman World', in D. Y.-M. Ng and M. Swetnam-Burland (eds), *Reuse and Renovation in Roman Material Culture: Functions, Aesthetics, Interpretations* (Cambridge: Cambridge University Press), pp. 84–111.

Kenney, E. J. 1961. *P. Ovidi Nasonis Amores, Medicamina faciei femineae, Ars amatoria, remedia amoris* (Oxford: Clarendon).

Kindberg, J. and R. Raja. 2018. 'A High-Definition Approach to the Forum of Caesar in Rome: Urban Archaeology in a Living City', in R. Raja and S. M. Sindbæk (eds), *Urban Network Evolutions: Towards a High-Definition Archaeology* (Aarhus: Aarhus University Press), pp. 21–25.

Kuttner, A. L. 1999. 'Culture and History at Pompey's Museum', *Transactions of the American Philological Association*, 129: 343–73.

Leitner, P. H. 2005. 'Nasonis Relegado: Zu den Hintergründen der Verbannung Ovids', *Zeitschrift der Savigny-Stiftung für Rechtsgeschichte*, 122: 150–65.

Lembke, K. 1994. *Das Iseum Campense in Rom: Studie über den Isiskult unter Domitian* (Heidelberg: Verlag Archäologie und Geschichte).

Lipps, J. 2018. *Die Stuckdecke des 'oecus tetrastylus' aus dem sog. Augustushaus auf dem Palatin im Kontext antiker Deckenverzierungen* (Rahden: Leidorf).

Liverani, P. 2007. 'Osservazioni sui Rostri del Foro Romano in età tardoantica', in A. Leone, D. Palombi, and S. Walker (eds), *Res bene gestae: Ricerche di storia urbana su Roma antica in onore di Eva Margareta Steinby* (Rome: Quasar), pp. 169–93.

Lorsch, R. S. 1997. 'Augustus' Conception and the Heroic Tradition Author(s)', *Latomus*, 56: 790–99.

LTUR = Eva Margareta Steinby (ed.). 1993–2000. *Lexicon topographicum urbis Romae*, 6 vols (Rome: Quasar).

Maderna, C. 1988. *Iupiter Diomedes und Merkur als Vorbilder für römische Bildnisstatuen: Untersuchungen zum römischen statuarischen Idealporträt* (Heidelberg: Verlag Archäologie und Geschichte).

McGinn, T. A. J. 1993. *Prostitution, Sexuality, and the Law in Ancient Rome* (Oxford: Oxford University Press).

Miles, M. M. 2008. *Art and Plunder: The Ancient Origins of Debate about Cultural Property* (Cambridge: Cambridge University Press).

Monterroso, A. 2008. 'Tres controversias sobre las catorce nationes de Coponio, quae sunt circa Pompeium', in E. La Rocca, P. Leon, and C. Parisi Presicce (eds), *Le due patrie acquisite: studi di archeologia dedicati a Walter Trillmich* (Rome: L'Erma di Bretschneider), pp. 277–85.

Monterroso Checa, A. and others. 2017. 'Curia Pompeia: secuencia edilicia desde la Arqueología de la Arquitectura', *Bullettino della Commissione archeologica comunale di Roma*, 118: 55–84.

—— 2020. 'Porticus Pompeiana: Forma, contenido y limitaciones de la investigación', in S. F. Ramallo Asensio and E. Ruiz Valderas (eds), *La 'porticus post scaenam' en la arquitectura teatral romana* (Murcia: Universidad de Murcia), pp. 31–46.

Moormann, E. M. 2014. 'Liefdesplaatsen in het kuise Rome van Augustus', *Lampas: Tijdschrift voor Classici*, 47: 224–45.

—— 2022. 'Some Observations on the Templum Pacis – a Summa of Flavian Politics', in M. Heerink and E. Meijer (eds), *Flavian Responses to Nero's Rome* (Amsterdam: Amsterdam University Press), pp. 127–59.

Moreno, P. 1981. 'Modelli lisippei nell'arte di età repubblicana ed augustea', in *L'art décoratif à Rome à la fin de la république et au début du principat* (Rome: École française de Rome), pp. 173–227.

Neumeister, C. 2010. *Das Antike Rom: Ein literarischer Stadtführer*, 4th edn (Munich: Beck).

Östenberg, I., S. Malmberg, and J. Bjørnebye. 2015. *The Moving City: Processions, Passages and Promenades in Ancient Rome* (London: Bloomsbury).

O'Sullivan, T. M. 2015. 'Augustan Literary Tours. Walking and Reading the City', in I. Östenberg, S. Malmberg, and J. Bjørnebye (eds), *The Moving City: Processions, Passages and Promenades in Ancient Rome* (London: Bloomsbury), pp. 111–22.

Pandey, N. B. 2018. *The Poetics of Power in Augustan Rome: Latin Poetic Responses to Early Imperial Iconography* (Cambridge: Cambridge University Press).

Papini, M. 2000. *Palazzo Braschi: la collezione di sculture antiche* (Rome: L'Erma di Bretschneider).

Pianezzola, E. 1991. *Ovidio, L'arte dell'amare* (Milan: Arnoldo Mondadori).

Poehler, E. E. 2016. 'Digital Pompeii: Dissolving the Fieldwork Library Research Divide', in E. W. Averett, J. M. Gordon, and D. B. Counts (eds), *Mobilizing the Past for a Digital Future: The Potential of Digital Archaeology* (Grand Forks: Digital Press at the University of North Dakota), pp. 201–08.

Poggio, A. 2018. 'Experiencing Art in the Saepta: Greek Artworks in a Monumental Space of Ancient Rome', in G. Adornato and others (eds), *Restaging Greek Art Works in Roman Times* (Milan: Universitarie di lettere economia diritto), pp. 191–207.

Quenemoen, C. K. 2006. 'The Portico of the Danaids: A New Reconstruction', *American Journal of Archaeology*, 110: 229–50.

Rutledge, S. H. 2012. *Ancient Rome as a Museum: Power, Identity, and the Culture of Collecting* (Oxford: Oxford University Press).

Sauron, G. 1994. *Quis deum? L'expression plastique des idéologies politiques et religieuses à Rome* (Rome: École française de Rome).

Simpson, C. J. 1987. 'The Adonea on the Palatine in the Age of Augustus: Ovid, Ars Amatoria 1.75–6', *Athenaeum*, 75: 244–48.

Slater, W. J. 1996. *Roman Theater and Society* (Ann Arbor: University of Michigan Press).

Spannagel, M. 1999. *Exemplaria principis: Untersuchungen zu Entstehung und Ausstattung des Augustusforums* (Heidelberg: Verlag Archäologie und Geschichte).

Stroh, W. 1979. 'Ovids Liebeskunst und die Ehegesetze des Augustus', *Gymnasium Heidelberg*, 86.3–4: 323–52.

Strazzulla, M. J. 1990. *Il principato di Apollo: mito e propaganda nelle lastre 'Campana' del tempio di Apollo Palatino* (Rome: L'Erma di Bretschneider).

Tosi, G. and L. Baccelle. 2003. *Gli edifici per spettacoli nell'Italia romana* (Rome: Quasar).

Tucci, P. L. 2017. *The Temple of Peace in Rome*, 2 vols (Cambridge: Cambridge University Press).

Versluys, M. J., K. Bülow Clausen, and G. Capriotti Vittozzi. 2018. *The Iseum Campense from the Roman Empire to the Modern Age: Temple – Monument – lieu de mémoire* (Rome: Quasar).

Villedieu, F. 2001. *Il giardino dei Cesari: dai palazzi antichi alla Vigna Barberini sul Monte Palatino* (Rome: Quasar).

3. FIND A LOVER IN AUGUSTAN ROME

Volk, K. 2002. *The Poetics of Latin Didactic: Lucretius, Vergil, Ovid, Manilius* (Oxford: Oxford University Press).

—— 2010. *Ovid* (Chichester: Wiley-Blackwell).

Welch, K. E. 2007. *The Roman Amphitheatre: From Its Origins to the Colosseum* (Cambridge: Cambridge University Press).

Westall, R. 1996. 'The Forum Iulium as Representation of Imperator Caesar', *Römische Mitteilungen*, 103: 83–118.

Zanker, P. 2000. 'Bild-Räume und Betrachter im kaiserzeitlichen Rom: Fragen und Anregungen für Interpreten', in A. H. Borbein and P. Zanker (eds), *Klassische Archäologie: Eine Einführung* (Berlin: Reimer), pp. 205–26.

—— 2009. 'The Irritating Statues and Contradictory Portraits of Julius Caesar', in M. Griffin (ed.), *A Companion to Julius Caesar* (Chichester: Wiley-Blackwell), pp. 288–314.

Zanovello, P. 2003. 'Il ruolo dei circhi e degli stadi', in G. Tosi and L. Baccelle (eds), *Gli edifici per spettacoli nell'Italia romana* (Rome: Quasar), pp. 835–99.

Zink, S. and H. Piening. 2009. 'Haec aurea templa: The Palatine Temple of Apollo and its Polychromy', *Journal of Roman Archaeology*, 22: 109–22.

THE ARCHAEOLOGY OF
CAESAR'S MILITARY VENTURES

4. THE ARCHAEOLOGY OF JULIUS CAESAR: NEW RESEARCH ON THE GALLIC WARS

Nico Roymans

Department of Archaeology, Classics and Near Eastern Studies,
Vrije Universiteit Amsterdam (n.g.a.m.roymans@vu.nl)

Manuel Fernández-Götz

School of History, Classics and Archaeology,
University of Edinburgh (M.Fernandez-Gotz@ed.ac.uk)

Introduction

The archaeology of Julius Caesar's military campaigns has experienced a significant surge in recent years, with new discoveries and the introduction of novel theoretical and methodological approaches. While the main evidence is still related to the territory of Gaul conquered by Caesar between 58 and 51 BC, research on other events such as his crossing of the English Channel to Britain in 55 and 54 BC,[1] or the Roman civil wars of 49–45 BC against political rivals,[2] such as Pompey the Great and his sons, is also providing exciting new insights. For example, the site of Puig Ciutat in north-east Iberia has been identified as a Late Roman Republic garrison destroyed during the military operations that preceded the Battle of Ilerda between the forces of Julius Caesar and the army of Pompey the Great in 49 BC.[3] In southern Spain, recent surveys have identified Caesarian battlefields at Ulia/Montemayor, related to combat in 48 and 45 BC and including the discovery of over 150 projectiles.[4]

Overwhelming military superiority and brutal violence against peoples that resisted domination were standard features of the Roman wars of conquest during the Late Republic.[5] Historical sources attest to various forms of mass violence, including large-scale enslavement, looting and destruction of indigenous settlements, massacres, and even cases of genocide. This use of brutal violence, combined with occasional clemency as part of the political strategy, is described in detail in the eight books of the *Commentarii de bello gallico*.[6] While it is generally accepted that Caesar's account of the Gallic Wars is infused with elements of personal propaganda and the rhetoric of an imperial ideology,[7] there is little doubt that many Gallic communities were dramatically affected by the conquest. This is best illustrated in Appian's and Plutarch's claims that Caesar killed one million and enslaved another million of his Gallic opponents.[8] Even if these numbers would be exaggerated, there is little doubt that the conquest must have had a significant demographic impact.

Having said this, there were significant regional variations within Gaul. At the beginning of Caesar's campaigns, there were around sixty recorded tribal groups (*civitates*) within independent Gaul (*Gallia Comata*), which were in turn subdivided into smaller entities (*pagi*) (Fig. 4.1).[9] While most of these groupings resisted the Roman invasion, others were actually allied to Caesar and even benefitted from the conquest, for example by seeing their territories increase at the cost of their neighbours. In addition, we need to take into account the complexity and fluidity of existing scenarios. Thus, pro- and anti-Roman factions could exist within the same *civitas*, and sometimes even the same family, and some groups changed sides during the course of the war. Both literary sources and the increasing amount of archaeological evidence highlight the diversity of Gallic communities in the years before, during, and after the Roman conquest.[10]

---

[1] Haselgrove and Fitzpatrick (in this volume).

[2] Maschek 2018.

[3] Pujol and others 2019.

[4] Quesada-Sanz and Moralejo-Ordax 2020.

[5] Badian 1968; Barrandon 2018; Fernández-Götz, Maschek, and Roymans 2020a.

[6] Raaflaub 2021; Roymans and Fernández-Götz 2015.

[7] Kraus 2009; Raaflaub 2017; Riggsby 2006; Schadee 2008.

[8] App., *Celt*. 1.2; Plut., *Caes*. xv.3.

[9] Arbabe 2017; Fichtl 2012.

[10] Brun and Ruby 2008; Fernández-Götz 2014; Haselgrove 2006; Ralston 2019.

Exploring the Materiality of the Gallic Wars: From the Nineteenth Century to the Present

The search for archaeological remains related to the Caesarian conquest of Gaul started to attract great interest after the mid-nineteenth century. The initial push came from the support given by the French emperor Napoleon III,[11] who was fascinated by Caesar's account and provided resources for work at sites named in the Gallic Wars, most notably Alesia, Gergovia, and Uxellodunum. This research was closely connected to the political atmosphere of the time, with the general rise of nationalism in Europe and the resorting to the past for modern political purposes. In the case of France, this was closely linked to the construction of collective memory and identity, at a time when the expression *nos ancêtres les Gaulois* ('our ancestors the Gauls') became popularized.[12] The best example of this close connection between modern politics and the ancient past was the erection in 1865 of a monumental statue of the Gallic leader Vercingetorix at the site of the *oppidum* of Alesia (Fig. 4.2), scene of the crucial Roman victory in 52 BC against the alliance of numerous indigenous tribes.

The excavations undertaken at Alesia from 1861 to 1865 represented a major enterprise,[13] uncovering ample material evidence for the siege and the battle described by Caesar.[14] The discoveries included weaponry, the remains of the siege works (which Napoleon III named 'contravallation' — facing the *oppidum* — and 'circumvallation' — facing outwards), and a number of supposed Roman camps (*castra*) as well as some smaller *castella* in the intervening gaps. More recent archaeological research at Alesia took place between 1991 and 1997 within the framework of a joint Franco-German project.[15] The new investigations confirmed only three of the Roman camps that the nineteenth-century excavations had claimed to discover: firstly, Camp C to the north on Bussy Hill (identified by two slingshot projectiles marked with the name of Caesar's lieutenant Labienus); secondly, Camp B to the south of the siege works, the largest of all the known camps and which might have been that of Caesar himself; and thirdly, the nearby and smaller Camp A

(Fig. 4.3). In contrast, the other camps identified under the patronage of Napoleon III are more suspicious and cannot be attributed with any certainty to the time of the siege. Finally, there are some military installations that have been either confirmed or newly found by the 1990s investigations, for example a possible but nowadays highly eroded camp on Mont Réa, as well as *castellum* 11 in the southern sector, and a previously unknown *castellum* at Fortin de l'Épineuse.

In general terms, there is a notable discrepancy between the number of confirmed archaeological structures identified with certainty at Alesia and what could be expected for a Roman army of between 40,000 to 60,000 men plus auxiliary troops.[16] This, however, is not surprising in itself considering the rather ephemeral nature of the installations and the post-battle activities and post-depositional processes that affect the preservation of battlefield remains, as has been amply attested for both ancient and modern case studies.[17] In addition, we need to take into account that, on occasions, the archaeological work can contradict or at least nuance some of the statements made by Caesar: thus, in the plain of Les Laumes the contravallation has three ditches and not two.[18]

While Alesia is without doubt the most important and best investigated battlefield in Gaul, other sites and types of evidence also deserve attention, including Roman military finds and structures identified within indigenous *oppida* (Fig. 4.4). A good example of the latter can be found at the important Treveran *oppidum* of Titelberg in Luxembourg, where a Roman military presence is attested since the Gallic Wars.[19] In general terms, fieldwork projects across the territories of ancient Gaul are constantly providing new insights, sometimes confirming, and other times nuancing or revising, earlier interpretations.[20] For example, the *oppidum* of Puy d'Issolud has been confirmed as Uxellodunum, site of the last major siege and battle of the Gallic Wars in 51 BC. The episode was narrated by Caesar's lieutenant Hirtius, who completed the writing of the *Commentarii*. The archaeological investigations at Puy d'Issolud have recovered, among other finds, numerous arrowheads, which testify

---

[11] Napoleon III 1865–1866.

[12] Dietler 1994; 1998; Olivier 2006.

[13] Napoleon III 1865–1866. For the wider context of the nineteenth century, see Olivier 2019.

[14] Caes., *B Gall.* VII.68–89.

[15] Reddé 2003; 2018a; Reddé and von Schnurbein 2001; see also Deyber 2008.

[16] Reddé 2013; 2018a.

[17] Cf. Roymans and Fernández-Götz 2018; Scott and McFeaters 2011.

[18] Reddé 2018a.

[19] Metzler and others 2018.

[20] Fitzpatrick 2020; Fitzpatrick and Haselgrove 2019; Poux 2008; Reddé 2018b.

4. THE ARCHAEOLOGY OF JULIUS CAESAR: NEW RESEARCH ON THE GALLIC WARS

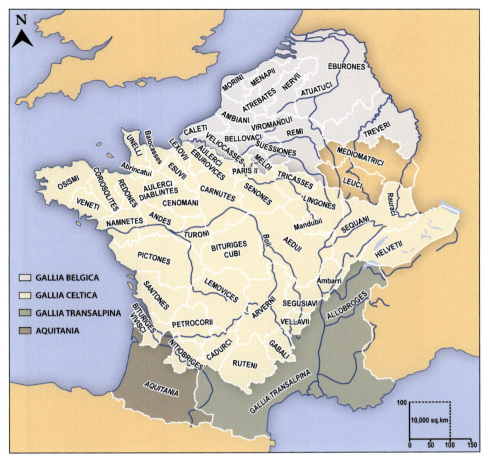

Figure 4.1. Gaul: tribal groups and major regional subdivisions on the eve of the Gallic Wars (after Ralston 2019, modified by authors).

Figure 4.2. Statue of Vercingetorix at Alesia, erected in 1865. Photo by Myrabella (CC BY-SA 4.0).

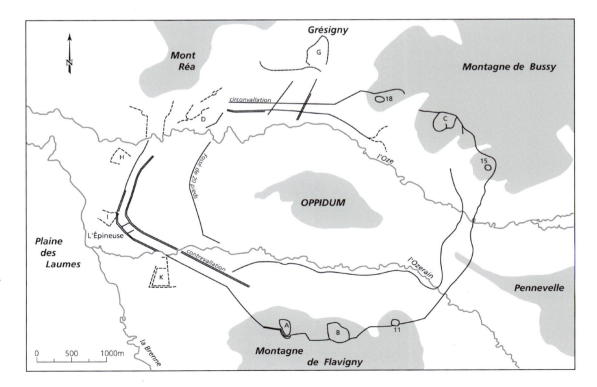

Figure 4.3. Topographical sketch map of the Siege of Alesia. From Reddé 2018a.

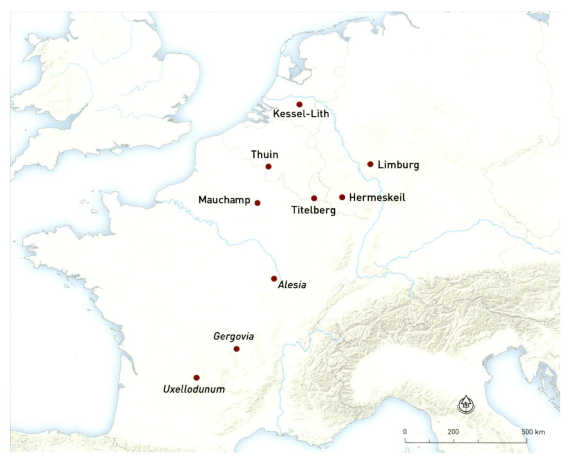

Figure 4.4. Location of key sites mentioned in the text. Map by Roymans and Fernández-Götz.

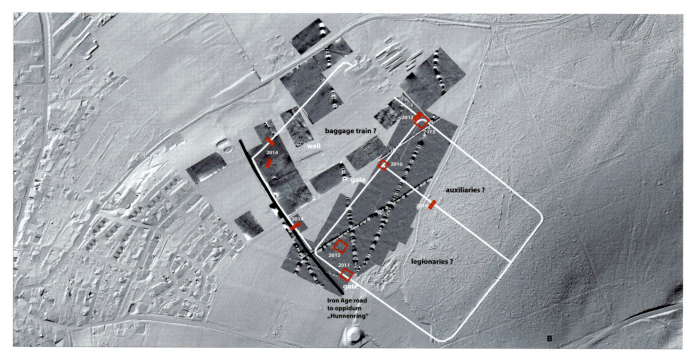

Figure 4.5. Map of the Caesarian military camp at Hermeskeil. Outlined in red are the excavation trenches opened between 2010 and 2015. From Hornung 2018.

to the attack suffered by the besieged Gauls when they tried to collect water from a spring below the *oppidum*.[21]

Other cases where archaeological work provides insights into key scenarios of the Gallic Wars include the Camp of Mauchamp, which was likely related to the Battle of the Aisne against the Belgae in 57 BC, and the famous Siege of Gergovia in 52 BC.[22] While these two previous sites have a long research tradition starting in the nineteenth century and continuing into recent decades, there are also some completely unexpected discoveries made in recent years. Thus, the last decade has witnessed the identification of a Caesarian military camp at Hermeskeil, located in the direct vicinity of the Treveran *oppidum* of Otzenhausen (Fig. 4.5),[23] as well as two Roman camps near Limburg, which could relate to one or two of Caesar's crossings of the Rhine in 55 and 53 BC.[24]

In what follows, we will focus, in a bit more detail, on the north-eastern regions of Gaul, where the research of the last years is fundamentally changing our archaeological knowledge of the conquest and its immediate aftermath.[25]

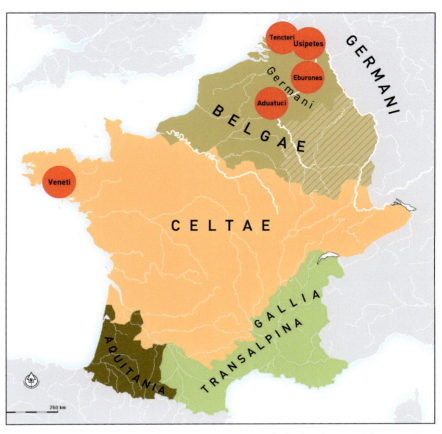

Figure 4.6. Gaul at the time of the Roman conquest, with the distribution of the cases of genocide/ethnocide described by Caesar in his *Commentarii*. From Roymans 2019a.

Caesar in the North: Landscapes of War and Terror

Until recently, the Caesarian conquest was almost totally intangible in the archaeological record of the Netherlands, Belgium, and the German Lower Rhine. In these regions, direct archaeological evidence of Roman army camps or battlefields from the 50s BC was absent, in contrast to the more central and southern areas of Gaul in which remarkable scenarios such as Alesia have been explored since the nineteenth century. One reason for this could be the scarceness of heavily defended *oppida* in the northernmost territories,[26] which Caesar could have used as winter camps for his army or as military targets.

However, the shortage of archaeological evidence does not mean that the societies of the northern periphery did not suffer significant consequences. On the contrary, according to Caesar's own writings, the so-called 'Germanic' frontier zone was probably the area of Gaul most dramatically affected by the Roman conquest.[27] In the north-eastern districts, Roman expansionism revealed itself in its most aggressive form, leading to profoundly negative effects on the lives of probably hundreds of thousands of people. In these regions, the emphasis was on destruction, mass enslavement, deportation, and even genocide of resistant groups. In fact, four of the five cases that, based on Caesar's description of the events, could be potentially classified as acts of genocide or ethnocide are clustered in the north-east of Gaul (Fig. 4.6).

---

21 Girault 2013.
22 For a summary, see Reddé 2019.
23 Hornung 2016; 2018.
24 Schallmayer, Schade-Lindig, and Meyer 2012.
25 Roymans 2019a; 2019b; Roymans and Fernández-Götz 2015; 2019.

---

26 Fernández-Götz 2014; Fichtl 1994; Roymans 1990.
27 Roymans 2004; 2019a; 2019b.

It is interesting to note that Caesar had no hesitations when describing the cruelty of his campaigns. He was, for example, very clear about the aim of his war against the Eburones: the campaigns were meant to annihilate this people and its name (*stirps ac nomen civitatis tollatur*),[28] which testifies to his awareness of genocidal practices. The strategy repeatedly described by Caesar was to travel with his army through the homeland of enemy tribes with the aim of destroying the crops in the fields, burning down as many settlements as possible, and murdering or enslaving the inhabitants. This must have had a dramatic impact on the physical appearance of the homeland of the affected populations; in fact, their lands would have been transformed into 'landscapes of war and terror'.[29]

Although these more negative aspects of the Roman conquest in the far north of Gaul were known since Antiquity due to Caesar's own writings, they have scarcely been the subject of serious modern research due to the lack of independent archaeological data. However, this situation has changed substantially in the last two decades. New archaeological, palaeobotanical, and numismatic evidence allows for the development of a more accurate picture of the conquest and its social and cultural impact on indigenous societies, as well as of Caesar's war narrative itself. The interest in the more destructive sides of the Caesarian conquest has also been influenced by wider theoretical trends and novel methodological approaches,[30] among which we can highlight the following:

1. The rise of postcolonial and decolonial perspectives, with their associated critical views of imperialism and militarism.[31]
2. The growth of conflict archaeology as a powerful subdiscipline, including its application to prehistoric and early historic periods.[32]

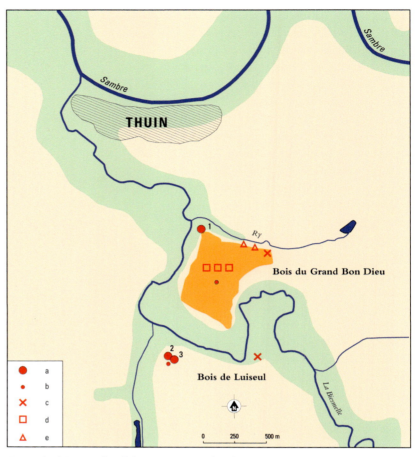

Figure 4.7. Topography of the Late Iron Age fortification at Thuin, including the location of gold finds and Roman lead sling bullets. a) gold hoards; b) isolated gold coin(s); c) concentration of sling bullets; d) iron tools; e) bronze ornaments and appliqués. From Roymans and Scheers 2012.

3. The development of advanced forms of critical reading of Caesar's narrative, which direct our attention to its role as an instrument of political communication and manipulation.[33]

In his account, Caesar described three different ways of annihilating a tribal group. In the case of the Aduatuci, the tribal group was defeated, enslaved, and deported after the conquest of a single fortification where the community had assembled. The Tencteri and Usipetes, for their part, were massacred on a large scale after a battle in which the Romans attacked their major camp, which included a significant non-combatant population. A final scenario is represented by the Eburones, who were dispersed over a large region when they were attacked in 53 and again in 51 BC by the Caesarian army that ravaged the countryside employing a 'scorched-earth' policy

---

[28] Caes., *B Gall.* VI.34.8.

[29] Cf. Hill and Wileman 2002.

[30] Roymans 2019a; Roymans and Fernández-Götz 2019.

[31] e.g. Madley 2017 for the case of nineteenth-century California; for Roman expansionism, cf. Fernández-Götz, Maschek, and Roymans 2020a; Padilla Peralta 2020.

[32] Cf. Dolfini and others 2018; Fernández-Götz and Roymans 2018.

[33] e.g. Johnston 2018; Riggsby 2006; Schadee 2008.

and slaughtered the population over a more prolonged time. These different scenarios have important implications for what we can expect in terms of archaeological evidence, as will be discussed in the sections below.

The Attack on Thuin and the Fate of the Aduatuci

Among the main 'crime scenes' of the Gallic Wars identified since the turn of the millennium is the Late Iron Age fortification of Thuin (Belgium), which has been interpreted as the *oppidum* of the Aduatuci that was attacked and conquered by the Roman army in 57 BC (Fig. 4.7). According to Caesar,[34] the Aduatuci had assembled at their *oppidum*, but after the Roman victory the entire population of 53,000 individuals was sold as slaves and deported to Italy, in what might perhaps be classified as a case of ethnocide (i.e. the destruction of a group's culture without the massacre of its people).[35]

The arguments for identifying the fortification of Thuin, which occupies a plateau of more than 13 ha, as the *oppidum* of the Aduatuci are manifold:[36]

Figure 4.8. Roman lead sling bullets from the Late Iron Age fortification at Thuin. From Roymans and Scheers 2012.

1. The location of the site within the territory that the written sources roughly attribute to the Aduatuci.
2. The existence of a radiocarbon date for charcoal from the rampart providing a date between 90 BC and AD 60.
3. The absence of finds within the site from the Early Roman period, which means that the fortification did not survive into Roman times.
4. The match of the topography with the description provided by Caesar.
5. The discovery of several hoards of indigenous gold coins that can be dated to the early 50s BC and which seem to reflect a single event. Our hypothesis is that the mass deportation of the Aduatuci after the fall of their *oppidum* meant that part of the portable wealth buried beforehand in the soil was never recovered.

6. Finally, and very importantly, the existence of several concentrations of Roman lead sling bullets, which indicate an attack on the fortification by the Roman army (Fig. 4.8). The sling bullets appeared in two separate concentrations: on the wall near the main entrance of the fortification and in the valley of the River Biesmelle.

Following their defeat, the Aduatuci no longer played any politically significant role, to the point that they soon disappeared from the northern Gallic tribal map.

Our identification of the fortification of Thuin as the *oppidum* of the Aduatuci besieged by Caesar has triggered new archaeological fieldwork by a team from the Université Libre de Bruxelles. Small-scale excavations and surveys in the interior of the *oppidum* produced mid-first-century BC gold coins, a complete Late Iron Age sword, and a new series of Roman lead sling bullets. Although, for the moment, the excavators try to avoid historical interpretations and keep open the option that the sling bullets might relate to a historically undocu-

---

34 Caes., *B Gall.* II.29–35.
35 Cf. Chalk and Jonassohn 1990.
36 See also Roymans and Scheers 2012, 20–24.

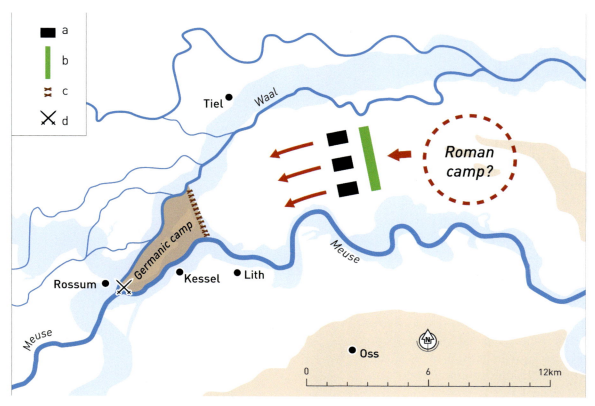

Figure 4.9. Palaeogeographic reconstruction of the Meuse–Waal confluence at Rossum in the early first century AD (Cohen and others 2012, except for the reconstruction of the Lower Waal between Tiel and Rossum), and hypothetical scenario of the Roman attack on the Germanic camp, based on Caesar's war account. a) Roman infantry column; b) Roman cavalry; c) open east flank of the Germanic camp, probably protected by a barrier of carts and wagons. From Roymans 2018.

mented Roman campaign in the early post-conquest period,[37] the new evidence collected so far strengthens our identification of the site as the *oppidum* of the Aduatuci. Geochemical analyses of the sling bullets show that the lead originated from mines in south-east Spain (regions of Murcia and Almería), which were exploited from the Republican period onward.[38] This fits very well with the information that Caesar's army included specialized units of slingers from the Balearic Islands,[39] who may have used lead that they brought from Iberia. Moreover, the mobile finds from within the fortification can be placed in La Tène D2, and the coin spectrum helps to narrow down the chronology even further since it consists almost exclusively of mid-first-century BC gold staters. If the *oppidum* had still been in use in the 40s or 30s BC, one would expect a different coin spectrum with a significant proportion of post-conquest bronzes and silver *quinarii*. However, these later emissions appear to be largely absent. Our proposal to identify Thuin as the *oppidum* of the Aduatuci conquered by Caesar is, therefore, more plausible than ever.

Genocide in the North? Kessel-Lith and the Massacre of the Tencteri and Usipetes

An even more spectacular crime scene is related to an event of the Gallic Wars that took place two years after the defeat of the Aduatuci: the massacre of the Germanic tribes of the Tencteri and the Usipetes in 55 BC.[40] Following Caesar, the Tencteri and Usipetes were two tribes from inner Germania who had given up their homeland due to the pressure of the Suebi.[41] In the winter of 56/55 BC, they crossed the Rhine and lived on the stores of the Menapii. They sent messengers stating that they did not want a conflict with the Romans and asked for permission to settle in Gaul. However, this request was rejected by Caesar.

---

[37] Paridaens 2020.
[38] Paridaens and others 2020.
[39] Caes., *B Gall*. II.7.

[40] Roymans 2018.
[41] Caes., *B Gall*. IV.4–15.

4. THE ARCHAEOLOGY OF JULIUS CAESAR: NEW RESEARCH ON THE GALLIC WARS

Figure 4.10. Human remains from a battle-related find complex dredged from the River Meuse at Kessel-Lith (The Netherlands), probably linked to Caesar's massacre of the Germanic Tencteri and Usipetes in 55 BC. From Roymans 2004.

The Tencteri and Usipetes gathered with all their possessions in an encampment, which probably took the form of a wagon fort and included men, women, and children. While most of their cavalry was away trying to collect grain in the territory of the Ambivariti, Caesar attacked their camp after arresting the delegates that tried to negotiate with him. In the absence of their leaders, the Germans panicked and tried to escape. Caesar subsequently ordered his troops to kill as many as possible, including women and children. The fleeing Germans were finally trapped at the confluence of the Rivers Rhine and Meuse. Here they were slaughtered in great numbers, or they drowned in the nearby river (Fig. 4.9).

While the population figures provided by Caesar for this event (430,000) are certainly heavily exaggerated, recent estimations by Roymans suggest that the number of casualties must nonetheless have been significant, probably reaching several tens of thousands.[42] The location of the massacre has recently been identified as the site of Kessel-Lith (The Netherlands), where a large Late Iron Age collection of finds, as well as numerous human remains, have been recovered over the years during large-scale dredging operations in an ancient bed of the Meuse. Initially interpreted as the result of votive offerings,[43] a reassessment of the evidence and the results of recent radiocarbon and isotopic analyses make it more plausible to connect a significant portion of the finds with a battle-related event. The plausibility of this interpretation results from the combination of historical, palaeogeographical, and archaeological data.[44] The main arguments can be summarized as follows:

1. The palaeogeographic reconstruction of the area around Kessel is consistent with the topographical description provided by Caesar for the place of the massacre.

2. The dating range of the recovered archaeological materials (including several La Tène D2 swords probably produced at the same workshop) falls within the historical date of the event in the mid-first century BC.

---

[42] Roymans 2018.

[43] Roymans 2004, chapter 7.

[44] For a more extensive discussion, see Roymans 2018.

3. The large amount of human skeletal remains, including bones of women, children, and elderly individuals, fits well with the anthropological profile that we can expect from Caesar's account (Fig. 4.10). Moreover, the bones of some of the victims present traces of weapon injuries.

4. The spread of the human bones in the ancient river-bed across a zone of some 3 km suggests a link to a major battle rather than a cult place interpretation.

5. The C-14 dating of human bones provides a clear clustering in the Late Iron Age.

6. Finally, several isotope analyses point to a non-local origin of the dead, as would correspond to populations that had just arrived from inner Germania.

Finally, we can pose the question of whether Caesar's destruction of the Tencteri and Usipetes can be qualified as an act of genocide. Genocide is generally defined as a practice involving the mass killing of a national, ethnic, or religious group in combination with the intent (successful or otherwise) to annihilate that group.[45] While some scholars have argued that it is anachronistic when applied to mass killings in pre-modern periods, others have employed it as a historical concept for cross-cultural comparative studies from Antiquity onwards.[46] Caesar does not explicitly state that he intended to destroy the Tencteri and Usipetes, but it is clear from his narrative that he must have realized that his actions would result de facto in at least their partial annihilation. Moreover, he included women and children as legitimate military targets. Although mass killing was an accepted practice against groups that resisted Roman domination and was not considered a crime in the value system of Late Republican Rome,[47] from a comparative, cross-cultural perspective it can be proposed that Caesar's actions against the Tencteri and Usipetes could be classified as a genocidal act. The same qualification can be used for Caesar's instructions to destroy the Eburones as a tribal group (see below).

A Depopulated Landscape? The Impact of the Conquest on Indigenous Settlement Patterns

In addition to identifying specific 'crime scenes', it is important to assess the demographic consequences of the conquest through the study of settlement patterns in the wider landscape.[48] Written sources suggest major regional differences in the direct demographic impact experienced by Gallic societies during and immediately after the Caesarian conquest. While in some regions the population seems to have remained fairly stable, in other areas the process of conquest was extremely violent, resulting in major disruptions. The latter scenario seems to apply to many tribal groups in the 'Germanic' frontier zone, which were confronted with a scorched-earth strategy. The Roman army practised this policy particularly against groups who avoided an open battle and turned to a sort of guerrilla warfare, such as the Menapii, Morini, and Sugambri, and above all the Eburones in the years after their revolt in 54 BC.[49] The Roman strategy was the large-scale burning to the ground of settlements, taking of prisoners, carrying off cattle, and destroying the harvest. These scorched-earth campaigns would have had a disastrous short-term impact on the subsistence and demography of the indigenous populations.

The interpretation of Caesar's narrative is, of course, not free of controversies. Although it is clear that both the Eburones and the Aduatuci did not survive the conquest period as tribal groups, there are differing opinions among ancient historians about the veracity of Caesar's affirmations and the demographic impact of the conquest. Some scholars take his account on the destruction of the above tribes very literally, whereas others see it as a rhetorical act of political propaganda.[50] While there are reasons to assume that their absence from the political map after the conquest was not necessarily due to complete genocide/ethnocide, but could be at least partly the result of a policy of *damnatio memoriae* by the Roman authorities, a substantial population decrease seems likely for these and some other tribal groups in north-east Gaul.

First of all, we need to take into account the radically altered tribal map of the Lower 'Germanic' frontier in the early post-conquest period, combined with reports of the substantial settlement of immigrant groups from the east bank of the Rhine (Fig. 4.11). This settlement of

---

[45] Cf. Bloxham and Moses 2010; Chalk and Jonassohn 1990.

[46] Kiernan 2007; van Wees 2010.

[47] Bellemore 2012.

[48] Roymans 2019a; 2019b.

[49] Cf. Caes., *B Gall.* vi.5–6, vi.43 and viii.24–25.

[50] e.g. Heinrichs 2008.

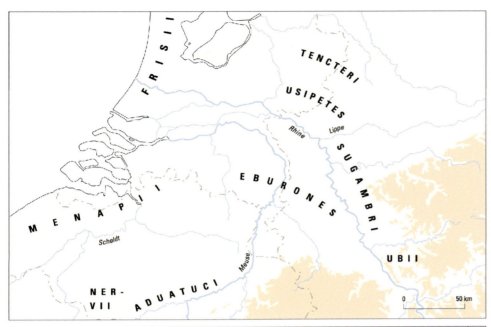

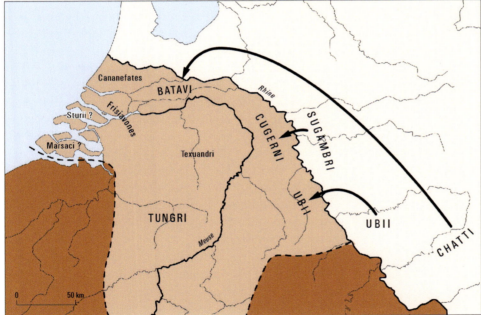

Figure 4.11. Tribal map of the 'Germanic' frontier zone in the Caesarian period (above) and the Augustan/Tiberian period (below). From Roymans 2019b.

new groups — the Batavians are even said to have moved to uninhabited land (*vacua cultoribus*) in the Dutch river area[51] — implies a phase of demographic decline in the preceding period.

In addition, the increasing amount of archaeological evidence seems to support — although sometimes also nuance — the model of a period of significant settlement discontinuity. While slaughtered people, stolen cattle, or destroyed harvests leave little or no archaeological trace, the systematic study of settlement evidence offers some possibilities for testing the historical model based on Caesar's account. If we assume that his activities caused a substantial depopulation in many regions, the most practical method is to investigate regional habitation trends of the first century BC, paying particular attention to possible discontinuities.[52] Although the chronological resolution of Late Iron Age material culture continues to pose some challenges, in general terms the quality of the dating system has improved considerably over the last two decades. This is due to the improved typo-chrono-

---

51 Tac., *Hist.* IV.12.

52 Roymans 2019a.

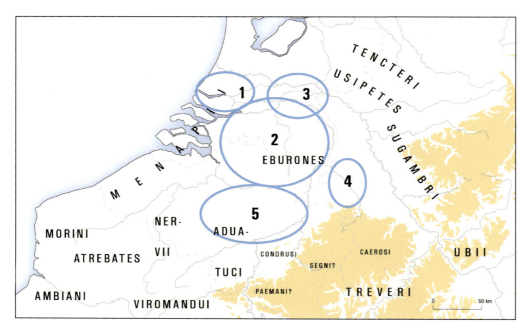

Figure 4.12. Five test regions with good settlement evidence for the investigation of demographic trends during the Late Iron Age and earliest Roman period. 1. South Holland; 2. Meuse/Demer/Scheldt region; 3. Dutch East River area; 4. Cologne hinterland; 5. Tongeren area. From Roymans 2019a.

logy of building structures and material culture (particularly glass bracelets and fibulae), as well as the systematic use of metal detectors that has led to the discovery of numerous coin hoards.

The settlement evidence from five well-explored test regions in the far north of Gaul allows some preliminary conclusions about the demographic impact of the Caesarian conquest to be established (Fig. 4.12). Typical of these regions is a decentralized settlement pattern, consisting of small sites of only a few contemporary farmhouses.

The first region is the province of South Holland in the Dutch coastal area, where we have a sample of about fifty, largely partially excavated, rural sites. A recent synthesis of the evidence concludes that almost every Roman settlement began in the Claudian period, which points to large-scale colonization of the land.[53] The architecture of the byre houses and the handmade domestic pottery types suggest that the new settlers came from the coastal areas north of the Rhine Delta. The results suggest a more or less total depopulation of the region, which according to the pottery evidence can be dated to the earlier first century BC.

The second test region is the sandy Meuse/Demer/Scheldt area of the southern Netherlands and northern Belgium. Thanks to the intensive archaeological research of the last few decades, we now have a relatively good understanding of the Late Iron Age and Early Roman habitation trajectory, with about forty settlements from the period that have been fully or partially excavated (Fig. 4.13). Most Roman settlements appear to be new foundations from the Augustan period, pointing to a substantial influx of settlers from another area.[54] The Augustan-period foundation of several new cult places of supralocal significance points in the same direction. While we know eight Roman cemeteries that began in the Late Iron Age, the absence in them of metal finds characteristic of the advanced stage of La Tène D2 suggests a discontinuity in their use between the Late Iron Age and the Roman period. Overall, the archaeological evidence indicates a substantial population decline in this region in the first century BC, with a recolonization in Augustan times.

The third region is the Dutch East River area, the homeland of the Batavians during the Roman Empire.[55] Here, some forty rural settlements from the Late Iron Age and/or the Early Roman period have been excavated.[56] Many Roman settlements were already inhabited in the final stage of La Tène D2, thus a generation earlier than in the Meuse/Demer/Scheldt region. However, in only four settlements can we observe a continuity from La Tène D1 (i.e. pre-Caesarian times) into the Roman period. The vast majority of known sites appear to have been new foundations from the period between c. 50–20 BC. The most plausible model for this region is that of a partial decrease in habitation around the

---

53 De Bruin 2019.

54 Hiddink and Roymans 2015.

55 Roymans 2004.

56 Heeren 2009.

4. THE ARCHAEOLOGY OF JULIUS CAESAR: NEW RESEARCH ON THE GALLIC WARS

Figure 4.13. Diagram of the period of use of excavated settlements, cemeteries, and cult sites from the Late Iron Age and earliest Roman period in the Meuse/Demer/Scheldt region. From Roymans 2019a.

mid-first century BC (probably linked to the Caesarian campaigns), followed shortly afterwards by an influx of immigrant groups. The coin evidence and the handmade pottery suggest that the immigrants came from the east bank of the Rhine.[57]

The fourth region is the lignite mining area in the hinterland of Cologne, an area inhabited in Caesarian times by the Eburones.[58] Some sixty-nine Roman rural settlements have been excavated here, almost all of them being new foundations from the Tiberian, and especially the Claudian, period. The few excavated Late Iron Age settlements had all been abandoned in the first century BC. Thus, the settlement record of this region indicates a substantial discontinuity and a demographic decline in the first century BC. Some scholars have also proposed that pollen diagrams suggest a reduction of human activity and an increase in arboreal pollen in the Cologne hinterland around the mid-first century BC, although the dating accuracy of these data remains problematic.[59] Be that as it may, overall the most plausible interpretation for this test region is a significant population decline around the time of the Caesarian conquest, probably linked to the punitive campaigns against the Eburones. However, the evidence also indicates that the region never became completely uninhabited, so we are speaking about a substantial, but not total, discontinuity.

Finally, the fifth and last case study is the fertile Hesbaye/Tongeren region in Belgium, where the majority of the thirty-four analysed sites from La Tène C/D seem to have been abandoned towards the end of La Tène D, with most Roman settlements being new foundations from the Augustan period onward.[60] This, again, suggests a significant population decline in the first century BC.

Overall, the first century BC seems to have been a period of substantial settlement abandonment and demographic decrease in the five test regions. Although a complete depopulation is also not observable (with perhaps the exception of region 1), all the case studies show a more or less pronounced discontinuity between La Tène D1 and the Roman period (Table 4.1). It is also interesting to analyse the repopulation patterns in the different regions. In the Batavian river area, the foundation of new settlements began in the period between 50–20 BC, whereas in the Meuse/Demer/Scheldt region and probably also the Hesbaye area it took place a generation later, in the Augustan period. Depopulation was most dramatic in South Holland and the Cologne hinterland, where recolonization is only observable in the Claudian period.

Table 4.1. Degree of settlement discontinuity in five test regions in the extreme north of Gaul.[61]

Region	Degree of discontinuity	Dating	Recolonization
South Holland	total(?) discontinuity	first c. BC	Claudian
Meuse/Demer/Scheldt area	substantial discontinuity	first c. BC	Augustan
Dutch East River area	partial discontinuity	mid-first c. BC	50–20 BC
Cologne hinterland	substantial discontinuity	first c. BC	Claudian
Hesbaye/Tongeren region	substantial discontinuity	first c. BC	Augustan

The Testimony of Coinage

A final aspect that we would like to mention is the enormous and systematic extraction of mobile wealth from Gallic groups by Caesar. The systematic plundering of precious metals was a key strategy of Roman warfare in the 'barbarian' frontiers.[62] At the time of the Roman conquest, northern Gaul was a region with a rich gold circulation in the form of coins and ornaments. Figure 4.14 shows the distribution of some gold series that were in full circulation in the mid-first century BC. By quantifying the number of coin dies used for each coin type, we get an idea of the size of the emissions, thereby assuming a production rate of at least one thousand coins per obverse die.[63] The volumes of the different emissions show a considerable variation, but it is clear that several hundred thousand coins must have been circulating in the northern half of Belgic Gaul at the time of the Caesarian conquest.

This intense circulation raises the question of what happened with all this gold. A first observation is that the conquest period corresponds with a significant peak

---

[57] Roymans and Habermehl 2023.

[58] Gaitzsch 2011; Joachim 2000; 2007.

[59] Kalis and Meurers-Balke 2007; Meurers-Balke and Kalis 2006.

[60] Martin 2017.

[61] Roymans 2019a.

[62] Badian 1968; Raaflaub 2021.

[63] Haselgrove 1984; Roymans and Scheers 2012.

4. THE ARCHAEOLOGY OF JULIUS CAESAR: NEW RESEARCH ON THE GALLIC WARS

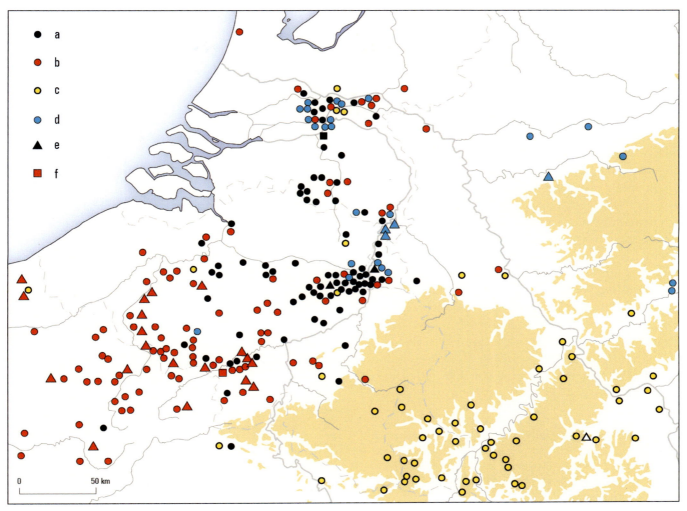

Figure 4.14. Distribution of some Late Iron Age gold coins that were in full circulation in the conquest period. a. staters type Scheers 31 ('Eburones'); b. staters type Scheers 29 ('Nervii'); c. staters type Scheers 30-IV/V ('Treveri'); d. electrum/silver rainbow staters type Lith; e. hoard find; f. sanctuary. Map by Roymans (based on Roymans and Scheers 2012, figs 9–11 and Hornung 2016, fig. 217, with additions).

Figure 4.15. Scheers 31 gold staters, ascribed to the Eburones, from the hoard of Amby. This hoard was probably buried during the Gallic Wars in the late 50s BC. From Roymans and Dijkman 2012.

in hoard deposition.[64] It seems plausible to associate this archaeological 'hoard horizon' with the extreme circumstances of war — with genocidal connotations — that Caesar describes for this northern region (Fig. 4.15). A second observation is that — in contrast to the situation in Britannia — there is hardly any evidence for a continuation of the production and circulation of gold coins in these northern regions in the post-conquest period.[65] We may conclude that after Caesar's departure gold circulation had almost disappeared in this frontier zone.

The most plausible interpretation is that the 'disappearance' of the native gold was a direct consequence of a systematic extraction of precious metals by Caesar via plundering, ransom payments, and forced tribute payments. This raises the question of the importance of the economic aspects of Caesar's campaigns in Gaul. Caesar's war narrative hardly informs us about this issue, but important information comes from later writers, in particular Suetonius. In his biography of Caesar, Suetonius accuses him of the large-scale plunder of Gallic *oppida* and sanctuaries and of enriching himself enormously with wealth stored there, most notably in the form of gold:

> In Gaul he pillaged shrines and temples of the gods filled with offerings, and oftener sacked oppida for the sake of plunder than for any fault. In consequence he had more gold than he knew what to do with, and offered it for sale throughout Italy and the provinces at a rate of 3000 sesterces a pound.[66]

Since the usual price of gold was 4000 sesterces, it is evident that Caesar greatly inflated the Italian gold market.

Conclusion: Caesar's Conquest as an Expression of a Predatory Political Economy

The case studies discussed above, from the identification of 'crime scenes' to the analysis of discontinuities in settlement patterns and coinage circulation, show some of the cruellest sides of Roman military expansionism. In a recent article, we introduced the concept of a 'predatory regime' to define the political economy of Late Republican and Early Imperial Rome, with Caesar's Gallic Wars as one of the prime examples.[67] Our use of the concept is based on the application by González-

Ruibal who, following Mbembe,[68] describes predatory regimes as being 'characterised by the militarization of power and trade, pillage as an economic strategy, the pursuit of private interest under public command and the conversion of brute violence into legitimate authority'.[69] The period of the Roman Late Republic was characterized by social and political violence, which was both internalized in the form of civil wars and externalized with the violent conquest of foreign lands.[70]

Rather than following a well-designed state strategy, the process of annexation and exploitation of new territories can often be characterized as pillage carried out in order to increase the personal wealth and prestige of certain elite factions and individuals. Caesar's enormous personal enrichment through the Gallic Wars serves as a case in point, but similar strategies are also observable in other areas, such as the Iberian Peninsula. Within this model, state gain was frequently just a secondary outcome of individual and familial agendas that used warfare and the extraction of external resources (both human, i.e. slaves, and non-human, e.g. minerals, grain, and textiles) as a means of reaching or consolidating their position at the top of Roman society. These asymmetric power dynamics and the 'dark sides' of the conquest need to be taken into account if we want to construct more inclusive narratives that acknowledge the suffering of millions of people.[71] This is not to demonize ancient Rome, which was not necessarily more violent than other state powers in Antiquity,[72] but to realize that all empires, ancient and modern, have both 'bright' and 'dark' sides, which are closely entwined. In the case of Late Republican and Imperial Rome, scholarship has traditionally placed more emphasis on the supposedly bright aspects, such as the spread of literacy, sumptuous villas, monumental public buildings, and high-quality tableware. However, the darker sides, including mass killing, exploitation, and enslavement, also need to be incorporated into our analysis.

As we have tried to show, archaeology can contribute to a more holistic understanding of the Roman expansion by providing data that illustrate not only the strategies and practices of the Roman military, but also the impact on indigenous societies at a local and regional level. The

---

64 Roymans and Scheers 2012; Roymans 2019c.

65 Roymans 1990, 127.

66 Suet., *Iul.* LIV.2.

67 Fernández-Götz, Maschek, and Roymans 2020a.

68 Mbembe 2001.

69 González-Ruibal 2015, 424.

70 Barrandon 2018; Maschek 2018; Lange and Vervaet 2019.

71 For recent discussions, see Fernández-Götz, Maschek, and Roymans 2020a; 2020b; Padilla Peralta 2020; Raaflaub 2021.

72 Eckstein 2006.

rapid development of conflict archaeology, new methodologies, and more detailed settlement studies hold great potential for the future. While processes of collaboration, integration, and hybridization undoubtedly existed, we cannot ignore that the Caesarian conquest was ultimately an aggressive imperialist act that brought with it the death and loss of liberty for hundreds of thousands of people. Aspects such as the partial genocide of the Eburones, Tencteri, and Usipetes, the massive sale of slaves through the southern markets, and the looting of numerous settlements and sanctuaries were acknowledged by the conquerors in their writings and should not be underestimated or sanitized by modern scholars. Acknowledging the complexities of history requires researching its most uncomfortable facets — a lesson that holds value not only for the past but also for our collective present and future.

Works Cited

Arbabe, E. 2017. *La politique des Gaulois: vie politique et institutions en Gaule chevelue (IIᵉ siècle avant notre ère-70)*, Histoire ancienne et médiéval, 150 (Paris: Éditions de la Sorbonne).

Badian, E. 1968. *Roman Imperialism in the Late Republic* (Ithaca: Cornell University Press).

Barrandon, N. 2018. *Les massacres de la République romaine* (Paris: Fayard).

Bellemore, J. 2012. 'The Roman Concept of Massacre. Julius Caesar in Gaul', in P. G. Dwyer and L. Ryan (eds), *Theatres of Violence: Massacre, Mass Killing and Atrocity throughout History* (New York: Berghahn), pp. 38–49.

Bloxham, D. and A. D. Moses (eds). 2010. *The Oxford Handbook of Genocide Studies* (Oxford: Oxford University Press).

Bruin, J. de. 2019. *Border Communities at the Edge of the Roman Empire: Processes of Change in the Civitas Cananefatium* (Amsterdam: Amsterdam University Press).

Brun, P. and P. Ruby. 2008. *L'âge du Fer en France: premières villes, premiers états celtiques* (Paris: La Découverte).

Chalk, F. and K. Jonassohn. 1990. *The History and Sociology of Genocide: Analyses and Case Studies* (New Haven: Yale University Press).

Cohen, K. M. and others. 2012. 'Rhine-Meuse Delta Studies Digital Basemap for Delta Evolution and Palaeogeography' (unpublished doctoral thesis, Utrecht University, Department of Physical Geography).

Deyber, A. 2008. 'Le champ de bataille d'Alésia à la lumière d'exemples comparables', in M. Reddé and S. von Schnurbein (eds), *Alésia et la bataille du Teutoburg: un parallèle critique des sources* (Ostfildern: Thorbecke), pp. 321–40.

Dietler, M. 1994. 'Our Ancestors the Gauls: Archaeology, Ethnic Nationalism, and the Manipulation of Celtic Identity in Modern Europe', *American Anthropologist*, 96: 584–605.

—— 1998. 'A Tale of Three Sites: The Monumentalization of Celtic Oppida and the Politics of Collective Memory and Identity', *World Archaeology*, 30: 72–89.

Dolfini, A. and others (eds). 2018. *Prehistoric Warfare and Violence: Quantitative and Qualitative Approaches* (New York: Springer).

Eckstein, A. M. 2006. *Mediterranean Anarchy, Interstate War, and the Rise of Rome* (Berkeley: University of California Press).

Fernández-Götz, M. 2014. *Identity and Power: The Transformation of Iron Age Societies in Northeast Gaul* (Amsterdam: Amsterdam University Press).

Fernández-Götz, M., D. Maschek, and N. Roymans. 2020a. 'The Dark Side of the Empire: Roman Expansionism between Object Agency and Predatory Regime', *Antiquity*, 94: 1630–39.

—— 2020b. 'Power, Asymmetries and How to View the Roman World', *Antiquity*, 94: 1653–56.

Fernández-Götz, M. and N. Roymans (eds). 2018. *Conflict Archaeology: Materialities of Collective Violence from Prehistory to Late Antiquity* (New York: Routledge).

Fichtl, S. 1994. *Les Gaulois du nord de la Gaule: 150–20 av. J.-C.* (Paris: Errance).

—— 2012. *Les peuples gaulois: IIIᵉ-Iᵉʳ siècle av. J.-C.* (Paris: Errance).

Fitzpatrick, A. P. 2020. 'Julius Caesar's Battle for Gaul: New Archaeological Perspectives', *Current World Archaeology*, 103: 38–41.

Fitzpatrick, A. P. and C. Haselgrove (eds). 2019. *Julius Caesar's Battle for Gaul: New Archaeological Perspectives* (Oxford: Oxbow).

Gaitzsch, W. 2011. 'Roman Villa Landscapes of the Lignite Mining Areas in the Hinterland of Cologne', in N. Roymans and T. Derks (eds), *Villa Landscapes in the Roman North* (Amsterdam: Amsterdam University Press), pp. 285–300.

Girault, J.-P. 2013. *La fontaine de Loulié au Puy d'Issolud: le dossier archéologique du siège d'Uxellodunum*, Collection Bibracte, 23 (Glux-en-Glenne: Centre archéologique européen du Mont Beuvray).

González-Ruibal, A. 2015. 'An Archaeology of Predation: Capitalism and the Coloniality of Power in Equatorial Guinea (Central Africa)', in M. Leone and J. Knauf (eds), *Historical Archaeologies of Capitalism* (New York: Springer), pp. 421–44.

Haselgrove, C. 1984. 'Warfare and its Aftermath as Reflected in the Precious Metal Coinage of Belgic Gaul', *Oxford Journal of Archaeology*, 3: 81–105.

—— (ed.). 2006. *Celtes et Gaulois: l'archéologie face à l'histoire, IV: Les mutations de la fin de l'âge du fer*, Collection Bibracte, 12.4 (Glux-en-Glenne: Centre archéologique européen du Mont Beuvray).

Heeren, S. 2009. *De romanisering van rurale gemeenschappen in de civitas Batavorum: De casus Tiel-Passewaaij*, Nederlandse Archeologische Rapporten, 36 (Amsterdam: Vrije Universiteit).

Heinrichs, J. 2008. 'Die Eburonen, oder: Die Kunst des Überlebens', *Zeitschrift für Papyrologie und Epigraphik*, 164: 203–30.

Hiddink, H. A. and N. Roymans. 2015. 'Exploring the Rural Landscape of a Peripheral Region', in N. Roymans, T. Derks, and H. A. Hiddink (eds), *The Roman Villa of Hoogeloon and the Archaeology of the Periphery* (Amsterdam: Amsterdam University Press), pp. 45–86.

Hill, P. and J. Wileman. 2002. *Landscapes of War: The Archaeology of Aggression and Defence* (Stroud: Tempus).

Hornung, S. 2016. *Siedlung und Bevölkerung in Ostgallien zwischen Gallischem Krieg und der Festigung der Römischen Herrschaft: Eine Studie auf Basis landschaftsarchäologischer Forschungen im Umfeld des Oppidums 'Hunnenring' von Otzenhausen (Lkr. St Wendel)*, Römisch-Germanische Forschungen, 73 (Darmstadt: Von Zabern).

—— 2018. 'Tracing Julius Caesar. The Late Republican Military Camp at Hermeskeil and its Historical Context', in M. Fernández-Götz and N. Roymans (eds), *Conflict Archaeology: Materialities of Collective Violence from Prehistory to Late Antiquity* (New York: Routledge), pp. 193–203.

Joachim, H.-E. 2000. 'Die Eburonen – Historisches und Archäologisches zu einem ausgerotteten Volksstamm caesarischer Zeit', *Jülicher Geschichtsblätter*, 67/68: 157–70.

—— 2007. 'Die späte Eisenzeit am Niederrhein', in G. Uelsberg (ed.), *Krieg und Frieden: Kelten, Römer, Germanen* (Darmstadt: Primus), pp. 48–58.

Johnston, A. C. 2018. 'Nostri and "the Other(s)"', in L. Grillo and C. B. Krebs (eds), *The Cambridge Companion to the Writings of Julius Caesar* (Cambridge: Cambridge University Press), pp. 81–94.

Kalis, A. J. and J. Meurers-Balke. 2007. 'Landnutzung im Niederrheingebiet zwischen Krieg und Frieden', in G. Uelsberg (ed.), *Krieg und Frieden: Kelten, Römer, Germanen* (Darmstadt: Primus), pp. 144–53.

Kiernan, B. 2007. 'Classical Genocide and Early Modern Memory', in B. Kiernan (ed.), *Blood and Soil: A World History of Genocide and Extermination from Sparta to Dafur* (New Haven: Yale University Press), pp. 42–71.

Kraus, C. S. 2009. 'Bellum Gallicum', in M. Griffin (ed.), *A Companion to Julius Caesar* (Oxford: Blackwell), pp. 159–74.

Lange, C. H. and F. J. Vervaet. 2019. *The Historiography of the Late Republican Civil War* (Leiden: Brill).

Madley, B. 2017. *An American Genocide: The United States and the California Indian Catastrophe, 1846–1873* (New Haven: Yale University Press).

Martin, F. 2017. 'Atuatuques, Condruses, Eburons: Culture matérielle et occupation du sol dans le territoire de la future civitas Tungrorum, de la fin de l'âge du Fer au début de l'époque gallo-romaine' (unpublished doctoral thesis, Université Libre de Bruxelles).

Maschek, D. 2018. *Die römischen Bürgerkriege: Archäologie und Geschichte einer Krisenzeit* (Darmstadt: Von Zabern).

Mbembe, A. 2001. *On the Postcolony* (Berkeley: University of California Press).

Metzler, J. and others. 2018. 'Comptoir commercial italique et occupation militaire romaine dans l'oppidum du Titelberg. Un état de la recherche (2017)', in M. Reddé (ed.), *Les armées romaines en Gaule à l'époque républicaine: nouveaux témoignages archéologiques*, Collection Bibracte, 28 (Glux-en-Glenne: Centre archéologique européen du Mont Beuvray), pp. 179–205.

Meurers-Balke, J. and A. J. Kalis. 2006. 'Landwirtschaft und Landnutzung in der Bronze- und Eisenzeit', in J. Kunow and H.-H. Wegner (eds), *Urgeschichte im Rheinland* (Cologne: Rheinischer Verein für Denkmalpflege und Landschaftsschutz), pp. 267–76.

Napoleon III. 1865–1866. *Histoire de Jules César* (Paris: Henri Plon).

Olivier, L. 2006. 'Il faut défendre la Gaule', in S. Rieckhoff (ed.), *Celtes et Gaulois, l'archéologie face à l'histoire*, I: *Celtes et gaulois dans l'histoire, l'historiographie et l'idéologie modern*, Collection Bibracte, 12.1 (Glux-en-Glenne: Centre archéologique européen du Mont Beuvray), pp. 153–69.

—— 2019. 'The Second Battle of Alesia: The 19th-Century Investigations at Alise-Sainte-Reine and International Recognition of the Gallic Period of the Late Iron Age', in A. P. Fitzpatrick and C. Haselgrove (eds), *Julius Caesar's Battle for Gaul: New Archaeological Perspectives* (Oxford: Oxbow), pp. 285–309.

Padilla Peralta, D. 2020. 'Epistemicide: The Roman Case', *Classica*, 33: 151–86.

Paridaens, N. 2020. 'L'oppidum du "Bois du Grand Bon Dieu" à Thuin: Résultats des recherches 2018–2019', *LUNULA: Archaeologia protohistorica*, 28: 145–48.

Paridaens, N. and others. 2020. 'Les balles de fronde en plomb découvertes sur l'oppidum de Thuin: caractérisation, origine et interprétation', *Signa*, 9: 111–23.

Poux, M. 2008. *Sur les traces de César: militaria tardo-républicains en contexte gaulois*, Collection Bibracte, 14 (Glux-en-Glenne: Centre archéologique européen du Mont Beuvray).

Pujol, A. and others. 2019. 'Archaeology of the Roman Civil Wars: The Destruction of Puig Ciutat (Catalonia, Spain) and Caesar's Campaign in Ilerda (49 BC)', in A. P. Fitzpatrick and C. Haselgrove (eds), *Julius Caesar's Battle for Gaul: New Archaeological Perspectives* (Oxford: Oxbow), pp. 227–40.

Quesada-Sanz, F. and J. Moralejo-Ordax. 2020. 'Tras las huellas de Julio César: los campos de batalla cesarianos de Ulia/Montemayor y el hallazgo de un carro de época ibérica', in P. C. G. Barba (ed.), *Actualidad de la investigación arqueológica en España II (2019–2020): conferencias impartidas en el museo arqueológico nacional* (Madrid: Museo arqueológico nacional), pp. 229–52.

Raaflaub, K. A. 2017. *The Landmark Julius Caesar: The Complete Works* (New York: Pantheon).

—— 2021. 'Caesar and Genocide: Confronting the Dark Side of Caesar's Gallic Wars', *New England Classical Journal*, 48: 54–80.

Ralston, I. 2019. 'The Gauls on the Eve of the Roman Conquest', in A. P. Fitzpatrick and C. Haselgrove (eds), *Julius Caesar's Battle for Gaul: New Archaeological Perspectives* (Oxford: Oxbow), pp. 19–47.

Reddé, M. 2003. *Alésia: L'archéologie face à l'imaginaire* (Paris: Errance).

—— 2013. 'L'avenir d'Alésia', in S. Krausz and others (eds), *L'Âge du Fer en Europe: mélanges offerts à Olivier Buchsenschutz* (Bordeaux: Ausonius), pp. 681–88.

—— 2018a. 'The Battlefield of *Alesia*', in M. Fernández-Götz and N. Roymans (eds), *Conflict Archaeology: Materialities of Collective Violence from Prehistory to Late Antiquity* (New York: Routledge), pp. 183–91.

—— 2018b. *Les armées romaines en Gaule à l'époque républicaine: nouveaux témoignages archéologiques*, Collection Bibracte, 28 (Glux-en-Glenne: Centre archéologique européen du Mont Beuvray).

—— 2019. 'Recent Archaeological Research on Roman Military Engineering Works of the Gallic War', in A. P. Fitzpatrick and C. Haselgrove (eds), *Julius Caesar's Battle for Gaul: New Archaeological Perspectives* (Oxford: Oxbow), pp. 91–112.

Reddé, M. and S. von Schnurbein (eds). 2001. *Alésia: fouilles et recherches franco-allemandes sur les travaux militaires romains autour du Mont-Auxois (1991–1997)* (Paris: De Boccard).

Riggsby, A. 2006. *Caesar in Gaul and Rome: War in Words* (Austin: University of Texas Press).

Roymans, N. 1990. *Tribal Societies in Northern Gaul: An Anthropological Perspective*, Cingula, 12 (Amsterdam: Amsterdam University Press).

—— 2004. *Ethnic Identity and Imperial Power: The Batavians in the Early Roman Empire* (Amsterdam: Amsterdam University Press).

—— 2018. 'A Roman Massacre in the Far North: Caesar's Annihilation of the Tencteri and Usipetes in the Dutch River Area', in M. Fernández-Götz and N. Roymans (eds), *Conflict Archaeology: Materialities of Collective Violence from Prehistory to Late Antiquity* (New York: Routledge), pp. 167–81.

—— 2019a. 'Conquest, Mass Violence and Ethnic Stereotyping: Investigating Caesar's Actions in the Germanic Frontier Zone', *Journal of Roman Archaeology*, 32: 439–58.

—— 2019b. 'Caesar's Conquest and the Archaeology of Mass Violence in the Germanic Frontier Zone', in A. P. Fitzpatrick and C. Haselgrove (eds), *Julius Caesar's Battle for Gaul: New Archaeological Perspectives* (Oxford: Oxbow), pp. 113–33.

—— 2019c. 'Late Iron Age Coin Hoards with Silver Rainbow Staters from Graetheide (NL) and the Mid-1st Century BC Hoard Horizon in the Lower Rhine/Meuse Region', *Germania*, 97: 65–92.

Roymans, N., T. Derks, and S. Heeren. 2020. 'Roman Imperialism and the Transformation of Rural Society in a Frontier Province: Diversifying the Narrative', *Britannia*, 51: 265–94.

Roymans, N. and W. Dijkman. 2012. 'The Gold and Silver Hoard of Maastricht-Amby', in N. Roymans, G. Creemers, and S. Scheers (eds), *Late Iron Age Gold Hoards from the Low Countries and the Caesarian Conquest of Northern Gaul* (Amsterdam: Amsterdam University Press), pp. 171–213.

Roymans, N. and D. Habermehl. 2023. 'Migration and Ethnic Dynamics in the Lower Rhine Frontier of the Expanding Roman Empire (60 BC–AD 20): A Historical-Anthropological Perspective', in M. Fernández-Götz, C. Nimura, P. W. Stockhammer, and R. Cartwright (eds), *Rethinking Migrations in Late Prehistoric Eurasia* (Oxford: Oxford University Press), pp. 292–312.

Roymans, N. and M. Fernández-Götz. 2015. 'Caesar in Gaul: New Perspectives on the Archaeology of Mass Violence', in T. Brindle and others (eds), *TRAC 2014: Proceedings of the Twenty-Fourth Annual Theoretical Roman Archaeology Conference* (Oxford: Oxbow), pp. 70–80.

—— 2018. 'The Archaeology of Warfare and Mass Violence in Ancient Europe. An Introduction', in M. Fernández-Götz and N. Roymans (eds), *Conflict Archaeology: Materialities of Collective Violence from Prehistory to Late Antiquity* (New York: Routledge), pp. 1–10.

—— 2019. 'Reconsidering the Roman Conquest: New Archaeological Perspectives', *Journal of Roman Archaeology*, 32: 415–20.

Roymans, N. and S. Scheers. 2012. 'Eight Gold Hoards from the Low Countries: A Synthesis', in N. Roymans, G. Creemers, and S. Scheers (eds), *Late Iron Age Gold Hoards from the Low Countries and the Caesarian Conquest of Northern Gaul* (Amsterdam: Amsterdam University Press), pp. 1–46.

Schadee, H. 2008. 'Caesar's Construction of Northern Europe: Inquiry, Contact and Corruption in *De bello gallico*', *The Classical Quarterly*, 58: 158–80.

Schallmayer, E., S. Schade-Lindig, and J. Meyer. 2012. 'Mit den Kelten kommen die Römer: Militäranlagen an der Lahn bei Limburg-Eschhofen', *Hessen Archäologie*, 2012: 95–101.

Scott, D. and A. P. McFeaters. 2011. 'The Archaeology of Historic Battlefields: A History and Theoretical Development in Conflict Archaeology', *Journal of Archaeological Research*, 19: 103–32.

Wees, H. van. 2010. 'Genocide in the Ancient World', in D. Bloxham and A. D. Moses (eds), *The Oxford Handbook of Genocide Studies* (Oxford: Oxford University Press), pp. 239–58.

5. Across the Rubicon to Rome: New Elements for the Identification of Caesar's Military Camp

Annalisa Pozzi

Ministero della Cultura (MIC) — Soprintendenza Archeologia Belle Arti e Paesaggio per le Province di Ravenna, Forlì-Cesena e Rimini (annalisa.pozzi@cultura.gov.it)

Cristian Tassinari

Professional archaeologist (Tecne S.r.l.) (cristiantass@libero.it)

Fonte cadit modico parvisque inpellitur undis puniceus Rubicon, cum fervida canduit aestas, perque imas serpit valles et Gallica certus limes ab Ausoniis disterminat arva colonis. Tum vires preabebat hiemps atque auxerat undas tertia iam gravido pluvialis Cynthia cornu et madidis Euri resolutae flatibus Alpes. Primus in obliquum sonipes opponitur amnem excepturus aquas; molli tum cetera rumpit turba vado faciles iam fracti fluminis undas.[1]

(The reddish Rubicon originates from a small source and proceeds with short waves, when the hot summer burns, and flows into the bottom of the valleys and arises, as an exact border, between the Gallic fields and the lands occupied by the Italic settlers. At that time, made stronger by winter, it had been increased by the third day of the new moon, with its sickle bringing much rain, and by the snow of the Alps that melted in the humid blows of the east wind. First the cavalry placed themselves across the current of the river, ready to withstand the impact of the waves, then the rest of the army passed, easily fording the waters of the river, whose violence had been broken).[2]

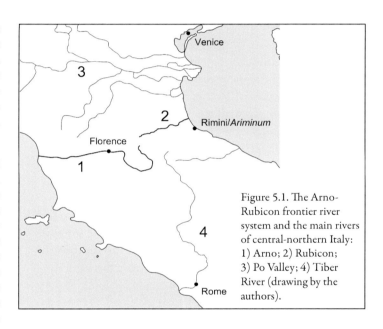

Figure 5.1. The Arno-Rubicon frontier river system and the main rivers of central-northern Italy: 1) Arno; 2) Rubicon; 3) Po Valley; 4) Tiber River (drawing by the authors).

Introduction

The Rubicon district links its name to one of the most emblematic events for Julius Caesar's political career. As is known, it is at the banks of the Rubicon that between 10 and 11 January 49 BC, the leader rejoined the troops returning from the Gallic military campaign, before embarking on the march towards Rome.[3] At that time, the river represented the border of the power of military and civil government of Rome, within which entry under arms was prohibited.[4] With the Arno, which flowed on the western side of the Apennines, the Rubicon formed a frontier river, as the first application of that defensive model that would subsequently be applied on a large scale along the northern and eastern borders of the Empire (Fig. 5.1).

Unfortunately, the only direct source of those events, *De bello civili*, written by the hand of Caesar himself, does not deal with the crossing of the river: the description passes from the exhortation to the troops in Ravenna, after the order of the Senate to dissolve the army, to the arrival in Rimini, where the tribunes of the plebs were

---

[1] Luc., *Bellum civile* I.213–23.

[2] This translation is by the authors.

[3] App., *B Civ.* II.35; Cass. Dio XLI.4; Plut., *Caes.* XXXI–XXXII.6; Suet., *Iul.* XXXII; Vell. Pat., II.4.

[4] The border had been set a few decades earlier by Sulla, at the end of a period of internal strife. On the function of the Rubicon as the border of Italy 'In ora fluvius Crustumium, Ariminum colonia cum amnibus Arimino et Aprusa, fluvius Rubico, quondam finis Italiae' (Plin., *HN* II.115). In Suetonius 'Consecutusque cohortis ad Rubiconem flumen, qui provinciae eius finis erat' (Suet., *Iul.* I.31). The description given by Plutarch is very similar (Plut., *Caes.* XXXII.6).

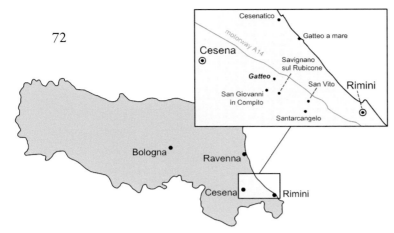

Figure 5.2. Geographical location of Gatteo with indications of the minor locations mentioned in the text (drawing by the authors).

waiting to rejoin the general.[5] Therefore, no mention of the Rubicon is present in the writings of Caesar, perhaps because he did not want to emphasize the subversive act, full of symbolic value, against the homeland.[6] All the words are in fact addressed to underline the ingratitude of the senators of Rome, diverted in judgement by Pompey Magnus, towards the years of sacrifices spent by the soldiers in the provinces.

This is the image that Caesar wants to give us of the situation; however, according to a literary tradition that refers to a lost work by the Roman politic and historian Asinius Pollio (from which Suetonius also draws),[7] the leader did not enjoy the full support of the troops, who were tricked into crossing the river. Leaving aside the real motivations of the parties involved, the topographical references in the sources are more important for our research. Suetonius's description is particularly interesting since he reports some details of Caesar's journey from Ravenna to the Rubicon.[8] Leaving aside the elements of dramatization of the story aimed at discrediting the leader,[9] we can instead isolate some indications of a geographical nature. Firstly, the journey that will lead Caesar to rejoin his cohorts took place between Ravenna and the Rubicon, along a minor and winding road network, avoiding crossing the border at the main consular ways. Secondly, at the point where the army was waiting for its general, there was a slender bridge, probably not strong enough to support the passage of an army, which crossed the river by fording.[10]

In the following parts of this contribution, we will demonstrate that the archaeological remains found in Gatteo belong to a site that controlled the paths along the valley since prehistoric time and that the remains of the Roman period can be associated with a military settlement. Subsequently, through an analysis of the geographical and environmental context and the itinerant network, we will prove that this river course corresponded to the ancient Rubicon River and that the site was inserted at the centre of a border road system, coinciding with the *limes* established by Publius Cornelius Sulla to mark the division between the Italic territory and the provincial one.

The Archaeological Excavations in Gatteo

As for the location of the Caesarean military camp, new food for thought comes from the recent excavations carried out in the territory of Gatteo, a small town in the Rubicon area, not far from Savignano sul Rubicone and Rimini (Fig. 5.2).

From an archaeological point of view, the area of Gatteo over the years had never revealed particular discoveries and therefore it was considered a territory where occasional finds testified to a scattered rural population of the Roman period.[11] Starting from the excavations

---

[5] Caes., *B Civ.* I. 5–8.

[6] The Civil War, which would oppose the senatorial aristocracy to the conqueror of Gaul, begins with a violated border. To understand the gravity of Caesar's gesture in its cultural resonances, it is necessary to go back to the myth of the foundation of the city, to the auspicious dispute between Romulus and Remus, and to the fratricide linked to the failure to respect the sacred pomerium. In the perspective of Caesar, faced with the general violation of law by the Senate, an outraged border could not represent an obstacle for those who intend to restore the legality of rights. About the sacred pomerium, see De Sanctis 2007; Maccari 2019; Magdelain 1976; Sisani 2014.

[7] Cf. Canfora 1999, 398–99, appendix 1.

[8] Suet., *Iul.* XXXI–XXXII.

[9] It's very difficult to believe that the general, who had demonstrated perfect geographical knowledge of Gaul, could get lost on the way between Ravenna and Rimini.

[10] The references to the winding paths ('per angustissimos tramites') and to the small bridge ('ponticulum') are in Suetonius (Suet., *Iul.* XXXI). In the next passage of the text, the crossing of the river is just mentioned ('prosilivit ad flumen et ingenti spiritu classicum exorsus pertendit ad alteram ripam'). Lucan outlines a river swollen by winter rains and crossed by fording (Luc., *Bellum civile* 1.217–23).

[11] The only evidence of some historical significance was represented by the fifteenth-century castle (Fig. 5.3, D), of which the perimeter wall with towers and access portal is preserved. Although the local tradition holds that the castle rests on the remains of a Roman *castrum* there are no elements to believe that the building is older than the medieval period and very recent archaeological excavations carried out outside the southern enclosure wall have highlighted the existence of stratigraphies dating between the Late Antiquity and the high medieval period.

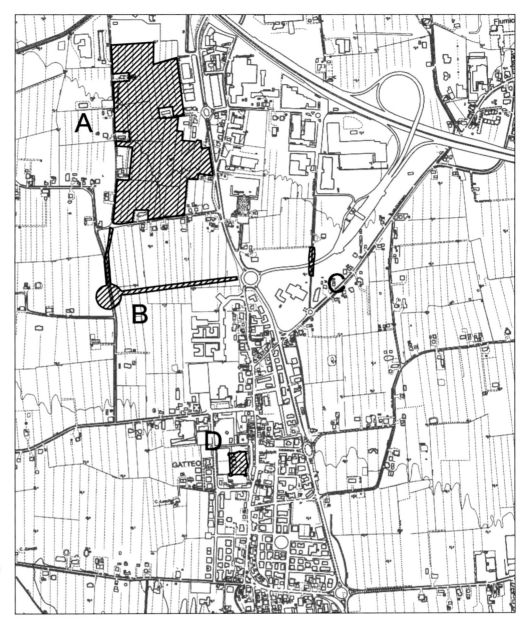

Figure 5.3. Areas of archaeological and historical interest: A) Sector A of 2018–2020 excavations; B) Sector B of 2018–2020 excavations; C) excavations for the *Valle del Rubicone* motorway exit; D) The fifteenth-century castle (drawing by the authors).

conducted in 2010 and 2011 relating to the construction of the motorway exit A14 *Valle del Rubicone*, the sector between the motorway and the centre of Gatteo has begun to reveal its historical and archaeological potential (Fig. 5.3).[12]

The excavation campaigns carried out in a vast area between 2018 and 2020 contributed to an increase in the archaeological evidence and to outline the picture of a territory with a strong settlement vocation, favoured by the geomorphological characteristics and by the presence of roads.

The latest research has focused on two areas: a large first sector of about four hectares where the construction of a logistics centre with an artisan building was planned and the second sector in correspondence with the preparation of a new road towards the A14 motorway exit (Fig. 5.3, A and B).[13]

---

[12] The excavations, carried out under the scientific direction of Dr Monica Miari of the Archaeological Superintendence of Emilia Romagna (Client: Autostrade S.p.A.; Archaeological Company in charge: Tecne S.r.l.), allowed documenting the remains of a settlement attributable to the Eneolithic and traces of later stages.

[13] The campaigns were conducted under the scientific direction of the Superintendency of Archaeology, Fine Arts, and Landscape of Ravenna (Client: Teddy S.p.A.; Archaeological Company in charge: Tecne S.r.l.). Archaeological checks were requested by the

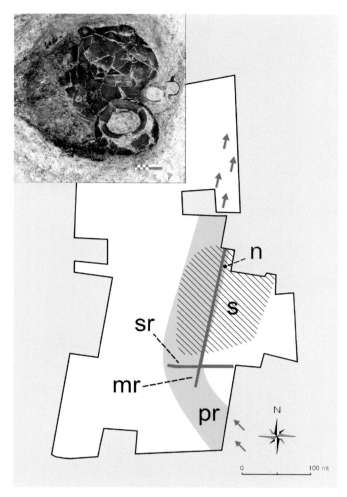

Figure 5.4. Main pre-Roman evidences: pr) prehistoric riverbed; s) Iron Age settlement; n) necropolis; mr) south-west/north-east main road; sr) west–east secondary road. Top left: a female tomb with a set of ceramic vases and a pair of amber earrings on the cinerary (drawing by the authors).

In Sector A, the main findings are attributable to the Prehistoric and Protohistoric periods. They are located in connection with the passage of a river, witnessed by an ancient riverbed with a south-west/north-east course, which favoured the supply of water and defined optimal settlement conditions. Some areas of fire and charred wooden traces with a straight path, arranged to the west of the riverbed, were attributable to a site that can be framed between the Neolithic and Eneolithic.[14]

Starting from the eighth century BC, an articulated settlement phase is identified, consisting of a village with housing and artisan frameworks. A small sepulchral nucleus, made up of six cremation tombs, was placed in relation to a road route directed towards the sea above a prehistoric riverbed.[15] The Villanovan settlement seems to reach its maximum expansion starting from the beginning of the seventh century BC when structures related to leather tanning appear.[16] In the same period, an east–west secondary road was traced, crossing the older axis and probably leading to a river ford. The course of the nearby river not only determined the layout of the main road from the hill to the sea, but also influenced the orientation of the housing structures.[17] To the north, on the side of the road, a nucleus of six cremation tombs, characterized by rich funerary equipment, was found (n, in Fig. 5.4). They cover a chronological period from the end of the eighth century BC to the middle of the following century and show affinity with the tombs of

---

Superintendency since previous excavation activities conducted in the area had returned traces of human presence; following the execution of some preventive trenches, an archaeological excavation was activated in extension and checks on all areas affected by the works.

[14] The chronology proposed is deduced from a possible comparison with similar attestations found in Riccione ('ex Conti Spina', in Berlinguer Street; cf. Miari and others 2018) and from an assessment relating to the level of outcrop, compatible with that on which the aforementioned Eneolithic remains were identified in 2011. The lack of materials and analysis on the wooden remains still does not allow for a better chronological specification.

[15] It is believed that by this time, the river course must have moved further east. The sandy sediments left by the riverbed ensured the drainage of the houses, also favoured by the excavation of numerous wells and cisterns.

[16] The estimated extension of the town, whose limits have been identified on the three north, south, and west sides, is about 1.5 ha. The artisan destination of the archaeological evidence linked to the processing of leathers is hypothesized on the basis of the characteristics. Large tanks covered with wood, probably used for the maceration of the skins, and deep pits with an elongated shape, inside which the skins fixed to the frames were immersed, are attested throughout the area. In relation to these pits from the Padanian Neolithic sites, interpreted as related to tanning, the standardization of the shape had already been highlighted in 1997 due to specific functional needs (Ferrari and Steffè 1997). Confirmation of this interpretation may come from the analysis of the samples carried out.

[17] The study of the evidence and materials recovered from the housing structures, still in the preliminary phase, will allow us to better frame the characteristics of the site, which presents elements partly related to the centre of Verucchio for the most ancient phases (the eighth and seventh centuries BC) and with the site of the Compito for the most recent phases (the seventh and sixth centuries BC). In particular, in the cultural component of the village, elements of central Italic and middle Adriatic tradition seem to emerge, which are in line with what is documented in the neighbouring territories (for an analysis of the Savio Valley and its territorial complexity, see Miari 2014; about the recent findings at S. Giovanni in Compito, see: Pozzi and Urbini (forthcoming)).

the Villanovan centre of Verucchio.[18] The history of the protohistoric village seems to close by the middle of the sixth century BC when a general change is felt in the nearby area of the Marecchia River, and the site of Verucchio re-emerges in importance (Fig. 5.5).[19]

In Sector A (Fig. 5.3), some evidence of Roman times has also come to light, a phase in which the Iron Age road patterns are maintained, even if slightly modified.[20] The direction of the main axis led to the conclusion that this road connected, with a straight stretch, the two stations located twelve *milia passum* from Rimini on the two consular roads: Ad Confluentes on Via Aemilia and Rubico Flumen on Via Popilia (Fig. 5.6).

Right from the start, the close relationship of this road with the Rubicon border was not lost, and from the analysis of the cartography, it emerges with great evidence that this straight line, geometrically drawn between the two consular roads, constituted a kind of barrier for the routes to Rimini (and therefore also towards Rome).

The hypothesis is that this *limes* road had some military checkpoints at the crossing points of the routes leading to the river fords. The oldest Roman structures found in the excavation are indeed located at the crossroad: these included a quadrangular wooden building surrounded by a portico or a palisade.[21] A few metres to the north-west, a well with a diameter of 2.20 m was discovered. It was too shallow to be useful for drawing water, so it was interpreted as a ritual

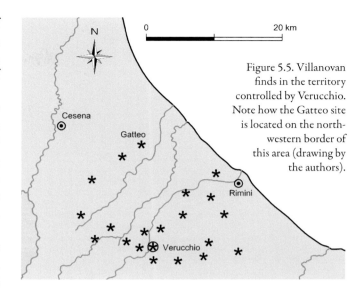

Figure 5.5. Villanovan finds in the territory controlled by Verucchio. Note how the Gatteo site is located on the north-western border of this area (drawing by the authors).

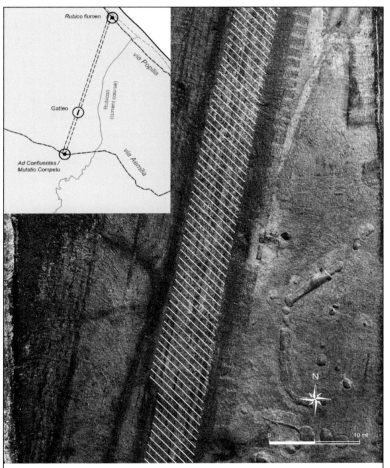

Figure 5.6. Stretch of the Roman road, recognized by the lateral ditches. Top left: the projection of the road axis towards the hill and towards the coast (drawing by the authors and photo by the Photographic Archive of the Superintendence of Archaeology, Fine Arts, and Landscape of Ravenna).

---

[18] Males are characterized as warriors through the deposition of weapons, whereas the role and prestige of women are emphasized by precious ornaments and placed in relation to spinning and weaving.

[19] The new organization of the Romagna area starting from the second half of the sixth century BC was influenced by cultural contribution coming from the central Italy. In the district of the Marecchia River, the sites of Verucchio and Rimini-Covignano stand out in terms of importance, while several sites, documented in the territory between the seventh and mid-sixth centuries BC, tend to run out.

[20] The east–west road is kept in its original position, while the valley road leading to the sea is shifted west by a few metres (perhaps resulting from further shifts in the riverbed). The road layouts are given by the lateral ditches; however, nothing remains of their surfaces, which must have been located at a higher level than the one where the remains emerged.

[21] Henceforth, it is referred to as Structure 9. The building is partially damaged in the southern part by the passage of a later Roman moat.

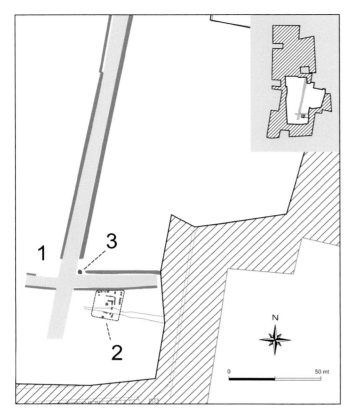

Figure 5.7. Gatteo. Sector A (warehouse area and east car park) evidence from the Late Latenian/Early Roman period: 1) crossroads; 2) Structure 9; 3) ritual pit; 4) forty-five degrees north-east oriented ditch; 5) human burial (drawing by the authors).

pit due to the position at the crossroads and the presence of an animal burial inside (Fig. 5.7).[22]

Alternatively, the plan of Structure 9, which recalls the so-called Gallo-Roman sanctuaries and the religious enclosures of the Celtic territory (Fig. 5.8),[23] and the evidence of ritual activities related to the pit[24] has suggested that these elements constituted a small religious complex, connected to the crossroad (*compitum*). However, this hypothesis encounters some chronological obstacles: the materials returned from these contexts would seem to direct the dating towards the Late Latenian period or to a phase of very early Romanization (third century BC),[25] a chronology that,

however, appears too high for the small place of worship (*fanum*).[26]

A different interpretation can be proposed: considering the position along the border road and the military vocation that the whole area acquired in Roman times, the wooden building could be recognized as a control structure, similar to the watchtowers known through the numerous examples found along the Rhine *limes*.[27] This hypothesis could explain the evolutionary dynamics of the next phase, when Structure 9 is inserted at the southwestern vertex of a triangular-shaped fence, which used the forty-five degree angled moat as its northern boundary. Outside this moat, a human tomb, devoid of a skull, was discovered: the rectangular pit was arranged parallel to the ditch and at a distance of 8.7 m from it. The tomb was of a very poor type, a simple pit without equipment and not inserted in a larger sepulchral context.[28] For this reason, it is considered an anomalous burial, the meaning of which is probably to be found in the relationship with the nearby oblique moat. The connection between the moat and human burial finds only one comparison in a military context, in the excavation of the Caesarian Grand Camp at Gergovie. In that case, the skeleton of a boy aged eight–fifteen found inside the moat delimits the camp on the east side. The dating of the tomb converges in the first half of the first century BC, but the burial still does not have a clear explanation, although the young age of the deceased leads us to exclude that it is a soldier involved in the clashes between Gauls and Romans.[29]

---

[22] It probably dates back to the Late Iron Age, but it was also used in the Roman period. At that time, it was only 1.10 m deep.

[23] The structure consists of a central cell, delimited by trenches of continuous foundations, with an external gallery. For examples of sacred enclosures in Celtic territory, see Lejars 2001.

[24] The deposit of animal bones could be linked to some ritual activities or collective consumption of meat, see Poux and Foucras 2008.

[25] The finds, which include coarse pottery of pre-Roman tradition, small fragments of the later north Etruscan workshops, and vases of certain Roman production (black-painted plates and amphorae), come mainly from the filling of the ditch.

[26] Faced with the area of diffusion (Gaul, Germany, southern Britain and Noricum) that has prompted scholars to consider these religious buildings as an expression of a Celtic tradition, their dating, never prior to the mid-first century BC, brings us to place them in the period of the Roman conquest (Fauduet 2010). The *fanum* that came to light in the 1940s in Heathrow has been dated to the third century BC, although not all scholars agree on the dating and evolution proposed by the discoverers (Lejars 2001, 246–47).

[27] Becker 2008.

[28] These elements lead us to hypothesize that the individual was not given much consideration and belonged to a low social category.

[29] Deberge and others 2015, 28–32. The burials could perhaps be linked to sacralization rituals of the limits of the enclosure, with a protective and apotropaic function. A vague reference could also be traced to the sacrifice of the pair of Gauls in the Forum Boarium attested for the years 228, 216, and 114 BC, always coinciding with the danger of Gallic invasion, see Fraschetti 1981. It should not be forgotten that in the period in which our tomb dates (third century

5. ACROSS THE RUBICON TO ROME

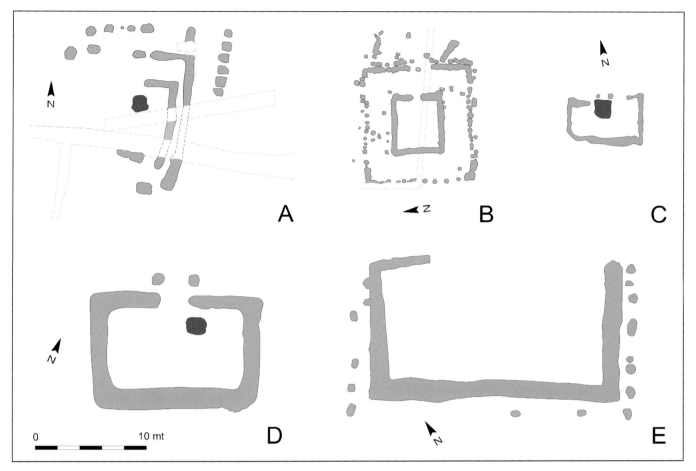

Figure 5.8. Comparison (at the same metric scale) between Structure 9 and some ritual complexes found in Celtic territory: A) Structure 9; B) Heathrow (reworked by Lejars 2001); C) cult enclosure of Clermont-Ferrand 'Le Brézet' (plan by G. Vernet, reworked by Poux and others 2002, 68, fig. 12); D) Corent (reworked by Poux and others 2002, 68, fig. 12); E) Lausanne-Vidy (reworked by Paunier 1989) (drawing by the authors).

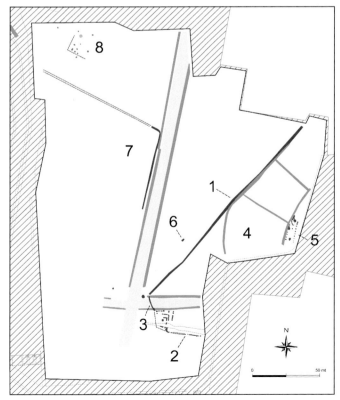

Figure 5.9. General plan of the Roman remains. Eastern enclosure: 1) oblique ditch; 2) south palisade; 3) west side moat; 4) internal fence; 5) rectangular building (Structure 147); 6) human burial. Western enclosure; 7) fence moat; 8) civil building with a well (Structure 35) (drawing by the authors).

Figure 5.10. Aerial view of the rectangular building, Structure 147, located in the internal part of the eastern closure (Photographic Archive of the Superintendence of Archaeology, Fine Arts, and Landscape of Ravenna).

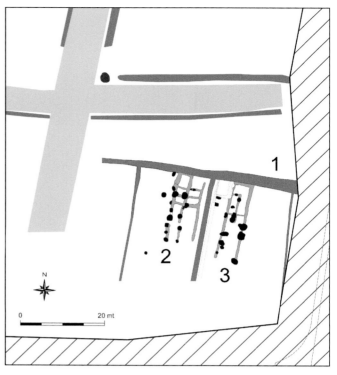

Figure 5.11. The layout at the crossroads in the first century AD: 1) northern closing moat; 2) Structure 12; 3) Structure 13 (drawing by the authors).

A palisade with postholes inserted within a continuous foundation trench delimited the south side of the triangular fence, and within this area, there was a more regularly shaped sector,[30] also delimited by moats. Other channels divided the space inside the enclosure into smaller sectors, and in the innermost part, a rectangular building was discovered,[31] outlined by two rows of postholes (Fig. 5.10). Some postholes located along the central axis of the building suggest a roof with a double-pitched roof, probably made of perishable material.

Two long stretches of a second enclosure, more regular in shape, have also been recognized to the west of the road (Fig. 5.9, no. 7). In this sector, extensive exploration was not conducted, however, through some small-scale excavations, wooden frameworks with continuous foundation trenches or with alignments of single postholes were ascertained. A pit has returned numerous small and medium-sized iron bars, interpreted as a reserve of metal for the needs inside the enclosure. Beyond the north boundary of this west enclosure, a probable hut (14 by 6.5 m), consisting of postholes has been identified (Fig. 5.9, no. 8). It was arranged with the central axis parallel to the north ditch of the enclosure and was flanked by a well (Structure 35). The recovery of black-painted ceramics confirmed the dating to the Republican period, while the discovery of a few loom weights would suggest the presence of females in the building.[32]

Although a tangible trace of the military presence has not emerged, in various parts of Europe, the large areas bordered by moats and palisades, sometimes even of irregular shape, are often traced back to military camps.[33]

BC), the surrounding territory had just been subdued and the Gallic threat was still very strong (Rimini was besieged again in 238 BC).

30   Perhaps quadrangular with rounded corners.

31   Structure 147 is 16 by 5.5 m.

32   On gender indicators within the camps, see Tomas 2011.

33   On some occasions, the ancient sources mention camps of irregular shape, almost always determined by the nature of the terrain or by some specific need. Thus we know the *castra necessaria*, where the topography made it necessary to build an irregular palisade (Hyg. (Ps.), *De metatione castrorum liber* LVI; Caes., *B Gall.* VII.83, and Caes., *B. Civ.* I.81); the *castra lunata*, in the shape of a crescent moon; the *castra semirotunda* on the curve of a river, on an isthmus or at the confluence of two rivers (Veg., *Mil.* I.23), and the

Figure 5.12. View of the timber buildings from the north-east. In the foreground Structure 13 (Photographic Archive of the Superintendence of Archaeology, Fine Arts, and Landscape of Ravenna).

In Ljubljana (ancient Emona), a training camp shaped very similarly to our eastern enclosure and equipped with a *clavicula* type gate was unearthed.[34] Scholars consider the general lack of artefacts a characteristic of military contexts and the cleanliness of the fillings a sign of the discipline with which the buildings were demolished after their use phase.[35]

In the next phase, datable to the first century BC, a new moment of arrangement occurs: the elements attributable to this period (palisades and ditches) are oriented more uniformly and over a wider extension.[36] In the

---

castra tumultuaria, on a prominence of the country. On the state of the matter in relation to the Spanish Republican encampments, see Morillo Cerdán 1991. On the documentation of the Roman Republican camps in Gaul, see Reddé 2008; 2018; Reddé and others 2006.

[34] It was dated to the Republican period and dismantled in the Early Imperial Age, see Gaspari 2010, 25–30.

[35] It is no coincidence that the sector that returns the most artefacts is that of the civil hut, where craftsmanship activities were probably carried out in the service of the field. In addition to weaving, very recent discoveries, still in progress, also seem to indicate the processing of leather as a second activity always linked to the needs inside the site. About this topic, see Kolbeck 2018.

[36] Currently, the installations extend over an area of 15 ha, including also the remains that came to light in Sector B Their orientation is influenced by the road and, indirectly, by the river course that must have been to the east.

south-east corner of Sector A, a large ditch that delimited the area to the north was identified, and against it, two rectangular wooden buildings, framed within a system of rectangular lots surrounded by channels, were placed (Fig. 5.11).

The two buildings show a similar construction technique, characterized by vertical poles inserted at the meeting points of the horizontal beams (Fig. 5.12).[37] These were located within continuous foundation trenches, 0.6–0.8 m wide and *c.* 20 cm deep. Inside, the buildings were divided into two long spans by a central foundation, while at some points, short transverse foundation trenches indicate further subdivisions into smaller spaces. Based on the absence of brick tiles, a double-pitched wooden roof is assumed.

Except for some iron finds, which can be connected to the locking elements of the wooden beams, the fillings of this area have restored the arch of an iron brooch, comparable with the later variants of the Alesia type fibula, with an arch moved by plates.[38] Although buildings with this plan and this construction technique are not a prerogative of the camps, it must be admitted that the most convincing comparisons come from sites with a strong

---

[37] Structure 11 (17.5 by 7 m) to the west; Structure 12 (19.5 by 5 m) to the east.

[38] Istenič 2005; Buora 2005.

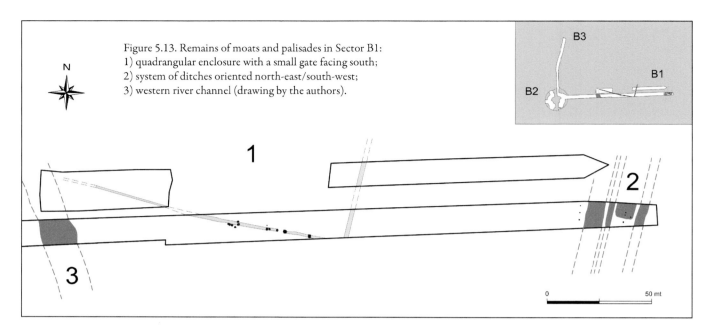

Figure 5.13. Remains of moats and palisades in Sector B1:
1) quadrangular enclosure with a small gate facing south;
2) system of ditches oriented north-east/south-west;
3) western river channel (drawing by the authors).

military component. The earth-and-wood barracks of the Salla/Zalalhövő military fort (Hungary) offer a convincing comparison[39] and further similarities can also be recognized with the timber phase of the building discovered in Gönyű (Győr, Győr-Moson-Sopron County, Hungary), a site interpreted as a station of military importance for the control of the Amber Road in the section between the auxiliary forts of Arrabona and Ad Statuas.[40]

The two comparisons and the connection with the road suggest how the two buildings could constitute a small station or military garrison along the road that defended the river border. Also the iron brooch, as an example attributable to the military, would indicate the frequentation of the area by soldiers.

Sector B of the excavations coincides with a road to be built soon and is divided into three parts: an east–west segment 400 m long and 14 m wide (Sector B1), a circular area with a diameter of 80 m (Sector B2), finally a north–south segment 170 m long and 12 m wide (Sector B3). In Sector B1, further stretches of palisade and moats oriented with the first-century BC system have come to light. A long palisade was identified for a linear development of 120 m and equipped with an opening, perhaps a small gate (2.5 m wide) (Fig. 5.13). These elements appeared to form a quadrangular perimeter between a river channel to the west and a system of

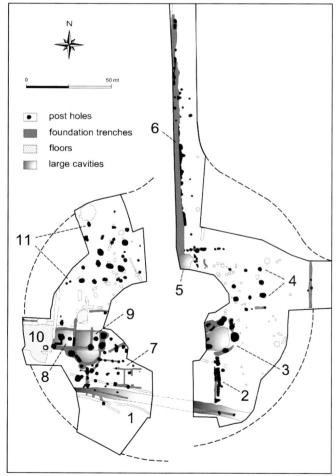

Figure 5.14. General plan of Sector B2: 1) *vallum*/southern limit;
2) double palisade; 3) south tower of the gate; 4) eastern gate;
5) north tower of the gate; 6) trench of the palisade; 7) Structure 3000;
8) Structure 3041; 9) Structure 3036; 10) courtyard with well;
11) pits grid (drawing by the authors).

---

[39] Mráv 2013, 52–55.
[40] Mráv 2013, 78–79.

Figure 5.15. View from the west of the tower and the double palisade (Photographic Archive of the Superintendence of Archaeology, Fine Arts, and Landscape of Ravenna).

parallel canals to the east, probably a temporary camp for light installations, such as tents.[41]

The western part (especially Sector B2) is the one that has returned the most evidence in terms of structural remains and quantity of finds;[42] it is also the area with the greatest settlement continuity. A 3.4 m wide moat, identified for 54 m in length, was attributable to the installation of the Late Republican period, but it probably maintained a limit function also in the following epochs. To the north of this ditch, some pits and alignments of postholes were arranged with the same orientation. The organization of a district with wooden buildings, canopies, and towers, on the other hand, was established starting from the Caesarian/Early Augustan Age, and it was easily recognizable because all its elements were oriented north–south or east–west. For the convenience of exposure, we can divide the findings into two parts: the first comprised all the elements of a defensive system oriented north–south; the second part comprised a housing quarter.

The defence system was composed of a succession of several elements: starting from the south, first a double palisade (Structure 3016), then a building with a trapezoidal plan with a large central cavity (Structure 3017), finally a building with a square plan, consisting of a grid of nine postholes (Structure 3018). Starting from this framework, a long foundation trench for the posts of a palisade developed in a north–south direction, on the edge of the local road, which is still in use. The double palisade (Fig. 5.14, no. 2) was composed of two rows of very close poles, which together formed a 14.5 m long and 1.9 m wide barrier. The trapezoidal building, called Structure 3017 (Fig. 5.14, no. 3 and Fig. 5.15), had a length of 9.8 m and a width of 10.9 m, which was reduced to 7.5 m at the west end. Along the perimeter, it was surrounded by postholes that reached 2 m in diameter and deepened up to 0.7–0.8 m.

In addition to wood, clay was also used in the construction of the building, as demonstrated by the numerous fragments of daub[43] recovered from the holes for the dismantling of the timber elements. The footprints of the reeds immersed in clay appear oversized, compared to what is usually recorded in the structures of civil buildings. This construction does not find many com-

---

[41] For comparison for these installations, see Szabó, Fábián, and Fodor 2020; Jones 2014.

[42] In the years preceding the excavation, some geophysical prospecting and surface reconnaissance had been carried out, through which, especially the western half of the roundabout, emerged as the richest point of pieces of evidence.

[43] For comparisons, see Niemeijer 2018, 501.

Figure 5.16. View from the north of the eastern gate (Photographic Archive of the Superintendence of Archaeology, Fine Arts, and Landscape of Ravenna).

parisons in the timber architecture of the Roman period, some similarities can instead be found with some elements of the masonry defensive walls, in particular with the corner towers of the *castra*.[44] Structure 3018, which extends beyond the line of palisades, measured about 8 m per side and could be interpreted as an eastern gate (Fig. 5.14, no. 4 and Fig. 5.16).[45]

As well as the trapezoidal tower, the gate was devastated by a fire, as a result of which the poles were removed and the pits ended up filling with fragments of daub, hardened by combustion. Few remains of a construction at the north-west corner (Structure 3025) of the door suggest the existence of a second watchtower, located at the point where a long foundation trench oriented in a north–south direction was grafted (Fig. 5.14, nos 5–6). This deep trench housed the horizontal beams and vertical poles of a defensive palisade, ascertained for a length of 70 m, from which protruded at least two square watchtowers.[46]

The housing district was also divided into sectors with specific characteristics (Fig. 5.17): from the south, firstly a rectangular building (Structure 3000, Fig. 5.14, no. 7) 16 by 7 m, which partially reused a palisade from the Republican period. It was divided into two long naves by a central row of poles to support the double-pitched roof. To the north of Structure 3000, two quadrangular wooden buildings were placed side by side in

---

[44] Corner towers of this shape are well known in the province of Dacia (Drobeta, Dimum, Sacidava, Capidava, Zeiselmauer, Odiavum (Almásfüzitő), Contra Aquincum/Budapest). For examples, see Băjenaru 2010. In relation to the chronology, the moment of abandonment and dismantling is well defined (sixth century AD), probably due to a fire. However, the moment of implantation is more uncertain, although comparisons direct us towards the Augustan Age or the Early Imperial Age. On a stratigraphic basis, a remodelling of the external perimeter of the tower has also been documented, which from the original trapezoidal shape was regularized to assume a square plan.

[45] Some gates of camps from the Early Imperial Age have this aspect. As an example, we can mention the north-east gate of the Augustan camp of Nijmegen (Driessen 2009, 1252), the gate of the fort of Lunt (AD 60; Barret and Perry 1992), the first phase of the *porta principalis dextra* in the *castellum* of Intercisa (the first and second centuries AD), supported by four poles (György and others 2011, 47), the gate of the Băneasa fort (early third century AD; Teodor and Dumitrașcu 2019). In this last site, the poles are driven into two continuous foundation trenches and not within individual pits.

[46] The absence of findings to the east of the palisade and gate confirms that this system constituted a limit and a barrier to the settlement area that developed to the west. This defence system is attested in the Augustan camp of Nijmegen (Willems 1991).

5. ACROSS THE RUBICON TO ROME

Figure 5.17. Aerial view of the southern part of the officer's housing district (Photographic Archive of the Superintendence of Archaeology, Fine Arts, and Landscape of Ravenna).

an east–west direction (Fig. 5.14, nos 8–9).[47] The nearly square buildings[48] had to have a wooden floor suspended above a large central cavity. The floor level was anchored to the horizontal beams, which were laid on special support surfaces, obtained in the sides of the foundation pit.[49] A third building without the central pit was to occupy the eastern end of this row, in the space between the north façade of Structure 3000 and the east side of Structure 3036.

A 12.6 m wide and empty space separated this block of buildings from an area occupied by wells for poles, neatly distributed in parallel rows,[50] composing a grid of 20 by 18.5 m (Fig. 5.14, no. 11). Numerous re-excavation interventions attested to a prolonged use of this sector, replacements of deteriorated poles, or additions to reinforce the structure. In the group of southern buildings, the major changes made over time mainly concerned Structure 3036; an apse, with a timber supporting structure, was added on the south side.[51] After the third century AD, its front was advanced towards the north, partly occupying the strip free from structures.[52] A long north–south canal forms a certain limit, towards the west, of this row, while a further continuation towards the north cannot be entirely excluded. Beyond the canal, there was a courtyard (or square) paved with a beaten floor of clay fragments with a well in the south-east corner. Finally, a curvilinear roadway, starting from the south side of the courtyard, led to the barracks Structure 3000 (Fig. 5.14, no. 10, Fig. 5.18).[53]

---

47 Structure 3041 to the west and Structure 3036 to the east.

48 7.60 by 6.70 m.

49 Probably this solution was determined for reasons of hygiene, to create a gap in which the air circulated between the ground and the floor. The numerous fragments of dolia and amphorae coming from these environments suggest their function as warehouses. During the first two centuries of the Roman Empire, the cavities in the basement level of the two wooden buildings were filled with ceramic discharges, descending from the south side of the pit. Table vases (plates and cups in Italic sealed, thin-walled ceramic glasses, jugs in common ceramic) and for food preservation are the most documented; among the non-ceramic finds, there are numerous parts of millstones.

50 Approximately one pole every 3.8 m.

---

51 The retreat of the building involved the dismantling of the north-west corner of Structure 3000; the building nevertheless remained alive and the corner was adapted with a curvilinear palisade that supported the apse of Structure 3036.

52 In the new environment created in front of Structure 3036 a domestic space is established.

53 A similar solution is also attested in the *principia* of the Porolissum Fort (Marcu 2009, 89–91; Opreanu and Lăzărescu 2016, 97–101), where the Via Praetoria ends with a curvilinear

Figure 5.18. View of the courtyard with brick fragments floor and a view of the well (Photographic Archive of the Superintendence of Archaeology, Fine Arts, and Landscape of Ravenna).

Scholars agree in considering this specific organization of buildings to be typical of wooden military architecture, as it is emerging from the excavations of the military sites of the Caesarian war in Gaul or the Augustan camps along the Rhine *limes* (Fig. 5.19). Alignments of wells, pits, and ovens have been discovered within the Caesarian sites of Lautagne, La Chaussée-Tirancourt, and Hermeskeil,[54] while blocks organized like in Gatteo have come to light in Oberaden,[55] Valgirmes,[56] Rödgen,[57] Dangstetten,[58] and Nijmegen.[59] Despite the possibility of variations, their planimetric solutions are perfectly comparable.

The rows (*strigae*) are always divided into two parts: in the first part, there are the buildings of greater constructive commitment; in the second part, the network of pits characterizes the area occupied by the soldiers' tents.

The more solid buildings, interpreted as barracks for officers,[60] were built with foundations of horizontal wooden beams or with palisades, held together by a mixture of reeds and clay; by contrast, the section reserved for soldiers was made up of modular elements (*contubernia*), intended to accommodate eight soldiers.[61] The grating of the pits has also been interpreted as a trace of the modular wooden canopy that protected the soldiers' tents from the rain and snow in winter camps (*hibernia*).[62]

For the timber construction attested in the Gatteo excavation, especially for the size of the facilities, there are not immediate comparisons in the local and regional

course. Also this site, where the basilica is not placed in axis with the centre axis of the Via Praetoria, could provide a comparison for the position of the apsed building Structure 3036, assuming that the complex found in Sector B2 corresponds to the centre settlement, as it emerges from the prospecting.

[54] Kielb Zaaraoui and others 2018; Bayard 2018; Hornung 2018; Reddé 2018, 290–93. Sites of this type are also known in the Balkan area, see Guštin 2015.

[55] Gaspari 2010, 117–18.

[56] Becker and Rasbach 2007, 108–09.

[57] Schönberger and Simon 1976.

[58] Kühlborn 1992, 59–72, fig. 31a–b.

[59] Driessen 2009; Niemeijer 2018.

[60] Timber buildings with a rectangular plan, believed to be barracks for officers, have come to light in the Insula XIII of Emona and in Brigentium/Bregenz (Oberhofer 2018); they are also attested in the *castrum* of Valkemburg (Glasbergen and Groenman-Van Waatering 1974), in the legionary fortress of Novae (Dyczek 2018a, 30–43; 2018b), and in the fort of Salla/Zalalhövő, Hungary (Redő 2005; Mráv 2013, 52–55).

[61] Each *contubernium* was subdivided into an antechamber (*arma*) and a rear chamber for sleeping (*papillio*). The *contubernia* had in common the rear part and were separated from the next row by an empty space, in which wells and channels for disposal were located.

[62] Morel 1991, 383; Reddé 2018, 296.

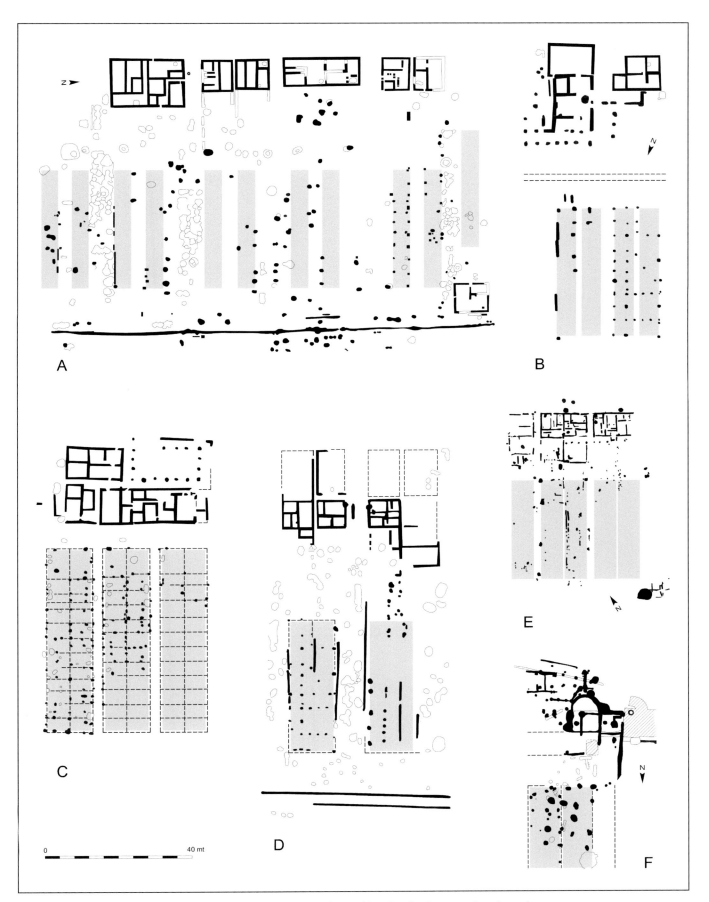

Figure 5.19. Comparative table between the neighbourhoods of some earth-and-wood camps:
A) Oberaden; B) Valgirmes; C) Rödgen; D) Dangstetten; E) Nijmegen; F) Gatteo (drawing by the authors).

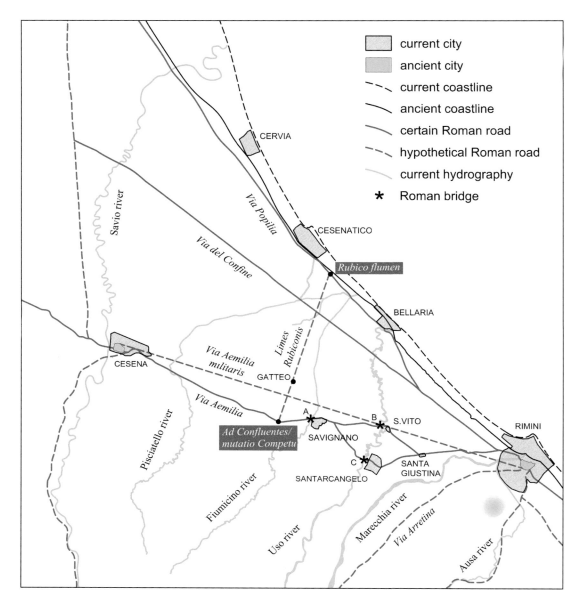

Figure 5.20. Current hydrography and Roman roads in the territorial area of the Rubicon River. The bridges are indicated with asterisks (drawing by the authors).

archaeological documentation,[63] while it is the military architecture that offers the most convincing examples. In addition to these considerations of a structural nature, some further indications of military attendance in the area are represented by the militaristic finds in the excavation: iron nails for footwear, bronze double buttons to fasten the belts,[64] pendants for equine harnesses, fragments of segmental armour,[65] and part of a blade razor.[66]

---

[63] Where a more durable construction technique, which uses brick masonry foundations, is attested for both rural complexes and *vici*.

[64] Comparisons in Radman-Livaja 2008, 298–300.

[65] Dyczek 2018c.

[66] Blade razors are rather rare finds, found almost exclusively in contexts of a military nature, see Ronc and Rusalen 2011. For a

Where Did Caesar Cross the Rubicon? The Hydrological Structure of the Area

One of the main difficulties encountered in the research is identifying the ancient course of the Rubicon since none of the currently existing rivers probably coincides with the ancient one. The radical transformations that the landscape of this sector of Emilia Romagna has undergone after the Roman period do not allow us to identify with certainty the path of the ancient river.[67]

---

recent discovery from Rimini, along the system of the Imperial walls, see Faedi and others 2020, 50–51.

[67] On the subject, see the numerous contributions by A. Veggiani, in particular Veggiani 1983; 1985; 1988; Veggiani and Roncuzzi 1969.

Figure 5.21. Roman stone bridge over the current Rubicon River (photo by the authors).

For this reason, several locations overlook the various waterways present in the area, each of which would revise the role of theatre in the event.

The hypotheses of the scholars have focused mainly on three streams: the Pisciatello, the Fiumicino, and the Uso River (Fig. 5.20).[68]

The first one is born on the north side of Mount Strigara (380 m high) and marks the border between the municipalities of Cesena and Montiano. It heads towards Cesenatico, and after receiving the Rigossa canal on the right, flows into the Adriatic south of Gatteo a Mare. Its course is called Urgon in the hilly area, and along its path, the church of Sanctus Martinus in Urgone is preserved. Both names are believed to derive from the Latin *Rubicon*.

The Fiumicino also originates on the north-east side of Mount Strigara but, with a path towards the north-east, it reaches the plains at Savignano sul Rubicone. With a north–south path, it flows into the sea with a single mouth, together with the Pisciatello River and the Rigossa canal. West of Savignano, the remains of a Roman stone bridge are preserved where the Via Aemilia crossed the river (Fig. 5.20, A and Fig. 5.21).[69] In 1933, the name Rubicon was attributed to this course with an institutional act to put an end to the long controversies.[70]

Finally, the Uso River, the one closest to Rimini, rises on the slopes of Mount Perticara and, after a long mountainous path, reaches the plain near Santarcangelo di Romagna. The mouth is located near Bellaria, and along its course, the remains of two bridges are preserved: one to the west of Santarcangelo, dating to the Roman Republican era and connected with the route of Via Aemilia (Fig. 5.20, C), the second one near San Vito and dating to the Augustan period (Fig. 5.20, B).[71]

---

[68] A summary of the various hypotheses is found in Tassinari 2006b, 207. See also Pecci 1889, with an extensive bibliography about the Rubicon.

[69] Conconi 1996, 171; Tassinari 2006a, 85–86.

[70] On the controversies between scholars from the eighteenth century AD onwards, see the work of Ravara Montebelli 2010, 15–46.

[71] Maraldi 2001; Cartoceti and De Cecco 2006.

The Roman Road Network and the Frontier River Road

As emerges from the numerous bridges that are preserved, the area is also characterized by an articulated road network dating to the Roman age (Fig. 5.20).[72] One of the oldest roads in this sector is the Via del Confine (which means 'border road' in Italian), a centurial axis from the Republican period that connected the south area of Ravenna with Rimini, by a straight path. The road, which can still be travelled for long stretches, is visible through aerial photos in the points where it is no longer preserved.[73]

The Via Aemilia was undoubtedly the most strategically important road axis. It was built in 187 BC by consul Marcus Aemilius Lepidus to connect the two cities located at the extremes of the Po Valley, Rimini/Ariminum and Piacenza/Placentia.[74] The road was born with a purely military purpose, to constitute a *limes* that presided over the chain of the Apennines and divided the Ligurians in the north-west of Italy from the Gallic Boii tribe in the north-east. In the stretch between Rimini and Savignano, the road shows two distinct paths: a southern one, passing through Santarcangelo and the Republican stone bridge over the Uso River;[75] a northern one passing over the Augustan bridge near San Vito.[76] To the east of Savignano sul Rubicone, the two paths joined and proceeded to the site of San Giovanni in Compito, where the road made a wide curve before continuing to Cesena. The locality of San Giovanni in Compito is archaeologically known from numerous excavations, and the ancient Roman itineraries also mention it as a *mutatio*[77] connected to Via Aemilia and located at twelve *milia passum* from Rimini — this measure corresponds to the actual distance of the site from the city.[78] In the *Tabula Peutingeriana*, the site is called Ad Confluentes, thus suggesting a convergence at this point of road axes and river courses (Fig. 5.22).[79] The existence of these two irregular paths, not very suitable for the speed of connection for military use, has recently led to the hypothesis that between Rimini and Cesena, there was a direct straight itinerary.[80] This direct road crossed the Uso River right at the point where Augustus had symbolically built a monumental stone bridge and placed a milestone to celebrate the restoration of Via Aemilia in 2 BC.[81]

The last important road for framing our survey area is Via Popilia, built in 120 BC by consul Publius Popilius Lenas to connect the cities located along the Adriatic coast. The Via Popilia used the route of the Via del Confine for the first six *milia passum*, and then it continued closer to the sea by exploiting the geological formation called Fossil Cliff (*falesia* in Italian). In the thirty-three *milia passum* that separated Ravenna from Rimini, the *Tabula Peutingeriana* places three stations: Rubico Flumen at twelve *milia passum* from Rimini, Ad Novas after a further three *milia passum*, and Sabis at eleven *milia passum* from Ravenna (Fig. 5.22).[82] On the basis of these indications, we can therefore place the mouth of the Rubicon 17.7 km away from Rimini along the Via Popilia, at a point located immediately north of Gatteo a Mare, not far from where the Rivers Pisciatello and

---

[72] For the road network of the Regio VIII, see Bottazzi 2000; Ortalli 2000; Quilici 2000. On the question of the Roman road network between the Savio and the Marecchia Rivers, see also Vullo 1993, 96–104.

[73] The infrastructure was also archaeologically investigated in 1977 at several points between Villalta and Ponte Rosso, where a milestone was also found. Based on the data collected, the road was 10 m wide and had a 'humpback' shape, with lateral ditches. The road surface consisted of a compact layer of pebbles, no more than 70 cm thick. The name has been attributed to the road in modern times, as it formed the border between the centuriation of Cesena and that of Ravenna. Ballerin 1993, 16–22; Farfaneti 2004, 66; Tassinari 2006b, 204–05.

[74] The bibliography on the Via Emilia is very extensive. For the latest acquisitions please refer to the exhibition catalogue held in Reggio Emilia (2017–2018), see Cantoni and Capurso 2017. See also Dall'Aglio 2006.

[75] Mansuelli 1941a, 121; Biondi 2005.

[76] For the question of *diverticula*, see Tassinari 2006a, 84–86 and Bondini and Tassinari 2017, 55–58.

[77] *Itinerarium Burdigalense.*

[78] For the excavations and findings on the site of the Compito, see Maioli 1998; Scarpellini 1979; 1998.

[79] The toponym Competu (from *compitum*, crossroads in Latin) is also preserved in the surname of the church of S. Giovanni in Compito, which still faces the road today, see Tassinari 2006a, 83.

[80] A kind of Via Aemilia Militaris, which originated from the Montanara Gate, the main *caput viarum* of Rimini in the Republican Age, and which avoided the centres of the territorial population by passing through the open plain, see Bondini and Tassinari 2017.

[81] About the milestone, see Mansuelli 1951; 1955; Tassinari 2006a, 85. For the celebratory inscription, see Herzig 1970, 70–71 n. 18.

[82] The attribution of the route to Via Popilia is based on the discovery of a milestone with the name of the consul, found in 1844 at the gates of Adria, see Alfieri 1964, 62; Basso 1986, 156–58; Bosio 1991, 59; Fogolari and Scarfi 1970, 78–79; Mansuelli 1941b, 39; Uggeri 1981, 43; Tassinari 2006b. North-west of Cesenatico, a section of the road was found in 2008, see Cesaretti, Curina, and Tassinari 2011, 592, 619–20, figs 2 and 4.

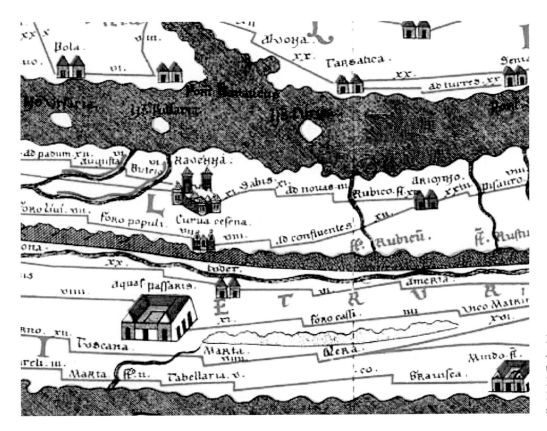

Figure 5.22. Section of the *Tabula Peutingeriana*, which includes the territory between Ravenna and Rimini and the path of the Rubicon River, with the homonymous road station at the mouth.

Fiumicino currently flow into a unified course.[83] This data would already be sufficient to exclude the course of the Uso, which flows much further south, from a possible identification with the ancient Rubicon, while the river that marked the ancient border of Rome will therefore be placed on the east side of our road route.[84]

Conclusions

With this preliminary dossier, we have tried to provide an interpretation of the archaeological finds carried out in the locality of Gatteo between 2018 and 2020. The conformation that the site assumes starting from the Late Republican period appears to us to be consistent only with a military destination of the structures found, through comparisons with the French sites of the Caesarian wars and with the Augustan camps in the north-eastern sector of the empire. Faced with the plurality of forms that these sites can show, often depending on the type of army they were intended to house, some structural types emerge to be specific to military architecture. The adherence to these models would demonstrate that the site of Gatteo constituted a Roman military base[85] at least from the first century BC, even if some elements could anticipate this function from the early stages of the Romanization of the territory. With the Roman victory near the Sentino River (295 BC) and the foundation of Sena Gallica (284 BC) and Ariminum (268 BC), the Roman penetration into the territory previously occupied by the Senones begins.[86] The Gatteo site is located along the border of the Senones' territory and at the centre of a triangular-shaped area that has

---

83 Lorenzo Braccesi supports this possibility, see Braccesi 2006.

84 Towards the coast, for a stretch of about 3 km the Rubicon route could be traced by two existing minor canals: Rigoncello and Rigossa. The latter is an Italian translation of *Rubico flumen*: Rigossa = Rigo Rossa (toponym existing in historical cartography) that is Rigo (rivulet or small river, equivalent of the Latin *rigum*) and Rosso (red, equivalent of the Latin *rubrum*).

85 As long as a plan that consists of a regular valley divided by the road axes does not emerge, we cannot properly speak of a *castrum*. Sites with similar characteristics found in archaeological excavations are considered camps for organizing soldiers, garrisons, or training centres for the army.

86 The Senoni Gauls' settlement in the current regions of Romagna and Marche in the north, from the Montone River towards the south, then from the Ager Decimanus, or the countryside south of Ravenna, up to the Esino River. In this regard, Polybius tells us: 'Beyond the Po, the Anari first settled, then the Boi, the Lingoni in the direction of the Adriatic, and finally, near the sea, the Senones' (Pol. II.17). Brizzi 2015; Curina and others 2015.

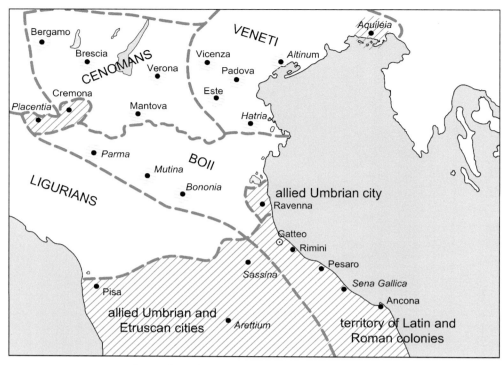

Figure 5.23. Northern Italy in the early stages of Romanization (drawing by the authors).

the coast as its eastern limit, the Marecchia Valley as its southern side, and a western side formed by the route connecting some territorial garrison centres (Fig. 5.23).[87] A military camp in this position, in addition to representing a barrier for possible raids against Ariminum/Rimini,[88] could serve as a base for the construction of territorial infrastructure, such as road construction or agricultural subdivision.[89]

In the first half of the first century BC, the structural complex appears marked by greater uniformity, with palisades and ditches that divide the land into a lot, in which elongated rectangular buildings, interpreted as barracks,

are placed. The site is also connected to the localities of Ad Confluentes/Mutatio Competu and Rubico flumen through a road that acts as a barrier for the crossing paths of a south-west/north-east river course, in which the ancient Rubicon can now be recognized with certainty, according to the toponym of the road station at the mouth. The realization of this system of garrisons on the road is connected to the definition of the Rubicon *limes* and it probably constitutes the first implementation of that frontier river,[90] which will be the form of defence most applied to the northern and eastern borders of the empire beyond in the following centuries.

Therefore, we propose to place the reunion between Caesar and the troops stationed along the banks of the Rubicon in this context, which represents the first concrete evidence of a military settlement located in a geographical position consistent with that handed down by literary sources.

Starting from the Augustan period, the site has undergone a radical reformation: first of all, the orientation dependent on the valley road and the course of the river is abandoned and the structures are aligned with the centurial network. This fact may have been due to the dismantling of the Rubicon *limes* by Augustus,[91]

---

[87] Sassina, Umbrians *civitas foederata* starting from 266 BC (Brizzi 2008); Curva Caesena, *oppidum* from the mid-third century BC (remains on the Garampo Hill, see Miari 2009; 2015); and Ravenna, *civitas foederata* with brick fortifications dating back to the third century BC (Manzelli 2001; 2015).

[88] The Boi besieged Rimini in 236 BC after a peace that had lasted for fifty years.

[89] The second of these activities, traditionally linked to the technicians (*mensores*) who were following the army, comes from some toponyms of the place: about 2 km south-west of the excavation area, along the road connecting to the site of the Compito, there is an agglomeration of houses called Termine and the toponym returns in two orthogonal streets, Via del Termine I and Via del Termine II, which are located a few hundred metres away from the excavation (Termine, from Latin *terminus*, means in Italian: border; limit).

[90] Graafstal 2017. On the *prolatio imperii* of Sulla, see Maccari 2016.

[91] With Augustus, the border of Italy was set in the Alps (Bonora Mazzola and Dolci 2008; Bigliardi 2004, 317–34). The interest in strengthening a military site like that of Gatteo could be part of a broader strategic plan, including the reform of the army (Speidel 2016) and the expansion of the nascent Empire towards enemy territories, against which the war aspirations that had animated the final phase of the Republic could be directed. Among the military enterprises conducted by Augustus during his principality, the *Res gestae divi Augusti* recall the return of the insignia from the Parthians, the victories in Macedonia, Dacia, Pannonia, Dalmatia, and Noricum (Parisi Presicce 2013). The military site of Gatteo on the Rubicon River was located right along the Adriatic route that led to the eastern expansion sector (on the subject, see Šašel Kos 2013),

5. ACROSS THE RUBICON TO ROME

but the removal of the river course to the east could have caused a change in the morphological structure of the area.

A military centre on the Rubicon in this historical moment no longer had a defensive motivation, but it could represent a valid logistical base, located between Rome and the provinces, thanks to its inclusion within a dense road network. New defensive needs, starting from the advanced Imperial period[92] and increasingly in Late Antiquity,[93] will determine the long frequentation and fortune of the site.

To conclude, this discovery, in addition to providing a first solution to the numerous issues related to the events of the Caesarian biography for the year 49 BC, requires us to reconsider all the Roman finds made in the area, starting with the rural farms that could be involved, in various ways, in the supply of food and goods for the army.[94] Further considerations will undoubtedly come from continuing analyses of the excavation records and future investigations in the area.

---

about halfway between Rome and Aquileia.

92 Starting from the third century AD, the north-eastern sector of the peninsula was suffering under the pressure of people of Germanic origin who were making raids. In AD 258, the Alemanni and Marcomanni went as far as Ravenna (Pavan 1987, 40), Rimini was stormed in AD 259–260 and in the same years many cities of Emilia show traces of fires and destruction (among these Ravenna and Sarsin, see Ortalli 2014. In the fourth century AD, the ancient authors also indicate an intense presence of armies, in particular along the land communications network of the Po Valley, see Sami 2011; 2015, 162–63).

93 When the site would again be on a border (that of the area of Byzantine influence). Probably the name Gatteo is connected to the Kastron Ghetteon mentioned in the *Descriptio orbis Romani* written by Giorgio Ciprio (the sixth and seventh centuries AD). The toponym returns in numerous localities between the Mugello Pass and the Romagna area (Gattaia — FI; S. Martino in Gattara — FC), confirming the importance of controlling this territory, through the cities located along the Apennine passages between the Tyrrhenian coast and the Adriatic.

94 Simon 2015.

Works Cited

Alfieri, N. 1964. 'Le vie di comunicazione in Italia settentrionale', in M. Vergnani (ed.), *Arte e civiltà romana nell'Italia settentrionale dalla repubblica alla tetrarchia*, I (Bologna: Alfa), pp. 55–70.

Băjenaru, C. 2010. *Minor Fortifications in the Balkan-Danubian Area from Diocletian to Justinian*, The Center of Roman Military Studies, 8 (Cluj-Napoca: Mega).

Ballerin, B. 1993. 'Il Rubicone e la litoranea antica: conferme archeologiche ad una tesi', *Romagna arte e storia*, 13: 5–31.

Barret, A. A. and J. G. Perry. 1992. 'Excavations at the Lunt Roman Fort (1988–91): The Western Defences', *Echos du monde classique: Classical Views*, 36: 201–09.

Basso, P. 1986. *I miliari della Venetia Romana* (Padua: Società archeologica veneta).

Bayard, D. 2018. 'L'occupation des oppida gaulois par l'armée romaine à la fin de la République: l'exemple du "camp César" de la Chaussée-Tirancourt', in M. Reddé (ed.), *L'armée romaine en Gaule à l'époque républicaine: nouveaux témoignages archéologiques*, Collection Bibracte, 28 (Glux-en-Glenne: Bibracte centre archéologique européen), pp. 155–78.

Becker, T. 2008. 'Nature and Function of Reconstruction on the Upper German-Raetian Limes Using the Example of Wooden Watch-Towers', in D. J. Breeze and S. Jilek (eds), *Frontiers of the Roman Empire: The European Dimension of a World Heritage Site* (Edinburgh: Historic Scotland), pp. 153–62.

Becker, A. and G. Rasbach. 2007. '"Städte in Germanien": Der Fundplatz Waldgirmes', in R. Wiegels (ed.), *Die Varusschlacht: Wendepunkt der Geschichte?* (Stuttgart: Theiss), pp. 102–16.

Bigliardi, G. 2004. 'Alpes, id est claustra Italiae: La trasformazione dei complessi fortificati romani dell'arco alpino centro-orientale tra l'età tardo-repubblicana e l'età tardo-antica', *Aquileia Nostra*, 75: 317–72.

Biondi, S. 2005. 'Il ponte romano di Santarcangelo di Romagna sul fiume Uso', *Studi Romagnoli*, 56: 11–17.

Bondini, A. and C. Tassinari. 2017. 'La via Aemilia a Rimini e la conquista della pianura padana', in G. Cantoni and A. Capurso (eds), *On the Road: Via Emilia 187 a.C.–2017* (Parma: Grafiche Step), pp. 53–59.

Bonora Mazzoli, G. and M. Dolci. 2008. *Le regioni dell'Italia romana: urbanistica e topografia nella divisione amministrativa di Augusto* (Milan: Campuscuem).

Bosio, L. 1991. *Le strade romane della Venetia e dell'Histria* (Padua: Editoriale Programma).

Bottazzi, G. 2000. 'La rete itineraria', in M. Marini Calvani (ed.), *Aemilia: La cultura romana in Emilia Romagna dal III sec. a.C. all'età constantiniana* (Venice: Marsilio), pp. 79–85.

Braccesi, L. 2006. 'Augusto, l'Italia e il ponte di San Vito: Addendum', in L. Braccesi (ed.), *Ariminum: storia e archeologia*, II (Rome: L'Erma di Bretschneider), pp. 99–101.

Brizzi, G. 2008. 'Conquista e penetrazione romana nella valle del Savio', in A. Donati (ed.), *Storia di Sarsina*, I (Cesena: Stilgraf), pp. 155–77.

—— 2015. 'Le operazioni belliche in Val Padana tra Annibale e la sconfitta di Boi e Insubri', in L. Malnati and V. Manzelli (eds), *Brixia: Roma e le genti del Po; un incontro di culture III–I secolo a.C.* (Prato: Giunti), pp. 112–13.

Buora, M. 2005. 'Osservazioni sulle fibule del tipo Alesia nell'arco alpino orientale e nell'alto Adriatico', *Vjesnik za arheologiju i historiju dalmatinsku*, 98: 83–91.

Canfora, L. 1999. *Giulio Cesare: il dittatore democratico* (Rome: Laterza).

Cantoni, G. and A. Capurso. 2017. *On the Road: Via Emilia 187 a.C.-2017* (Parma: Grafiche Step).

Cartoceti, M. and E. De Cecco. 2006. 'I ponti di San Vito', in L. Braccesi (ed.), *Ariminum: storia e archeologia* (Rome: L'Erma di Bretschneider), pp. 83–98.

Cesaretti, C., R. Curina, and C. Tassinari. 2011. 'Nuovi dati sul popolamento antico e sulle infrastrutture territoriali nella fascia litoranea a nord di Rimini', *Studi Romagnoli*, 61: 587–626.

Conconi, M. 1996. 'Il ponte di Savignano sul Rubicone', *Atlante tematico di topografia antica*, 5: 171–78.

Curina, R. and others. 2015. 'La Cisalpina tra III e I secolo a.C. alla luce dell'archeologia', in L. Malnati and V. Manzelli (eds), *Brixia: Roma e le genti del Po; un incontro di culture III–I secolo a.C.* (Prato: Giunti), pp. 42–54.

Dall'Aglio, P. L. 2006. 'La via Emilia', in P. L. Dall'Aglio and I. Di Cocco (eds), *La linea e la rete: formazione storica del sistema stradale in Emilia-Romagna* (Milan: Panini), pp. 77–82.

Deberge, Y. and others. 2015. 'Témoignages de la Guerre des Gaules dans le bassin clermontois, nouveaux apports', *Revue archéologique du Centre de la France*, 54: 28–32.

De Sanctis, G. 2007. 'Solco, muro, pomerio', *Mélange de l'École française de Rome*, 119: 503–26.

Driessen, M. 2009. 'The Early Flavian Timber *castra* and the Flavian-Trajanic Stone Legionary Fortress at Nijmegen (The Netherlands)', in Á. Morillo, N. Hanel, and E. Martín (eds), *Limes XX: XXth International Congress of Roman Frontier Studies*, Anejos de Gladius, 13 (Madrid: Poliferno), pp. 1245–56.

Dyczek, P. 2018a. 'Novae – Western Sector (Section XII), 2011–2018: Preliminary Report on the Excavations of the Center for Research on the Antiquity of Southeastern Europe, University of Warsaw', *Novensia*, 29: 27–72.

—— 2018b. 'Wooden Barracks of the First Cohort of the legio VIII Augusta from Novae (Moesia inferior)', in C. S. Sommer and S. Matešić (eds), *Limes XXIII: Akten des 23. Internationalen Limeskongresses in Ingolstadt 2015* (Mainz: Nünnerich-Asmus), pp. 530–36.

—— 2018c. 'Segmental Armour from the Fortress of the First Italic Legion in Novae', in L. Kocsis (ed.), *The Enemies of Rome: Proceedings of the 15th International Roman Military Equipment Conference, Budapest 2005*, Journal of Roman Military Equipment Studies, 16 (Oxford: Oxbow), pp. 191–99.

Faedi, M. and others. 2020. 'I materiali del Periodo I', in A. Bondini and others (eds), *Il monastero ritrovato: continuità di devozione a Rimini nel complesso dell'ex Leon Battista Alberti*, Documenti ed Evidenze di Archeologia, 15 (Urbino: Ante Quem), pp. 41–51.

Farfaneti, B. 2004. 'La via del Confine', *Atlante tematico di topografia antica*, 13: 65–79.

Fauduet, I. 2010. *Les temples de tradition celtique: nouvelle édition revue et argumentée*, Collection des Hespérides (Paris: Errance).

Ferrari, A. and G. Steffè. 1997. 'Formigine, loc. Cantone di Magreta', *Archeologia dell'Emilia Romagna*, 1: 20–21.

Fogolari, G. and B. M. Scarfi. 1970. *Adria Antica* (Venice: Alfieri).

Fraschetti, A. 1981. 'Le sepolture rituali del Foro Boario', in M. Torelli and C. Guittard (eds), *Le délit religieux dans la cité antique: actes de la table ronde de Rome (6–7 avril 1978)*, Publications de l'École française de Rome, 48 (Rome: École française de Rome), pp. 51–115.

Gaspari, A. 2010. *'Apud horridas gentis...': Beginnings of the Roman Town of Colonia Iulia Emona* (Ljubljana: Žnidarič).

Glasbergen, W. and W. Groenman-Van Waatering. 1974. *The Pre-Flavian Garrisons of Valkenburg Z. H.: Fabriculae and Bipartite Barracks* (Amsterdam: North-Holland Publishing Company).

Graafstal, E. 2017. 'River Frontiers or Fortified Corridors?', in N. Hodgson, P. Bidwell, and J. Schachtmann (eds), *Roman Frontier Studies 2009: Proceedings of the XXI International Congress of Roman Frontier Studies* (Oxford: Archaeopress), pp. 186–93.

Guštin, M. 2015. 'Roman Camps Following the Route to Segestica and the Western Balkans', in J. Istenič, B. Laharnar, and J. Horvat (eds), *Evidence of the Roman Army in Slovenia* (Ljubljana: Present), pp. 221–34.

György, T. and others. 2011. *Fejér megye várai az őskortól a kuruc korig*, Magyarország várainak topográfiája, 3 (Budapest: Miskolc).

Herzig, H. E. 1970. *Le réseau routier des régions VI et VIII d'Italie* (Bologna: Cappelli).

Hornung, S. 2018. 'Le camp militaire de Hermeskeil. Une nouvelle perspective sur la conquête césarienne et ses conséquences à l'est de la Gaule Belgique', in M. Reddé (ed.), *L'armée romaine en Gaule à l'époque républicaine: nouveaux témoignages archéologiques*, Collection Bibracte, 28 (Glux-en-Glenne: Bibracte centre archéologique européen), pp. 113–34.

Istenič, J. 2005. 'Brooches of the Alesia Group in Slovenia', *Arheološki vestnik*, 56: 187–212.

Jones, R. H. 2014. '*Known Unknowns*: "Invisible" People on Temporary Camps', in R. Collins and F. McIntosh (eds), *Life in the Limes: Studies of the People and Objects of the Roman Frontiers Presented to Lindsay Allason-Jones on the Occasion of her Birthday and Retirement* (Oxford: Oxbow), pp. 172–83.

Kielb Zaaraoui, M. and others. 2018. 'Les camps militaires tardo-républicains de Lautagne (Valence, Drôme)', in M. Reddé (ed.), *L'armée romaine en Gaule à l'époque républicaine: nouveaux témoignages archéologiques*, Collection Bibracte, 28 (Glux-en-Glenne: Bibracte centre archéologique européen), pp. 45–72.

Kolbeck, B. 2018. 'A Foot in Both Camps: The Civilian Suppliers of the Army in Roman Britain', *Theoretical Roman Archaeology Journal*, 1: 1–19 <https://doi.org/10.16995/traj.355>.

Kühlborn, J.-S. 1992. *Das Römerlager in Oberaden*, III: *Die Ausgrabungen im nordwestlichen Lagerbereich und weitere Baustellenuntersuchungen der Jahre 1962–1988*, Bodenaltertümer Westfalens, 27 (Münster: Aschendorff).

Lejars, T. 2001. 'Les installations cultuelles celtiques: un aperçu de la recherche en France', in S. Vitri and F. Oriolo (eds), *I Celti in Carnia e nell'arco alpino centro orientale: atti della Giornata di studio; Tolmezzo, 30 aprile 1999* (Trieste: Comunita Montana della Carnia), pp. 245–77.

Maccari, A. 2016. 'Habebat ius proferendi pomerii (Gell., Noctes Atticae, XIII, 14): l'evoluzione dello ius prolationis dalle origini a Silla', *Rivista di studi classici e orientali*, 62: 161–84.

—— 2019. 'Pomerium, verbi vim solam intuentes, postmoerium interpretantur esse: la critica storica e antiquaria e la manipolazione del passato', *Rivista di studi classici e orientali*, 65: 139–59.

Magdelain, A. 1976. 'Le pomerium archaïque et le mundus', *Revue des études latines*, 54: 71–109.

Maioli, M. G. 1998. 'Lo scavo archeologico in proprietà Teodorani', in D. Scarpellini (ed.), *Gli scavi archeologici di S. Giovanni in Compito* (Cesena: Il Ponte Vecchio), pp. 15–17.

Mansuelli, G. A. 1941a. *Ariminum: Italia romana, municipi e colonie* (Rome: Istituto di studi romani).

—— 1941b. 'La rete stradale e i cippi miliari della regione ottava', *Atti e memorie della Regia deputazione di storia patria per l'Emilia e Romagna*, 7: 33–69.

—— 1951. 'Il nuovo cippo augusteo della via Aemilia', *Studi Romagnoli*, 2: 303–06.

—— 1955. 'S. Mauro Pascoli – Cippo miliare della Via Aemilia', *Notizie degli scavi di antichità*, 9: 10–13.

Manzelli, V. 2001. 'Le mura di Ravenna repubblicana', *Atlante tematico di topografia antica*, 9: 7–24.

—— 2015. 'Ravenna nel III secolo a.C.', in L. Malnati and V. Manzelli (eds), *Brixia: Roma e le genti del Po; un incontro di culture III–I secolo a.C.* (Prato: Giunti), pp. 104–05.

Maraldi, L. 2001. 'Il ponte di San Vito sul torrente Uso: analisi tecnica e strutturale', *Atlante tematico di topografia antica*, 10: 79–88.

Marcu, F. 2009. *The Internal Planning of Roman Forts of Dacia* (Cluj-Napoca: MEGA).

Miari, M. 2009. 'Il periodo formativo: alle origini della città', in S. Gelichi, M. Miari, and C. Negrelli (eds), *Ritmi di transizione: il colle Garampo tra civitas e castrum; progetto archeologico e primi risultati* (Borgo San Lorenzo: All'insegna del Giglio), pp. 15–25.

—— 2014. 'Nuovi rinvenimenti riguardo alla presenza umbra in Romagna', in *Gli Umbri in età preromana: atti del XXVII Convegno di Studi Etruschi ed Italici; (Perugia-Gubbio-Urbino 2009)* (Pisa: Serra), pp. 215–29.

—— 2015. 'Sarsina', in L. Malnati and V. Manzelli (eds), *Brixia: Roma e le genti del Po; un incontro di culture III–I secolo a.C.* (Prato: Giunti), pp. 102–03.

Miari, M. and others. 2018. 'Il sito di Riccione (RN) via Berlinguer: strategie di insediamento e sfruttamento di un'area pericostiera dal Neolitico al Bronzo recente', in M. Bernabò Brea (ed.), *Protostoria dell'Emilia Romagna*, II (Florence: Istituto italiano de preistoria e protostoria), pp. 529–37.

Morel, J. M. A. W. 1991. 'Tents or Barracks?', in V. A. Maxfield and M. J. Dobson (eds), *Roman Frontier Studies 1989: Proceedings of the XVth International Congress of Roman Frontier Studies* (Exeter: University of Exeter Press), pp. 376–86.

Morillo Cerdán, A. 1991. 'Fortificaciones campamentales de época romana en España', *Archivo español de arqueología*, 64: 135–90.

Mráv, Z. 2013. 'The Roman Army along the Amber Road between Poetovio and Carnuntum in the 1st Century A.D. – Archaeological Evidence: A Preliminary Research Report', *Communicationes archaeologicae Hungariae*, 2010–2013: 49–100.

Niemeijer, R. 2018. 'Buildings and Building Materials from the Large Augustan Camp on the Hunerberg in Nijmegen', in C. S. Sommer and S. Matešić (eds), *Limes XXIII: Akten des 23. Internationalen Limeskongresses in Ingolstadt 2015* (Mainz: Nünnerich-Asmus), pp. 497–504.

Oberhofer, K. 2018. 'Moving out from Brigantium (Bregenz/A): A Wooden Construction as an Indicator of the Military Fort's Demolition', in C. S. Sommer and S. Matešić (eds), *Limes XXIII: Akten des 23 Internationalen Limeskongresses in Ingolstadt 2015* (Mainz: Nünnerich-Asmus), pp. 521–28.

Opreanu, C. H. and V.-A. Lăzărescu. 2016. 'The Province of Dacia', in C. H. Opreanu and V.-A. Lăzărescu (eds), *Landscape Archaeology of the Northern Frontier of the Roman Empire at Porolissum: An Interdisciplinary Research Project* (Cluj-Napoca: MEGA), pp. 49–114.

Ortalli, J. 2000. 'Le tecniche costruttive', in M. Marini Calvani (ed.), *Aemilia: La cultura romana in Emilia Romagna dal III sec. a.C. all'età constantiniana* (Venice: Marsilio), pp. 86–92.

—— 2014. 'Crisi urbana e invasioni barbariche: spunti archeologici dall'Italia Cispadana del III secolo d.C.', in S. F. Ramallo Asensio and A. Quevedo Sánchez (eds), *Las ciudades de la Tarraconense oriental entre los s. II–IV d.C.: evolución urbanística y contextos materiales* (Murcia: Editum), pp. 13–50.

Paunier, D. 1989. *Le vicus gallo-romain de Lousonna-Vidy: le quartier occidental, le sanctuaire indigène, rapport préliminaire sur la campagne de fouilles, 1985* (Lausanne: Institut d'archéologie et d'histoire ancienne de l'Université de Lausanne).

Parisi Presicce, C. 2013. 'Arte, imprese e propaganda: l'Augusto di Prima Porta 150 anni dopo la scoperta', in E. La Rocca and others (eds), *Augusto* (Milan: Electa), pp. 118–29.

Pavan, M. 1987. 'Aquileia città di frontiera', *Antichità Altoadriatiche*, 29: 17–55.

Pecci, A. 1889. 'Note storico-bibliografiche intorno al fiume Rubicone', *Bibliofilo*, 10: 129–42.

Poux, M. and S. Foucras. 2008. 'Banquets gaulois, sacrifices romains dans le sanctuaire de Corent', in S. Lepetz and W. Van Andringa (eds), *Archéologie du sacrifice animal en Gaule romaine, rituels et pratiques alimentaires: actes du colloque de Paris, Muséum Histoire Naturelle*, Archéologie des plantes et des animaux, 2 (Montagnac: Mergoil), pp. 165–86.

Poux, M. and others. 2002. 'L'enclos cultuel de Corent (Puy-de-Dôme): festins et rites collectives', *Revue archéologique du Centre de la France*, 41: 57–110.

Pozzi, A. and L. Urbini (forthcoming). 'La sepoltura di San Giovanni in Compito: elementi piceni nella Romagna dell'età del Ferro', Atti del Convegno Internazionale di Studi Piceni (Ancona).

Quilici, L. 2000. 'Le infrastrutture', in M. Marini Calvani (ed.), *Aemilia: La cultura romana in Emilia Romagna dal III sec. a.C. all'età constantiniana* (Venice: Marsilio), pp. 93–101.

Radman-Livaja, I. 2008. 'Roman Belt-Fittings from Burgenae', *Journal of Roman Military Equipment Studies*, 16: 295–308.

Ravara Montebelli, C. 2010. *Alea iacta est: Giulio Cesare in Archivio* (Cesena: Il Ponte Vecchio).

Reddé, M. and others (eds). 2006. *L'architecture de la Gaule romaine: les fortifications militaires*, Documents d'archéologie française, 100 (Bordeaux: Ausonius).

Reddé, M. 2008. 'Les camps militaires républicains et augustéens: paradigmes et réalités archéologiques', *Saldvie*, 8: 61–71.

—— 2018. *L'armée romaine en Gaule à l'époque républicaine: nouveaux témoignages archéologiques*, Collection Bibracte, 28 (Glux-en-Glenne: Bibracte centre archéologique européen).

Redő, F. 2005. 'Strategical Significance of Salla and its Effect on the Development of the Inner Pannonian Municipium', in L. Borhy and P. Zsidi (eds), *Die norisch-pannonischen Städte und das römische Heer im Lichte der neuesten archäologischen Forschungen*, II: *Internazionale Konferenz über norisch-pannonische Städte*, Aquincum Nostrum, 2 (Budapest: Pro Aquinco Stiftung), pp. 133–44.

Ronc, M. C. and C. Rusalen. 2011. 'Il rasoio romano di Aosta: nuova attribuzione e nuovi spunti', *Bollettino/Notiziario della Soprintendenza per i Beni e le Attività culturali della Valle d'Aosta*, 7: 84–89.

Sami, D. 2011. 'Archeologia a Cesenatico', *Studi Romagnoli*, 61: 11–33.

—— 2015. 'A Passage of Troops? Late Roman Small Finds from Ad Novas-Cesenatico (North-East Italy)', *Aquileia Nostra*, 86: 153–65.

Šašel Kos, M. 2013. 'The Roman Conquest of Illyricum (Dalmatia and Pannonia) and the Problem of the Northeastern Border of Italy', *Studia Europaea Gnesnensia*, 7: 169–200.

Scarpellini, D. 1979. *Il Compito e la ceramica romana*, Quaderni degli Studi Romagnoli, 11 (Faenza: Fratelli Lega).

—— 1998. *Gli scavi archeologici di S. Giovanni in Compito* (Cesena: Il Ponte Vecchio).

Schönberger, H. and H.-G. Simon. 1976. *Römerlager Rödgen: Das Augusteische Römerlager Rödgen*, Limesforschungen, 15 (Berlin: Mann).

Simon, B. 2015. 'The (Grain) Supply System of the Early Imperial Roman Army', in L. Borhy, K. Tankó, and K. Dévai (eds), *Studia archaeologica Nicolae Szabó LXXV annos nato dedicata* (Budapest: L'Harmattan), pp. 237–50.

Sisani, S. 2014. 'Qua aratrum ductum est: La colonizzazione romana come chiave interpretativa della Roma delle origini', in T. D. Stek and J. Pelgrom (eds), *Roman Republican Colonization: New Perspectives from Archaeology and Ancient History*, Papers of the Royal Netherlands Institute in Rome, 62 (Rome: Palombi), pp. 357–404.

Speidel, M. A. 2016. 'Actium, Allies, and the Augustan Auxilia: Reconsidering the Transformation of Military Structures and Foreign Relations in the Reign of Augustus', in C. Wolff and P. Faure (eds), *Les auxiliaires de l'armée romaine: des alliés aux fédérés; actes du sixième Congrès de Lyon (23–35 octobre 2014)*, Collection études et recherches sur l'Occident romain (Lyon: Centre d'études et de recherches sur l'Occident romain), pp. 79–95.

Szabó, M., B. Fábián, and F. Fodor. 2020. 'Research on Roman Temporary Camps near Brigetio (Komárom-Szőny): Results of the Excavations Conducted on the BRI V, VI (–VII), X–XI, XIII–XIV, XIX, XXII–XXIII, XXX and XXXII Archaeological Sites', in G. I. Farkas, R. Neményi, and M. Szabó (eds), *The Danube Limes in Hungary: Archaeological Research Conducted in 2015–2020* (Pécs: Kontraszt Plusz), pp. 77–112.

Tassinari, C. 2006a. 'La via Popilia', in P. L. Dall'Aglio and I. Di Cocco (eds), *La linea e la rete: formazione storica del sistema stradale in Emilia-Romagna* (Milan: Panini), pp. 202–12.

—— 2006b. 'Rimini-Cesena', in P. L. Dall'Aglio and I. Di Cocco (eds), *La linea e la rete: formazione storica del sistema stradale in Emilia-Romagna* (Milan: Panini), pp. 83–87.

Teodor, E. S. and E. Dumitraşcu. 2019. 'Excavations at the Eastern Gate of the Băneasa Roman Fort', *Cercetări Arheologice*, 26: 103–24.

Tomas, A. B. 2011. 'Reading Gender and Social Life in Military Spaces', in F. M. Stępniowski and A. Maciałowicz (eds), *Światowit: Annual of the Institute of Archaeology of the University of Warsaw*, VIII (Warsaw: Instytut Archeologii), pp. 139–52.

Uggeri, G. 1981. 'Aspetti della viabilità romana nel delta padano', *Padusa*, 17: 40–58.

Veggiani, A. 1983. 'Degrado ambientale e dissesti idrogeologici indotti dal deterioramento climatico nell'alto Medioevo in Italia: i casi riminesi', *Studi Romagnoli*, 34: 123–46.

—— 1985. 'Le vicende idrografiche del Rubicone della Rigossa tra Gambettola e Montiano nei tempi storici', *Studi Romagnoli*, 36: 305–13.

—— 1988. 'Il ponte antico di San Vito. Variazioni del clima e mutamenti dei corsi d'acqua e delle strade dall'antichità al medioevo tra Marecchia e Pisciatello', in C. Curradi (ed.), *San Vito e Santa Giustina: contributi per la storia locale* (Rimini: Maggioli), pp. 33–68.

Veggiani, A. and A. Roncuzzi. 1969. 'Ricerche geomorfologiche per la localizzazione degli antichi insediamenti umani nel territorio di Cesenatico', *Studi Romagnoli*, 20: 3–24.

Vullo, N. 1993. 'L'età romana', in P. L. Dall'Aglio (ed.), *Storia di Bellaria, Bordonchio, Igea Marina: ricerche e studi sul territorio dalle origini al XIII secolo* (Rimini: Ghigi), pp. 83–109.

Willems, W. J. H. 1991. 'Early Roman Camps on the Kops Plateau at Nijmegen (NL)', in V. A. Maxfield and M. J. Dobson (eds), *Roman Frontier Studies 1989: Proceeding of the XVth International Congress of Roman Frontier Studies* (Exeter: University of Exeter Press), pp. 210–14.

6. Caesar in Britain: Britain in Rome

A. P. Fitzpatrick
School of Archaeology and Ancient History, University of Leicester (af215@leicester.ac.uk)

Colin Haselgrove
School of Archaeology and Ancient History, University of Leicester (cch7@leicester.ac.uk)

Introduction

In 55 and 54 BC Julius Caesar mounted expeditions to Britain. The news that the ocean had been crossed for the first time was greeted with great acclaim in Rome. It was one of the reasons why Caesar was awarded a supplication in 55 BC and it would have been usual for this to be followed by the award of a triumph. In contrast, the popular perception in Britain today is that Caesar's expeditions were military failures that had little lasting effect and little attention is paid to them.

Some of the reasons why there is so little interest today are readily explicable. For many students of Republican Rome, Britain remains a remote island at the end of the world. In Britain the expeditions fall between modern fields of study: prehistory and history; and the classical world and provincial Roman studies. The later history of Roman Britain as a frontier province has also often led to the assumption by British scholars that a substantial military garrison should be anticipated during the Republic. Measured against this anachronistic expectation, Caesar's expeditions will inevitably be regarded as failures. In addition, Britain lies outwith the dominant tradition in archaeological studies of Caesar's war for Gaul which has understandably concentrated on France. There the Gauls described by Caesar and studied by Napoleon III have become inextricably linked with national identity.[1] However, Caesar's Gaul encompassed not only modern France but also Belgium, Luxembourg, parts of the Netherlands, and Switzerland.

In Britain, many studies have concentrated on identifying where individual events during the expeditions to the island described in Caesar's commentaries took place (Fig. 6.1). This can lead to a certain parochiality. Because the first expedition lasted for only five weeks and the second only a few months, there has also often been an implicit assumption that neither would have left many archaeological traces. This assumption risks becoming a self-fulfilling prophecy.[2]

In this context, it is readily understandable why studies of the expeditions and their significance continue to rely on written sources of which Caesar's accounts are, of course, by far the most important. In this regard, the many works of Thomas Rice Holmes on Caesar were particularly important in shaping perceptions in Britain. Rice Holmes published a Latin edition, an English translation of the *Commentaries*, and a number of discursive works.[3] These books were very popular and were reprinted many times; as a result, the views of Rice Holmes — with which he brooked no argument — became widely accepted. In many regards, his works effectively ended the discussion about the expeditions to Britain until after World War II.

Like Theodor Mommsen, Rice Holmes was an admirer of Caesar, often uncritically so, but World War II brought a sea-change in opinion. Caesar's *Commentaries* came to be viewed in Britain with, at best, suspicion and often outright disbelief. This view was propounded most notably by Courtenay Stevens and much of it stemmed from the significance of the date at which Caesar's first command in Gaul would end. Stevens outlined the importance of this date in a paper published before World War II, and after it, he developed his argument in a series of articles.[4]

---

[1] Olivier 2019.

[2] This chapter is based on a systematic review of the expeditions for the project 'In the Footsteps of Caesar: The Archaeology of the First Roman Invasions of Britain', funded by the Leverhulme Trust at the University of Leicester. The archaeological evidence will be set out in the authors' forthcoming *Julius Caesar in Britain*. O'Donnell's 2019 translation of the *War for Gaul* is used but Loeb editions are used elsewhere unless stated.

[3] Rice Holmes 1899; 1907; 1908; 1914; 1923.

[4] Stevens 1938; 1947; 1951; 1952; 1953.

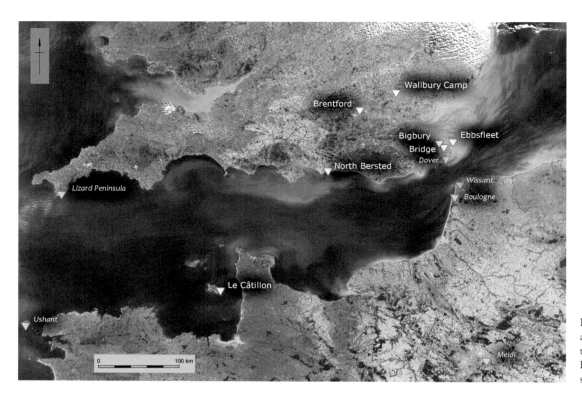

Figure 6.1. Selected sites and places mentioned in the text. Drawing by Andrew Fitzpatrick (over a NASA satellite image base).

Stevens argued that Caesar intended to invade Britain to demonstrate that the war in Gaul was not finished and so his command should be extended. In 56 BC he intended to do this by requisitioning the fleet of the Veneti of Armorica and using their ships to cross the Channel. The objective was to conquer not just all of Britain but Ireland too. According to Stevens, when the Veneti learnt of Caesar's plan, they rebelled. When their revolt ended with the destruction of their fleet, Caesar was forced to conceal his intentions. In order to do so, his commentary for 56 BC was essentially a confection that concealed his ambitions. Stevens also suggested that after the Britons in the south-east of the island were defeated in 54 BC, the terms Caesar used in the peace settlement showed that he intended to make Britain a province. Remarks by Cicero were also held to show that there had been high hopes that the wealth of Britain would prove to be as lucrative as that of Gaul. Ultimately, the revolt in Gaul in the winter of 54/53 BC precluded a return to Britain, and the denouement of Caesar's plans came in 51 BC when 'Gaul was declared a province from "mare nostrum" to Oceanus — but no further. Of Britain there is not a word. The provisional had become factual: it is the final concession of failure in Britain.'[5]

Steven's reading of Caesar's *Commentaries* differed from Michel Rambaud's more subtle, though equally cynical, formulation of 'déformation historique' published in 1953. The conclusion of Stevens's 1952 paper 'The "Bellum Gallicum" as a Work of Propaganda' makes clear how his service as an intelligence officer during World War II had influenced his thinking. During the war, Stevens had written propaganda for use in print and on the airwaves:

> When I made propaganda for the British government during the last war, there were two types of it, the 'White', in which our aim was to slant the truth but rigorously to tell it, and the 'Black' in which we permitted ourselves to swerve deliberately from it in the pursuit of the objective. In both 'White' and 'Black', Caesar has shown himself, as I have tried to demonstrate, supreme. Across the ages as an old propagandist, I salute my master![6]

Steven's argument rapidly superseded the uncritical admiration of Rice Holmes and became the new orthodoxy in Britain.[7] For example, for a generation Sheppard Frere's book *Britannia: A History of Roman Britain* was the standard text on Roman Britain. It was first published in 1967 and ran to a fourth edition that appeared in 1999. In the 1974 second edition Frere wrote 'Caesar

---

[5] Stevens 1947, 8.

[6] Stevens 1952, 179.

[7] e.g. Lazenby 1959.

had come and gone. The future denied him the opportunity of ever returning, but this failure to complete his work was only to be certificated by the passage of time.'[8]

Others developed Stevens's thesis. In his essay 'Britain and Julius Caesar', which is still the most recent extended treatment of the subject, Steven's schooltime friend Christopher Hawkes followed him and argued that Caesar deliberately concealed his plan for the British campaign in 54 BC.[9] Stephen Mitchell proposed that Caesar was motivated by a desire to control the trade in tin from Cornwall in south-west England and that 'we can go further and assume with him [Stevens] that the original intention in 56 was to launch a two-pronged attack on south-west and south-east Britain'.[10] Also, 'the expedition of 55 was unsuccessful and almost disastrous in its results' and 'this was an army of conquest, not a reconnaissance force'.[11] It would seem that by 1983 nothing in Caesar's *Commentaries* about Britain was beyond doubt.

The rehabilitation of Caesar as an artful reporter and the subsequent upsurge in Caesarian studies has, as yet, had relatively little impact in Britain on how Caesar's expeditions are viewed. Most recent works on the British Iron Age still present what is essentially Steven's view. For Tim Champion, 'Caesar's expeditions across the Channel undoubtedly boosted his reputation in Rome, even if they did not result in formal conquest and incorporation of any part of Britain'.[12]

Britain in the War for Gaul: History and Archaeology

In 2013 Birgitta Hoffman could answer her own question as follows: 'what physical evidence do we have for Caesar's presence? The short answer to this is: none.'[13] Like most writers, she restricted her considerations to 55 and 54 BC, but as Stevens argued, Caesar's campaigns in Gaul had begun to cast a shadow over Britain before 55 BC. There is extensive archaeological evidence for cross-Channel connections between Gaul and central southern and south-east England in the last centuries BC. The gold coinage of Belgic Gaul circulated widely

Figure 6.2. Gallo-Belgic E (Scheers class 24) coin found at Pakenham, Suffolk. Mid-first century BC. Diameter 16 mm. Reproduced with the permission of the Portable Antiquities Scheme/the Trustees of the British Museum under a Creative Commons Share-Alike agreement (CC BY 3.0).

in south-east England; trade and exchange between Armorica and central southern England is well documented; and a new funerary rite, cremation burial, was also adopted.[14] Caesar stated that within living memory Diviciacus, the king of the Suessiones, had exercised authority over much of Belgic Gaul and even over Britain.[15] Clearly, events in Gaul would affect Britain.

57 and 56 BC

Evidence for the type of authority that Diviciacus enjoyed and its territorial remit has long been sought in the distributions of Iron Age coins. One of the most important series of gold coins issued in Belgic Gaul in the first century BC is distinctive because its reverse side is plain. Known as Scheers class 24 and commonly attributed to the Ambiani of the Somme Valley, this coinage was struck in enormous numbers (Fig. 6.2). Although the exact chronology of individual types is disputed, a sudden and dramatic increase in the number of coin dies has often been associated with paying the soldiers who fought in the Belgic coalition of 57 BC against Caesar.[16] These coins are found in Britain in large numbers and it is likely that many — though by no means all — of them reflect the aid that Caesar would later use to help justify his expedition in 55 BC.[17]

Caesar's remark about Diviciacus holding authority on both sides of the Channel was made in his description of the Belgic alliance of 57 BC. Caesar also stated that the Bellovaci demanded that they should command the campaign. When it ended in failure, the leaders

---

8 Frere 1974, 55.
9 Hawkes 1977.
10 Mitchell 1983, 95.
11 Mitchell 1983, 91–92.
12 Champion 2016.
13 Hoffmann 2013, 21.

14 For coins, see Haselgrove 1984; 2019. For trade and exchange, see Cunliffe and de Jersey 1997. For cremation burial, see Fitzpatrick 2011.
15 Caes., *B Gall.* II.4.
16 Scheers 1977; Haselgrove 1984; 2019; Sills 2003; 2017.
17 Caes., *B Gall.* IV.20.

Figure 6.3. Visualization of the warrior found at North Bersted burial, West Sussex by Grant Cox, ArtasMedia. Reproduced by permission of the Novium Museum, Chichester.

of the Bellovaci fled to Britain.[18] It is possible that the burial of one of those leaders has been found at North Bersted, near Chichester, West Sussex on the south coast of England (Fig. 6.3).[19]

This man probably grew up in Gaul and the way in which the weapons buried with him were damaged deliberately is typical of contemporary burial rites in Normandy. The Gaulish bronze helmet was adorned by a unique bronze crest that may represent the outstretched wings and tail of a fighting bird. It may not be a coincidence that a series of bronze coins attributed to the Bellovaci show men wearing helmets surmounted by cockerels and that most of the British coins inspired by these types have been found around Chichester.

The massive Iron Age coin hoard found at Le Câtillon on Jersey in the Channel Islands also has a British connection. The Le Câtillon II hoard contained almost seventy thousand coins, the great majority of which are base silver issues struck by the Coriosolites, but there are also small numbers of similar coins issued by other Armorican nations, some gold coins issued in the Lower Seine Valley, and a few from Britain.[20] Precisely when this great hoard was buried is a matter for debate. Competing chronologies based on the same historical evidence, see the Gaulish coins as being buried in 56 BC, while a different chronology for the British coins requires the Gaulish coins in the hoard to have been withdrawn from circulation for up to two decades before the hoard was buried, it is suggested, in the 40s BC. If the British coins were in circulation by 56 BC, they could well be associated with the help which Caesar stated that the Armorican coalition sought from Britain.[21]

The discoveries at North Bersted and Le Câtillon sit comfortably alongside the extensive evidence for trade and exchange between the nations of Armorica and central southern England in the Late Iron Age. The maritime considerations in crossing the Channel at this time were assessed by Sean McGrail. The practicalities of seafaring that he set out provide important perspectives on Stevens's suggestion, supported by both Mitchell and Barbara Levick, that Caesar intended to use the fleet of the Veneti to sail to Britain.[22] The shortest, most reliable, and safest crossing of the Channel is by the Strait of Dover with a landing in the county of Kent in south-east England. Crossings further to the west become progressively more difficult, with the sailing that passes the westernmost tip off Brittany near Ushant (Île d'Ouessant) to the Lizard Peninsula in Cornwall being the most hazardous. In 56 BC Caesar was already experienced in naval campaigns and was familiar with Atlantic waters from his campaign in Iberia in 61 BC.[23] His experience makes it improbable that he would have attempted to cross the Channel in unfamiliar ships, let alone by the longest and least reliable crossing. In 55 BC he took the shortest crossing to Britain, across the Strait of Dover.

---

[18] Caes., *B Gall*. II.14.
[19] Fitzpatrick 2020.
[20] de Jersey 2016; 2019; Mahrer 2021. The Le Câtillon II hoard was found in 2012, following an earlier discovery nearby in 1957. The slightly later Le Câtillon I hoard also contains British coins.
[21] Caes., *B Gall*. III.9.10.
[22] McGrail 1983; Mitchell 1983; Levick 1998.
[23] Schulz 2000.

Figure 6.4. View of Dover harbour. The medieval castle overlooks what was originally a small natural harbour at the mouth of the narrow Dour Valley. It is possible that an Iron Age hillfort lies under the castle's earthworks. © Andrew Fitzpatrick.

55 BC: Britain

In the spring Caesar left his provinces to campaign in the present-day Low Countries against the Germans who had crossed the River Rhine.[24] Caesar then did what no Roman general had done before. First, he crossed the Rhine and then the Channel. In many regards the two expeditions were similar; both lasted for only a few weeks but each involved major logistical achievements.[25]

Caesar spent perhaps twenty-one days in Britain. Citing the support given by Britons to the Gauls as one of his reasons for the expedition, he sailed in September. This was towards the end of the campaigning season and not long before the equinox after which the crossing the Channel would become much more hazardous. He took just two legions, an unknown number of auxiliaries, and some cavalry, who never arrived in Britain.[26] This small force was not an army of occupation and it did not take provisions for an extended stay or heavy equipment. If it had remained into the winter, the Britons would have been able to surround the camp and starve the Romans into submission. Caesar was clear that both he and the Britons understood this. As he put it, 'If there wasn't time to fight, he still thought it would be very useful for him just to visit the island, see the people there, and learn the places, ports and approaches.'[27] He stated that little was known about Britain and its people or, tellingly, 'which ports could handle a large number of boats.'[28]

For over a century, it has been believed that Caesar set sail from Boulogne and intended to land at Dover (Fig. 6.4). Caesar described how on reaching Britain he saw Britons on all the hills and that later the steep ground allowed a spear to be thrown down to the shore. As this was not a suitable place to land, he sailed on to a location usually believed to be between Walmer and Deal. Before Rice Holmes wrote, many places had been suggested for the landing site but he vigorously championed Boulogne as the port of embarkment and Dover as the intended port of disembarkment. The image that Rice Holmes conjured of Britons lining the White Cliffs of Dover ready to repel the Romans became famous.

There is little evidence to suggest that the image is correct.[29] Rice Holmes assumed that the Gauls and Britons had ports with quays and jetties and that, like many medieval harbours, they would be located close to the mouth of a river. There is no evidence for the existence of such Iron Age ports in northern France or Britain. Instead, landing sites were sheltered bays and open beaches with gently sloping profiles on which boats were beached by the falling tide. Caesar himself described how the hulls of the ships of the Veneti were less steep than those of the Romans in order to help them take the shallows and low tides.[30] There is no archaeological evidence to suggest a Late Iron Age port at Dover but there was one c. 10 km to the west, on the beach below the cliffs at East Wear Bay, Folkestone.[31]

Caesar would not have needed to reach the shore at Dover before seeing that the army would have had to land on a small beach and then fight its way uphill through

---

[24] Hulot 2018; Roymans and Fernandez-Götz (in this volume).

[25] After spending ten days building a bridge across the Rhine, Caesar spent only eighteen days in Germany. Schade-Lindig 2020 considers the first archaeological evidence for the expedition.

[26] Caesar mentioned arrows and slings being used and it is usually assumed that this indicates the presence of auxiliaries. The cavalry may have numbered approximately five hundred; a figure Caesar used regularly.

[27] Caes., *B Gall.* IV.30–34.

[28] Caes., *B Gall.* IV.20.

---

[29] Fitzpatrick 2019.

[30] Caes., *B Gall.* III.13.

[31] Parfitt 2013, 36–37; Weston 2020.

Figure 6.5. View along Walmer Beach looking north towards Deal. It would have been almost impossible to bring a Roman transport or galley ashore here without excavating a trench in the beach front at the same time as defenders overlooked and attacked the ships. © Andrew Fitzpatrick.

a narrow valley.[32] This would also have been clear to Volusenus, who reconnoitred the coast before the fleet sailed. It is more likely that Caesar always intended to land at the northern end of the white cliffs, at or near Kingsdown.[33] Here, the cliffs fall rapidly to a wide, open, beach that is backed by higher ground. From Kingsdown the beach extends to Walmer, where the higher ground falls away, to Deal. This beach is over 5 km long.

Only when the fleet got close would it have become apparent that the shore here was unsuitable for disembarking the army. Today, the beach between Kingsdown and Deal comprises loose shingle stones and it has a high, steep, face (Fig. 6.5).

In 55 BC the beach is likely to have been similar because the shingle derives from the flint nodules in the chalk of the White Cliffs from where it is transported north by longshore drift. This process has been ongoing since the land bridge with the Continent was broken at the end of the last Ice Age. North of Deal, the shingle forms a coastal spit called the Deal spit or the Sandwich Bay spit. Romano-British settlements sited in the lee of the spit indicate that by the second century AD the spit reached as far north as Worth. Consequently, it must already have extended well beyond Deal in the first century BC. The steeply sloping and unstable face of the beach between Kingsdown and Deal would have made it difficult for soldiers to gain a footing and almost impossible to land a ship without the risk of it breaking its keel unless a trench was excavated into the beach face to reduce the angle at which the vessel would rest.

In fact, Caesar did not describe the Britons lining cliffs (*praeceps*) but high grounds or heights (*collibus*).[34] Nor is it clear that the place Caesar intended to land was the same one as the heights on which the Britons stood because the higher ground at the landing site was described as *montibus*. *Montibus* is usually translated as mountain but it can also mean 'heaped-up' or 'towering'.[35] This could describe the shingle shore at Kingsdown or Walmer just as well as, if not better than, the one at Dover. When the army did land Caesar described fighting in shallow water. This description is incompatible with the shore at Kingsdown or Walmer today but it is consistent with a location further north around Worth. If so, the landing place now lies below land reclaimed from the sea. The marshes that had developed in the lee of the Deal spit were reclaimed progressively, with the process perhaps starting as early as the Romano-British period. The modern landscape of the Lydden Valley between Deal and Worth is one created by reclamation.

---

[32] The valley of the River Dour is just *c.* 1 km wide.

[33] A fuller account of the coastal change, land reclamation, and the landing sites is given in Fitzpatrick 2019.

[34] The association with Dover is so famous as to beguile even the most sceptical commentator. O'Donnell (2019, 96) comments, 'Caesar clearly chooses to say "hills" rather than used the word available for "cliffs", but the setting is unmistakable'. In 54 BC Cicero described the White Cliffs as 'muratos mirificis molibus' (Cic., *Att.* IV.16.7).

[35] Lewis and Short 1879.

6. CAESAR IN BRITAIN: BRITAIN IN ROME

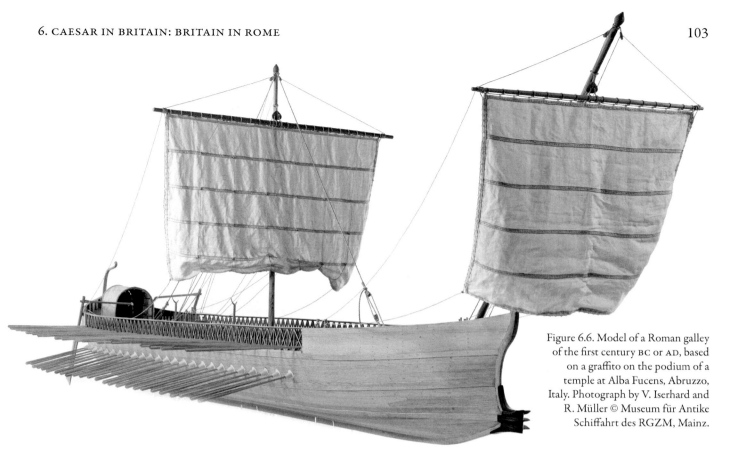

Figure 6.6. Model of a Roman galley of the first century BC or AD, based on a graffito on the podium of a temple at Alba Fucens, Abruzzo, Italy. Photograph by V. Iserhard and R. Müller © Museum für Antike Schiffahrt des RGZM, Mainz.

Once the army had fought its way ashore, a battle described in dramatic detail by Caesar, it did not venture far beyond its camp. Instead, Caesar had to combat the forces of nature. The ships carrying the cavalry, whose departure from Gaul had been delayed, were forced to turn back because of a storm. This storm also damaged the fleet. Some of the transports that were riding at anchor in deeper water were damaged beyond repair and the rest lost their rigging and anchors, which rendered them unseaworthy. The transports were brought ashore and after most of them had been repaired, the legions returned to Gaul.

Caesar had been in Britain, like Germany, for only a matter of weeks. As with Germany, nature had been subjugated. Just as the Rhine had been bridged, the sea had been crossed twice — despite the damage to the fleet caused by the storm. In Germany Caesar measured his success against honour and expediency.[36] It was also expedient to reconnoitre Britain and to secure honour, but for himself as much as for Rome. He was successful in both objectives.

54 BC: Britain

The Fleet

Before Caesar left to winter in Cisalpine Gaul, he gave orders to repair as many ships as possible and to build many new ones. He specified that the transports should have a shallower draught so that they could be beached more easily and those for the cargo and the mules were to be broader in the beam. All the transports were to have oars. The legions worked on the ships through the winter even though some of their winter bases were far inland. By the spring around six hundred new transports and twenty-eight new warships had been built (Fig. 6.6). Caesar remarked that sixty ships were built in the territory of the Meldi. As the Meldi inhabited the region of Meaux (Seine-et-Marne), those ships were probably built on the River Marne, c. 40 km north-east of Paris, and some 200 km from the sea (see Fig. 6.1).

Caesar drew not only on the lessons learnt that summer but also in Armorica the preceding one. Building the fleet was a massive logistical undertaking. It required bringing Mediterranean shipwrights to Belgic Gaul, collecting and preparing the materials needed to build the ships, training the skilled craftsmen in the legions how to make parts for the vessels and how to fit them, and hiring sailors to captain and steer the ships, and oversee their

---

[36] Caes., *B Gall.* IV.19.

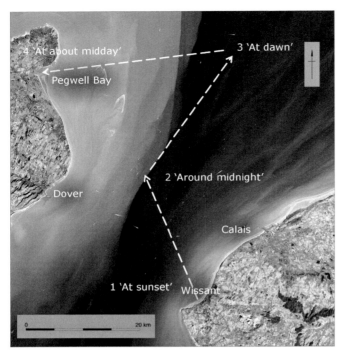

Figure 6.7. Timeline of the fleet's crossing to Britain, 4–5 July 54 BC, in Caesar's own words (*B Gall.* v.8).

1. 4 July *c.* 20:00 GMT, 'Caesar sailed at sunset'.
2. 4 July, *c.* 00:00 GMT, 'Carried on a light southwest wind, he lost headway around midnight when the wind dropped'.
3. 5 July, *c.* 4:00 GMT, 'Drifting farther with the current at dawn he saw Britain on his left. Then following the change of tide, he pressed with oars to reach that part of the island he had learned the previous summer was best for landing'.
4. 5 July, 12:00 GMT, 'They all reached Britain about midday'.

Drawing by Andrew Fitzpatrick (over a NASA satellite image base).

fitting out. Caesar ordered that the ship's tackle should be brought from Spain.[37] Caesar had stated previously that the ships of the Veneti had leather sails so this tackle would have comprised linen sails and rigging.[38]

The magnitude of the shipbuilding project for 54 BC is rarely recognized. Its scale dwarfs the building of the bridge across the Rhine. It required careful planning and an immense investment of skill and labour. The very considerable cost of it was borne by Caesar personally.

---

[37] Caes., *B Gall.* v.1.

[38] It is quite possible that this came from the port of Cartagena Nova (Carthagena) where the sails and rigging will have been made up as sets. In Antiquity the city was so famous for items made from the fibres of the variety of broom plant (*Stipa tenacissima*) that grows in the district that it was known as Carthago spartaria. The ropes used in ship's rigging were one well-known product (Plin., *HN* XIX.26–30 and XXXI.94).

This investment in the fleet indicates that the second expedition should be seen as a naval campaign as much as one on land. The expedition had a different purpose from the previous year. It was to conquer those parts of Britain closest to the Continent and make them subject to Rome. After the army left in 55 BC, only two of the British nations that had promised to send hostages to Caesar in Gaul had done so and during the winter Mandubracius, a prince of the Trinobantes nation, came to Gaul seeking Caesar's protection against the aggression of Cassivellaunus, who was the leader of a neighbouring nation.

The new fleet comprised almost eight hundred ships, almost ten times as many as the previous year and the army included five legions. The notional complement of a Late Republican legion is much debated but many scholars agree that it was around five thousand men. In addition, there were two thousand cavalrymen and an unknown number of auxiliaries. It is unlikely that any of the legions were at full strength but the army could have comprised over twenty thousand soldiers. In addition, there were the non-combatants. Ancient writers rarely mentioned them and so there is considerable uncertainty about their relative and absolute numbers.[39] Nonetheless, the muleteers, servants, and sutlers could have amounted to a number not far short of another legion. There were also well over two thousand horses. The cavalry would have had some remounts and there were also horses for the small number of legionary cavalry and the officers. There would also have been double this number of mules. Unlike the previous year, the force travelled with its baggage, heavy equipment, and probably also food and fodder for a longer period. Lastly, there would have been several thousand sailors, most of whom would have remained at the naval base with the fleet.

On this basis, the force could have approached *c.* thirty thousand men and *c.* five thousand horses and mules. While these figures are notional, they demonstrate the order of magnitude of the undertaking. To muster and transport the army across the Channel was a huge logistical exercise. As Gerald Grainge demonstrated in his consideration of the naval constraints on the Claudian army when it sailed for Britain almost a century later, it would have required a landing place whose front was several kilometres wide.[40]

While this force was large enough to defeat the coalition of Britons in the south-east of the island, its cor-

---

[39] e.g. Erdkamp 1988; Roth 1999.

[40] Grainge 2002.

6. CAESAR IN BRITAIN: BRITAIN IN ROME

ollary was that only three legions, two thousand cavalry, and an unknown number of auxiliaries and allied nations were left to hold Gaul, to supply the force in Britain, and to ensure that it could land safely on its return. Such a division of the legions was not tenable in the long-term. As in Britain the previous year, the small force in Gaul could be surrounded and a revolt elsewhere in Gaul would also effectively isolate the army in Britain. Mindful of this possibility, Caesar took most of the leaders of the Gaulish nations to Britain as hostages.[41]

The land Campaign

The whole fleet set sail at the same time, and despite being carried off-course when the wind dropped, all of it made landfall at the same time, and the whole army disembarked the same day (Fig. 6.7). This landing place has attracted much less scholarly attention than the one of the previous year, partly because as the landing was unopposed, it lacked drama. Caesar described how they had learnt the previous year where the best place for disembarkation was.

A location near Worth has often been suggested but recent discoveries suggest that it was further north in Pegwell Bay on the Isle of Thanet. The Wantsum Channel, which separates Thanet from the mainland of Kent, was long thought to be a wide sea channel in the first century BC,[42] but a recent study of its landscape history indicated that the Wantsum was probably only a relatively small river; as with the Lydden Valley north of Deal, much of the marshland around it was reclaimed in the medieval period (Fig. 6.8).

The Ebbsfleet Peninsula forms the south-eastern tip of Thanet, and a large defensive enclosure of first-century BC date has been discovered at Ebbsfleet not far from the modern shore of Pegwell Bay (Fig. 6.9). This bay is by far the largest on the east coast of Kent, and its gently shelving shore and the nearby coastal topography correspond well with incidental comments made by Caesar. The size and shape of the defensive ditch are similar to the siegeworks built at Alesia in 52 BC and a few certain or possible Republican weapons have been found.[43]

After choosing the site for the camp, at first light the next day Caesar led most of the army inland. As usual, his speed was intended to deny his opponents time to prepare and to choose the most advantageous ground

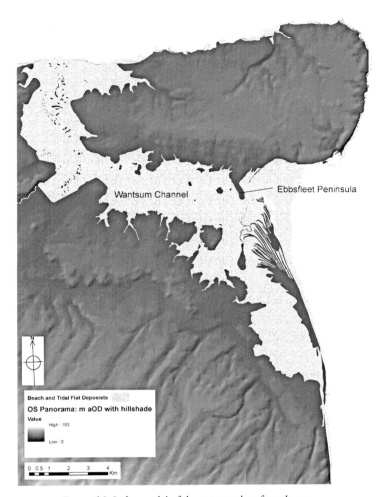

Figure 6.8. Lidar model of the topography of north-east Kent and the location of selected places mentioned in the text. Lidar render: Matt Beamish © University of Leicester.

for battle. And as usual, the better trained, better disciplined, and better armed Romans won the day, the decisive engagement coming after the Britons retreated to an old hillfort that they had refortified hastily. That hillfort has long been identified as Bigbury near Canterbury because it is one of the very few hillforts in east Kent.[44]

On this occasion Caesar's *celeritas* came at a price. The next morning, he learnt that the fleet had been badly damaged in a storm in which the ships broke their anchors and then collided. The underlying reason for this damage is likely to have been that the transports were still close to the shore because there had not yet been time to move them into deeper water so that they could swing at anchor and not collide. Nearly all the ships needed repairing and so Caesar decided to bring them all ashore and protect them with a ditch that was connected to the camp. The defence at Ebbsfleet runs

---

41 Caes., *B Gall.* v.5.
42 e.g. Hawkes 1977.
43 Andrews and others 2015; Fitzpatrick 2018; 2019.

44 Thompson 1983.

Figure 6.9. The Ebbsfleet enclosure looking east towards Pegwell Bay and the chalk cliffs at Ramsgate. In the foreground, part of the landward side of the defence is under excavation. The fields beyond it under the cereal crop are on the Ebbsfleet Peninsula. The area between those fields and the coast was reclaimed in the medieval period and this land masks the first-century BC shoreline. © Dean Barkley.

along a low ridge parallel to the shore, and it is suggested to be part of that defensive work, the shoreline along which the ships were repaired having been reclaimed in the medieval period. The ditches at Ebbsfleet and Alesia differ from the V-shaped ditches of Caesarian camps in having steep sides and broad, flat, bases because their purpose was to protect large areas (Fig. 6.10).

Caesar remarked that Labienus was to guard the ports in Gaul and ensure the corn supply. This suggests that the force in Britain was to be supplied from the main port in Gaul and that the naval base was the supply depot for the campaign.[45] The size of Pegwell Bay makes it likely that the main port of departure in Gaul, from which the army embarked in a day, was similar in size. This suggests that the large, open, beach at Wissant was used rather than the estuary of the Liane at Boulogne. Wissant also lies below the headland of Cap Gris Nez which is a prominent landmark for sailors. In the terminology used by Alfons Labsich, both ports will have functioned as operational bases while also serving as magazines for food.[46] On arrival in Britain, the supplies will have been tran-

shipped at the naval base and then carried forward along the River Thames to the advancing army.

Caesar stated that when he returned to the site of the first battle after completing the defences of the naval base, he learnt that the Britons had appointed Cassivellaunus to lead their coalition against the Romans. This did not change the Britons' fortunes. They were again defeated, and the Romans then built a camp. In 2010 a polygonal enclosure some 35 ha in size was located by Lidar 1.5 km away on the opposite side of the valley from Bigbury.[47] At present, the enclosure can only be suggested to date to the first centuries BC/AD but its angular form recalls that of some later Republican bases and it could be the camp built at the time of the second battle near Bigbury.[48] A few other finds in east Kent may be related to the early days of the expedition, notably a bronze Coolus helmet used as the container for a cremation burial found at Bridge not far from Canterbury (Fig. 6.11).[49] This type of helmet is Gaulish,[50] so its owner may have been a Gaulish cavalryman.

---

[45] Caes., B Gall. v.9.

[46] Labish 1975; Erdkamp 1988, 46–52; 2010; Roth 1999, 169–77.

[47] Sparey-Green 2013.

[48] Christopher Sparey-Green kindly shared his 2021 paper on these sites in advance of its publication.

[49] Farley and others 2014.

[50] Pernet 2010.

6. CAESAR IN BRITAIN: BRITAIN IN ROME

Caesar then led the army *c.* 75 km to the west. This was to the lowest crossing point of the Thames, which was also close to the territory of Cassivellanus on the north side of the river. The army probably followed a route broadly similar to Watling Street, the Roman road between Canterbury and London, though the exact course of this road changed many times.[51] This route is both direct and close enough to the Thames or its tributaries to have allowed the army to be reprovisioned during the march by ships sailing from the naval base.

The Thames was forded in the area of modern Greater London. At present, it is not possible to reconstruct the topography of this area in the first century BC in any detail because of the extensive changes since then. As the sea level was lower, the tidal head will have been further east than today, and the river channel in London is likely to have been narrower. This is because the rising tide effectively dams the flow of tidal rivers and causes them to widen. Extensive land reclamation, the dredging and embanking of the Thames, and the canalization of its tributaries have caused other changes. That said, a cluster of first-century BC coin hoards in the area of Brentford in west London comprised only of potin coins made in east Kent and all ending with the same type of coin, have long been suggested to have been buried as the Roman army approached the lowest crossing point because these coins are not common finds in Greater London.[52] Other hoards suggested to be 'flight hoards' buried at the time of the Caesarian campaigns include some of the hoards of torques buried at Snettisham, Norfolk, in East Anglia. Many of the gold and potin coins found there are from Kent.[53]

Figure 6.10. The defensive ditch at Ebbsfleet under excavation. The pit in the base of the ditch is a well associated with the Iron Age settlement that was cut away above this point when the ditch was dug. The tip of a pilum was found in the lower fills of the ditch. © Andrew Fitzpatrick.

Figure 6.11. Gaulish Coolus type helmet found with a cremation burial at Bridge, near Canterbury, Kent. Height 145 mm. Reproduced with the permission of Canterbury Museums and Galleries.

The Britons could not prevent the Romans from crossing the Thames and they retreated north until they were defeated decisively at an *oppidum* of Cassivellaunus not far from the territory of the Trinobantes. Cassivellaunus was not present himself but he had to sue for peace. For many years the site of the battle has been identified as Wheathampstead close to the later Roman town of Verulamium,[54] but field survey has demonstrated that there is little evidence for an *oppidum* there. Caesar

---

51 Tatton Brown 2001.

52 Allen 1971; Holman 2016 is more cautious. Some of the British potin coins found in France arrived with soldiers returning from Britain, see Gruel and Haselgrove 2007.

53 Sealey 1979. Subsequent finds are summarized in Joy 2015.

54 Wheeler and Wheeler 1936.

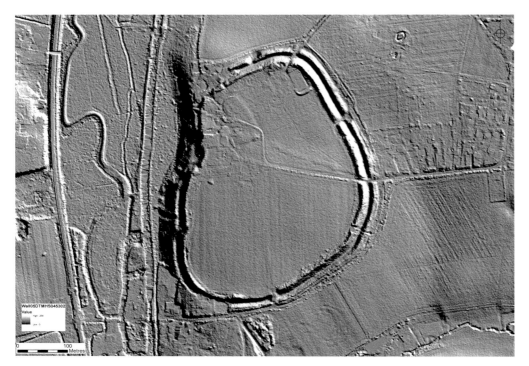

Figure 6.12. The Iron Age hillfort at Wallbury, Essex, considered to be the most likely site of the decisive battle in 54 BC. The west (left side) of the fort is protected by a cliff and below it is the River Lea, now canalized. The land between the river and the railway embankment is marshland. Lidar render: Matt Beamish © University of Leicester.

described this *oppidum* of Cassivellaunus in the same way as the hillfort in Kent — 'well defended by nature and engineering' — but added that it was also protected by marshes. The systematic inspection of all the hillforts in the region revealed that only one, Wallbury Camp near Stansted, Essex, is well defended and sited next to extensive marshes today (Fig. 6.12). It is also close to the presumed boundary of the territory of the Trinobantes. On this basis, it is considered likely that Wallbury Camp was the site of the decisive battle.

The Peace Settlement

Little is known of the peace settlement that Caesar enforced. He wrote only that he took hostages and determined what annual tribute Britain should pay to Rome, though in reality only a small part of south-east England had submitted to him.[55] As we have seen, Stevens took *vectigalis* to mean provincial taxation that was payable in perpetuity,[56] but in the Late Republic a range of terms was used to describe taxation, which could be paid in other ways. *Vectigalis* could mean tribute that was set for a defined period and it could also serve as an indemnity against further conflict.[57] As a system of taxation that was compatible with Rome did not exist in Britain, it is likely that the *vectigalis* imposed by Caesar was tribute payable over a defined period. As Caesar was responsible for ensuring that it was collected, it may be suspected that it was liable until the end of his command in Gaul. In Gaul, *vectigalis* appears to have been set towards the end of 52 BC, suggesting that it was determined when the end of campaigning was in sight, and Gaul's future as a Roman province had been determined. The tribute from the Britons would most easily have been transferred as bullion, quite likely gold, as it was used much more extensively in British Iron Age coinage than silver.

There is little evidence for high-level contact between Rome and Britain after 54 BC. It is likely that aspects of the peace settlement fell in abeyance during the Civil War and its aftermath. It was only after Octavian had achieved undisputed control that he could begin to organize the western provinces and formalize diplomatic relations with the neighbouring nations. He is reported to have considered returning to Britain on several occasions in the 30s and 20s BC but did not do so. However, in the 20s BC a sudden and dramatic change in the style of British Iron Age coinage indicates that diplomatic relations had been renewed. In the following decades evidence begins to emerge for the presence of Romans in Iron Age Britain. The *Res gestae divi Augusti* records that some British kings were made friendly kings and Strabo stated that some of them made sacrifices on the

---

[55] Caes., *B Gall.* v.22.

[56] Stevens 1947, 7.

[57] e.g. Losada 1965; de Souza 1998; Ñaco del Hoyo 2010.

6. CAESAR IN BRITAIN: BRITAIN IN ROME

Capitol.[58] It is likely that this renewal of formal relations was achieved by Octavian, by now Augustus, by drawing on the personal relationships that his adoptive father had instituted when he took hostages in 54 BC. Creighton has suggested that boys given as hostages to Caesar returned to Britain to assume the thrones of their nations,[59] but it is perhaps more likely that diplomatic arrangements with existing kings were agreed when the administration of Gaul was reorganized and were implemented by Agrippa rather than Augustus. Ultimately the network of friendly kings in south-east Britain would provide Claudius with a justification to invade Britain, and this time it was intended that Rome would occupy Britain and make it a province.

To Cross the Ocean

During the later Republic, Rome fought many foreign wars but these often did not lead to major shifts in territorial power. Even when Cyprus and Egypt could have been translated into provinces with relative ease, they were not. Sometimes the decisions not to create a province was taken after extensive debate in the Senate and it has been suggested that for much of this time extracting revenue was considered more important than imposing direct rule.[60] Much of the rapid expansion of Rome's territorial dominance from the 70s BC onwards was achieved on the initiative of individuals such as Pompey. He was appointed to the command against Mithridates VI in 66 BC, but after the death of Mithridates in 63 BC (albeit not at Roman hands) Pompey spent the next year reorganizing the eastern part of the empire. This was largely done by extending existing provinces, annexing new ones, formalizing arrangements with Crete and Cyrene, which had been recently conquered and annexed respectively, and recognizing friendly kings. Direct military conquests were responsible for only a small part of this settlement which was undertaken with little reference to the Senate and bore little relation to the command to which Pompey had been appointed. Less than a decade later, several holders of the imperium were acting simultaneously on a largely individual basis.

In or shortly after 55/54 BC, the poet Catullus observed this in his *Carmen* XI. In it, Catullus portrayed himself as a member of a general's staff (which in real life he had been) who wonders where he might travel to before asking two of his comrades to take a message to his mistress. The poem starts with a priamel of the peoples that Catullus might encounter:

> Furius and Aurelius, fellow soldiers of fortune,
> whether Catullus will make his way to the farthest Indians,
> where the shore is pounded by the far-resounding Eastern wave,
>
> or reach the Hyrcanians or soft Arabs,
> or even the Scythians and arrow-bearing Parthians,
> or the plains that are coloured by the seven-mouthed Nile
>
> or whether he will scale the lofty Alps,
> viewing the monuments of mighty Caesar,
> the Gallic Rhine (that horrible river) and the farthest Britons
>
> all of these places, wherever the will of the gods may lead,
> you, who are ready to brave them together,
> just take a brief message to my girl,
> no good words.[61]

While this priamel has sometimes been described as a 'romantic travelogue', the peoples in it are those that Catullus the soldier might face in the conflicts that Rome had been engaged with in 55 BC, some of them at the ends of the world ('extremos Indos' and 'ultimos Britannos').[62] Opinion is divided as to whether Catullus was complimenting or criticizing Caesar in the third stanza but as he was consistently critical of politicians and generals, and Caesar was sometimes singled out, it seems likely that Catullus was being ironic. The Alps, the Rhine, and Britain are monuments to an excessive personal ambition that later in the poem Catullus juxtaposed with the excesses of the sexual conquests of his own mistress.

All the campaigns in 55 BC were criticized at the time for their personal ambition, or avarice, or both. When Crassus left to campaign against the Parthians in November, it was widely seen as a brazen attempt to accrue even more wealth and to renew his military glory. Ateius Captio had supported Cato in his attempt to block the *Lex Trebonia* that awarded Crassus and

---

[58] *R. Gest. div. Aug.* XXXII.1; Str. IV.3.

[59] Creighton 2000.

[60] e.g. Steele 2013, 211–25.

[61] Translation by Shapiro 2012.

[62] It has been argued that the peoples in the second and third stanzas represent the respective conquests of Pompey and Caesar and that they are compared with Alexander the Great, see Krebs 2008. However, as Shapiro (2012) has pointed out, it is not clear why Catullus would refer to Pompey's eastern campaigns almost a decade after them.

Pompey the five-year commands of their provinces. When that was unsuccessful, he tried to arrest Crassus in order to prevent him leaving Rome, and, after being thwarted again, he cursed Crassus as he left. Plutarch stated that Crassus thought that the only thing in which Caesar exceeded him was in military achievement.[63]

> He would not consider Syria nor even Parthia as the boundaries of his success, but thought to make the campaigns of Lucullus against Tigranes and those of Pompey against Mithridates seem mere child's play, and flew on the wings of his hopes as far as Bactria and India and the Outer Sea.[64]

In the spring of that year, Aulus Gabinius had left his province of Syria at Pompey's instruction to invade Egypt and restore Ptolemy XII Auletes to the throne. Gabinius did so on the receipt of at least part of a huge bribe.[65] After Ptolemy has been restored, Gabinius left Roman soldiers in Egypt. In July Caesar's legions crossed the Rhine and in September they sailed for Britain. While Caesar offered reasons for those campaigns, neither Germany nor Britain posed an immediate threat to Transalpine Gaul. Like Crassus and Pompey, Caesar was using his imperium as he saw fit, the personal interests and ambitions of all three of them being legitimated by Rome's destiny as the territorial world power.

The previous year Cicero had lavished public praise on Caesar and his victories in Gaul in his speech *On the Consular Provinces*.[66] As is well known, the praise was not entirely sincere. In delivering *in Vatinum* earlier that year, he had acknowledged both Caesar's violence in Gaul and his passion for glory.[67] Cicero reiterated that desire for glory even in *On the Consular Provinces*.[68] In 55 BC, by the time that Caesar's report of his successes was read to the Senate, Cicero had retreated from public life, but other senators were publicly critical. One was Caesar's long-standing critic Cato. He opposed the award of a supplication, arguing that instead of being celebrated, Caesar should be surrendered to the Germans for detaining their ambassadors before battle.

Several Roman and Greek historians also made clear their understandings of the nature of Caesar's ambition.[69] In Plutarch's words, it was to carry 'Roman supremacy beyond the confines of the inhabited world'.[70] Dio, as often when commenting on Caesar, was slightly sceptical. Writing about the expedition to Britain in 55 BC, he stated that:

> So he sailed back to the mainland and put an end to the disturbances [in Gaul]. From Britain he had won nothing for himself or for the state except the glory of having conducted an expedition against its inhabitants; but on this he prided himself greatly and the Romans at home likewise magnified it to a remarkable degree. For seeing that the formerly unknown had become certain and the previously unheard-of accessible, they regarded the hope for the future inspired by these facts as already realized and exulted over their expected acquisitions as if they were already within their grasp; hence they voted to celebrate a thanksgiving for twenty days.[71]

In many regards, a comment by Florus encapsulated the opinions about Caesar's motives: 'He sought a reputation and not a province'.[72]

Britain may have been beyond the inhabited world but, conveniently, on a clear day it is readily visible from France. The Strait of Dover is only 33 km wide but because it is so narrow the sea currents are strong and, unlike the Mediterranean, it has a large tidal range. Caesar personally understood tidal ranges but the unfamiliar waters posed difficulties for him and all those who sailed with him. In 55 BC the ships carrying the cavalry were forced back by a storm, in 54 BC when the wind dropped the tide took the fleet far off course, and in both years the fleets were seriously damaged by storms. In 55 BC Caesar reported how long the shortest crossing took and in 54 BC he gave the distance of the most convenient crossing as about thirty Roman miles. By comparison, crossing the Adriatic from Brundisium is a voyage of over 100 km. The distance required to cross beyond the inhabited world was, it would seem, a relative distance and not an absolute one.

As Schulz has suggested, the seed of conquering the Ocean may have been sown in 68 or 61 BC when Caesar

---

[63] Plut., *Cras.* XIV.4.

[64] Plut., *Cras.* XVI.2. Crassus was following Pompey in trying to emulate Alexander the Great and reach the end of the world, see Welch and Mitchell 2013.

[65] Said to be 10,000 talents. Ptolemy had already paid 6000 talents to Caesar and Pompey in 59 BC to be recognized as a friendly king.

[66] Cic., *Prov. cons.* XXXII–XXXV.

[67] Cic., *Vatin.* XV.

[68] Cic., *Prov. cons.* XXXV.

---

[69] Vell. Pat. II.46.1; Plut., *Caes.* XXIII.2; Flor., *Epit.* I.45.16–18; Cass. Dio XXXIX.53; XL.1.

[70] Plut., *Caes.* XXIII.2.

[71] Cass. Dio. XXXIX.53.

[72] Flor., *Epit.* I.45.19.

6. CAESAR IN BRITAIN: BRITAIN IN ROME

served in Hispania Ulterior.[73] By then, Caesar may well have seen the monument that Pompey had erected in the Pyrenees in 72–71 BC to commemorate his role in ending the Sertorian Wars. This did not stand on a battlefield but astride the via Domitia, the road from Rome to Gaul and Spain as it crossed the Pyrenees in the pass of Col de Panissars.[74] Pliny stated that the monument was decorated with a representation of Pompey and an inscription that celebrated the subjection of 876 *oppida* between the Alps and the boundary of Hispania Ulterior.[75]

Britain in Rome

It may not have been a coincidence that in 55 BC the news that Caesar had led a Roman army beyond the inhabited world reached Rome shortly after Pompey dedicated his theatre-temple complex in September. Paid for by the booty from his eastern campaigns and displaying statues of the nations he had defeated and a giant one of himself, the complex monumentalized the claim that he had made in his triumph in 61 BC to have conquered the world.[76] The theatre-temple complex took years to build, and the games that celebrated its opening were lavish. But in almost the same moment that Pompey commemorated his conquest, Caesar redefined the world.

The complex was probably opened on 12 August of the pre-Julian Roman civil calendar.[77] It is believed that Caesar landed in Britain on 23 August and as the following year it took a minimum of twenty-seven days for a letter from Britain to arrive in Rome, the news that Caesar had landed in Britain is likely to have reached Rome around 20 September.[78]

Caesar was awarded a supplication of unprecedented length — twenty days — for the campaigns in Gaul, Germany, and Britain that year. Although they were not celebrated in a triumph until almost a decade later, Caesar's commentaries ensured that the intellectual triumph of providing the first detailed description of Britain and Germany was celebrated shortly after the expeditions. The detailed account of Britain was included in the commentary for 54 BC and that of Germany in the one for 53 BC after he had crossed the Rhine for the second time. The two accounts are very different in character.[79]

The one of Britain was written in the Greek geographical tradition. In addition to the ethnographic passages, the account of the size and shape of Britain was based on personal knowledge. Writing in *c.* 80 BC Posidonios probably included an ethnography of northern Europe in his *History* that provided the first reliable description of Britain, superseding calculations that derived ultimately from Pytheas.[80] Caesar made it clear that his description of the size and shape of the island was based on knowledge gained from questioning Britons. The statement that exact measurements were made of the length of the nights indicates that the latitude of the island was calculated. This would have allowed Britain to be situated in the geographical framework that Eratosthenes created and so incorporated into the known world.

An intellectual triumph was not at the expense of booty. While the importance of booty to the finances of Rome is debated,[81] it was undoubtedly an expectation for individual soldiers. In the summer of 54 BC Cicero remarked in a letter to Atticus that 'there isn't a grain of silver on the island [Britain] nor any prospect of booty apart from captives'.[82] This view may have been formed the preceding year as Cicero had made the same remark to Trebatius, who is thought to have been on his way to Gaul, perhaps in late June 54 BC (and so before army landed), 'I hear there is not an ounce of gold nor silver in Britain. If that is true, my advice is to lay hold of a chariot and hurry back to us at full speed.'[83] However, for a triumphant general booty, even if modest in value, also had symbolic capital.

In 46 BC Germany and Britain were included in the Gaulish triumph. This was the first of the four to be celebrated and was regarded as the most lavish.[84] As the format of the triumphal procession is relatively well

---

[73] Schulz 2000.

[74] Castellvi, Nolla, and Rodà 2008.

[75] Plin., *HN* III.18; VII.96; XXXVII.16.

[76] Temelini 2006; Russell 2015, 153–86.

[77] Based on the evidence of the calendars of Amiternum and Allifae. Cicero delivered *in Pisonum* shortly before the games and referred to the crossing of the Rhine but not to Britain. Cic., *Pis.* XXXIII; Marshall 1975, 91–92; 1985, 81–82; Russell 2015, 194–96.

[78] For the dates, see Ramsey and Raaflaub 2017, 10 and 34–36.

---

[79] Krebs 2008; 2018.

[80] Kidd 1988, 308–09. Some of Posidonios's account is preserved in Diodorus Siculus's *Library of History*.

[81] e.g. Ñaco del Hoyo 2010; Rowan 2013.

[82] Cic., *Att.* IV.16.7.

[83] Cic., *Fam.* VII.7.1.

[84] Deutsch 1926.

understood,[85] it is possible to suggest how Britain was represented in it. As the victorious general processed in his chariot, his army marched behind him and the spoils of war were paraded in front of him, the general riding between the two as the defender of Rome and the victor beyond it. The spoils, including the enemy's arms, bullion, works of art and other valuables, models of cities conquered, and paintings of battles won, were carried on wagons and biers at the head of the procession. They were followed by gifts from allies, then the animals that were to be sacrificed afterwards, then musicians and dancers, and finally the prisoners, the most important of whom walked before the general's chariot.

In Britain gold torques were a traditional medium of displaying wealth and there are many such finds of first-century BC date. Gaulish torques had been displayed in Roman triumphs over the Gauls in the third and second centuries BC but are not mentioned in subsequent triumphs over them.[86] This may simply be because no detailed accounts survive of those triumphs but it has also been suggested that as torques had become a type of Roman *dona militaria* they were no longer a suitable spoil of war.[87] The increasing reliance on allies and provinces, which from 121 BC included Transalpine Gaul, to provide cavalry may also have made it less appropriate to display Gaulish torques.[88]

This would not have been a consideration for Britain. If British torques were displayed as booty, they may have carried been on British chariots. Caesar gave a detailed description of how these chariots were used in war and called them *essidis*. Chariots are shown on coins issued on Caesar's behalf and they may allude to his success in Britain.[89] Lucan, in his vision of the Gallic triumph, envisaged Gauls and 'fairhaired Britons' following wheeled vehicles and it has been suggested that these vehicles were British.[90] In his triumph over Mithridates

and Tigranes in 63 BC Lucullus paraded ten chariots with scythes on their axles, the vehicles having presumably been captured and shipped to Rome. As chariots could usually be dismantled easily in order that they could be carried over difficult terrain (by the horses that usually pulled them), their transportation over long distances would not have been difficult.

Caesar stated that as well as hostages, he brought a great number of prisoners back from Britain and in Lucan's vision Britons were paraded, even though this will have been after almost a decade in captivity.[91] It was traditional to display the names of the conquered nations on placards. The Trinobantes's name will have been paraded and probably those of the Cenimagi, Segontiaci, Ancalites, Bibroci, and the Cassi. These nations had sent ambassadors and surrendered to Caesar after he undertook to protect the Trinobantes. In 61 BC Pompey paraded the names of the kings he had conquered and although Caesar only named one British leader as having surrendered to him, in view of the role of Cassivellaunus as leader of the British coalition in 54 BC, it must be likely that his name was carried through Rome.

However, the most prominent captive was not a king, a queen, or another person, but the ocean. Caesar appears to have been the first general to include representations of rivers in a triumph and it is believed that these were statues. As rivers were regarded as living beings they were paraded as prisoners.[92] The Rhône, Rhine, and Nile were represented in Caesar's triumphs but the ocean was apparently afforded prominence by being made of gold and the description of it as 'captive' suggests that it was in chains. While the representation symbolized Britain, it signified Caesar's success in going beyond the inhabited world.

On the last day of his triumphs, Caesar inaugurated the Temple of Venus Genetrix in the Forum Iulium (Westall 1996). The land for the forum had been bought at the time of the British expeditions and the temple and almost all the offerings in it were opulent. There was, though, at least one exception. This was a *thorax*, or breastplate, made of British pearls.[93] The following century Pliny described how the pearls found in the Mediterranean compared unfavourably with those from the Red Sea and that: 'It is established that small pearls

---

85 e.g. Östenberg 2009.

86 Triumphs over the Gauls were celebrated by Domitius Ahenobarbus and Fabius Maximus in 120 BC, Marius in 101 BC (over the Cimbri in this context), and Caius Pomptinus in 54 BC.

87 Maxfield 1981, 60–61; Östenberg 2009, 108–11.

88 On auxiliaries, see Pernet 2010. The later first-century statue of a soldier found at Vachères, Ales-de-Haut-Provence, shows him wearing a torque, see Barruol 1996.

89 RRC 448/2 issued in 48 BC shows a standing warrior and a seated driver in a chariot being pulled at speed by two (not four) horses and RRC 482 issued in 44 BC shows a trophy, a carnyx, two spears, and an unhitched chariot at rest, see Piggott 1952; 198 and 208–11; Östenberg 2009, 37.

90 Östenberg 2009, 37, though Lucan (III.76–78) called the

vehicles *currus* not *essidis* despite the word *essidis* having entered popular usage in Rome, cf. Nice 2003.

91 Caes., *B Gall.* v.22.

92 Östenberg 2009, 230–45.

93 Deutsch 1924; Flory 1988.

of poor colour grow in Britain, since the late lamented Julius desired it to be known that the breastplate which he dedicated to Venus Genetrix in her temple was made of British pearls.'[94] The breastplate symbolized the weapons mounted on the trophies that were erected on the sites of battles, and the pearls symbolized the sea. The pearls were probably not from British oysters (the European flat oyster, *Ostrea edulis*) rather than freshwater mussels (*Margaritifera margaritifera*) or saltwater blue mussels (*Mytilus edulis*), both of which are native to Britain — although it would have been difficult to obtain large numbers of pearls from either species.

This breastplate of small and badly coloured pearls might have appeared incongruous amongst the grandeur of the triumphs and the temple but, like the golden representation of captive ocean, its true value lay in the way that it signified that Caesar had achieved his ambition. He had defeated the Britons but his triumph was in crossing the outer sea.

---

94 Plin., *HN* ix.116.

Works Cited

Allen, D. F. 1971. 'British Potin Coins: A Review', in M. Jesson and D. Hill (eds), *The Iron Age and its Hillforts*, Southampton University Monograph Series, 1 (Southampton: University of Southampton), pp. 127–54.

Andrews, P. and others. 2015. *Digging at the Gateway: Archaeological Landscapes of South Thanet*, Oxford Wessex Archaeology Monograph, 8, 2 vols (Oxford: Oxford Archaeology).

Barruol, G. 1996. 'La statue du guerrier de Vachères (Alpes-de-Haute-Provence)', *Revue archéologique de Narbonnaise*, 29: 1–12.

Castellvi, G., J.-M. Nolla, and I. Rodà. 2008. *Le trophée de Pompée dans les Pyrénées (71 avant J.-C.): Col de Panissars; Le Perthus, Pyrénées-Orientales (France), La Jonquera, Haut Empordan, (Espagne)*, Gallia suppléments, 58 (Paris: Centre national de la recherche scientifique).

Champion, T. 2016. 'Britain before the Romans', in M. Millett, L. Revell, and A. Moore (eds), *The Oxford Handbook of Roman Britain* (Oxford: Oxford University Press), pp. 150–78.

Creighton, J. 2000. *Coins and Power in Late Iron Age Britain* (Cambridge: Cambridge University Press).

Cunliffe, B. and P. de Jersey. 1997. *Armorica and Britain: Cross-Channel Relationships in the Late First Millennium BC*, Oxford University Committee for Archaeology Monograph, 45 (Oxford: Oxford University Committee for Archaeology).

Deutsch, M. E. 1924. 'Caesar and the Pearls of Britain', *Classical Journal*, 19: 503–05.

—— 1926. 'Caesar's Triumphs', *Classical Weekly*, 19: 101–06.

Erdkamp, P. 1988. *Hunger and the Sword: Warfare and Food Supply in Roman Republican Wars (264–30 BC)* (Amsterdam: Gieben).

Farley, J. and others. 2014. 'A Late Iron Age Helmet Burial from Bridge, near Canterbury, Kent', *Proceedings of the Prehistoric Society*, 80: 379–88.

Fitzpatrick, A. P. 2011. 'Les pratiques funéraires de l'Âge du fer tardif dans le Sud d'Angleterre', in P. Barral and others (eds), *L'Âge du fer en Basse-Normandie: gestes funéraires en Gaul au second Âge du fer; actes du XXXIIIᵉ colloque international de l'Association française pour l'étude de l'Age du fer, Caen, 20–24 mai 2009*, 2 vols (Besançon: Presses universitaires de Franche-Comté), pp. 15–30.

—— 2018. 'L'enceinte d'Ebbsfleet sur l'île de Thanet (Kent). Un camp césarien en Angleterre', in M. Reddé (ed.), *L'armées romaines en Gaule à l'époque républicaine: nouveaux témoignages archéologiques*, Bibracte, 28 (Glux-en-Glenne: Bibracte-Centre archéologique européen), pp. 273–84.

—— 2019. 'Julius Caesar's Landing Sites in Britain and Gaul in 55 and 54 BC: Critical Places, Natural Places', in A. P. Fitzpatrick and C. Haselgrove (eds), *Julius Caesar's Battle for Gaul: New Archaeological Perspectives* (Oxford: Oxbow), pp. 135–58.

—— 2020. 'A Man Who Fought Caesar?', *British Archaeology*, 171: 21–22.

Flory, M. B. 1988. 'Pearls for Venus', *Historia*, 37: 498–504.

Frere, S. 1974. *Britannia: A History of Roman Britain* (London: Routledge).

Grainge, G. 2002. *The Roman Channel Crossing of A.D. 43: The Constraints on Claudius's Naval Strategy*, British Archaeological Reports, British Series, 332 (Oxford: Archaeopress).

Gruel, K. and C. Haselgrove. 2007. 'British Potin Coins Abroad: A New Find from Central France and the Iron Age in Southeast England', in C. Gosden and others (eds), *Communities and Connections: Essays in Honour of Barry Cunliffe* (Oxford: Oxford University Press), pp. 240–62.

Haselgrove, C. 1984. 'Warfare and its Aftermath as Reflected in the Precious Metal Coinage of Belgic Gaul', *Oxford Journal of Archaeology*, 3: 81–105.

—— 2019. 'The Gallic War in the Chronology of Iron Age Coinage', in A. P. Fitzpatrick and C. Haselgrove (eds), *Julius Caesar's Battle for Gaul: New Archaeological Perspectives* (Oxford: Oxbow), pp. 241–66.

Hawkes, C. F. C. 1977. 'Britain and Julius Caesar', *Proceedings of the British Academy*, 63: 125–92.

Hoffmann, B. 2013. *The Roman Invasion of Britain: Archaeology versus History* (Barnsley: Pen & Sword).

Holman, D. 2016. 'A New Classification System for the Flat Linear Potin Coinage', *British Numismatic Journal*, 86: 1–67.

Hulot, S. 2018. 'César génocidaire? Le massacre des Usipètes et des Tenctères (55 av. J.–C.)', *Revue études anciennes*, 120: 73–99.

Jersey, P. de. 2016. 'Colbert de Beaulieu, the Coriosolites and the Jersey Hoards', *Revue belge de numismatique*, 162: 159–78.

—— 2019. 'The Island of Jersey: Focus of Resistance or Field of Last Resort?', in A. P. Fitzpatrick and C. Haselgrove (eds), *Julius Caesar's Battle for Gaul: New Archaeological Perspectives* (Oxford: Oxbow), pp. 267–83.

Joy, J. 2015. 'Snettisham: Shining New Light on an Old Treasure', *British Archaeology*, 144: 18–25.

Kidd, I. G. 1988. *Posidonius*, II: *The Commentary*, 1: *Testimonia and Fragments 1–149*; 2: *Fragments 150–293* (Cambridge: Cambridge University Press).

Krebs, C. 2008. 'Magni Viri: Caesar, Alexander and Pompey in Cat. 11', *Philologus*, 152: 223–29.

—— 2018. 'The World's Measure: Caesar's Geographies of Gallia and Britannia in their Contexts and as Evidence of his World Map', *American Journal of Philology*, 139: 93–122.

Labisch, A. 1975. *Frumentum commeatusque: Die Nahrungsmittelversorgung der Heere Caesars* (Meisenheim am Glan: Hain).

Lazenby, J. F. 1959. 'The Conference of Luca and the Gallic War: A Study in Roman Politics 57–55 BC', *Latomus*, 18: 67–76.

6. CAESAR IN BRITAIN: BRITAIN IN ROME

Levick, B. 1998. 'The Veneti Revisited: C. E. Stevens and the Tradition on Caesar the Propagandist', in K. Welch and A. Powell (eds), *Julius Caesar as Artful Reporter: The War Commentaries as Political Instruments* (Swansea: Classical Press of Wales), pp. 61–83.

Lewis, C. T. and C. Short. 1879. *A Latin Dictionary: Founded on Andrews' Edition of Freund's Latin Dictionary* (Oxford: Clarendon).

Losada, L. A. 1965. 'The Aetolian Indemnity of 189 and the Agrinion Hoard', *Phoenix*, 19: 129–33.

McGrail, S. 1983. 'Cross-Channel Seamanship and Navigation in the Late First Millennium BC', *Oxford Journal of Archaeology*, 2: 299–337.

Mahrer, N. 2021. 'Le Câtillon II: Conserving Britain's Largest Iron Age Hoard', *Current Archaeology*, 373: 44–51.

Marshall, B. A. 1975. 'The Date of Delivery of Cicero's in Pisonem', *Classical Quarterly*, 25: 88–93.

—— 1985. *A Historical Commentary on Asconius* (Columbia: University of Missouri Press).

Maxfield, V. A. 1981. *The Military Decorations of the Roman Army* (London: Batsford).

Mitchell, S. 1983. 'Cornish Tin, Iulius Caesar, and the Invasion of Britain', in C. Deroux (ed.), *Studies in Latin Literature and Roman History*, III, Collection Latomus, 180 (Brussels: Revue d'études latines), pp. 80–99.

Ñaco del Hoyo, T. 2010. 'The Republican "War Economy" Strikes back: A "Minimalist" Approach', in N. Barrandon and F. Kirbihler (eds), *Administrer les provinces de la République romaine* (Rennes: Presses universitaires de Rennes), pp. 161–74.

Nice, A. 2003. 'C. Trebatius Testa and the British Charioteers: The Relationship of Cic. Ad Fam. 7.10.2 to Caes. BG 4.25 and 33', *Acta classica*, 46: 71–96.

O'Donnell, J. J. 2019. *The War for Gaul: A New Translation; Julius Caesar* (Princeton: Princeton University Press).

Olivier, L. 2019. 'The Second Battle of Alesia: The 19th-Century Investigations at Alise-Sainte-Reine and International Recognition of the Gallic Period of the Late Iron Age', in A. P. Fitzpatrick and C. Haselgrove (eds), *Julius Caesar's Battle for Gaul: New Archaeological Perspectives* (Oxford: Oxbow), pp. 285–309.

Östenberg, I. 2009. *Staging the World: Spoils, Captives, and Representations in the Roman Triumphal Procession* (Oxford: Oxford University Press).

Parfitt, K. 2013. 'Folkestone before Folkestone: Prehistoric Times', in I. Coulson (ed.), *Folkestone to 1500: A Town Unearthed* (Canterbury: Canterbury Archaeological Trust), pp. 9–30.

Pernet, L. 2010. *Armement et auxiliaires gauloise (IIe et Ier siècles avant notre ère)*, Protohistoire européenne, 12 (Montagnac: Monique Mergoil).

Piggott, S. 1952. 'Celtic Chariots on Roman Coins', *Antiquity*, 26: 87–88.

Ramsey, J. T. and K. A. Raaflaub. 2017. 'Chronological Tables for Caesar's Wars (58–45 BCE)', *Histos*, 11: 162–217.

Rambaud, M. 1953. *L'art de la déformation historique dans les 'commentaires' de César*, Études anciennes, 4 (Paris: Les belles lettres).

—— 1965. *De bello gallico: secundus tertiusque libri*, Erasme, 12 (Paris: Presses universitaires de France).

Rice Holmes, T. 1899. *Caesar's Conquest of Gaul* (London: Macmillan).

—— 1907. *Ancient Britain and the Invasions of Julius Caesar* (Oxford: Clarendon).

—— 1908. *Caesar's Commentaries on the Gallic War: Translated into English by T. Rice Holmes* (London: Macmillan).

—— 1914. *C. Iuli Commentarii rerum in Gallia gestarum vii, A. Hirti Commentarius viii* (Oxford: Clarendon).

—— 1923. *The Roman Republic and the Founder of the Empire* (Oxford: Clarendon).

Roth, J. P. 1999. *The Logistics of the Roman Army at War (264 B.C.–A.D. 235)*, Columbia Studies in the Classical Tradition, 23 (Leiden: Brill).

Rowan, C. 2013. 'The Profits of War and Cultural Capital: Silver and Society in Republican Rome', *Historia*, 62: 361–86.

Russell, A. 2015. *The Politics of Public Space in Republican Rome* (Cambridge: Cambridge University Press).

Schade-Lindig, S. 2020. *Archäologie am Greifenberg bei Limburg a. d. Lahn: Spuren von der Jungsteinzeit bis zur Römischen Republik*, Hessen-Archäologie. Sonderband, 4 (Darmstadt: Theiss).

Scheers, S. 1977. *Traité de numismatique celtique*, II: *La Gaule Belgique*, Annales littéraires de l'Université de Besançon, 195 (Paris: Les belles lettres).

Schulz, R. 2000. 'Caesar und das Meer', *Historische Zeitschrift*, 271: 281–309.

Sealey, P. R. 1979. 'The Later History of Icenian Electrum Torcs', *Proceedings of the Prehistoric Society*, 45: 165–78.

Shapiro, S. O. 2012. 'Love and War and the Ends of the Earth (Catullus 11)', *Mediterranean Chronicle*, 2: 31–50.

Sills, J. 2003. *Gaulish and Early British Gold Coinage* (London: Spink).

—— 2017. *Divided Kingdoms: The Iron Age Gold Coinage of Southern England* (Norwich: Rudd).

Souza, P. de. 1998. 'Late Hellenistic Crete and the Roman Conquest', *Post Minoan Crete: Proceedings of the First Colloquium on Post-Minoan Crete Held by the British School at Athens and the Institute of Archaeology, University College London, 10–11 November 1995*, British School at Athens Studies, 2 (London: British School at Athens), pp. 112–16.

Sparey-Green, C. 2013. 'Recent Research on Bigbury Camp and its Environs, Canterbury, Kent', *Epistula*, 5: 10.

—— 2021. 'Bigbury Camp and its Associated Earthworks: Recent Archaeological Research', *Archaeologia Cantiana*, 142: 31–58.

Steele, K. 2013. *The Later Roman Republic 146 to 44 BC: Conquest and Crisis*, Edinburgh History of Ancient Rome, 3 (Edinburgh: Edinburgh University Press).

Stevens, C. E. 1938. 'The Terminal Date of Caesar's Command', *American Journal of Philology*, 59: 169–208.

—— 1947. '55 and 54 B.C.', *Antiquity*, 21: 3–9.

—— 1951. 'Britain between the Invasions (B.C. 54–A.D. 43): A Study in Ancient Diplomacy', in W. F. Grimes (ed.), *Aspects of Archaeology in Britain and Beyond: Essays Presented to O. G. S. Crawford* (London: Edwards), pp. 332–44.

—— 1952. 'The "Bellum Gallicum" as a Work of Propaganda', *Latomus*, 11: 3–18, 165–79.

—— 1953. 'Britain and the Lex Pompeia Licinia', *Latomus*, 12: 14–21.

Tatton-Brown, T. 2001. 'The Evolution of "Watling Street" in Kent', *Archaeologia Cantiana*, 121: 121–33.

Temelini, M. A. 2006. 'Pompey's Politics and the Presentation of his Theatre-Temple Complex, 61–52 BCE', *Studia humaniora tartuensia*, 7: 1–14.

Thompson, F. H. 1983. 'Excavations at Bigberry, near Canterbury 1978–80', *Antiquaries Journal*, 63: 237–78.

Welch, K. and H. Mitchell. 2013. 'Revisiting the Roman Alexander', *Antichthon*, 47: 80–100.

Westall, R. 1996. 'The Forum Iulium as Representation of Imperator Caesar', *Römische Mitteilungen*, 103: 83–118.

Weston, A. 2020. 'Republican Dressel 1 Amphorae from East Wear Bay, Folkestone', *Archaeologia Cantiana*, 141: 47–58.

Wheeler, R. E. M. and T. V. Wheeler. 1936. *Verulamium: A Belgic and Two Roman Cities*, Reports of the Research Committee of the Society of Antiquaries of London, 11 (London: Society of Antiquaries of London).

NEW DISCOVERIES

7. Excavating the Forum Iulium: The Danish-Italian Excavations between Longue Durée Perspectives and High-Definition Narratives

Laura Di Siena
Accademia di Danimarca (laura.disiena@outlook.it)

Jan Kindberg Jacobsen
Accademia di Danimarca (jaki@glyptoteket.dk)

Gloria Mittica
Accademia di Danimarca (mittica@acdan.it)

Giovanni Murro
Accademia di Danimarca (giomurro@hotmail.com)

Claudio Parisi Presicce
Sovrintendenza Capitolina ai Beni Culturali, Direzione Musei archeologici e storico-artistici (claudio.parisipresicce@comune.roma.it)

Rubina Raja
Department of History and Classical Studies and Centre for Urban Network Evolutions (UrbNet), Aarhus University (rubina.raja@cas.au.dk)

Sine Grove Saxkjær
Centre for Urban Network Evolutions (UrbNet), Aarhus University (klasgs@cas.au.dk)

Massimo Vitti
Sovrintendenza Capitolina ai Beni Culturali, Direzione Musei archeologici e storico-artistici (massimo.vitti@comune.roma.it)

Introduction

In early 2019 and throughout 2021, excavations were conducted in Rome's historical centre in the area best known as Caesar's Forum, a monumental public square laid out in the Late Republican period — but which attests to activity both much earlier and later.[1] The excavations were carried out in the south-eastern end of Caesar's Forum, in an area where it was expected that archaeological remains covering several thousand years would be encountered, from as far back as the Late Bronze Age through to the early 1930s, when the demolition of the so-called Alessandrino Quarter and the layout of a new central road, Via dell'Impero (today's Via dei Fori Imperiali), conducted under Mussolini, led to a new urban layout in this central part of Rome. The excavations have up until now produced new insights into the development of the area over a period of *c.* 2600 years. From the discovery of Archaic walls and graves from the sixth century BC to Late Republican drainage channels, parts of Caesar's Forum in its third-century AD phase, and Late Antique deposits. What is more, the excavations have unearthed remains of medieval activities of the ninth and tenth centuries AD as well as outlined architectural developments and daily life in the Alessandrino Quarter from the second half of the sixteenth century till its destruction in 1931 and 1932.

Open and Closed Spaces

Reconstructing past events starts at surface level. During the logistic installation of the excavation site, which included the erection of security fencing and creating office facilities, a few objects were picked up on the surface the first day of the excavation (Fig. 7.1). Among these were a few small change coins minted in Singapore in 2016 and a small contemporary carved wooden figure

---

[1] The excavations are undertaken as a collaboration between Sovrintendenza Capitolina ai Beni Culturali, the Danish Institute in Rome, and Centre for Urban Network Evolutions, Aarhus University. The project is directed by Jan Kindberg Jacobsen, Claudio Parisi Presicce, and Rubina Raja. The project has been funded by the Carlsberg Foundation since 2017 and Aarhus University Research Foundation with a flagship grant since 2019. Further support comes from Centre for Urban Network Evolutions, directed by Rubina Raja under the grant DNRF119. For publications on the earlier phases of the project cf. Corsetti and others 2020–2022; Egelund 2018; Jacobsen and Raja 2018; Jacobsen and others 2019–2020; 2020; 2021; 2022; Sauer 2018; 2021a; Saxkjær and Mittica 2018.

Figure 7.1. Small coins (5 cents and 50 cents) minted in Singapore in 2016.
Photo: Sovrintendenza Capitolina/the Caesar's Forum Project.

Figure 7.2. Modern carved wooden turtle.
Photo: Sovrintendenza Capitolina/the Caesar's Forum Project.

of a turtle. They might not seem of much, but they do, in their own right, tell us about central functions of the areas today — as a tourist hotspot — where people mingle, both visitors and sellers of tourist goods. These seemingly unimportant small surface finds exemplify one of the challenges surrounding urban archaeology. Cities with their roads, squares, and houses are constantly being cleaned out leaving little if any material traces from ongoing daily life in private and public spaces. Whatever context may have been deposited stands little chance of long durée survival in the face of urbanistic transformation processes. How, then, did the carved turtle survive the *c.* fifty thousand daily passing tourists as well as everyday public sanitation? It did so because it as well as the coins were deposited in an enclosed area of 30 by 12 m alongside the busy Via dei Fori Imperiali. Fenced off by the Roman authorities in 2009, the area had remained inaccessible for almost two decades until the new excavations were initiated, absorbing and conserving material evidence from the open public space just beyond its limits. This case exemplifies the reoccurring challenges in the excavation of reconstructing past events in open public and private spheres on the basis of information preserved in inaccessible closed environments (Fig. 7.2).

Before Caesar's Forum

From the area that later would be known as Caesars's Forum, the earliest traces of human activities are datable to between the thirteenth and the eleventh centuries BC.[2] The location was an amalgamation of favourable geological conditions for agricultural activities and a generally strategically important topographical setting.[3] The earliest datable archaeological evidence was found in the regions of the Aventine, Capitoline, and Palatine Hills and consists of sporadic finds of pottery, postholes, levelling works, and a series of wheel-tracks, all dating to the second millennium BC.[4] From impasto fragments found in the archaeological stratigraphy, it is evident that levelling operations with wooden posts and wattle-and-daub walls were implemented not only at Caesar's Forum, but also on the summit of the Capitoline Hill.[5] These elements, datable to the Recent Bronze Age, attest to a widespread attempt to create a terraced area.[6] The aforementioned wheel-tracks as well as a few postholes, belonging to a hut structure, have partly been destroyed by three cremation graves datable to the eleventh–tenth centuries BC, providing a *terminus ante quem* of the wheel-tracks and postholes in the twelfth century BC.[7] The three cremation graves belonged to a group of ten tombs dated to the eleventh and tenth centuries BC. Four of them were inhumations tombs, of which two were identified as burials of female individuals, and six cremation tombs, of which five have been ascribed to adult males and one to a child of unspecified gender.[8] The nutrition analyses attested to a varied diet and the accompanying grave goods indicated that the individuals were of elevated social status.[9]

These tombs are, together with contemporary burials from the area of Augustus's Forum, interpreted as

---

[2] De Santis and others 2010, 261–62; Meneghini 2009, 12.

[3] Brock and others 2021.

[4] Meneghini 2009, 11; Forsythe 2005, 80. On the geology of Rome, see Marra and others 2018 with further references.

[5] Lugli and Rosa 2001; Cazzarella and others 2007.

[6] De Santis and others 2010, 261, fig. 2.

[7] De Santis and others 2010, 262.

[8] De Santis 2019, 401–02; De Santis and others 2010, 263–72.

[9] Catalano and others 2021.

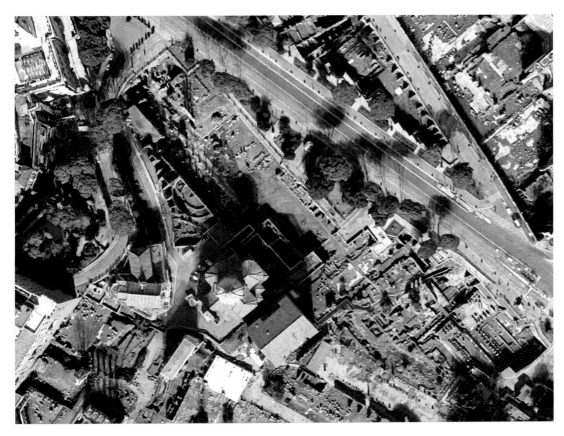

Figure 7.3. Aerial photo with an indication of the current excavation area at the Forum of Caesar. Photo: Sovrintendenza Capitolina/ the Caesar's Forum Project.

being a part of a greater necropolis area located between the Capitoline and Quirinal Hills.[10] During the eighth and ninth centuries BC, the settlement pattern in Rome developed from small villages to larger centres each covering areas up to 200 ha.[11] As a consequence, the cemetery was moved from the lower forum area to the higher area of the Esquiline Hill, thereby leaving the lower valley for domestic and productional purposes.[12] Nevertheless, two infant burials dating to the mid-eighth and last half of the eighth century BC have been discovered at Caesar's Forum.[13] These burials were situated inside a hut, both enclosed with significant grave contents, stipulating the well-known Latial practice of *suggrundaria*.[14] Later on, from the beginning of the ninth century and throughout the eighth and seventh centuries BC, as huts were being constructed in the area, it was once again levelled, however, this time with soil.[15] During the latter part of the seventh century BC, the area was partially drained, and domestic stone constructions were being used instead of the former wattle-and-daub walls.[16] Although the constructions have been obliterated over time, the evidence for the edifices is to be found in a well and from a pit containing archaeological material from a kiln.[17] This evidence imposes organized, domestic, and production-orientated functions in the area for this point in time.

The excavations conducted in 2005–2008 produced one of the most detailed examinations of the development of and societal networks in central Rome during the Archaic period so far. The finds included two Archaic houses, related wells, and streets in the south-eastern area of Caesar's Forum.[18] They were constructed in the sixth century BC and underwent several architectural transformations until a fire largely destroyed them in the early fourth century BC.[19] During the fourth and third centuries BC, the area was partly rebuilt and populated until the first sod was cut for Caesar's Forum in 54 BC.[20]

---

10 Meneghini 2009, 12.

11 Fulminante 2018. On the succeeding wave of urbanization emerging in Archaic Rome, see Sauer 2021b.

12 Cazzella 2001, 268; Fulminante 2018, 103.

13 De Santis and others 2010, 278.

14 Fulminante 2018, 198–99.

15 Meneghini 2015, 14.

16 Hopkins 2014, 30; Sauer 2020–2022.

17 Ricci 2013; Meneghini 2015, 14.

18 Delfino 2010a; 2014, 64–92.

19 Delfino 2010a, 293–94.

20 Delfino 2010a, 295–302; 2014, 93–134; Di Giuseppe 2010.

Towards Caesar's Forum — a Representative Space of the Late Republican Period

From the Roman politician and writer Marcus Tullius Cicero, we know that he, together with the Roman writer Gaius Oppius, acquired the area that would later become Caesar's Forum on behalf of Caesar from private owners of the Roman upper class (Fig. 7.3). Immediately prior to this, Republican elite houses occupied the area. According to Cicero, they paid the enormous sum of 60,000,000 sestertii for the grounds.[21] The Roman writers Pliny the Elder and Suetonius set the price even higher, namely at 100,000,000 sestertii.[22] This substantial price difference has led to hypothesizing a potential second round of land purchases during a subsequent construction phase or even real estate speculation on Cicero's part against Caesar's interests.[23] While Cicero and Oppius had bought the area in 56 BC, the construction of Caesar's Forum only began in 54 BC. The construction of Caesar's Forum was a prestige project, intended to underline Gaius Julius Caesar as one of the most important men in Late Republican Rome.[24] Primarily, the space became pivotal to how central Rome developed from then on — and basically Caesar's Forum, in Antiquity called Forum Iulium, was the forerunner of the Imperial fora, of which the first was that of Augustus, located right next to Caesar's Forum (Fig. 7.4). Caesar's vision for this area changed Rome forever, eradicating elite private houses for his public square and power demonstration.[25]

Before the construction of Caesar's Forum could begin, two majorly invasive changes to the area had to be undertaken. Firstly, the elite houses located in the area had to be demolished and, secondly, the area needed to be levelled to even out the sloping from the Capitoline as well as from the Quirinal Hill.[26] This large-scale levelling needed to even out a height difference of between 3 to 5 m over 50 m at the northern end of the Caesar's Forum area, creating an even space at a height between 14 and 15 m above sea level. As a consequence, the operation effectively demolished all remains of previous phases in the area towards the Capitoline and Quirinal Hills. Fortunately, sizeable parts of the southern-eastern forum were spared, and later excavations here have revealed important stratigraphic sequences dating between the Early Iron Age and the Republican period (see above as well).[27]

Other preparatory activities prior to the forum's construction were the removal of the grave contents that had appeared during the levelling of the area. The graves were cut into the geological substratum and were of a sub-circular shape, corresponding to some intact Iron Age graves found nearby in the 1998–2008 excavations.[28] Additionally, the graves were filled with coarse-grained sand similar to what has been noted underneath the tufa-stone blocks covering the forum square, indicating that the forum's construction was simultaneous with the emptying of the graves. The disturbance of graves during the initial construction work would inevitably have invoked some rites of purification to restore the *pax deorum*.[29] In this regard, the content of the graves can substantiate the activities to the time of Caesar.[30] For example seashells of the species *Cerastoderma glaucum* and *Glycymeris violacescens* occur at the bottom of some of the emptied graves. Often seashells denote a ritual significance in sanctuary contexts, and these might therefore potentially also be reminiscences of ritual performances linked to water cults at Caesar's Forum.[31] Staying within the interpretation of these as ritual objects, the intact seashells could also be linked to the ritual destruction of a ceramic vessel after which a single fragment was deposited as a *pars pro toto* of a larger vessel.[32]

The latest discovery of a filled well, located in connection with a Republican house and contemporary with the initial construction phase of Caesar's Forum, reflects, through the finds of tiles and painted wall plaster, the general demolition of private houses.[33] The well

---

21 Cic., *Att.* IV.17; Palombi 2016, 35–37; Raja and Rüpke 2021.

22 Plin., *HN* XXXVI.24; Suet., *Iul.* XXVI.2.

23 Coarelli 1974, 103; Tortorici 1991, 104–05; 2012, 6–11.

24 Raja and Rüpke 2021.

25 While the circumstances regarding the acquisition of private property prior to the construction of Caesar's Forum as well as Augustus's Forum are known from ancient writers, no sources are preserved when it comes to the construction of the subsequent Fora of Nerva and Trajan nor the construction of Templum Pacis, but similar purchases must have taken place, cf. Palombi 2016, 38–43.

26 The limits of the levelling have been identified in the area towards the Clivo Argentario and behind the cella of the temple to Venus Genetrix, see Ammerman and Terrenato 1996, 35–46; Ammerman and Filippi 2000, 27–38.

---

27 For a general overview, see De Santis and others 2010.

28 Delfino 2010b, 172; De Santis and others 2010.

29 On the argument, see Serlorenzi and Di Giuseppe 2009, 573–98; Carandini 2003, 410.

30 Delfino 2010b, 173.

31 Delfino 2010b, 173.

32 The ritual reading of deposits contemporary with the construction of Caesar's Forum is treated at length in Delfino 2010b.

33 Rizzo 2002, 27–28; Bertoldi and Ceci 2013, 45–47.

7. EXCAVATING THE FORUM IULIUM

was preserved by the superimposed tufa-stone pavement on the forum square. A significant quantity of pottery was excavated from the well-preserved well. The composition suggests that the material was deposited within a limited time span, possibly in connection with the demolition of the Republican houses — an interpretation that is further supported by the find of tiles and wall-plaster fragments. Additionally, the find of a possibly intentionally deposited seashell in the well indicates the sacred significance of the deposition of the material.[34]

The excavation campaigns from 2005–2008 produced detailed, albeit topographically partial insights into the long-term architectural and functional transformation of houses. As mentioned above, the 2005–2008 excavations revealed remains of two private buildings and a road in the south-eastern area of Caesar's Forum. Both buildings were originally constructed in the sixth century BC, but underwent several restoration phases over the centuries and are believed to have remained in use up until 54 BC.[35] This complex development leading up to the construction of Caesar's Forum is yet to be encountered in the new Danish-Italian excavation.

Within the new excavation, during the spring of 2021, a limited excavation trench (Area C) was opened up in an area just a few metres to the east of the mentioned houses uncovered in the 2005–2008 excavations. The trench revealed a picture fundamentally different from that found in the previous excavations. In fact, in Area C extensive earth removal works related to agricultural activities of the ninth and tenth centuries AD had erased all structures and archaeological stratigraphy for the period ranging from the end of the sixth century BC until the ninth century AD (Fig. 7.5), Such a situation had already been encountered in earlier excavations and has been interpreted as the early medieval layout of cultivation trenches on the Caesar's Forum square in the aftermath

Figure 7.4. View of the Forum of Caesar and the Temple of Venus Genetrix seen from the south. Photo: Sovrintendenza Capitolina/the Caesar's Forum Project.

Figure 7.5. Profile in the *domus terrinee* area showing a direct transition from early medieval layers to Archaic layers. Photo: Sovrintendenza Capitolina/the Caesar's Forum Project.

---

34 Delfino 2010b, 171–72.

35 Delfino 2014, 64–93.

Figure 7.6. Small Etruscan bucchero jugs during excavation and after conservation. Sixth century BC. Photo and drawing: Sovrintendenza Capitolina/the Caesar's Forum Project.

Figure 7.7. *Doppia olla* graves found during the excavation in 2021. Sixth century BC. Photo: Sovrintendenza Capitolina/the Caesar's Forum Project.

of the spoliation of the open space's marble flooring which occurred during the centuries leading up to the ninth century AD.[36] In fact the 2021 excavation also revealed traces of similar trenches.

The layers in which the cultivation trenches were cut exclusively contained archaeological material from the Archaic period, mainly consisting of impasto pottery and Etruscan bucchero. Two orthogonal walls found just in front of the southern limit of the trench (USM 3069) and in the eastern part of the trench (USM 3076) also date to a sixth-century Archaic phase. Two small bucchero jars (Fig. 7.6) were excavated close to USM 3069. The finding of these complete vessels indicates that we are looking at a small, preserved part of a floor level inside a dwelling. The excavation brought to light many fragments of Archaic roof tiles, most of which surely belonged to the same building as the walls. In the outer southern part of the excavation's Area C and at a lower level, four infant burials were excavated during autumn 2021 (Fig. 7.7). Three of the burials belong to the category of so-called *doppia olla* graves, in which the body of the deceased was placed inside two *impasto olla* vessels arranged rim-to-rim. The first biological anthropological observations indicate that two of the *doppia olla* graves contained individuals of perinatal age (one–two years). The third *olla* was block-lifted and is awaiting further analysis. The fourth burial was a pit grave containing a child aged two–three years. All four burials were found to be oriented north-east/south-west. Burying young children and infants in close proximity to domestic dwellings was a distinct burial costume in Latium between the eighth and sixth centuries BC[37] and occurs, although in a more sporadic manner, throughout pre-Roman Italy.[38] However, it is entirely unique to find as many as four graves situated closely together, out of which the three sixth-century *doppia olla* graves further-

---

[36] Santangeli Valenzani 2001, 273–76.

[37] Rathje and van Kampen 2001, 386–88; De Santis 2001; De Santis, Fenelli, and Salvadei 2009, 736–38; Nizzo 2011; Fulminante 2018; Modica 2019; D'Acri and Mogetta 2020.

[38] Tabolli 2018.

7. EXCAVATING THE FORUM IULIUM

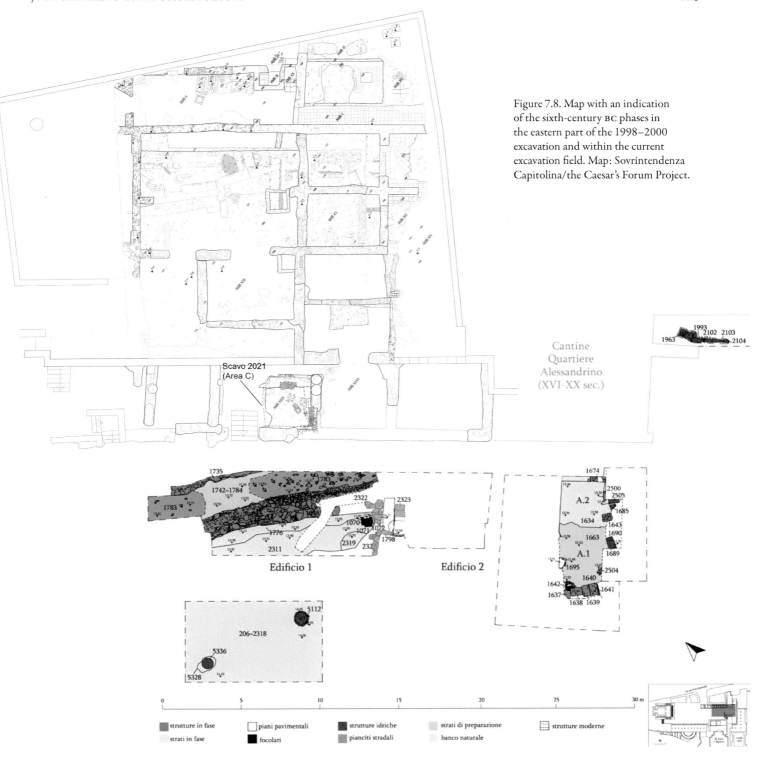

Figure 7.8. Map with an indication of the sixth-century BC phases in the eastern part of the 1998–2000 excavation and within the current excavation field. Map: Sovrintendenza Capitolina/the Caesar's Forum Project.

more appear to have been laid down contemporarily. The fourth pit grave was partly covered by one of the *doppia olla* graves and must therefore date *terminus ante quem* the three *doppia olla* graves. The lack of associated grave goods does, however, not permit a precise date for the pit grave. In the case of all *olla* graves, an accumulation of fragmented Archaic roof tiles and stones were found to have been placed at a level of 10–15 cm above the graves. The unorganized nature in which materials had been placed in these piles might indicate that they served as protection against subsequent animal disturbance rather than as intended grave markers. New parts of the excavation were initiated in March 2022 and will extend the excavation area in a southerly direction to clarify whether

Figure 7.9. Sixth-century BC contexts with postholes in Area A. Photo: Sovrintendenza Capitolina/the Caesar's Forum Project.

the graves form part of a larger grave cluster. Some circumstances from the 2021 excavation speak for such a possibility: an aryballos (oil container) of Etruscan-Corinthian manufacture was found in the south-eastern part of the trench on a slightly lower level than the *doppia olla* graves, but without any stratigraphical relation to these. The aryballos can, based on shape and decoration, be dated to the last quarter of the seventh century BC, and similar vessels are well known from Archaic graves in Latium and Etruria.[39] This vessel might belong to a so far unidentified grave beyond the current limits of the excavation field. In addition, several piles like the just mentioned grave protection accumulations were identified but not excavated in the northern part of the trench, indicating a possible continuation of the grave cluster in this direction. In relation to this, a few preliminary notes can be made on a possible continuation of an Archaic urban setting within the wider excavation area.

In their own right, the Archaic walls in Area C and the excavated graves show that the Archaic phase continues beyond the eastern limits of the 2005–2008 excavations. Previous excavations in 1931 and 1932 as well as between 1961 and 1970 have likewise revealed Archaic remains in the area of the Temple of Venus Genetrix and

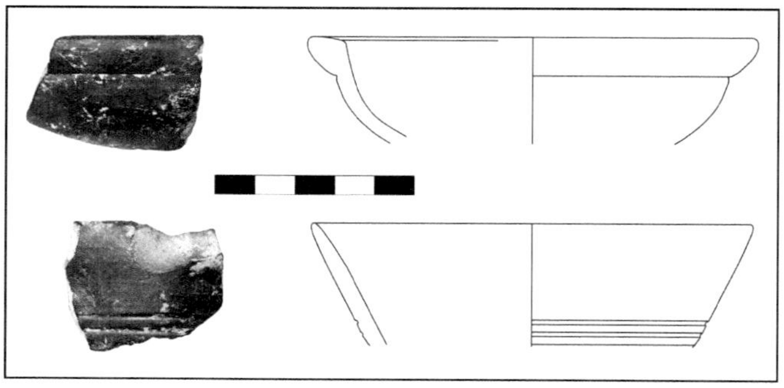

Figure 7.10. Bucchero fragments from bowl and cup. Sixth century BC. Photo and drawing: Sovrintendenza Capitolina/the Caesar's Forum Project.

behind the Curia, indicating sporadic but consistent evidence for the existence of an extensive Archaic urban setting in the Caesar's Forum area.[40] Preliminary results from the 2021 excavation provide partial evidence for the continuation of the Archaic phase in an eastwards direction beyond Area C (Fig. 7.8). At the eastern limits of the excavation's Area A, a small area of *c.* 80 by 80 cm revealed a few postholes and a covering layer at 13.45 m above sea level (Fig. 7.9). Associated impasto and bucchero ceramics provide a provisional date for the

---

[39] e.g. Franco 2019, 330, no. g125.56 (Esquilino). For the specific type and general distribution, see Gabrielli 2010, 27 (Type A.4).

[40] Temple of Venus Genetrix: Meneghini 2009, 241; Coarelli 2014, 163. Curia: Amici and others 2007, 138–57.

Figure 7.11. Granite columns, eastern part of Caesar's Forum. Photo: Sovrintendenza Capitolina/the Caesar's Forum Project.

area of the sixth and fifth centuries BC. In the remaining part of Area A, the excavation is still to reach lower levels in order to provide a detailed reading of potential Archaic remains in the area. The same is the case for Area B, a direct southern continuation of Area A. However, Area B holds several deeply dug cisterns and vertical sewers from the Renaissance. A limited number of bucchero fragments have come to light doing the excavation of these, indicating that their construction intercepted underlying Archaic phases (Fig. 7.10). Secondarily deposited Archaic material is otherwise entirely absent from Areas A and B.

Adding New Pieces to the Forum of Caesar

Whereas the extensive earth removal works related to agricultural activities of the ninth and tenth centuries AD had eliminated the Forum of Caesar in the *domus terrinee* area, the excavation Areas A and B had been less affected during the early medieval period and in consequence parts of the forum were uncovered during the 2021 excavations. Specifically, a section of the inner part of the eastern portico of the forum has been brought to light. The marble paving on the foundation of the portico, the *crepidoma*, had already been stripped prior to the early medieval period, but the underlying concrete fundament could be exposed over a length of *c.* 9 m from Area A to Area B. Directly in front of the *crepidoma*, three large columns in grey granite were brought to light in a horizontal position following the orientation of the *crepidoma* (Fig. 7.11). The columns were not in their precise fall-position since they had been partly incorporated into an early medieval wall.[41] The Forum of Caesar was equipped with these granite columns during a third-century AD rebuilding initiated by Emperor Diocletian or Emperor Maxentius after a fire in AD 283.[42] They seem to have fallen in connection with an earthquake either shortly before AD 484 or 508.[43] Just to the west of the *crepidoma* and partly covered by the granite columns, two Roman sewer channels came to light some 30 cm below the *crepidoma*. The sewers have a height of *c.* 2.2 m and were 0.5 m wide. They start in Area A and are orientated in the direction of the Forum of Augustus. Both must belong to an articulated water disposal system that kept the Forum of Caesar dry. At the current stage of our investigations, the recovered sewers can be ascribed to

---

[41] A few medieval walls have been identified. Further excavations need to be undertaken in order to interpret these remains more closely.

[42] On the rebuilding and its attribution, see Meneghini 2010.

[43] For the argument, see Galadini and others 2013.

Figure 7.12. Caesarean sewer with fill. Photo: Sovrintendenza Capitolina/the Caesar's Forum Project.

two different chronological phases: a Caesarean-period sewer displaying masonry in *opus reticulatum* with *cubilia* (bricks) of red tuff; and an Augustan sewer likewise displaying a wall construction composed of *opus reticulatum* made with *cubilia* in yellow tuff and with roofing in cast concrete. Although the masonry uses the same construction technique, it has been possible to differentiate the chronology through the details of the latticework of the *opus reticulatum*. In detail, the Caesarean sewer presents *cubilia* arranged with greater regularity on thicker and more homogeneous mortar bedding, while the Augustan sewer shows a less regular finish as well as extremely thin and differently styled mortar beddings. The reasons for this phase of remodelling of the water disposal network are still to be clarified through further research. However, there is a need to explore further whether the most recent sewers, which also perforate the concrete core of the *crepidoma*, are related to the Forum of Augustus to the east.[44]

The sewer's concrete roofing was broken through in the early medieval period and again in modern times when the construction of a sixteenth-century water cistern pierced the Caesarean sewer. In October 2021, a limited part of the fill within the Caesarean sewer was excavated. The fill layers predominantly contained ceramics from the fifth and sixth centuries AD, together with some limited amounts of later Republican to first-century AD ceramics. In addition, a notable quantity of cow leg bones were found. These had been sawn through vertically and should be understood as remains from the production of objects on bone. The fill did not contain pottery from the early medieval period, meaning that the penetration of the roofing of the sewer had not compromised the fill below (Fig. 7.12). Beyond the excavation field, the roofing of the two sewers running towards the Forum of Augustus was found to be intact, and the continuation fill of the Caesarean sewer could be clearly seen occupying two-thirds of the height of the sewer. A mud deposit of *c.* 8 cm covered the top of the fill (Fig. 7.13). In February 2022, a limited excavation was conducted in the sewer. Studies of the excavated material are still pending, but it can — in a very preliminary manner — be observed that the vast majority of the material dates to the Late Republican/Early Imperial periods; however, pottery datable until the sixth/seventh century was also found, indicating that the sewer continued to function up to this point in time.

---

[44] Corsetti and others 2020–2022.

Figure 7.13. Mud deposits inside the Caesarean sewer. Photo: Sovrintendenza Capitolina/the Caesar's Forum Project.

Farms and Flooding during the Early Medieval Period

By the second half of the ninth century AD, what was once the open square of Caesar's Forum was transformed into what seems to be small farm plots and connected gardens with orchards and vineyards.[45] As we saw above, cultivation trenches were dug out in sixth-century BC deposits. This was hardly a coincidence. The soil of the Archaic layers being fairly compact and clayey provided good growth conditions, and medieval farmers would have been well aware of this. In addition, the medieval occupation at the site consisted of one-storey single-room houses, the so-called *domus terrinee*. The *domus terrinee* were simple rural dwellings constructed by the farmers themselves without relying on specialized crafts or external workers. These house constructions were by no means a new invention. They are well known from outside Rome, where they have been well documented at sites like Portus and Tusculum. The novelty rather consisted in the fact that agricultural activities moved from the surroundings of Rome to occupying the central Roman area in pace with the demographic and political decline of the city.

Aside from the *domus terrinee* houses on Caesar's Forum, recent excavations conducted in connection with the construction of the Metropolitana C have produced clear traces of a contemporary phase in today's Piazza Venezia, a few hundred metres from Caesar's Forum, adding to a growing understanding of this period.[46] On the Forum of Caesar, the houses were erected on the level of the Roman Forum, and previous excavations permit a partial reconstruction of ground plans and construction techniques.[47] The walls were constructed reusing stone elements from Roman buildings, including marble fragments, granite columns, and turf stone. The roofing was made in perishable materials, straw or wood, and the floor was beaten earth. Remains of hearths have been identified inside and outside of the *domus terrinee* structures on Caesar's Forum, leading to the interpretation that cooking would have been taking place inside during winter and outside during summertime.

The farmers were confronting a constant problem of moist soil and seasonal flooding. The excavations of the Roman drainage channels in Area A, discovered in 2021 and described above, show that this side's channels, leading water to the Cloaca Maxima, went out of use in the sixth or seventh century AD. It is not clear when the Cloaca Maxima ceased to function, but it is evident that by the ninth century AD, the farmers on Caesar's Forum would have had to invent ways of counteracting the flooding problems. The excavation in Area C has permitted a detailed description of how soil, taken from Late Antique contexts, was reused during the ninth and tenth centuries AD to cover up mud deposits brought in by seasonal flooding. The procedure was conducted regu-

---

[45] On the *domus terrinee* houses on the Forum of Caesar, see Meneghini and Santangeli Valenzani 2004, 45–51 and 178–79.

[46] Serlorenzi 2010, 155–56.

[47] Santangeli Valenzani 2001, 278, fig. 8.

larly, as evident from the archaeological stratigraphy that shows clearly recognizable interchanging layers of mud with a thickness of *c.* 10 cm and layers of gravel-rich soil with a corresponding thickness of *c.* 10 cm. A preliminary study of the material from the gravel infills reveals that *c.* 97 per cent of the pottery dates to the Roman Imperial and Late Antique periods, whereas the last 3 per cent consists of medieval pottery from the ninth and tenth centuries AD. Among the latter, the best dating indications are provided from the glazed ware classes known as *ceramica vetrina sparsa* and *ceramica vetrina passante*.[48] A similar chronological division of the pottery has already been observed in the case of infills at the so-called *domus terrinee ambiente* III and *ambiente* XII, excavated on Caesar's Forum between 1998 and 2000. Here, the medieval infills contained up to 94.1 per cent of Roman residual fragments.[49] In the present state of research, we do not know from where the soil used as infill in Area C was taken. However, there are strong reasons to suggest that the soil was taken from one location, even though mud deposits vertically separated the infills. This is due to the fact that the infills contain ceramics of the same date and function, and, what is more, the animal bones in the infills almost all have a distinct green colouration, indicating that they were subject to the same soil conditions.

Scholars dealing with the social and spatial organization of agricultural activities during the early medieval period recognize two types of dwellings belonging to different social stratifications. Farmers would be living in the described *domus terrinee*, whereas an aristocratic upper class would be dwelling in more pleasurable houses, that is, the so-called *domus solarate*.[50] Given the high level of disturbance caused by constructions of later periods, the difference between a *domus solarate* and a *domus terrinee* rarely rests on the architectural remains, but rather on an analysis of the associated material culture.[51] A *domus solarate* is known from the Nerva's Forum area, where the presence of medieval stemmed drinking glasses has been taken as a clear indication of elevated social status. In contrast, medieval drinking glasses or other vessels are totally absent from the material excavated in 2021; neither does it occur among the material excavated in the *domus terrinee* area between 1998 and 2000. However, fragments from stemmed drinking glasses have been attested in contexts in an area *c.* 30 m to the south-east of the *domus terrinee* area excavated between 1998 and 2000.[52] These contexts and the related excavation documentation are still undergoing examination, hence a detailed reading is still pending. However, the preliminary results show that the contexts contain sporadic evidence of medieval ceramics from the ninth and tenth centuries AD in the form of *ceramica vetrina sparsa* and *ceramica vetrina passante*, whereas the majority of the pottery can be dated to the fifth and sixth centuries AD.[53] The chronological coherency between these contexts and the *domus terrine*, together with presence of glass vessels, does suggest that a *domus solarate* might have been located in this area.

Lost and Found — The Alessandrino Quarter

The farmers of the early medieval period eventually succumbed to the invasiveness of the seasonal flooding and abandoned the area of Caesar's Forum, and a thick layer of mud slowly covered gardens and structures over the course of the next five centuries. The excavations in 2021 produced a limited number of ceramics datable to the twelfth and thirteenth centuries AD, but these were found as residual material in later Renaissance contexts. Therefore, it is unclear whether activities were taking place in the area during this period or if the fragments came from somewhere else. The Renaissance brought a turn of events. In the 1570s, a new area in the old Roman centre arose: the Alessandrino Quarter. This constitutes the latest historical phase at the Caesar's Forum site, and the residential quarter existed more than three centuries before Mussolini demolished its last parts on 28 October 1932.[54]

In the sixteenth century, Rome underwent rapid population growth, which demanded new residential areas. Construction projects in uninhabited areas had already begun to see the light of day at the beginning of

---

[48] On the chronology, see Paroli 1990.

[49] Delfino 2013, 129–36. A similar situation is noted on the Forum of Trajan where extensive early medieval mud deposits have been recorded as well, cf. Bernacchio and others 2021, 344–45; Meneghini 2017, 288–89; Santangeli Valenzani 2007, 151–55.

[50] De Luca 2001.

[51] Boschetti and others 2022.

[52] As an integrated part of the excavation project, the material from the 1998–2000 excavations has been prepared for publication, Jacobsen and others (forthcoming).

[53] Corsetti and others 2020–2022.

[54] On the Alessandrino Quarter, see Bernacchio 2017; Jacobsen and others 2021; Meneghini 2000; 2016–2017, 460–62; Meneghini and Santangeli Valenzani 2010, 141–230; Molinari and Spagnoli 1990; Pocino 2008; Cederna 1979.

7. EXCAVATING THE FORUM IULIUM

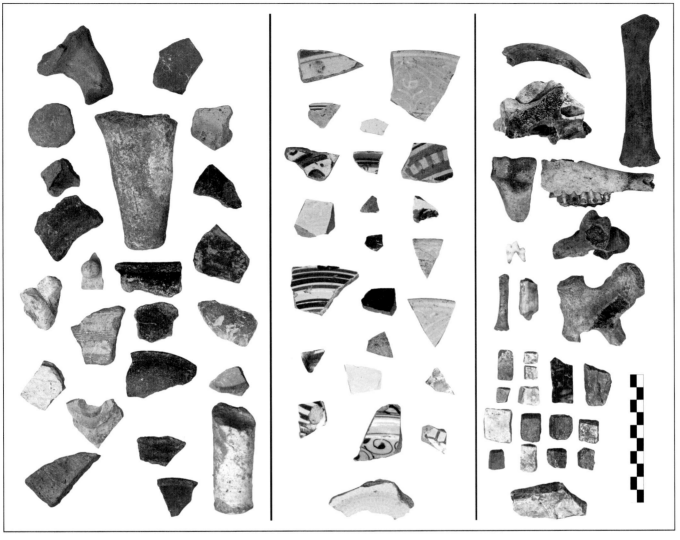

Figure 7.14. Archaeological material from Renaissance infills datable from the Roman period to the second half of the sixteenth century. Photo: Sovrintendenza Capitolina/the Caesar's Forum Project.

the sixteenth century under the then papal government. This elicited a much-needed development of the urban nature of Rome.[55] The transformation of the urban landscape included draining the aforementioned swamp area, called *I Pantani*, which was conducted by Comune di Roma in the years 1582 and 1584. The land retrieval consisted of a deposition of a uniform layer of soil in the moist area, creating a new elevated dry surface. An approach that effectively copied the one used by farmers during the early medieval period in the *domus terrinee* area. This layer of Renaissance infill has been encountered in the 2021 excavations, where it has a thickness ranging from 1–2 m. Extensive archaeological material has been collected, ranging from the Roman period till the second half of the sixteenth century AD (Fig. 7.14). Similar infills from the Renaissance excavated in the area of the Templum Pacis show the same broad chronological range.[56] Simultaneously, the previously essential Cloaca Maxima, which gradually was both clogged and collapsed several places, was restored in order to prevent reoccurring floods from the Tiber.[57] Spoliation, which was the main source of building materials for the medieval *domus terrinee* houses, is again found within the barring external walls of the Alessandrino buildings of the second half of the sixteenth century, but now as an

---

[55] De Amici 1993; De Luca 2020, 11.

[56] Fogagnolo 2013.

[57] Antognoli and Bianchi 2009, 123–25.

Figure 7.15. Fragment of marble frieze with a depiction of a Nike figure. Late second century AD. Photo: Sovrintendenza Capitolina/the Caesar's Forum Project.

occasional phenomenon, exemplified by sporadic finds of Roman marble pieces and tiles (Fig. 7.15). The main volume of the walls was, however, made of worked and unworked tuff stone with the occasional inclusion of fragments from Renaissance ceramics (Fig. 7.16).[58]

Two of the major promoters of the urban transformation project were the Della Valle family, the then official owners of the Caesar's Forum area, and Cardinal Michele Bonelli (1541–1598), who simply went by the title Cardinal Alessandrino. The latter of two gave name to both the residential area and its main street, Via Alessandrina. In 1584, the Della Valle family obtained authorization to inaugurate new streets, i.e. Via della Salara Vecchia, Via Cremona, and Via Bonella, establishing an area encompassing a total of thirty-five houses by 1590.[59]

The excavations, and the Alessandrino Quarter at large, generally lack contextual remains from the earlier sixteenth-century phase of the area, since these were lost due to the rebuilding activities during the following centuries. However, with one notable exception. In Area A, a vertical sewer was found (Fig. 7.17). During the second half of the sixteenth century, a group of objects had been discarded into the sewer, which seems to have gone out of use shortly after.[60] Most of the material consisted of fragments from decorated and white painted plates, of which many could be reconstructed into complete or semi-complete vessels. A number of small and still intact medicine containers in clay had also been discarded. In addition, some 1500 fragments of thin-walled vessels were found, of which most belong to narrow-necked glass bottles and so-called *urinari* vessels, urinals. During the Middle Ages and Renaissance, *urinari* were used to study urine. These vessels, as well as the medicine containers, point towards medical practices. In addition, the sewer contained a number of minor — probably personal — objects such as clay toy figures, spindle whorls, devotional medals, and coins. Of the latter can be noted a silver coin minted by Pope Giulio III (1500–1555) and a bronze coin minted during the papacy of Leone X (1513–1521) (Fig. 7.18).

Discarding objects was a known procedure against disease spreading during the Renaissance.[61] The objects from the sewer appear to result from this kind of action. At Piazza Venezia, some 325 m north of the vertical sewer, a similar although much larger medical cesspit was excavated in 2009 during the construction of the Metropolitana C in central Rome.[62] The discarded objects originally came from the Hospital of the Congregazione dei Fornari di Santa Maria di Loreto, founded in 1564. Both deposits date to the second half of the sixteenth century AD, and the many similarities between objects found in the two deposits clearly indicate that the material found in the sewer originally must have been in use at the Renaissance-period hospital in Piazza Venezia.

Cisterns and sewers from later periods have provided limited but detailed insights into daily life in the Alessandrino Quarter. One of these is context 1216, which came to light in a closed-off cistern in Area B during summer 2021. The context contained a rich and functionally varied archaeological material, which provides a cross-section of the material culture and activi-

---

[58] Jacobsen and others (forthcoming).

[59] Meneghini 2009, 237–38.

[60] On context and interpretation, see Boschetti and others 2023.

[61] Boschetti and others 2023.

[62] Serlorenzi 2010, 151–54; De Luca, Ricci, and Serlorenzi 2012; De Luca and Ricci 2013.

7. EXCAVATING THE FORUM IULIUM

Figure 7.16. Renaissance ceramics found in walls of the Alessandrino phase. Second half of the sixteenth century. Photos and drawings: Sovrintendenza Capitolina/the Caesar's Forum Project.

Figure 7.17. Vertical sewer in Area A. Photo: Sovrintendenza Capitolina/the Caesar's Forum Project.

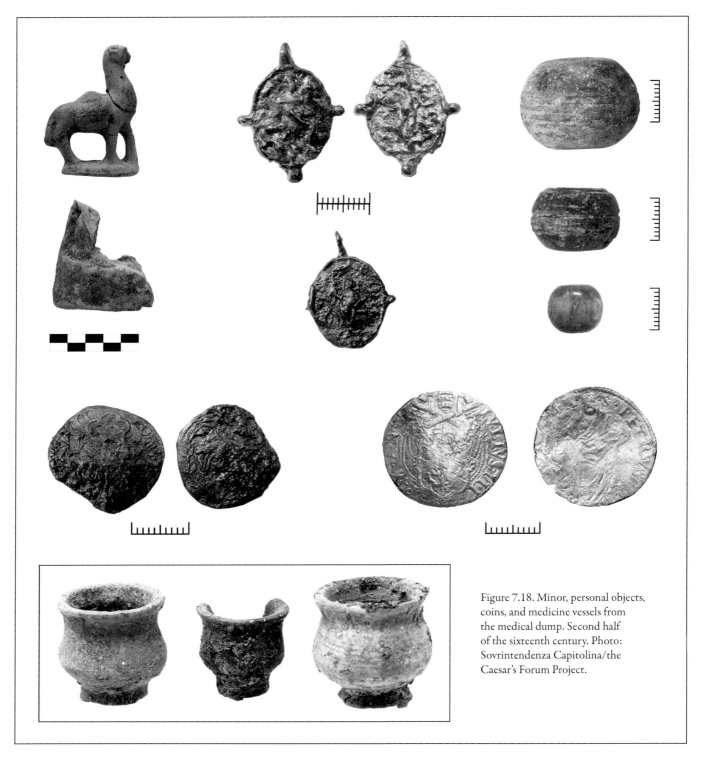

Figure 7.18. Minor, personal objects, coins, and medicine vessels from the medical dump. Second half of the sixteenth century. Photo: Sovrintendenza Capitolina/the Caesar's Forum Project.

ties between the latter part of the seventh century and the first half of the eighteenth century (Fig. 7.19). The ceramic fragments are composable into some 110 complete or semi-complete vessels, of which most are related to cooking and eating. In addition, large glass bottles for storing oil and wine, personal objects, and even a portable ceramic toilet came to light together with a large number of animal bones. An interesting find from the sewer are fragments from a Chinese porcelain plate (Fig. 7.20). The painted letters on the underside of the vessel relate to the reigns of Emperor Kangxi (1662–1722) or Yongzheng (1723–1735). Rich archaeological material from several other cisterns and sewers, of which the latest was excavated in March 2022, is currently undergoing study and

7. EXCAVATING THE FORUM IULIUM

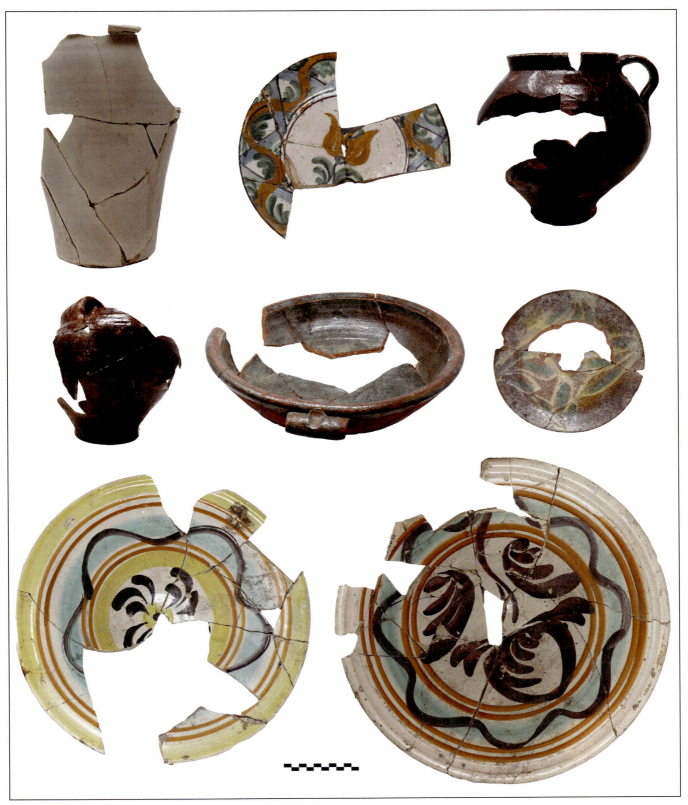

Figure 7.19. Vessels from the basin in Area B. Latter part of the seventeenth century and first half of the eighteenth century. Photo: Sovrintendenza Capitolina/the Caesar's Forum Project.

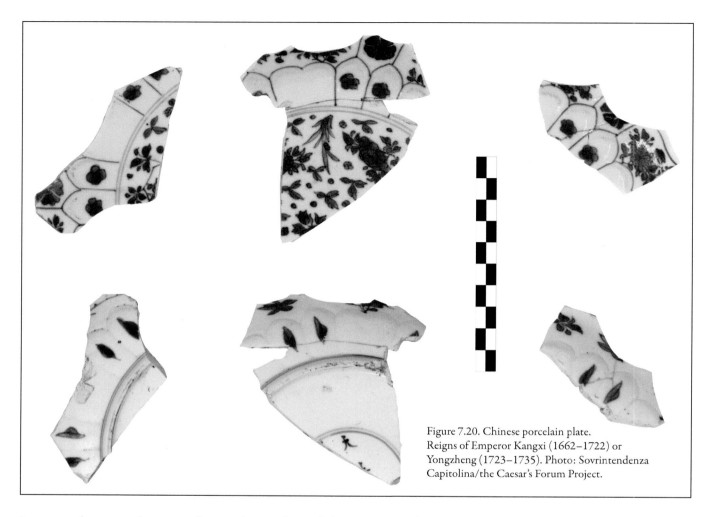

Figure 7.20. Chinese porcelain plate. Reigns of Emperor Kangxi (1662–1722) or Yongzheng (1723–1735). Photo: Sovrintendenza Capitolina/the Caesar's Forum Project.

is expected to contribute to a firm understanding of the activities in the Alessandrino buildings during the seventeenth and eighteenth centuries as well as the associated material culture.

Conclusion

The excavations conducted in 2019 and again in 2021 have shown that the buildings underwent massive reconstructions during the nineteenth century.[63] These reshaped the interior division of the buildings, existing steps to underlying basements were sealed off, while others were created. The buildings were furnished with modern sanitary installations such as water toilets and a new internal sewer system during this process. These activities erased much of the earlier evidence for room functions and daily life. The installation of modern sanitation in the buildings went hand in hand with developing a public waste management system. A circumstance that unfortunately deprives us of the hugely informative waste dumps that we know from earlier periods. However, a single exception was found in the remains of a brick-built cesspit, which had been partly destroyed probably on the occasion of the demolitions in 1932. A number of objects were found in the pit, which, when viewed together, showed that the pit accommodated waste from various rooms in the building: porcelain plates, drinking glasses, and spoons probably originated from a kitchen together with animal bones. Several shirt bottoms, small change coins, and minor pieces of jewellery could very well have originated from clothes washing, whereas medicine bottles, fragments from chandeliers, and porcelain figures show a broader spectrum of life in the building during the latter part of the nineteenth and early twentieth centuries.[64]

The Alessandrino Quarter, encompassing the houses in the area stretching from Piazza Venezia to

---

[63] For a detailed description of the rebuilding, see Jacobsen and others 2020; Corsetti and others 2022.

[64] Corsetti and others 2022.

the Colosseum, was demolished in 1931–1932, leaving space for the construction of the Via dell'Impero, today's Via dei Fori Imperiali. During the same years, extensive and hastily conducted excavations brought a vast part of the area of the Imperial fora to light, including a substantial part of Caesar's Forum itself.[65] The houses in the excavation area, which corresponds to the former plots occupied by Via Cremona 43 and 44, were demolished in September 1932, and the current excavations have given insights into the practical arrangements of the demolition works and uncovered remains belonging to the workers conducting the work.

While work continues in the spring and summer of 2022, we already have gained much new knowledge about central Rome across three millennia — the current excavations have even yielded information about the period when Caesar's Forum was laid out — a rare glimpse of a period not often intercepted in the area which the location is named after. What is more, the appearance of the eastern colonnade of the Forum of Caesar has established the topographical boundaries of the complex, and in effect, Caesar's Forum is now the first Imperial forum visible in its full extension. Although material studies and data processing of the excavation results are still ongoing, a comprehensive preliminary framework of the longue durée urban development in the area has already been established. In an overall perspective, the most invasive force in compromised structures and depositions from previous periods was the transformation of private space into public domain and the reverse. These asynchronous events brought a shift and far-reaching changes to the urban texture as they put a halt to the gradual architectural, functional, and cultural development of the area when the very purpose of this vast space was redefined. The demolition of private houses leading up to the construction of the Forum of Caesar and the demolition of — again — private houses prior to the construction of the Via dei Fori Imperiali were separated in time by two millennia but caused similar negative impacts on the preservation of archaeological remains from the centuries prior to both events. With respect to the 1932 demolitions, the excavations of some of the last standing remains of the Alessandrino Quarter have, for the first time, permitted a detailed description of the architectural, functional, and material-cultural development of the Alessandrino Quarter from its emergence during the second half of the sixteenth century AD until the early part of the twentieth century AD. As such these new results form a basis for contextualizing data from older and potential future excavations of remains from the modern phase in the forum areas at large. The 2007–2009 excavations on the Forum of Caesar permitted a partial outline of the transformation of domestic architecture in the area between the sixth century BC till the demolition of houses immediately prior to the construction of the forum. In the current state of excavation and data assessment, a similar chronological phase cannot be identified in the present excavation. Two competing explanations for this obliteration need to be balanced when addressing this void: the 2021 excavations in the *domus terrinee* area (Area C) revealed a direct transition in the archaeological stratigraphy from early medieval layers to Archaic layers, clearly showing that extensive earth and supposedly structure removals had taken place in the process of turning the area into fertile farmland. The stratigraphy in the *domus terrinee* area does not reveal whether this activity caused the removal of remains pertaining to the described phase or if these had already been cleared out when preparing the area for the construction of the Forum of Caesar. The assessment of the ceramic material from the *domus terrinee* area in particular and from the larger excavation Areas A and B provide us with some indications. The *domus terrinee* area has not produced any residual ceramics datable to the period, indicating that remains from the period had not been encountered where fields were laid out during the early medieval period. Except for a few fragments, this is mirrored in the pottery from excavation Areas A and B, contributing to a picture of general absence of evidence between the end of the Archaic period and the time of the construction of the forum. The upcoming 2022 excavations will provide a definitive answer to the question.

---

65   For an outline of the destruction of the Alessandrino Quarter, see Parisi Presicce 2009; Salsano 2003, 194; Racheli 1983, 91–92.

Works Cited

Ammerman, A. J. and D. Filippi. 2000. 'Nuove osservazioni sull'area a nord del Comizio', *Bullettino della Commissione archeologica*, 101: 27–38.

Ammerman, A. J. and N. Terrenato. 1996. 'Nuove osservazioni sul Colle Capitolino', *Bullettino della Commissione archeologica*, 97: 35–36.

Amici, C. M. and others. 2007. *Lo scavo didattico della zona retrostante la curia (foro di Cesare): campagne di scavo 1961–1970* (Rome: Bonsignori).

Antognoli, L. and E. Bianchi. 2009. 'La Cloaca Maxima dalla Suburra al Foro Romano', *Studi romani*, 57.1–4: 89–125.

Bernacchio, N. 2017. 'I Fori Imperiali nel Rinascimento e nell'età moderna', in N. Bernacchio and R. Meneghini (eds), *I Fori dopo i Fori: la vita quotidiana nell'area dei Fori imperiali dopo l'antichità* (Rome: Gangemi), pp. 31–48.

Bernacchio, N. and others. 2021. 'Lo scavo del tratto settentrionale di via Alessandrina (2016–2020): considerazioni preliminari', *Bullettino della Commissione archeologica*, 122: 342–52.

Bertoldi, T. and M. Ceci. 2013. 'Un contesto tardo-repubblicano dal Foro di Cesare', in M. Ceci (eds), *Contesti ceramici dai Fori Imperiali*, British Archaeological Reports, International Series, 2455 (Oxford: Archaeopress), pp. 45–59.

Boschetti, C. and others. 2022. 'Glass in Rome during the Transition from Late Antiquity to the Early Middle Ages: Materials from the Forum of Caesar', *Journal of Heritage Science*, 10.95: 1–14 <https://doi.org//10.1186/s404994-022-00729-y>.

—— 2023. 'Disease control and the disposal of infectious materials in Renaissance Rome: Excavations in the area of Caesar's Forum', *Antiquity*, 2023: 1–17 <https://doi.org/10.15184/aqy.2023.34>.

Brock, A. L. and others. 2021. 'On the Banks of the Tiber: Opportunity and Transformation in Early Rome', *Journal of Roman Studies*, 111: 1–30.

Carandini, A. 2003. *La nascita di Roma: dei, lari, eroi e uomini all'alba di una civiltà*, II (Turin: Einaudi).

Catalano, P. and others. 2021. 'Analisi contestuale di alimentazione e salute nel Lazio nella I età del Ferro (II periodo laziale ca. X–IX sec. a.C.)', in I. Damiani, A. Cazzella, and V. Copat (eds), *Preistoria del cibo: l'alimentazione nella preistoria e nella protostoria*, Studi di preistoria e protostoria, 6 (Florence: Istituto italiano di preistoria e protostoria), pp. 83–94.

Cazzella, A. 2001. 'Sviluppi verso l'urbanizzazione a Roma alla luce dei recenti scavi nel Giardino', *Bullettino della Commissione archeologica*, 102: 265–68.

Cazzella, A. and others. 2007. 'Testimonianze della media età del Bronzo sul Campidoglio', in *Atti della XL Riunione Scientifica: strategia di insediamento fra Lazio e Campania in età preistorica e protostorica* (Florence: Instituto italiano di preistoria e protostoria), pp. 803–14.

Cederna, A. 1979. *Mussolini urbanista: lo sventramento di Roma negli anni del consenso* (Rome: Laterza).

Coarelli, F. 1974. *Guida archeologica di Roma* (Milan: Mondadori).

——. 2014. *Rome and Environs: An Archaeological Guide* (Berkeley: University of California Press).

Corsetti, F. L. and others. 2020–2022. 'The Danish-Italian Excavations on Caesar's Forum 2021. Report', *Analecta Romana Instituti Danici*, 45: 267–80.

—— 2022. 'The Last Days of the Alessandrino District', *Journal of Contemporary Archaeology* <https://journal.equinoxpub.com/JCA/article/view/22264> [accessed 25 January 2023].

D'Acri, M. and M. Mogetta. 2020. 'The Regional Setting: Nonadult Burials from Contemporary Settlements in Latium Vetus', in M. Mogetta (ed.), *Elite Infant Burial Practices and Urbanization Processes at Gabii, Italy: The Area D Tombs and their Contents*, Journal of Roman Archaeology Supplementary Series, 108 (Portsmouth, RI: Journal of Roman Archaeology), pp. 125–40.

De Amici, A. R. 1993. 'I Pantani e la Suburra: forme della crescita edilizia a Roma tra XVI e XVII secolo', in M. Coppa (eds), *Inediti di storia dell'urbanistica* (Rome: Gangemi), pp. 101–45.

De Luca, I. 2001. 'La domus del Foro di Nerva: le fasi di vita (IX–X secolo)', in M. S. Arena and others (eds), *Roma: dall'antichità al Medioevo; archeologia e storia nel Museo nazionale romano, Crypta Balbi* (Milan: Electa), pp. 578–79.

De Luca, E. 2020. *L'area della Suburra in età moderna: genesi ed evoluzione dell'abitato* (Rome: Quasar).

De Luca, I. and M. Ricci. 2013. 'Le ceramiche dell'Ospedale dei Fornari', *Bollettino di archeologia on line*, 4: 163–91.

De Luca, I., M. Ricci, and M. Serlorenzi. 2012. 'Scavi Metro C Roma Madonna di Loreto: ceramiche dal "butto" di un ospedale tra '500 e '600', in *Atti del XLIV Convegno Internazionale della Ceramica 2011* (Albenga: Centro ligure per la storia della ceramica), pp. 239–48.

De Santis, A. 2001. 'Le sepolture di età protostorica a Roma', *Bullettino della Commissione archeologica*, 102: 269–80.

De Santis, A. and others. 2010. 'Le fasi di occupazione nell'area centrale di Roma in età protostorica: nuovi dati dagli scavi nel Foro di Cesare', *Scienze dell'antichità*, 16: 259–84.

De Santis, A., M. Fenelli, and L. Salvadei. 2009. 'Implicazioni culturali e sociali del trattamento funebre dei bambini nella protostoria laziale', in G. Bartoloni and G. M. Benedettini (eds), *Sepolti tra i Vivi: atti del convegno internazionale; evidenza ed interpretazione di contesti funerari in abitato*, Scienza dell'antichità, 14 (Rome: Quasar), pp. 725–41.

7. EXCAVATING THE FORUM IULIUM

De Santis, A. 2019. 'Ricchi corredi femminili: necropoli nell'area del Foro di Cesare. Museo Nazionale Romano, Palazzo Altemps', in I. Damiani and C. Parisi Presicce (eds), *La Roma dei Re: il racconto dell'archeologia* (Rome: Gangemi), pp. 401–04.

Delfino, A. 2010a. 'Le fasi arcaiche e alto-repubblicane nell'area del Foro di Cesare', *Scienze dell'antichità*, 16: 285–302.

—— 2010b. 'I riti del costruire nel Foro di Cesare', in H. Di Giuseppe and M. Serlorenzi (eds), *I riti del costruire nelle acque violate: atti del convegno internazionale, Roma, Palazzo Massimo 12–14 giugno 2008* (Rome: Scienze e lettere), pp. 167–81.

—— 2010c. 'Il primo Foro di Cesare', *Scienze dell'antichità*, 16: 335–47.

—— 2013. 'Contesti ceramici da due domus terrinee del Foro di Cesare', in M. Ceci (eds), *Contesti ceramici dai Fori Imperiali*, British Archaeological Reports, International Series, 2455 (Oxford: Archaeopress), pp. 129–38.

—— 2014. *Forum Iulium: l'area del Foro di Cesare alla luce delle campagne di scavo 2005–2008; le fasi arcaica, repubblicana e cesariano-augustea*, British Archaeological Reports, International Series, 2607 (Oxford: Archaeopress).

Di Giuseppe, H. 'Incendio e bonifica prima del Foro di Cesare. Il contributo della ceramica', *Scienze dell'antichità*, 16: 303–20.

Egelund, L. 2018. 'A Space for Caesar: The Heart of Rome and Urban Development', R. Raja and S. M. Sindbæk (eds), *Urban Network Evolutions: Towards a High-Definition Archaeology* (Aarhus: Aarhus University Press), pp. 45–50.

Fogagnolo, S. 2013. 'Contesti ceramici del XVII e del XVIII secolo nell'area dell'aula di culto del Foro della Pace', in M. Ceci (a cura di), *Contesti ceramici dai Fori Imperiali*, British Archaeological Reports, International Series (Oxford: Archaeopress), pp. 139–50.

Forsythe, G. 2005. *A Critical History of Early Rome: From Prehistory to the First Punic War* (Berkeley: University of California Press).

Franco, M. 2019. 'Il Gruppo 125 e gli altri corredi funerari con ceramiche importate e d'imitazione greca', in I. Damiani and C. Parisi Presicce (eds), *La Roma dei Re: il racconto dell'archeologia* (Rome: Gangemi), pp. 401–04.

Fulminante, F. 2018. 'Infancy and Urbanization in Central Italy during the Early Iron Age and Beyond', in E. Herring and E. O'Donoghue (eds), *The Archaeology of Death: Proceedings of the Seventh Conference of Italian Archaeology Held at the National University of Ireland, Galway, April 16–18, 2016*, Papers in Italian Archaeology, 7 (Oxford: Archaeopress), pp. 197–206.

Gabrielli, R. 2010. *Ceramica etrusco-corinzia del Museo archeologico di Tarquinia*, Archeologia, 155 (Rome: G. Bretschneider).

Galadini, F. and others. 2013. 'I terremoti del 484–508 e 847 d.C. nelle stratigrafie archeologiche tardoantiche e altomedievali dell'area romana', *Bollettino di archeologia on line*, 4: 139–62.

Hopkins, J. N. 2014. 'The Creation of the Forum and the Making of Monumental Rome', in E. C. Robinson (ed.), *Papers on Italian Urbanism in the First Millennium B.C.* (Portsmouth, RI: Journal of Roman Archaeology), pp. 29–61.

Jacobsen, J. K. and R. Raja. 2018. 'A High-Definition Approach to the Forum of Caesar in Rome: Urban Archaeology in a Living City', in R. Raja and S. M. Sindbæk (eds), *Urban Network Evolutions: Towards a High-Definition Archaeology* (Aarhus: Aarhus University Press), pp. 21–25.

Jacobsen, J. K. and others. 2019–2020. 'Excavating Caesar's Forum: Present Results of the Caesar's Forum Project', *Analecta Romana Instituti Danici*, 44: 239–45.

—— 2020. 'Practicing Urban Archaeology in a Modern City: The Alessandrino Quarter of Rome', *Journal of Field Archaeology*, 46: 36–51.

—— 2021. 'High-Definition Urban Narratives from Central Rome: Virtual Reconstructions of the Past and the New Caesar's Forum Excavations', *Journal of Urban Archaeology*, 3: 65–86.

—— 2022. 'Digging Caesar's Forum: Three Thousand Years of Daily Life in Rome', *Current World Archaeology*, 113: 32–39.

—— (forthcoming). *Foro Di Cesare*, II: *I materiali ceramici dallo scavo del 1998–2000*, Rome Studies, 2 (Turnhout: Brepols).

Lugli, F. and C. Rosa. 2001. 'Prime evidenze di opere di terrazzamento del Capitolium nell'età del Bronzo recente', *Bullettino della Commissione archeologica*, 102: 281–90.

Marra, F. and others. 2018. 'Rome in its Setting: Post-Glacial Aggradation History of the Tiber River Alluvial Deposits and Tectonic Origin of the Tiber Island', *PLoS ONE*, 13.3: e0194838 <https://doi.org/10.1371/journal.pone.0194838>.

Meneghini, R. 2000. 'L'origine di un quartiere altomedievale romano attraverso i recenti scavi del Foro di Traiano', in G. P. Brogiolo (ed.), *Congresso nazionale di archeologia medievale*, II: *Musei civici, Chiesa di Santa Giulia, Brescia 28 settembre-1 ottobre 2000* (Florence: All'insegna del giglio), pp. 55–59.

—— 2009. *I fori imperiali e i Mercati di Traiano: storia e descrizione dei monumenti alla luce degli studi e degli scavi recenti* (Rome: Libreria dello stato).

—— 2010. 'La trasformazione dello spazio architettonico del Foro di Cesare nella tarda antichità', *Scienze dell'antichità*, 16: 503–12.

—— 2015. *Die Kaiserforen Roms* (Darmstadt: Von Zabern).

—— 2016–2017. 'Fori imperiali e restauro. Gli interventi della sovrintendenza ai beni culturali di Roma capitale nell'ultimo decennio (2006–2017)', *Atti della Pontificia Accademia romana di archeologia*, 89: 429–62.

—— 2017. 'Roma. Fori Imperiali. "I pantani": le origini e il riscontro archeologico di un celebre toponimo medievale', *Archeologia medievale*, 44: 285–92.

Meneghini, R. and R. Santangeli Valenzani. 2010. *Scavi dei Fori Imperiali: Foro di Augusto (L'area centrale)*, Bullettino della Commissione archeologica comunale di Roma. Supplementi, 20 (Rome: L'Erma di Bretschneider).

Molinari, M. C. and E. Spagnoli. 1990. 'Il rinvenimento di Via Alessandrina', *Annali dell'Istituto italiano di numismatica*, 37: 135–64.

Modica, S. 2019. *Rituali e Lazio antico: deposizioni infantili e abitati* (Milan: CUEM).

Nizzo, V. 2011. '"Antenati bambini". Visibilità e invisibilità dell'infanzia nei sepolcreti dell'Italia tirrenica dalla prima età del Ferro all'Orientalizzante: dalla discriminazione funeraria alla costruzione dell'identità', in V. Nizzo (ed.), *Antropologia e archeologia a confronto: rappresentazioni e pratiche del sacro; atti dell'Incontro internazionale di studi* (Rome: Editorial Service System), pp. 51–93.

Palombi, D. 2016. *I Fori prima dei Fori: storia urbana dei quartieri di Roma antica cancellati per la realizzazione dei Fori Imperiali* (Monte Campatri: Espera).

Parisi Presicce, C. 2009. 'Scavi archeologici, sterri e demolizioni per l'apertura di via dell'Impero', in F. Betti and others (eds), *Via dell'Impero: nascita di una strada* (Rome: Palombi), pp. 13–18.

Paroli, L. 1990. 'Ceramica a vetrina pesante alto medievale (Forum Ware) e medievale (Sparse Glazed). Altre invetriate tardo-antiche e alto medievali', in L. Saguì and L. Paroli (eds), *Archeologia urbana a Roma: il progetto della Crypta Balbi*, V: *L'esedra della Crypta Balbi nel Medioevo (XI–XV secolo)* (Florence: All'Insegna del Giglio), pp. 314–56.

Pocino, W. 2008. 'L'Antiquario Francesco Martinetti e il Tesoro di via Alessandrina', *Strenna dei Romanisti*, 69: 531–44.

Racheli, A. M. 1983. 'L'urbanistica nella zona dei Fori Imperiali: piani e attuazioni (1873–1932)', in L. Barroero and others (eds), *Via dei Fori Imperiali – la zona archeologica di Roma: urbanistica, beni artistici e politica culturale* (Rome: Marsilio), pp. 61–163.

Raja, R. and J. Rüpke. 2021. 'Creating Memories in and of Urban Rome. The Forum Iulium', in T. A. Hass and R. Raja (eds), *Caesar's Past and Posterity's Caesar*, Rome Studies, 1 (Turnhout: Brepols), pp. 53–66.

Rathje, A. and I. van Kampen. 2001. 'The Distribution of Space and Materials in Domestic Architecture in Early Rome', in R. Brandt and L. Karlsson (eds), *From Huts to Houses: Transformations of Ancient Societies* (Stockholm: Åström), pp. 383–88.

Ricci, M. 2013. 'La ceramica d'impasto del Foro di Cesare', in M. Ricci (ed.), *Contesti ceramici dai Fori Imperiali*, British Archaeological Reports, International Series (Oxford: Archaeopress), pp. 11–24.

Ricco, S. 2002. 'Lo scavo dei Fori Imperiali', in S. Rizzo (ed.), *Roma città del Lazio* (Rome: De Luca Editori d'Arte), pp. 24–28.

Salsano, F. 2003. 'Conseguenze sociali degli sventramenti nella Roma fascista: le trasformazioni del tessuto urbano', *Rivista storica del Lazio*, 18: 173–200.

Santangeli Valenzani, R. 2001. 'I Fori Imperiali nel Medioevo', *Römische Mitteilungen*, 108: 269–83.

Sauer, N. 2018. 'The Archaic Period on the Forum of Caesar: The Urbanisation of Early Rome', in R. Raja and S. M. Sindbæk (eds), *Urban Network Evolutions: Towards a High-Definition Archaeology* (Aarhus: Aarhus University Press), pp. 39–44.

—— 2020–2022. 'Looking for Domestic Architecture in Archaic Rome', *Analecta Romana Instituti Danici*, 45: 7–41.

—— 2021a. 'The Forum of Caesar: A Historiographical Review', in T. A. Hass and R. Raja (eds), *Caesar's Past and Posterity's Caesar* (Turnhout: Brepols), pp. 213–41.

—— 2021b. 'Urbanism in Archaic Rome: The Archaeological Evidence', *Journal of Urban Archaeology*, 4: 33–41 <https://doi.org/10.1484/J.JUA.5.126596>.

Saxkjær, S. G. and G. P. Mittica. 2018. 'Caesar's Forum: Excavating Italian Iron Age', in R. Raja and S. M. Sindbæk (eds), *Urban Network Evolutions: Towards a High-Definition Archaeology* (Aarhus: Aarhus University Press), pp. 35–38.

Serlorenzi, M. 2010. 'Le testimonianze medievali nei cantieri di piazza Venezia', in R. Egidi, F. Filippi, and S. Martone (eds), *Archeologia e infrastrutture il tracciato fondamentale della linea C della metropolitana di Roma: prime indagini archeologiche* (Florence: Olschki), pp. 131–65.

Serlorenzi, M. and H. Di Giuseppe. 2009. 'La via Campana. Aspetti topografici e rituali', in V. Jolivet and others (eds), *Suburbium*, II: *Il suburbio di Roma della fine dell'età monarchica alla nascita del sistema delle ville (V–II secolo a.C.)* (Rome: École française de Rome), pp. 573–98.

Tabolli, J. 2018. *From Invisible to Visible: New Methods and Data for the Archaeology of Infant and Child Burials in Pre-Roman Italy and Beyond*, Studies in Mediterranean Archaeology, 149 (Uppsala: Åström).

Tortorici, E. 1991. *Argiletum: commercio, speculazione, edilizia e lotta politica dall'analisi topografica di un quartiere di Roma di età repubblicana* (Rome: L'Erma di Bretschneider).

—— 2012. 'Roma nell'età di Cesare. La politica urbanistica', in E. Tortorici (ed.), *Topografia antica*, II: *Tradizione, tecnologia e territorio* (Acireale: Bonanno), pp. 1–42.

8. The So-Called Aquinum Portrait of Julius Caesar: From its Discovery to Research Development

Giuseppe Ceraudo

Dipartimento di Beni Culturali, Università del Salento (giuseppe.ceraudo@unisalento.it)

After more than ten years from the start of the annual excavation campaigns (July 2009), the site of the Triumviral colony of Aquinum has now assumed greater importance in the Italian archaeological landscape.[1] The two buildings, the Roman theatre[2] and the monumental *thermae*,[3] which are gradually coming to light within the archaeological area in the territory of Castrocielo (FR), present a very peculiar architecture, adding to our knowledge of the Roman city and confirming its greatness, which has already been attested in literary sources.[4] All this has aroused interest and curiosity within the scientific community and among the general public. In fact, a series of relevant findings, such as precious marble floors, mosaics,[5] mosaic inscriptions,[6] four column shafts in *pavonazzetto* marble,[7] and a portrait attributed to Julius Caesar (the main subject of this article) have allowed the archaeological site in Aquinum to rise to national and international prominence — to the extent that it has been referred to as a 'lucky archaeological find' in the media.[8]

However, these discoveries are not just about luck, as they have been made by the extensive scientific research developed within the Ager Aquinas Project over the last two decades.[9]

This premise defines the history of the investigations conducted at Aquinum, which led to the discovery of the marble head in September 2018, known as the so-called 'Caesar of Aquinum'. This research project starts from a consolidated method, with field and laboratory activities pursuing a multidisciplinary approach and with an integrated and systematic use of non-invasive investigations (remote and proximal sensing), as part of an updated methodology of ancient topography.

Today, the area of the ancient city, gradually abandoned between the Late Imperial Age and the Early Middle Ages,[10] is occupied by a varied typology of houses: villas, cottages, and farmhouses.

Aerial images from the last century show how the whole area was occupied by fields planted with wheat, various olive groves, and vineyards, which have now almost completely disappeared (Fig. 8.1).[11] The eastern part, close to the edge of the ancient lakes, particularly in the central and southern sector, is characterized by intense residential urbanization, which made activities on the ground difficult. During the 1960s, the construction of the A1 Highway broke the topographical unity

---

[1] This article partly builds on Ceraudo 2020a, 249–74.

[2] Ceraudo 2020b, 125–37.

[3] Ceraudo 2019a; 2019b.

[4] Cicero and Strabo speak respectively of Aquinum as *frequens municipium* and μεγάλη πόλις (Cic., *Phil.* ii.105–06; Str. v.3.9). On the size and importance of Aquinum in the Imperial Age, see Ceraudo 2019a, 89–112; 2019b, 51–57.

[5] Inside some of the rooms in the spa building, mosaic floors have been identified with erotic/Nilotic scenes (Ceraudo and Vincenti 2015, 257–66) or with representations of exotic and fantastic animals (Ceraudo and Vincenti 2018, 461–70).

[6] On the mosaic inscriptions brought to light inside the two *frigidaria* in the baths, cf. Ceraudo, Molle, and Nonnis 2013, 101–09; 2019, 1–53.

[7] For the marble columns, see Fochetti 2020, 191–203.

[8] Caldarola 2018, 145–68; 2019, 260–66.

---

[9] On the project, see Ceraudo 2012, 94–103. The project, which aims to study the Roman city and its territory, is part of the research programmes run by the Laboratory of Ancient Topography and Photogrammetry of the Department of Cultural Heritage of the University of Salento in Lecce. These programmes have been launched in conjunction with the Superintendence of Archaeology, Fine Arts, and Landscape of the provinces of Frosinone and Latina, with the support of the Castrocielo municipality.

[10] For the phases of abandonment of the Roman city, see Corsi, Ceraudo, and Murro 2018, 185–89.

[11] The difference in the type of crops within the urban area of Aquinum can be clearly seen by comparing the historical aerial images of the 1940s, 1950s, and 1960s with those taken recently (see Fig. 8.1).

Figure 8.1. Aerial views of Aquinum in the Castrocielo area in comparison: A) zenith aerial photo from 1966; B) zenith aerial photo from 2016. Photos: LabTAF Photographic Archive.

8. THE SO-CALLED AQUINUM PORTRAIT OF JULIUS CAESAR

Figure 8.2. Perspective aerial view from 2022 of the southern sector of the Triumviral colony of Aquinum; the Autostrada del Sole has irreparably damaged the topographical unity of the ancient town, destroying a considerable part of the amphitheatre (on the right, obscured by trees). Photo: LabTAF Photographic Archive.

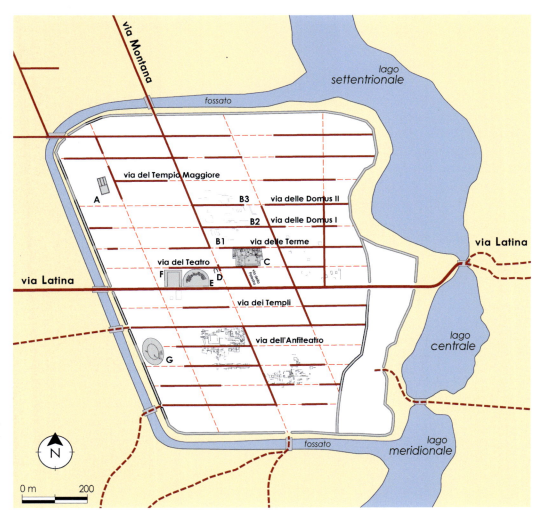

Figure 8.3. Schematic representation of the urban layout and the main monuments of Aquinum. Letter A indicates the major temple (so-called Capitolium); letters B1, B2, and B3 indicate the blocks north of the Via Latina affected by the presence of domus; C = central or Vecciane thermal baths; D = apsidal building (so-called 'Temple of Diana'); E = theatre; F = porticus duplex; G = amphitheatre. Figure: author

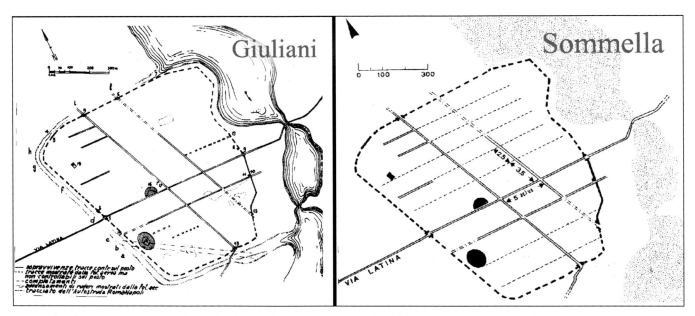

Figure 8.4. Schematic representation of the urban layout of Aquinum by Giuliani (1964) on the left and by Sommella (1988) on the right. Figure: author

of the Roman city, dividing the south-western corner of the city from the rest of the town and destroying a considerable part of the amphitheatre. More recently, the construction of a horse-riding centre and a motocross track has obliterated an enormous sector in the southern part of the urban area (Fig. 8.2).

The Roman city is mainly characterized by the path of the Via Latina, which crossed it in an east–west direction and divided it into two parts;[12] by the defensive system formed by the walls and a large moat on three sides;[13] by the regular but not orthogonal arrangement of the internal road axes, which generated blocks in the shape of a parallelogram; by the presence of monumental remains of some ancient buildings,[14] which have been inserted into an aerial photogrammetric map,[15] thus

Figure 8.5. View of the non-orthogonal intersection of two urban road axes identified at the modern Casale Pascale: in white limestone 'Via del Teatro', in dark lava stone 'Via della Palestra'. Photo: LabTAF Photographic Archive.

allowing some aspects of the Forma Urbis of Aquinum to be redesigned (Fig. 8.3).

Regarding this particular aspect, which has considerably helped to predict the presence of infrastructure and the typology of the pre-existing structures in the ancient urban area, we relied on the first reconstruction of the blocks put forward by Giuliani, made available thanks to aerial photographic imagery taken by the Royal Air Force in 1944 in a seminal article published in 1964

---

[12] About the Via Latina in the territory of Aquinum, see Ceraudo 2004c, 155–81; 2007b, 105–19.

[13] The fourth side, the eastern one, was naturally defended by the presence of three lakes, as evidenced by Grossi (Grossi 1907, 22), drained and reclaimed towards the end of the sixteenth century by Giacomo Boncompagni (duke of Sora from 1579 to 1612), after having bought the fiefs of Aquino from the d'Avalos in 1583 (Coldagelli 1969). It seems to confirm a stucco preserved in the Hall of the 18 Countries inside the Boncompagni-Viscogliosi Castle of Isola Liri, which reproduces Aquino and its territory around the end of the sixteenth century with the lakes having already dried up. For verified sources on the ancient lakes that characterized the Aquinas landscape, see Murro 2018.

[14] Ceraudo and Murro 2018a.

[15] Ceraudo 1999, 161–68.

8. THE SO-CALLED AQUINUM PORTRAIT OF JULIUS CAESAR

Figure 8.6. Vertical aerial view from 2017 of the central section of the urban map of Aquinum north of Via Latina (below in the photo); in the field at the centre of the frame — now owned by the Municipality of Castrocielo and where the annual excavation campaigns were started in 2009 — traces of two *decumani* and several domus are visible. Photo: LabTAF Photographic Archive.

(Fig. 8.4),[16] even though the lack of photogrammetric requirements of the photos did not allow us to define the exact dimensions of the blocks.

A recent survey has defined the precise dimensions of the largest blocks, equal to 212 by 140 m (6 by 4 *actus*).[17] A further internal division, with 70 m (2 *actus*) — tall blocks, was also identified. This reconstruction is based on the indisputable presence of fourteen *decumani* in addition to the *Decumanus Maximus* constituted by the Via Latina: seven identified to the north (of this) and six to the south (of it). The scheme presents a variation from the fourth *decumanus* north, up to the line of the walls, where the last two blocks are wider; these blocks measure 4.5 *actus*, divided in half (270 feet/*c*. 80 m) and are affected by the presence of a large temple,[18] the so-called 'Capitolium' (see Fig. 8.3).[19]

An attempt to reconstruct the width of the blocks is more complex due to the location, not always consistent,

---

[16] As part of local studies, the first interesting works were published in the early years of the last century. The first, by Eliseo Grossi (Grossi 1907), provides useful information on some elements of the Aquinas topography that have now disappeared, in particular walls and moats; the second, on the other hand, edited by Rocco Bonanni (1922), contains significant information and observations, especially about the centre in the Middle Ages. Later surveys in the region were carried out by Michelangelo Cagiano de Azevedo, whose precious and accurate work (Cagiano de Azevedo 1949) would be integrated into the monographic volume on Aquinum with the first schematic representation of the city plan. The events that involved Cassino and Montecassino during World War II also caused massive devastation in the whole surrounding area. Aquino and the surrounding area — partly due to the presence of a small airport — suffered violent bombings, documented by the photos of the Allied Forces of 1944 and 1945, which fortunately did not cause significant damage to the surviving monuments. Last but not least, the contribution by Fulvio Cairoli Giuliani was crucial to the most recent stages of research conducted at Aquinum (1964, 41–49).

[17] The new research corrects the measures proposed by Paolo Sommella (1988, 170–71, fig. 47).

[18] Ceraudo 2004b, 13–17.

[19] Murro 2010, 85–146.

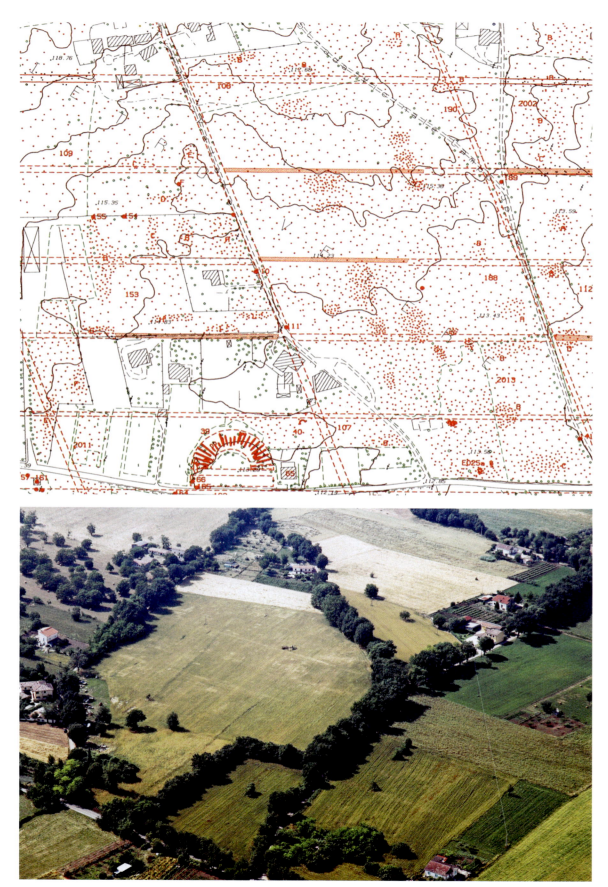

Figure 8.7. Extract from the Archaeological Map of Aquinum prior to the start of the excavation campaigns, with the area owned by the Municipality of Castrocielo as against the archaeological traces in a perspective aerial photo from 2005. LabTAF Photographic Archive.

8. THE SO-CALLED AQUINUM PORTRAIT OF JULIUS CAESAR

and the discontinuity and fragmentary nature of the cardines identified so far. In fact, only five have been recognized with certainty and almost all only on the basis of the surviving modern roads and field boundaries coinciding with ancient paths: the Cardo Maximus, the so-called 'Via Montana', which follows Via Civita Vetere in the northern part and Via Saudoni (contrada San Pietro Vetere) in the southern part; the eastern cardo, identified on the basis of the survival of Via Campo Spinello and the western cardo, reconstructed thanks to a trace in aerial images in a field to the east of the so-called 'Capitolium'.[20]

These elements seem to confirm the constant width of six *actus* for the blocks adjacent to the Cardo Maximus. In this reconstruction, there are some irregularities, which do not always seem to fit within this module. These are to be recognized in the line of the walls on the western side, where Via Santa Maria Maddalena still runs, in some cadastral parcels with the same orientation as the cardines, and in 'Via della Palestra' (Fig. 8.5), the only ancient road with a north-west/south-east orientation excavated to date, at the main entrance on the south side of the *palaestra* of the Vecciane thermal baths. This data suggests a much more complex system than the one reconstructed so far, and only by carrying on with the research activity will we be able to define its structure definitively.

In addition to the reading and image interpretation of a considerable number of aerial photos (already presented in various articles on Aquinum),[21] a specific aerial reconnaissance programme of the territory was launched in 2005, with a complete work of photographic documentation gathered at low altitude and with oblique views along the whole area of the ancient cities. Among the aerial images shot, some of these made it possible to shed light on a sector currently owned by the Municipality of Castrocielo in the centre of the ancient city and near the intersection of the two main roads,[22]

where recent archaeological excavations are concentrated (Fig. 8.6). The favourable combination of several factors (the agricultural harvesting of the fields and the choice of the best period for the aero-photographic reading of the traces) have made it possible to reconstruct the road network of a new large sector of the ancient city.

Prior to these aerial shots, the reconnaissance had identified areas with a high concentration of ancient material; aerial photographs have shown that these areas included the remains of isolated buildings aligned along some urban road axes ('Via delle Domus I' and 'Via delle Domus II') (Fig. 8.7). The presence of several residential complexes (*domus*) within three residential blocks (Fig. 8.3, B1-B2-B3) could therefore be hypothesized.

In the same aerial photos, the identification of the traces of four *decumani* north of the Via Latina (Fig. 8.8) at a regular distance of two *actus*, allowed further confirmation of the correct reconstruction of the urban layout scheme. However, it also raised some questions about the absence of archaeological traces in the ground (specifically in the southern sector) in which the investigations were concentrated.

In 2008, an aerotopographic, geophysical, and aerial reconnaissance, as well as field surveys conducted in the central area of the ancient Aquinum, explored a sector that had never returned valuable elements for the reconstruction of the urban layout of the city. With the start of the excavation campaigns in 2009, the first two topographical tests were carried out near the two *decumani* reconstructed north of the Via Latina (Fig. 8.9) but not found in the aerial photos. At the end of the first excavation campaigns, the discovery — at the hypothesized locations — of two roads paved with white limestone made it possible to demonstrate the reconstruction of the layout of the blocks and to understand that all the traces of the road axes so far identified on the aerial images were attributable only to the routes of *glareate* routes (see Figs 8.1, 8.5, 8.10–8.11); the cobbled streets are not clearly visible, though they have been detected only in some cases, above all thanks to the geophysical surveys carried out in various sectors of the city.[23]

---

[20] Ceraudo 2004, 17, fig. 5.

[21] In all these years, after the careful work done on historical aerial photos from the zeniths, the amount of data also recovered from perspective aerial images is considerable: in addition to the oblique photos taken by French colleagues at the beginning of the 1980s, and kindly made available by Gérard Chouquer, aerial surveys were made in collaboration with the Helicopter Operators Unit of the Rome Fire Brigade; cf. Ceraudo 2001, 161–75; 2003, 178–84; 2004b, 18–23.

[22] In 2001, the Municipality of Castrocielo inherited some buildings in San Pietro Vetere, in the centre of the Roman city and abutting (?) the Via Latina, with almost 6 ha of land and with an old

farmhouse (now restored and transformed into the Met@teca; see Ceraudo and others 2018a, 6–9). In 2012, the first plot of land was enlarged by acquiring land east of the archaeological area. Finally, in 2017, more land was purchased adjacent to the initial lot, near the theatre and the so-called 'apsidal building'. Today, the land owned by the municipality north of the Via Latina and the land bordering it constitute the Archaeological Area of Aquinum and have reached a total extent of about eight hectares.

[23] Ceraudo, Piro, and Zamuner 2010, 96–100; Piro, Ceraudo,

Figure 8.8. Oblique aerial view from 2005 with the traces of four *decumani* north of the Via Latina. Photo: LabTAF Photographic Archive.

Figure 8.9. Oblique aerial view from 2012 of the north of the field owned by the Municipality of Castrocielo with the two excavations open in correspondence with the points where the presence of two *decumani* had been assumed. Photo: LabTAF Photographic Archive.

In the block between the two excavated roads, conventionally named 'Via del Teatro' and 'Via delle Terme' (see Fig. 8.3.C), the excavations have identified a huge public spa building (Fig. 8.11): the Central or Vecciane Thermal Baths, from the name of the magistrate who promoted its construction.[24] The structures are arranged according to the double east–west and north-west/south-east orientation, like all the urban roads in Aquinum.[25]

---

and Zamuner 2011, 127–38; Piro and others 2012; Ceraudo and others 2018b, 1–14.

[24] Ceraudo, Molle, and Nonnis 2019.
[25] Ceraudo 1999, 161–68.

Figure 8.10. Aerial zenith view from 2018 of the access from 'Via delle Terme' to the women's sector of the Terme Vecciane: the junction of the paved road with the *glareata* is clearly visible at the entrance to the spa building. Photo: LabTAF Photographic Archive.

Figure 8.11. Perspective aerial view from 2018 of the Balneum of M. Veccius placed inside the block between the two road axes brought to light at the end of the tenth excavation campaign; the arrows indicate the points where the paved section ends and the *glareata* section begins. Photo: LabTAF Photographic Archive.

Figure 8.12. Perspective aerial view from 2018 of the theatre and the continuation towards the west of 'Via del Teatro'. Photo: LabTAF Photographic Archive.

Figure 8.13. The (partially disturbed) intersection of 'Via del Teatro' and Cardo Maximus. At the intersection, continuing towards the west, you can see how the road, tangential to the apse of the so-called 'Temple of Diana', changes material (and colour) depending on the different type of paving stones used. Photo: LabTAF Photographic Archive.

8. THE SO-CALLED AQUINUM PORTRAIT OF JULIUS CAESAR

Figure 8.14. Zenith aerial view from 2015 of a sector to the west of the theatre (some of the walls are visible in the lower right part of the frame) and the traces of a structure identified on private land to the left of the vineyard. Photo: LabTAF Photographic Archive.

Figure 8.15. Detail of Fig. 8.14 in which two clear linear traces can be seen at an angle and parallel to each other. The emphasis on this image also highlighted the presence of possible central pillars equidistant from the walls and placed at a regular distance between them (elaborated by Giovanni Murro). Photo: LabTAF Photographic Archive.

Figure 8.16. Zenith aerial view from 2016 of the central sector of the city north of the Via Latina with the theatre, the so-called 'apsidal building' and the Vecciane Baths: in A the area where the new excavation has been opened. Photo: LabTAF Photographic Archive.

In addition to the spa, almost completely excavated,[26] investigations were also possible around and near other monuments still visible but rarely studied. Recent tests carried out in the area of the theatre (Fig. 8.3.E) have made it possible to identify part of the stone elements of an annular corridor and the external pillars (Fig. 8.12).[27]

While investigations carried out at the so-called 'Temple of Diana' (Fig. 8.3.D),[28] an imposing apsidal building with the same orientation as the urban cardines, have promptly confirmed the presence of two fundamental road axes already hypothesized in the reconstruction of the road network: the one close to the eastern side, the Cardo Maximus ('Via Montana'), and the one in proximity to the apse and corresponding to 'Via del Teatro' (Fig. 8.13).

The research activities at Aquinum have continuously evolved in recent years, following the aerial survey approach, through the use of new technologies: the use of drones was added to the information derived from the study of traditional aerial photos (historical and recent, vertical and oblique).

The UAV sector is forging ahead thanks to the ever-increasing use of reliable and cost-effective drones in archaeology.[29] Thanks to drones, archaeological documentation has greatly evolved through multiple application areas such as, for example, aerial photogrammetric survey and the topography of archaeological areas, surveys of monuments and excavations, mapping and monitoring of large portions of the territory; a flexible tool that lends itself to a wide range of uses for the documentation, conservation, prevention, and protection of archaeological landscape. Last but not least, in my opinion, the most interesting aspect is the enormous potential these tools have to improve our knowledge of the territory.

---

[26] Ceraudo 2019a, 89–112; 2019b.

[27] Ceraudo 2020b, 125–37.

[28] Murro, Vitale, and Tulumello 2018, 111–29.

[29] Ceraudo, Guacci, and Merico 2017, 29–38.

Figure 8.17. The discovery of the three marble heads from the southern *crepidoma* of 'Via del Teatro', the upper one attributed to Julius Caesar. Photos: author

Figure 8.18. The portrait head attributed to Julius Caesar.

In addition to the advantages in terms of cost-effectiveness, repeatability, and autonomy of operations, the use of remote sensing with drones[30] has provided us with a formidable research opportunity for Aquinum, through constant monitoring of large portions of the ancient town,[31] strategic areas, and areas of specific interest, with the aim of acquiring data through the identification of new archaeological traces and by exploiting the advantageous possibility of replicating flights at different times of the year with the seasonal harvesting of the fields or at different times of the day to take advantage of the best lighting conditions.[32] The excavation of the last monumental complex discovered — a porticus duplex west of the theatre (Fig. 8.3.F) where the marble portrait attributed to Julius Caesar originates from — is the result of the combination of tradition and innovation.

In June 2015, a field was documented with a fixed wing UAV about 50 m west of the theatre. Here, a series of traces on the ground were able to be identified, which led to the start of the investigation in this sector (Fig. 8.14).

In addition to the trace of the first *decumanus* north of the Via Latina, the continuation of 'Via del Teatro', the paved road that runs behind the so-called 'Temple of Diana' and the theatre, and other visible traces (Fig. 8.15), the field also features two clearly perceptible linear traces running parallel to each other, in a north–south direction for about 40 m, with an angle straight to the east for another 15 m. Selective filtering and image enhancement[33] have highlighted the north-western corner of a large structure, with central pillars equidistant from the walls, directing the interpretation towards a large arcade complex, tentatively identified as a duplex porticus.

In September 2018, a new excavation sector was opened (Fig. 8.16). The choice to intervene at this point arose precisely from the observation of the anomalies detected.[34] In fact, the investigations began with the aim of intercepting

---

[30] With the use of multirotor and fixed-wing UAVs, crossing data with geophysical prospecting and experimenting with new image processing techniques for aerial photographs.

[31] Ferrari, Guacci, and Merico 2015, 66–68; Guacci and Merico 2021, 171–74.

[32] Flight planning and aerial image acquisition require an extremely short turnaround time, allowing for adequate photogrammetric coverage of areas of several hectares in a few minutes. Ease of use enables numerous flights, on-the-spot data verification and retakes. The possibility of replicating flights is essential for a more complete coverage of the archaeological context with numerous high-quality images taken under different conditions and with different exposures.

[33] Murro 2015, 69–81.

[34] In 2017, the municipality finally acquired the plot of land with the theatre hence the need to start the procedures to enclose the area in a stable form, as was previously the case with the land on which the Vecciane Baths stand.

Figure 8.19. The north-eastern corner of the porticus duplex with reticulated and cementitious masonry, the central pillars and the limestone channel that was meant to delimit the internal open space. Photo: LabTAF Photographic Archive.

the paved road (the extension towards the west of 'Via del Teatro') and of verifying the hypothetical continuation of the arcaded structure with the possible presence of the north-eastern corner in an effort to better understand the urban layout of this area of the Roman city.

The excavation has identified the *crepidoma* in blocks of local travertine and the white limestone paving of 'Via del Teatro'. At the edge of the paved road, from the southern *crepidoma*, three marble heads unexpectedly emerged from the ground (Fig. 8.17). The first fragmentary head belongs to a bearded male figure, probably relating to Hercules or to a boxer; the second head relates to a male portrait with his head covered (*velato capite*); the third head represents the most important find because of its high level of stylistic quality. This is a perfectly preserved male portrait of a mature man, slightly larger than life-size. The attribution is uncertain, but many somatic elements have led us to believe that the portrayed character could have been Julius Caesar (Fig. 8.18).[35] This hypothesis has stirred great media interest.

The following year, other fortunate discoveries were made. During the 2019 campaign, about 10 m west of the point where the head of Caesar had been identified, part of another marble head with the triumphal crown of Emperor Augustus was also found. Five medium-sized marble fragments were found, matching each other and pertaining to part of the head which is larger than life-size; once reassembled, these made it possible to reconstruct the upper part of the head and the entire left side including the ear. This find is attributable to a portrait of Octavian Augustus.

The portrait represented the first emperor in the so-called 'Prima Porta type', created after the attribution of the title of Augustus in 27 BC. The size and the quality of the crown and hair indicate an official portrait placed in a particularly prominent location in the city. The Augustus of Aquinum stands out for the presence of the laurel crown on the head — quite rare in representations

---

[35] For a detailed description of the head/portrait of the so-

called 'Caesar of Aquinum', see the article in this volume by Giovanni Murro, who coordinated all the excavation and documentation activities of the porticus.

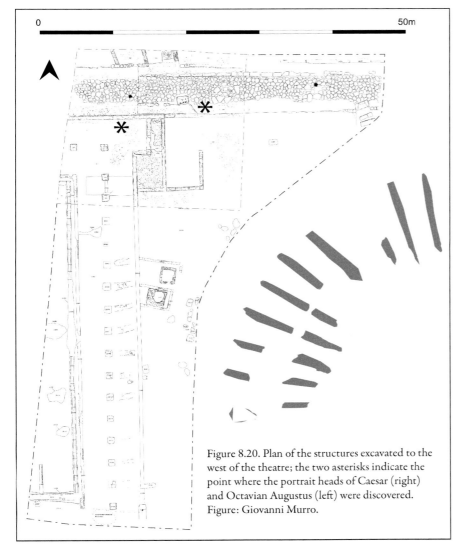

Figure 8.20. Plan of the structures excavated to the west of the theatre; the two asterisks indicate the point where the portrait heads of Caesar (right) and Octavian Augustus (left) were discovered. Figure: Giovanni Murro.

of the first emperor — as the emperor was most often portrayed wearing his civic crown (oak leaves) instead.[36]

The most important data that emerged from the excavations was certainly the effectiveness of the research method used at Aquinum. In fact, in the southern sector, near the road, the most important discovery was made, relating to the city's topography. Here, an angular part of the structure hypothesized through the analysis of aerial images was brought to light: a porticus duplex with cementitious walls and walls in *opus reticulatum* with *cubilia* in local travertine, the central row of the pillars of the colonnade, and the remains of a channel in limestone for the disposal of rainwater coming from the roof of the porticus (Fig. 8.19).[37]

The excavation data, building technique, architectural decoration,[38] and some stamps on the roof tiles of the porticus allow us to date the structure to the Augustan Age, in the decades between the first century BC and the first century AD (Fig. 8.20).[39]

---

[36] For the sake of comparison, albeit with some doubts about its authenticity, a specimen in the National Archaeological Museum of Florence, see Romualdi 1987, 65–67, cat. 14, pl. 55–57; Boschung 1993, cat. 98, pl. 105, 225, 3. An article signed by his colleague E. Polito entitled 'Una testa colossale di Augusto laureato da Aquinum' is currently being prepared.

[37] In addition to the walls, the excavation made it possible to highlight two pillars relating to the northern arm and sixteen of the eastern arm (with a distance between pillar and pillar of approximately 2.90–3.00 m). The quadrangular bases had to be covered with small coloured marble slabs (numerous strips of ancient red marble and *pavonazzetto* marble were found) and supported columns made of masonry with bricks shaped like one-fourth of a circular arc, in turn covered with white stucco and fluted, as evidenced by the remains exposed. Along the entire band of pillars on the eastern side, connected to the bases of the pillars, the collapsed remains of the colonnade are visible for an approximate height of the columns of about 3.20 m; to this the height of the capitals (about 0.60 m), roughly cut in local travertine, also stuccoed and probably attributable to the Corinthian order must be added, as evidenced by two specimens found inside the porticoed space.

[38] Several fragments of sima slabs have been recovered, including an intact specimen characterized by a lion protome drip and *anthèmion* decoration with a sequence of palmettes in relief; this presents residues of red and white on the surface, remains of the polychrome decoration in the exposed parts of the artefact. These slabs refer to the Roman-Lazio and Campania cultural environment and must have constituted the fictile architectural decoration of the porticus, similar terracottas are widely documented in Lazio and Campania contexts of the Late Republican Age (Pensabene 1999, 7–11, 19–33; Rescigno 1999, 268–78, 287–90) and their use, used for the cladding of wooden entablatures, is attested both in public buildings, especially sacred ones, as well as in private buildings. Even if the terracottas coming from the porticus of Aquinum seem more recent and can be dated to the first century BC, it is possible to refer to the Late Republican terracottas that belonged to the temple in summa *cavea* of the Pietravairano theatre, for which research into the origin of the matrices in a Sidician environment was put forward; for the temple/theatre of Pietravairano (Caserta) cf. Tagliamonte and others 2021, 191–212, in particular for the architectural decoration pp. 199–201 signed by D. Panariti.

[39] Five brick stamps with the name of a *T(itus) Umbrius* (or

Giuseppe Ceraudo

Figure 8.21. Perspective aerial view from 2018 of the central sector of the city along the Via Latina with the apsidal building, the theatre, and the corner of the porticus duplex: the field in which structures of a large building on the continuation of the arcaded building is indicated by the letter A. Photo: LabTAF Photographic Archive.

Figure 8.22. The field south of the Via Latina (top in the photo). The emphasis on this image has highlighted the presence of buried structures, probably including a large temple, which seem to have the same orientations and alignments as the newly discovered porticus duplex. Photo: LabTAF Photographic Archive, elaborated by Giovanni Murro.

8. THE SO-CALLED AQUINUM PORTRAIT OF JULIUS CAESAR

The precise comparison between photointerpretation and excavation data has been significant for continuing the research. The exposed structures are part of the north-east corner and the eastern side of the porticoed building identified thanks to the aerial images and traces found in the opposite corner;[40] the excavation, therefore, allowed a specific confirmation thanks to the exact correspondence of different measurements within a logic of symmetry and modularity of the structure. At the moment, the attribution of the arcade complex is not certain yet. The proximity to the theatre and the central position in the urban layout of the city allow us to make interesting hypotheses. It is a public building with a large open space of about 40 m on each side: a square enclosure, defined on three sides by the monumental porticus duplex,[41] rebuilt on the basis of the visible remains and comparisons with the canonical typology of the porticus extensively treated by Vitruvius.[42] The building had to be large, facing the Via Latina, which it overlooked, and from which one had to enter (see Fig. 8.3). For the moment we do not know if the central area was free or there were one or more buildings inside. If so, they certainly must have been civil or religious buildings with majestic architecture that could use the porticus duplex as a scenic backdrop. Inside this monumental complex, the four marble heads recovered during the excavations of 2018 and 2019 could have been located. The discovery of the portrait of Augustus and the one attributed to Caesar (or maybe a local magistrate?)[43] could advance the hypothesis of a sacral function of the porticoed space in which the statues were placed.[44] This is an interesting element borrowed from the eastern Hellenistic world, typical of large Asian complexes, which had already been introduced to Rome according to a model widely spread across the Roman world starting from the second century BC and also found in an Italic environment, such as Minturnae.[45]

The stratigraphic sequence of excavation indicates the chronological period of operation of the structure: from its construction in the Augustan Age to its abandonment which probably occurred during the fifth century, according to the materials recovered in the excavation.

The presence of rubble, fragments of stucco, and numerous fragments of roof tiles in the collapsed layers that came into contact with the floor levels would seem to suggest first abandonment and then a slow decay of the building, which must have been followed by the stripping of the decorative apparatus.

Throughout this central part of the ancient city, in proximity to the Via Latina, there are a series of monuments that occupy an entire block (2 *actus*) in height and are located in a focal point in the centre of the urban area; from the porticus, towards the east, there are other large spaces reserved for other buildings of a public, civil, and religious nature, such as the theatre[46] and the so-called 'apsidal building'.[47] Also south of the *Decumanus Maximus*, in the block facing the theatre and the porticus duplex, we can place other notable public buildings, identified through the analysis of aerial images and geophysical prospects (Figs 8.21–8.22): the most interesting of which, all within a large rectangular space (in turn defined by arcades, of about 25 by 40 m), is what can be recognized as a large temple from its planimetric articulation. This reconstruction can support the hypothesis, already advanced a few years ago, regarding the location of a temple in this sector and near the forum area.[48]

Umbricius) have been identified on some fragments of tiles, probably from the original batch of the roof covering: *T. Umbrians* (---?); cf. Molle 2020, 59–60. The dating of this type of stamp at the end of the first century BC, however, characterized by an onomastic formula without surname, would confirm the dating suggested for the construction of the porticus, which (as mentioned) could be traced back to the Augustan Age.

[40] Murro 2015, 69–81.

[41] Covered passage with double aisle (overall 7.50 m wide) with a central row of columns.

[42] Vitr., *De arch.* v.9.4; v.11.1–2; v.1.1.

[43] See Giovanni Murro (in this volume).

[44] From Appian, we know that Augustus, as early as in 36 BC (after the victory over Sextus Pompeius in Naulochos) was worshipped in Italy, see La Rocca 2011, 199, and that a portrait statue of the emperor inside a public building could symbolically represent the loyalty of the city towards the prince, which should certainly not be surprising. It is therefore not unlikely that the statue of Augustus (with other statues of divinities and illustrious personalities, including local ones) could have been placed inside a building (Augusteo?) in Aquinum, which was specially intended for the cult of the emperor.

---

[45] For example, that of Minturnae in which, in the period following the fire of 191 BC, in a central position, around the Capitolium, a double phi-portico was built towards the Via Appia, see Johnson 1935, 44–51; for an updated plan, see Bankel 2015, 13–25.

[46] The theatre was tangential to the eastern side of the porticus with which it had to be connected, as well as to a lateral passage — near the two buildings close to the Via Latina — as suggested by a large element of limestone in the doorstep.

[47] Perhaps the remains of a temple, for which a certain functional attribution is still lacking. For a preliminary analysis of the building, see Murro, Vitale, and Tulumello 2018, 111–29, in particular pp. 111–14, which highlight the hypothesis of a building with administrative functions, such as a curia or a religious building (*aedes Augusti*) probably connected to the basilica.

[48] Ceraudo 2007a, 42–43.

The sequence of buildings described so far, located north and south of the Via Latina, has characterized this sector of the city and constituted an important element in the urban and monumental landscape of the late first century BC: this well-structured layout appears in fact as an important witness to the cultural and architectural vivacity of the time, in keeping with the role that Aquinum had assumed by now in the Augustan Age, the most important city on the Via Latina between Rome and Capua. Therefore, it is not a question of 'random coincidences': it is the increasingly in-depth topographical knowledge of the ancient city that has enabled the achievement of extraordinary results, a natural consequence of the validity of the method. Precisely because of this, within a structured system and with a multidisciplinary approach applied in a systematic way, the numerous recent discoveries have given great visibility to the archaeological area of Aquinum in the territory of Castrocielo thanks to its lucky finds.

Works Cited

Bankel, H. 2015. 'La pianta complessiva di Minturnae e i due templi nel c.d. Foro Repubblicano. Un rapporto preliminare', in G. R. Bellini and H. von Hesberg (eds), *Minturnae: nuovi contributi alla conoscenza della Forma Urbis* (Rome: Quasar), pp. 13–25.

Bonanni, R. 1922. *Ricerche per la storia di Aquino* (Alatri: Isola).

Boschung, D. 1993. *Die Bildnisse des Augustus*, Das römische Herrscherbild, 1.2 (Berlin: Mann).

Cagiano de Azevedo, M. 1949. *Aquinum (Aquino): Regio I; Latium et Campania*, Italia romana: municipi e colonie, 9 (Rome: Istituto di studi romani).

Caldarola, G. 2018. 'Incrementare la conoscenza di un sito archeologico: dall'online all'offline: il caso di Aquinum', in A. Falcone and A. D'Eredità (eds), *Archeosocial: l'archeologia riscrive il web; esperienze, strategie e buone pratiche* (Mozzecane: Dielle), pp. 145–68.

—— 2019. 'Communication on an Archaeological Excavation in Progress: Aquinum Site', in E. Proietti (ed.), *Developing Effective Communication Skills in Archaeology* (Pennsylvania: IGI Global), pp. 260–66 (259–85).

Ceraudo, G. 1999. 'Il contributo dell'aerofotogrammetria per la ricostruzione dell'impianto urbano di Aquinum', in M. T. Onarati (ed.), *Terra dei Volsci: annali del Museo archeologico di Frosinone* (Frosinone: Museo archeologico di Frosinone), pp. 161–68.

—— 2001. 'Nuovi dati sulla topografia di Aquinum attraverso la fotointerpretazione archeologica e la ricognizione diretta', *Daidalos*, 3: 161–75.

—— 2003. 'Aquinum', in M. Guaitoli (ed.), *Lo sguardo di Icaro: le collezioni dell'Aerofototeca nazionale per la conoscenza del territorio* (Rome: Campisano), pp. 178–84.

—— 2004a. *Ager Aquinas: aerotopografia archeologica lungo la valle dell'antico Liris* (Marina di Minturno: Caramanica).

—— 2004b. 'Aquinum: la città romana', in G. Ceraudo (ed.), *Ager Aquinas: aerotopografia archeologica lungo la valle dell'antico Liris* (Marina di Minturno: Caramanica), pp. 13–23.

—— 2004c. 'La via Latina tra Fabrateria Nova e Casinum: precisazioni topografiche e nuovi spunti metodologici', in G. Ceraudo (ed.), *Archeologia aerea: studi di aerotopografia archeologica*, I (Rome: Libreria dello stato), 155–81.

—— 2007a. 'Progetto Ager Aquinas: 10 anni di ricerche: risultati e prospettive', in G. Ceraudo and A. Nicosia (eds), *Spigolature Aquinati: studi storico-archeologici su Aquino e il suo territorio* (Aquino: Museo della Città), pp. 39–48.

—— 2007b. 'Miliari della via Latina nel territorio di Aquino', in G. Ceraudo and A. Nicosia (eds), *Spigolature Aquinati: studi storico-archeologici su Aquino e il suo territorio* (Aquino: Museo della Città), pp. 105–19.

—— 2012. 'Progetto "Ager Aquinas": Indagini aerotopografiche finalizzate allo studio della Città Romana di Aquinum (Lazio, Italia)', in F. Vermeulen and others (eds), *Urban Landscape Survey in Italy and the Mediterranean* (Oxford: Oxbow), pp. 94–103.

—— 2019a. 'Il balneum di Marcus Veccius ad Aquinum. Considerazioni sull'edificio termale e sulle sue potenzialità ricettive', *Atlante tematico di topografia antica*, 29: 89–112.

—— 2019b. *Le Terme Centrali o Vecciane di Aquinum* (Foggia: Claudio Grenzi).

—— 2020a. 'Considerazioni topografiche a margine della scoperta del cosiddetto Cesare di Aquinum: la fortuna è nel metodo', *Rendiconti della Pontificia Accademia di Archeologia*, 91: 249–74.

—— 2020b. 'Gli edifici da spettacolo di Aquinum tra distruzione, ricerca e valorizzazione', *Atlante tematico di topografia antica*, 30: 125–37.

Ceraudo, G. and others. 2018a. 'Dallo scavo All'esperienza immersiva: il progetto Metateca nell'area archeologica di Aquinum', *Archeomatica*, 2: 6–9.

—— 2018b. 'Geoprospecting Survey in the Archaeological Site of Aquinum (Lazio, Central Italy)', *Surveys in Geophysics*, 39: 1–14.

Ceraudo, G., P. Guacci, and A. Merico. 2017. 'The Use of UAV Technology in Topographical Research: Some Case Studies from Central and Southern Italy', *SCIRES-IT*, 7.1: 29–38.

Ceraudo, G., C. Molle, and D. Nonnis. 2013. 'L'iscrizione musiva delle Terme Centrali di Aquinum', *Orizzonti: Rassegna di archeologia*, 14: 101–09.

—— 2019. 'L'iscrizione musiva di M. Veccius M. f. nelle terme centrali di Aquinum', *Rendiconti della Pontificia Accademia di Archeologia*, 40: 1–53.

Ceraudo, G. and G. Murro. 2018a. *Aquinum: guida ai monumenti e all'area archeologica* (Foggia: Grenzi).

—— 2018b. 'Le terme centrali di Aquinum: primi dati sul sistema di gestione dell'acqua', in M. Buora and S. Magnani (eds), *I sistemi di smaltimento delle acque nel mondo antico: atti del convegno, Aquileia, 6–8 aprile 2017* (Trieste: Editreg), pp. 567–86.

Ceraudo, G., S. Piro, and D. Zamuner. 2010. 'Integrated GPR and Archaeological Investigations to Study the Site of Aquinum (Frosinone, Italy)', in *Proceedings of the XIII International Conference on Ground Penetrating Radar* (IEEE), pp. 96–100 <https://doi.org/10.1109/ICGPR.2010.5550247>.

Ceraudo, G. and V. Vincenti. 2015. 'Le terme centrali di Aquinum (FR): considerazioni preliminari sulle fasi e sulle pavimentazioni', in C. Angelelli and others (eds), *Atti del XX Colloquio dell'Associazione italiana per lo studio e la conservazione del mosaico, Roma, 19–22 marzo 2014* (Tivoli: Scripta Manent), pp. 257–66.

—— 2018. 'Nuovi pavimenti dalle terme centrali di Aquinum', in *Atti del XXIII Colloquio dell'Associazione italiana per lo studio e la conservazione del mosaico, Narni 15–18 marzo 2017* (Rome: Quasar), pp. 461–70.

Coldagelli, G. 1969. 'Boncompagni, Giacomo', *Treccani, Dizionario biografico degli Italiani*, 11: 689–92.

Corsi, C., G. Ceraudo, and G. Murro. 2018. 'Terme centrali di Aquinum: nuovi dati per la definizione dell'abitato tra Tardoantico ed età longobarda', in F. Sogliani and others (eds), *VII Congresso nazionale di archeologia medievale*, I: *Teoria e metodi dell'archeologia medievale* (Sesto Fiorentino: All'insegna del giglio), pp. 185–89.

Ferrari, V., P. Guacci, and A. Merico. 2015. 'Archeologia aerea e telerilevamento di prossimità con sistemi aeromobili a pilotaggio remoto', *Archeologia aerea studi di aerotopografia archeologica*, 9: 6–68.

Fochetti, B. 2020. 'Quattro fusti di colonna in pavonazzetto dalla palestra delle terme', in G. Ceraudo (ed.), *Spigolature aquinati: dieci anni di scavi nell'area archeologica di Castrocielo* (Monteroni di Lecce: Esperidi), pp. 191–203.

Giuliani, C. F. 1964. 'Aquino', *Quaderni dell'Istituto di Topografia Antica dell'Università di Roma*, 1: 41–49.

Grossi, E. 1907. *Aquinum: ricerche di topografia e di storia; con due tavole e sette incisioni* (Rome: Loescher).

Guacci, P. and A. Merico. 2021. 'Il contributo delle immagini aeree da APR per la conoscenza della città antica di Aquinum', *Archeologia aerea studi di aerotopografia archeologica*, 13: 171–74.

Johnson, J. 1935. *Excavations at Minturnae*, I: *Monuments of the Republican Forum* (Rome: International Mediterranean Research Association).

La Rocca, E. 2011. 'Dal culto di Ottaviano all'apoteosi di Augusto', in G. Urso (ed.), *Dicere laudes: elogio, comunicazione, creazione del consenso; atti del convegno internazionale* (Pisa: ETS), pp. 179–204.

Molle, C. 2020. 'Epigrafia "minore" dagli scavi di Aquinum', in G. Ceraudo (ed.), *Spigolature aquinati: dieci anni di scavi nell'area archeologica di Castrocielo* (Monteroni di Lecce: Esperidi), pp. 51–70.

Murro, G. 2010. *Monumenti antichi di Aquino: la Porta San Lorenzo e il cosiddetto Capitolium*, Ager Aquinas: Storia e archeologia nella media valle dell'antico Liris, 4 (Aquino: Museo della Città).

—— 2015. 'Post-produrre, leggere, interpretare. Tecniche di enfatizzazione dell'immagine nella fotointerpretazione aerea; il caso di Aquinum', *Archeologia aerea studi di aerotopografia archeologica*, 9: 69–81.

—— 2018. 'Aquinum. La città romana', in G. Ceraudo and G. Murro (eds), *Aquinum: Guida ai monumenti e all'area archeologica* (Foggia: Grenzi), pp. 13–19.

Murro, G., V. Vitale, and G. Tulumello. 2018. 'Aquinum: il cd. edificio absidato: notizie preliminari (campagna di scavo 2014–2015)', *Siris*, 18: 111–29.

Pensabene, P. 1999. *Terrecotte del Museo nazionale romano*, I: *Gocciolatoi e protomi di sime* (Rome: L'Erma di Bretschneider).

Piro, S., G. Ceraudo, and D. Zamuner. 2011. 'Integrated Geophysical and Archaeological Investigations of Aquinum in Frosinone, Italy', *Archaeological Prospection*, 18: 127–38.

Piro, S. and others. 2012. 'A GPR Array System for Fast Archaeological Mapping: Stream X at Aquinum Roman Site (Castrocielo, Italy)', *25th Symposium on the Application of Geophysics to Engineering and Environmental Problems 2012: (SAGEEP 2012); Tucson, Arizona, USA, 25–29 March 2012* (Denver: Environmental and Engineering Geophysical Society), pp. 322–39.

Rescigno, C. 1999. 'Museo Civico Archeologico di Norma: le terrecotte architettoniche del santuario di Diana', in L. Quilici and S. Quilici Gigli (eds), *Città e monumenti nell'Italia antica*, Atlante Tematicodi Topografia Antica, 7 (Rome: L'Erma di Bretschneider), pp. 267–90.

Romualdi, A. 1987. 'I ritratti romani di epoca repubblicana e giulio-claudia del Museo archeologico di Firenze', *Mitteilungen des Deutschen Archäologischen Instituts: Römische Abteilung*, 94: 43–90.

Sommella, P. 1988. *Italia antica: l'urbanistica romana* (Rome: Jouvence).

Tagliamonte, G. and others. 2021. 'I Romani nella media valle del Volturno: il santuario del Monte San Nicola a Pietravairano (CE)', in T. D. Stek (ed.), *The State of the Samnites*, Papers of the Royal Netherlands Institute in Rome, 69 (Rome: Quasar), pp. 191–212.

9. The So-Called 'Caesar' of Aquinum: A Preliminary Analysis

Giovanni Murro

Accademia di Danimarca (giomurro@hotmail.com)

The Context of Discovery

In 2018 and 2019, the University of Salento[1] carried out archaeological excavations to the west of the theatre.[2] The archaeological presence in the area was revealed thanks to traces from photo interpretation,[3] which showed elements from a porticoed structure.

The excavation revealed a large porticus duplex, adjacent to the theatre and characterized by a rich architectural apparatus. The porticus has walls in *opus reticulatum* (Figs 9.1–9.2). The bases of the building's colonnade, currently visible, are made of brick covered with white stucco. The original roof had a double sloping roof. Numerous fragments of sima slabs, characterized by a vegetal ornament and a lion head drip, dating to the first century BC (Fig. 9.3), come from the collapsed layers of the roof.[4] The excavation yielded important data on the planimetry of the monument, a Roman derivation of the Hellenistic *diplè stoà*, and new elements on Aquinum's town planning.[5]

The excavation campaigns also involved the paved road north of the porticus. The road axis, the first *decumanus* north of the Via Latina, connected some important public monuments of the city. The stratigraphy that covered the road was partially made of parts of collapsed walls. These covered the levels of the last frequentation of the area, datable from materials — especially coins — to the fifth and sixth centuries AD. Along the south side of the road, the excavation has identified silt-sandy levels characterized by various fragments of limestone and marble pertinent to an accumulation of building material. Two marble heads and two fragments of another head were found in this area (Fig. 9.4).[6] The latter pertains to a bearded male head in white marble (Figs 9.5–9.6). Its most significant parts are a piece of the back and side of the head and a small piece of the neck and right ear.

The hair is curly and enlivened by the use of the drill, which emphasizes the *chiaroscuro* effect. The beard is thick, with a well-defined volume. The back of the head is less detailed. The difference is so evident, for example, in the use of the drill interrupted near the ear, which also suggests a reworking of the surfaces. There anatomical detail is eloquent on both fragments: the 'cauliflower' ear, common among those who practice contact sports. Several formal and technical details, such as the extensive use of the drill, suggest it could date back to the late second century. The statue, probably representing Hercules, was perhaps part of the theatre or decoration, together with other examples, of a building complex where the athletic/heroic theme was represented.

During the excavation, a well-preserved male portrait (*velato capite*) in Luni marble was also found (Fig. 9.7). The piece has a very classical formal conception, and the features of the young man presented canonical iconographic models. It is a statue that transmits values of honesty and moral rigour more or less consciously: the face is soft and strongly idealized without chiaroscuro contrasts. The forehead is smooth and forms a uniform plane with the eyebrow arch. The eyes have a smooth bulb, and the eyelids are arched and well defined. The mouth is small and closed, with two slight lateral dimples. The veil is devoid of dynamic volumes except in the lower portions, near the ears. The rear part of the head is flat, and this detail allows us to hypothesize that the statue's point of view was essentially frontal. The part uncovered by the veil shows the orderly hair, made up of rich curves, alternating

---

[1] The history of the Ager Aquinas Project is well summarized in Ceraudo 2012, 94–104. For an update, see the article by G. Ceraudo in this volume.

[2] The building is currently being excavated.

[3] Murro 2015, 71–83, in particular 79–80.

[4] For a chronological and typological classification, see Pensabene 1999. The analysis of the leonine protomes would allow us to date the typology to the Late Republican period, i.e., the first century BC.

[5] On the subject, see the article by G. Ceraudo in this volume.

[6] The Aquinum finds were the subject of the exhibition 'Heads Up! New Discoveries from the Roman Empire', held at Ny Carlsberg Glyptotek from 10 October 2019 to 15 March 2020. In the same period, various technical analyses were conducted on the portraits in an attempt to detect polychromy.

Figure 9.1. Aquinum, aerial view of the porticus duplex west of the theatre. Photo: Giovanni Murro.

with almost geometric precision. Under the veil, a smooth diadem holds the hair. It is a statue with a more iconic than realistic character, in which the characterizing physical elements seem almost absent. We can tentatively date it to the second century until its restoration gives us greater readability. The purpose of the statue was probably to be part of a decorative programme that involved the structures to the west of the theatre.

The So-Called 'Caesar' of Aquinum: Characteristics and Style

The most significant find, the subject of this preliminary analysis,[7] is a head in white marble,[8] which was named 'Caesar' by the discoverers through visual association and stylistic aspects.

It is a well-preserved male portrait, missing only the nose and a small part of the upper lip, fractured (already) in Antiquity as evidenced by the degree of abrasion of the surfaces. The head, slightly larger than life-size, has an insertion at the base of the neck in the shape of a pine cone, meant for insertion into a statue (Figs 9.8–9.9). The portrait represents a mature man, probably around fifty years old, with a mildly elongated face and a slightly enlarged skull. His face has strong features defined by soft sculptural planes. Few but significant transitions, together with expression lines, indicate authoritative and virile ageing. His head is slightly turned to the right. His forehead has a relatively high hairline to emphasize incipient baldness, further accentuated by the lateral receding hairline. The hair is thin and sticks to the head uniformly and compactly. The hair strands, densely distributed, start from the apex of the head and are orientated forward to cover his receding hairline. The eyes

---

[7] A more accurate analysis is postponed until after the restoration, currently in progress. The cleaning revealed red and blue pigments in the hair area.

[8] From the autopsy analysis, it is possible to hypothesize that it may be Parian marble, though specialized analyses are under way for a more precise characterization of the material.

9. THE SO-CALLED 'CAESAR' OF AQUINUM: A PRELIMINARY ANALYSIS

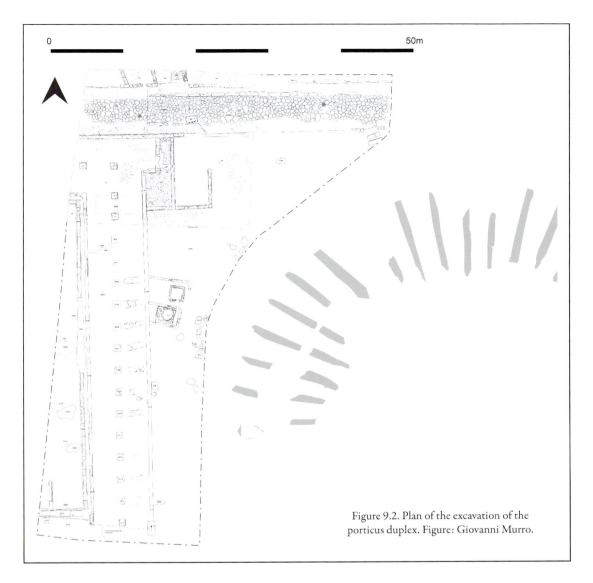

Figure 9.2. Plan of the excavation of the porticus duplex. Figure: Giovanni Murro.

Figure 9.3. Sima slab with leonine protome coming from the collapsed layers of the roof of the porticus. Photo: Giovanni Murro.

Figure 9.4. The context of the discovery of the marble heads along the paved road north of the porticus. Photo: Giovanni Murro.

Figure 9.5. Fragment of the head of Hercules, right part.

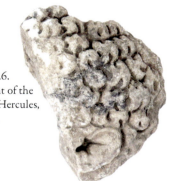

Figure 9.6. Fragment of the head of Hercules, left part.

Figure 9.7. Marble head of a young adult with his head covered (*velato capite*).

Figure 9.8. Marble head of the so-called 'Caesar' of Aquinum, front view.

Figure 9.9. Marble head of the so-called 'Caesar' of Aquinum, right side view.

The sculptures on this page are reproduced courtesy of the Municipality of Castrocielo (FR). Photos: Giovanni Murro.

have a smooth bulb, and the eyelids are arched and well defined. The lacrimal glands are visibly defined, while the lower and upper eyelids are protruding. The latter, in particular, is delimited at the top by a groove that extends to the outer limit of the orbital cavity without however coming out of it. The eyebrow arch is pronounced and has a frown that gives the face a melancholic expression. The chin is slightly receding but well defined, while the jaw appears slightly accentuated. The mouth and lip commissures are finely delineated. The mouth is quite small and slightly open. The anatomical definition of the neck is very accurate, characterized by well-defined folds. The Adam's apple is prominent, and the sternocleidomastoid muscles are clearly highlighted. A series of standard features, such as the high and receding hairline, the wrinkles on the forehead at the corners of the eyes, the rather deep nasolabial folds, and the slightly drooping labial commissures, gives the face a mature look.

Figure 9.10. Portrait of Julius Caesar from Tusculum. Archaeological Museum of Turin. Wikimedia Commons.

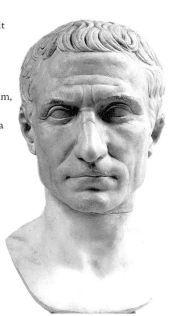

Figure 9.11. Portrait of Julius Caesar 'Chiaramonti-Pisa', kept in the Hall of Busts in the Pio Clementino Museum, Vatican City, inv. no. 713. Wikimedia Commons.

Figure 9.12. Presumed portrait of Julius Caesar, National Roman Museum. From Johansen 1987.

Stylistic Notes and Comparisons

In an important significant contribution to the so-called 'Hero of Cassino', F. Coarelli underlined — borrowing a phrase by C. Ginzburg — that the work of identifying an ancient portrait in the absence of definitive arguments must be carried out through a circumstantial procedure.[9] In the case of the Aquinum head, this method appears to be the only possible one, lacking — in the current state of research — the evidence beyond any doubt. In addition to those aspects relating to its attribution, the portrait from Aquinum has a particular historical and artistic importance, which manifests itself in the excellent technique, probably attributable to a workshop in Rome, and in the mixture between the physiognomic individualization of the face and different details of evident Hellenistic derivation. The stylistic features adopted, typical of Hellenistic pathos give the portrait evocative elements of psychological introspection: the refined execution technique, the torsion of the neck, the slight inclination of the head, and the accentuated demarcation of the interlabial line represent the distinctive features which echoes the 'malerisch-pathetische Richtung II' stylistic category defined by Schweitzer (e.g. the portrait of Pompey).[10]

The visual effects of the Aquinum head seem to reside precisely in the mixture of realism, idealization, and the progressive affirmation of psychological characteristics.[11] These aspects, stylistically the most interesting of the piece, distance the portrait from a possible association with Caesar. Many of the features, such as the marked and raised cheekbones, the well-defined jaw, and the frown, which characterize the dictator in portraits attributable to him with greater certainty (Figs 9.10–9.15), are, instead, significantly more nuanced in the so-called 'Caesar of Aquinum' portrait. Although the general lines are the expression of precise currents of Late Republican portraiture summarized in the Caesar of Tusculum,[12] there are no precise iconographic parallels with the latter (which is the only one made when Caesar was still alive) nor with other portraits attributable to him.[13]

The stylistic-iconographic structure of the Aquinum portrait sees the accentuated Caesarian realism fade to

---

9 Coarelli 1995, 269.

10 Schweitzer 1948, 86–91.

11 The set of characteristics suggests that it is not improbable to insert the work in a moment of stylistic transition, between the marked definition of the facial features of the portraits of the period of Caesar and the years immediately following his death, and the progressive and linear softening of the same, usual in the portraiture of the Second Triumvirate.

12 Borda 1943–1944, 347–49; Schweitzer 1948, 92 n. 14, fig. 152, 154–55, 106–09; Simon 1952, 123; Giuliani 1986, 202, fig. 59; Johansen 1987, 24, figs 15a–b; Megow 1987, 92–95, tabs. 82,4 and 83,3; Framarin 1995, 257–62.

13 For an overview of the portraits of Caesar, see Johansen 1967, 7–68; 1987, 17–40. For comments on the Caesar portraits and their historical context, see Zanker 2009, 288–314.

Figure 9.13. Portrait of Julius Caesar on a modern bust, National Archaeological Museum of Naples, Naples, Farnese Collection, inv. no. 6038. Photo courtesy of the National Archaeological Museum of Naples. Photo: Luigi Spina.

Figure 9.14. Presumed portrait of Julius Caesar kept at the Musée départemental Arles antique in Arles. Wikimedia Commons.

Figure 9.15. Portrait of Julius Caesar, Opera del Duomo Museum, Florence, inv. no. 20. From Johansen 1987.

Figure 9.16. Portrait of Pompey the Great, Augustan copy of an original from 70–60 BC. The National Archaeological Museum of Venice. Photo: Carole Raddato.

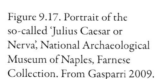

Figure 9.17. Portrait of the so-called 'Julius Caesar or Nerva', National Archaeological Museum of Naples, Farnese Collection. From Gasparri 2009.

Figure 9.18. Male portrait, British Museum of London. From Vessberg 1941.

Figure 9.19. Male portrait from Palestrina, National Roman Museum. From Vessberg 1941.

Figure 9.20. Male portrait, Museo Gregoriano Profano. From Vessberg 1941.

Figure 9.21. Male portrait from Rome, via Prenestina, Museo Nazionale Romano. Wikimedia Commons.

leave room for introspection, and in this latter characteristic, it is perhaps possible to identify an inspiration also for another famous model, the Pompeian one,[14] and in particular the Pompey of Venice, whose melancholic gaze is quite reminiscent of our portrait (Fig. 9.16). The most precise comparisons must be sought in the panorama of Late Republican portraits inspired by the Late Hellenistic tradition, which merges with the stylistic and cultural structure of the Roman portrait.

The so-called 'Julius Caesar or Nerva', a male portrait from the Farnese collection datable to between 40 and 30 BC,[15] is one of the best comparisons (Fig. 9.17). It shares its general iconographic structure with the Aquinum head, i.e., the realistic definition of expression lines and the compact hair.

Two portraits deserve particular attention, both for chronological affinity and stylistic analogies: the first is a portrait from the British Museum, similar to the Aquinum head insofar as its physiognomic features and expression of strong pathos are concerned (Fig. 9.18);[16] the second is a portrait from Palestrina preserved in the National Roman Museum,[17] with numerous similar features to the portrait from Aquinum, such as the frown, the hollow of the eye sockets, the protuberant arched eyebrows (Fig. 9.19), the shape of the head, and the hair (whose technique is similar to other portraits from the same period).[18]

Another element that unites all three heads is the fairly elongated neck and the small portion of the collarbone at the base, a detail that recurs in many portraits from the Caesarian period. The male head preserved in the Museo Gregoriano Profano is a good example (Fig. 9.20).[19] The so-called 'Caesar' of Aquinum has remarkable similarities, due to the strong imprint of caesarian figurative language and the overall definition of the details, with a portrait found on the Via Prenestina in Rome and preserved in the Museo Nazionale Romano

Figure 9.22. Male head from Dalmatia, Ny Carlsberg Glyptotek. From Johansen 1994.

Figure 9.23. Male head, probably from Venice, Ny Carlsberg Glyptotek. From Johansen 1994.

(Fig. 9.21).[20] The accentuated pathos and the *chiaroscuro* effect are elements that allow yet another stylistic comparison with a head from Dalmatia depicting a young adult, which was purchased by the Ny Carlsberg Glyptotek in 1901 (Fig. 9.22).[21] A slightly later head, datable to the end of the first century BC, has the same iconographic structure as the Aquinum head. Since the early 1900s, this head has also been in Copenhagen, probably originally from Palazzo Giustiniani-Recanati in Venice (Fig. 9.23).[22]

Notes for an Attribution

The man portrayed, adhering to the artistic taste of the urban ruling classes,[23] has chosen a form of idealized self-representation much closer to the Hellenistic plastic-pathetic late tradition than to the strong veristic style, typical for contemporary Roman portraiture. In any case, it is a portrait of 'Caesarian' inspiration, probably made shortly after the dictator's death. Its remark-

---

[14] For the role of the portrait of Pompey, see Coarelli 1995, 271–72; Zanker 1982.

[15] Coraggio 1999, 63–66, fig. 29. See also the article by the same author, in Gasparri 2009, 64, with bibliography.

[16] Vessberg 1941, tav. LI, 2; Smith 1892–1904; Hinks 1935, 15.

[17] National Roman Museum, Rome, inv. no. 115217; Vessberg 1941, tav. LIII, 1–2.

[18] A similar technique used on the hair seems to allow comparisons with the famous toga portrait of Copenhagen (Vessberg 1941, pl. LVIII) and a head portraying an old man, also kept at the Ny Carlsberg Glyptotek (Poulsen 1937, cat. 20; 1951, cat. 561).

[19] Vessberg 1941, tav. LI, 1; Felletti Maj 1953, 33.

[20] I. N. 125277, see Felletti Maj 1953, 48 n. 73.

[21] Poulsen 1951, cat. 457 (I. N. 1837); 1973, cat. 13; Johansen 1994, 52 n. 14.

[22] The piece, which was purchased by Paul Arndt in 1900, has more softened features, partly due to the acid used to clean the surfaces (cf. Poulsen 1951, cat 594; 1973, cat. 14; Johansen 1994, 54, no. 15).

[23] On the relationship between artistic language and ideology in the Republican era, see La Rocca 1990, 289–495.

Figure 9.24. Denarius of Lepidus and Octavian from 43 BC (lot 177, Sovereign Rarities Ltd).

Figure 9.25. Denarius of Lepidus and Octavian from 42 BC. Reproduced courtesy of Classical Numismatic Group.

Figure 9.26. Denarius of Lepidus and Octavian from 42 BC. Reproduced courtesy of Classical Numismatic Group.

able quality leads to the hypothesis that the portrait may be attributed to a workshop in the capital. The solutions adopted for the physical features suggest that the creation of the portrait took place in a particular historical and social context, inspired by the *Zeitgesicht* phenomenon. The result is a successful form of 'mimetic imitation', in which the individual characteristics overlap perfectly with those of a socially authoritative model, which finds its highest expression in Caesar, and perhaps even earlier, in Pompey. The style and aesthetic taste of the portrait has a Caesarian connotation. Distinct elements of a mature *sachliche stil* and clean-cut pathetic components, typically Hellenistic, converge in it. The historical context is linked to Caesar, but not only: 'Caesarian' is

the area of discovery, the Lower Liri Valley. While we have no direct evidence for Aquinum, the relationship between Caesar and the nearby colony of Interamna Lirenas (of which he was the patron)[24] appears to be defined. So who was the man in the portrait? There can be no certainty about this. He belonged to a high social rank, probably the equestrian class. Although the tendency towards idealization dulls the veristic traits, the latter emphasizes his maturity in the figure and, consequently, the value attributed to age and experience necessary to hold certain political positions.

If we wanted to identify the portrait with a politician in Aquinum who had made a fortune in the capital, it is not possible to make definitive associations due to the small range of persons from the city known from that time. Based solely on chronology, there is the possibility that the portrait could depict a member of the *Barronii gens*.[25] The historical-political context suggests the name of P. Barronius Barba, who made his fortune in Rome assuming the position of *aedilis curulis*. He was related to Marcus Barronius Sura,[26] another prominent figure in the colony, a rich representative of the equestrian class with an equally prestigious career.[27] It is a name with possible connections, but the dataset is too small to be able to suggest a persuasive hypothesis.

The investigation of the personality in question can only rely on fleeting clues and, against a wide spectrum of possibilities, it is not possible to advance a precise attribution. However, it is legitimate to put forward a suggestion, which concerns a man not originally from Aquinum but who, for a period of time was likely interested in it. The starting point for an attempt at an argument is the historical and political context in which the portrait was made: in the short text of the *Liber coloniarum* reference is made to Aquinum and *muro ducta colonia, a triumviris deducta*.[28] The triumvirate in question is the second,

---

[24] *CIL* X, 5332; Giannetti 1969, 59; Launaro and Patterson 2020, 216–24.

[25] The family is almost certainly originally from Aquinum, as the frequent number of attestations of the name seems to demonstrate, see Licordari 1982, 18.

[26] On the personage and his involvement in the production of purple in the colony, see Virno Bugno 1971, 681–95. On the interpretation of the tanks bearing the name of Barronius Sura, F. Coarelli has rightly attributed them to fountains.

[27] Marcus Barroius Sura was a *duovir quinquennalis*, *augur*, *tribunus militum*, and *praefectus fabrum*, as known from an honorary inscription dedicated to him (probably together with a statue) from the city decurions, see *CIL* X, 5401 = ILS 6291.

[28] *Liber coloniarum* CCXXIX.

9. THE SO-CALLED 'CAESAR' OF AQUINUM: A PRELIMINARY ANALYSIS

as would seem to be confirmed by a passage by Cicero referring to March 44 BC[29] written at the end of the same year,[30] in which the city is still defined as a *municipium*. It has also been speculated that Aquinum was on the list of eighteen cities whose lands were promised to the soldiers of the triumvirs on the eve of the Battle of Philippi.[31] This possibility is also reinforced by the geographical characteristics of the *ager aquinas*: a very extensive plain rich in resources and potentially available lands, located in an environment extremely favourable to the establishment of new settlers.[32] Furthermore, the data from archaeological surveys allows us to see how the number of rustic settlements, usually of small and medium size, increases starting from the Late Republican Age, a time in which a reorganization of the territory is made through a new *centuriatio*,[33] which overlaps with a previous settlement model based on more or less regular layouts though with a different orientation.[34] The city, which in this historical moment appears closely linked to the triumvirs,[35] experienced demographic growth and at the same time an important phase of monumentalization and general urban improvement.

If we compare the Aquinum portrait with the iconography of some coins dating back to 43–42 BC (Figs 9.24–9.26),[36] the figure that is evoked is that of the most improbable — or at least the most 'difficult' — among the three most important personalities of the time: Marcus Aemilius Lepidus. As mentioned earlier,

this is the most unlikely scenario: the greatest criticality concerns the recognition of precise physiognomic characteristics, given the generic nature of the monetary portraits and the lack, already noted by Bernouilli, of a homogeneous iconographic tradition regarding this personality, identified several times in portraiture and glyptic,[37] but without any compelling arguments. The second problem is political: the unfortunate outcomes of this personage's career are known, decidedly disliked by Octavian, who soon relegated him to the role, purely honorary, of *pontifex maximus* and then erased his political history. In addition to the demolition of this 'tarnished triumvir',[38] there are, however, some elements that are worth reflecting on.

If Augustus's intolerance towards Lepidus and the systematic *damnatio memoriae* reserved to him by the historiography linked to the emperor is evident,[39] it is equally clear that he was a trustworthy man of Caesar, to the point of becoming his *magister equitum* in 46 BC, enjoying therefore a deep-rooted reputation as a loyal Caesarian. From this point of view, the homage cannot be considered entirely improbable, likely not later than 36 BC both for historical reasons and for the stylistic aspects of the piece, by a 'passionate city' towards a personage of such great importance.[40]

A hypothetical tribute paid in one of the colonies would not constitute an isolated case: apart from the well-known inscription from the theatre of Terracina with Lepidus as the protagonist,[41] other episodes of tolerance by the emperor are known and must be interpreted

---

[29] Cic., *Phil.* II.105–06.

[30] Fedeli 1986; Molle 2011, 19–20.

[31] See Pais 1925, 363, 384–87; Keppie 1983, 137–39.

[32] An apparently contrasting piece of data, however, is the epigraphic one: for the *ager aquinas* the inscriptions referable with a good margin of certainty to the veterans are, in the current state of studies, very rare, such as the inscription *CIL* X, 5407, referring to Caius Aiedius, a soldier probably originally from Bononia or the Umbrian-Picene region.

[33] Ceraudo 2004, 43–47. For an updated summary, see Bellini, Murro, and Trigona 2012, 573–81.

[34] An update on the diachronic development of the organization of the territory, based above all on new excavation data, in Bellini and Murro 2019, 157–66.

[35] This bond of enthusiastic loyalty appears implicit precisely in Cicero (*Phil.* II.105–06). When the Arpinate tells of the passage of Mark Antony in the city, blaming the stupidity of the inhabitants of Aquinum. In Cicero, too, it is noted (*Fam.* IX.24.1) how Aquinum, once linked to him, had turned its back on him. For comments on the source, see Molle 2011, 24–25.

[36] Crawford, 495/2b, 495/2c, 495/2d; Sydenham 1323; Sear 1523.

[37] A sardonyx specimen from the Chesterfield Museum and Art Gallery has been associated with Lepidus, see Furtwängler 1900, vol. I, plate XLVII. 30 and vol. II, 226; Boardman and others 2009, n. 296. A similar association has been made for a carnelian by the Kunsthistorisches Museum in Vienna, see Zwierlein-Diehl 1973, n. 358; for a glass specimen from the Musée d'Art et d'Historie in Geneva, see Vollenweider 1979, no. 154; for one in black jasper from the Metropolitan Museum of New York, see Richter 1956, no. 473. For a general examination, with updated bibliography, see Gołyźniak 2020.

[38] The term has been borrowed from the title of Richard D. Weigel's essay *Lepidus: The Tarnished Triumvir* published in 1992.

[39] The case of the *Historiae* by Velleius Paterculus is emblematic of the precise 'strategy of oblivion' adopted by the Augustan historiography. The question is further discussed in Rohr Vio 2004, 235–56. More recently the topic was dealt with by Fasolini 2015, 43–64.

[40] Tibiletti 1976, 51–66.

[41] Recently G. L. Gregori hypothesized — on account of the use of the name — that the inscription could be interpreted as a form of praise to Lepidus, see Cassieri, Gregori, and Refalo-Bistagne 2020, 1724–2134.

as elements of an attempt made by Octavian/Augustus — who was capable of skilfully alternating cruelty and 'soft power' — to achieve consensus.[42] The presence of various bricks bearing a stamp with the name 'LEPIDI' in a rectangular cartouche,[43] coming both from the urban area and from the suburbs, is a fact that could take on a certain significance: even though the brand is commonly associated with a manufacturer named Lepidius, this does not rule out the connection with the family of the *pontifex maximus* and the economic interests that he could have in the area. Finally, the discovery in 2019 of the fragments of a colossal head of Augustus in the northern part of the porticus would not constitute an obstacle. The statue of the emperor could amount to a significant element of a precise propaganda strategy, where the physical — and moral — oversizing of the emperor would aim, also in this case, to further diminish, posthumously, the importance covered by a character who, up to the Battle of Naulochus, had played an extraordinary political role.

---

[42] In this regard, it is worth remembering the homage, narrated in Plut., *Brut.* LVIII.5, 2–4, paid to Brutus by the city of Mediolanum.

[43] On the diffusion in the *ager aquinas*, see Molle 2010, 42–44. It must be said that the number of known specimens has increased in recent years, with widespread attestation on buildings of a certain importance.

Works Cited

Bellini, G. R. and G. Murro. 2019. 'Paesaggi agrari di Aquinum: resti e contesti nella trasformazione diacronica del territorio', in A. Russo Tagliente, G. Ghini, and Z. Mari (eds), *Atti del Convegno: Roma 8–9 giugno 2015*, Lazio e Sabina, 12 (Rome: Quasar), pp. 157–66.

Bellini, G. R., G. Murro, and S. L. Trigona. 2012. 'L'ager di Aquinum: la centuriazione', in G. Ghini and Z. Mari (eds), *Atti del Convegno 'ottavo incontro di studi sul Lazio e la Sabina', Roma 30–31 marzo, 1 aprile 2011*, Lazio e Sabina, 8 (Rome: Quasar), pp. 573–81.

Bernouilli, J. J. 1882–1894. *Romische Ikonographie*, II (Stuttgart: Spemann).

Boardman, J. and others. 2009. *The Marlborough Gems Formerly at Blenheim Palace, Oxfordshire* (Oxford: Oxford University Press).

Borda, M. 1943–1944. 'Il ritratto tuscolano di G. Cesare', *Atti della Pontificia Accademia romana di archeologia: rendiconti*, 20: 347–82.

Cassieri, N., G. L. Gregori, and J.-B. Refalo-Bistagne. 2020. 'Le ultime acquisizioni dal teatro di Terracina e l'eccezionale iscrizione del triumviro M. Emilio Lepido', *Mélanges de l'Ecole française de Rome: antiquité*, 131.2 <http://doi.org/10.4000/mefra.9174>.

Ceraudo, G. (ed.). 2004. *'Ager Aquinas': Aerotopografia archeologica lungo la valle dell'antico Liris* (Marina di Minturno: Armando Caramanica editore).

——. 2012. 'Progetto "AgerAquinas": Indagini aerotopografiche finalizzate allo studio della Città Romana di Aquinum (Lazio, Italia)', in F. Vermeulen and others (eds), *Urban Landscape Survey in Italy and the Mediterranean* (Oxford: Oxbow), pp. 94–103.

Coarelli, F. 1995. 'Il ritratto di Varrone: un tentativo di paradigma indiziario', in A. Frova, G. Cavalieri Manasse, and E. Roffia (eds), *Splendida Civitas nostra: studi archeologici in onore di Antonio Frova* (Rome: Quasar), pp. 269–80.

Coraggio, F. 1999. 'Sui bronzi della collezione Farnese: una pagina di storia del collezionismo cinquecentesco', *Rivista dell'Istituto nazionale d'archeologia e storia dell'arte*, 22: 23–68.

Fasolini, D. 2015. 'Marco Emilio Lepido nella narrazione di Velleio Patercolo. Silenzi, reticenze e maldicenze nella storiografia d'epoca augustea', in A. Valvo and G. Migliorati (eds), *Ricerche storiche e letterarie intorno a Velleio Patercolo* (Milan: Educatt), pp. 43–64.

Fedeli, P. 1986. *M. Tulli Ciceronis in M. Antonium orationes Philippicae XIV, edidit Paulus Fedeli* (Leipzig: Teubner).

Felletti Maj, B. M. 1953. *Museo nazionale romano: i ritratti* (Rome: Libreria dello stato).

Framarin, P. 1995. 'Ritratto di Cesare di Aglié', in G. Sena Chiesa (ed.), *Augusto in Cisalpina: ritratti augustei e giulio-claudi in Italia settentrionale* (Milan: Cisalpino), pp. 257–62.

Furtwängler, A. 1900. *Die antiken Gemmen: Geschichte der Steinschneidekunst im Klassischen Altertum*, III (Leipzig: Giesecke & Devrient).

Gasparri, C. 2009. *Le sculture Farnese*, II: *I ritratti* (Milan: Electa).

Giannetti, A. 1969. *Ricognizione epigrafica compiuta nel territorio di Casinum, Interamna Lirenas ed Aquinum*, Rendiconti lincei. Scienze morali, storiche e filologiche, 24 (Rome: Bardi).

Ginzburg, C. 1986. *Miti, emblemi, spie; morfologia e storia* (Turin: Einaudi).

Giuliani, L. 1980. 'Individuum und Ideal. Antike Bildkunst', in B. Hüfler (ed.), *Bilder vom Menschen in der Kunst des Abendlandes: Jubiläumsausstellung der Preußischen Museen 1830–1980* (Berlin: Mann), pp. 43–52.

—— 1986. *Bildnis und Botschaft: Hermeneutische Untersuchungen zur Bildniskunst der römischen Republik* (Frankfurt: Suhrkamp).

Gołyźniak, P. 2020. *Engraved Gems and Propaganda in the Roman Republic and under Augustus* (Oxford: Archaeopress).

Hinks, R. P. 1935. *Greek and Roman Portrait Sculpture* (London: Trustees of the British Museum).

Johansen, F. S. 1967. 'Antichi ritratti di Caio Giulio Cesare nella scultura', *Analecta Romana Instituti Danici*, 4: 7–68.

—— 1987. 'The Portraits in Marble of Gaius Julius Caesar', in J. Frel and others (eds), *Ancient Portraits in the P. Getty Museum*, I (Malibu: J. Paul Getty Museum), pp. 17–40.

—— 1994. *Roman Portraits: Catalogue*, I (Copenhagen: Ny Carlsberg Glyptotek).

Keppie, L. J. F. 1983. *Colonisation and Veteran Settlement in Italy, 47–14 B.C.* (London: British School at Rome).

La Rocca, E. 1990. 'Linguaggio artistico e ideologia politica a Roma in età repubblicana', in C. Ampolo (ed.), *Roma e l'Italia: radices imperii* (Milan: Scheiwiller), pp. 289–495.

Launaro, A. and J. Patterson. 2020. 'New Epigraphic Evidence from Interamna Lirenas (Central Italy)', *Epigraphica*, 82: 213–41.

Laurenzi, L. 1940. 'Problemi della ritrattistica repubblicana', *Aevum*, 14: 367–84.

Licordari, A. 1982. 'Ascesa al senato e rapporti con i teritori d'origine. Italia: regio I (Latium)', in *Epigrafia e ordine senatorio: atti del Colloquio internazionale AIEGL, Roma, 1981* (Rome: Edizione di storia e letteratura), pp. 9–57.

Megow, W. R. 2005. *Republikanische Bildnis-Typen* (Frankfurt: Lang).

Molle, C. 2010. 'Varia epigraphica tra Aquinum ed Interamna Lirenas', in H. Solin (ed.), *Le epigrafi della Valle di Comino: atti del sesto convegno epigrafico cominese; Atina, 31 maggio 2009* (S. Donato Val di Comino: Associazione 'Genesi').

—— 2011. *Le fonti letterarie antiche su Aquinum e le epigrafi delle raccolte comunali di Aquino*, Ager Aquinas-Storia e archeologia nella media valle dell'antico Liris, 5 (Aquino: Amministrazione comunale).

Murro, G. 2015. 'Post-produrre, leggere, interpretare. Tecniche di enfatizzazione dell'immagine nella fotointerpretazione aerea; il caso di Aquinum', *Archeologia aerea: studi di aerotopografia archeologica*, 9: 69–81.

Pais, E. 1925. *Serie cronologica delle colonie romane e latine*, II: *Dall'età dei Gracchi a quella di Augusto*, Accademia nazionale dei Lincei, 6 (Rome: Tipografia della R. Accademia nazionale dei Lincei).

Pensabene, P. 1999. *Terrecotte del Museo nazionale romano*, I: *Gocciolatoi e protomi di sime* (Rome: L'Erma di Bretschneider).

Poulsen, F. 1951. *Catalogue of Ancient Sculpture in the Ny Carlsberg Glyptotek* (Copenhagen: Ny Carlsberg Glyptotek).

Poulsen, V. 1973. *Les portraits Romains*, I (Copenhagen: Ny Carlsberg Glyptotek).

Richter, G. M. A. 1956. *Catalogue of Engraved Gems: Greek, Etruscan, and Roman* (Rome: L'Erma di Bretschneider).

Rohr Vio, F. 2004. 'Marco Emilio Lepido tra memoria e oblio nelle Historiae di Velleio Patercolo', *Rivista di cultura classica e medio-evale*, 46.2: 235–56.

Salomies, O. 1996. 'Senatori oriundi del Lazio', in H Solin (ed.), *Studi storico-epigrafici sul Lazio antico*, Acta Instituti Romani Finlandiae, 15 (Rome: Institutum Romanum Finlandiae), pp. 23–127.

Schweitzer, R. 1948. *Der Bildniskunst der römischen Republik* (Leipzig: Koehler & Amelang).

Simon, E. 1952. 'Das Caesarportrat im Castello di Agliè', *Archaeologischer Anzeiger*, 67: 123–38.

Smith, A. H. 1982–1904. *Catalogue of Sculpture in the Department of Greek and Roman Antiquities, British Museum*, III (London: British Museum).

Tibiletti, G. 1976. 'Città appassionate dell'Italia Settentrionale Augustea', *Athenaeum*, 63: 51–66.

Vessberg, O. 1941. *Studien zur Kunstgeschichte der römischen Republik* (Lund: Gleerup).

Virno Bugno, L. 1971. 'M. Barronio Sura e l'industria della porpora ad Aquino', *Rendiconti dell'Accademia dei Lincei*, 29: 685–95.

Vollenweider, M.-L. 1979. *Catalogue raisonné des sceaux, cylindres, intailles et camées*, II: *Les portraits, les masques de theatre, les symboles politiques* (Mainz: Von Zabern).

Zanker, P. 'The Irritating Statues and Contradictory Portraits of Julius Caesar', in M. Griffin (ed.), *A Companion to Julius Caesar* (Oxford: Wiley-Blackwell), pp. 288–314.

Zwierlein-Diehl, E. 1973. *Die antiken Gemmen des Kunsthistorischen Museums in Wien*, I: *Die Gemmen von der minoischen Zeit bis zur frühen römischen Kaiserzeit* (Munich: Prestel).

10. L'IMMAGINARIO CESARIANO TRA VISIONI CLASSICISTICHE E IDEOLOGIE NAZIONALISTICHE: IL CASO DI UN RITRATTO EMERSO DALLE ACQUE DEL RODANO

Mario Denti

Université Rennes 2, IUF (mario.denti@wanadoo.fr)

Introduzione

Un episodio piuttosto significativo dell'uso (e dell'abuso) dell'immaginario cesariano nella cultura contemporanea è rappresentato dal modo in cui un ritratto di età tardo-repubblicana raffigurante un personaggio maschile ignoto, ritrovato quindici anni fa nelle acque del Rodano ad Arles, è stato trasformato in un'immagine di Giulio Cesare, caricandolo di precisi significati ideologici. Nel presente lavoro[1] abbiamo inteso esaminare questo episodio, decostruendone l'architettura, illustrando sulla base di quali percorsi concettuali esso è stato costruito, a livello sia scientifico che culturale: per un verso, esaminando i risvolti metodologici nell'ambito della ricerca storico-artistica e archeologica contemporanea sul ritratto greco-romano; per un altro, approfondendo le ricadute di questo tipo di approcci nella costruzione della cultura contemporanea.

Come vedremo, un unico filo rosso unisce e determina questi aspetti, basati su una serie di attitudini intellettuali interconnesse, che possiamo riconoscere come costruite fondamentalmente su almeno tre elementi: l'inerziale riproposizione di una tradizione storiografica di tipo attribuzionistico, fondata su approcci classicistici[2] e formalistici; la rinuncia a dialogare con le discipline storiche, sostituite da una fede acritica nei confronti delle cosiddette 'scienze esatte', lasciando così ai margini l'opportunità di capire la cultura figurativa ellenistico-romana nel quadro delle scelte politiche, dei caratteri culturali e dei contesti istituzionali che ne furono alla radice;[3]

il ricorso, risorgente in maniera più o meno cosciente, a categorie e a ideologie di tipo etnico-nazionalistico nell'interpretazione dei fenomeni storico-archeologici, particolarmente presente nel percorso storico-culturale della Francia moderna e contemporanea.[4]

Sarà innanzi tutto utile ricordare brevemente il quadro dei fatti che hanno caratterizzato il caso di studio in questione, il ritratto detto *de César* conservato nel Musée départemental Arles antique (Fig. 10.1, 10.2 e 10.6). A seguito della sua scoperta nel 2007 grazie a un importante programma di archeologia subacquea, la scultura è stata immediatamente mediatizzata in quanto immagine di Caio Giulio Cesare. Due anni dopo viene infatti pubblicato il bel catalogo della mostra allestita ad Arles, dal significativo titolo *César. Le Rhône pour mémoire. Vingt ans de fouilles dans le fleuve à Arles*.[5] Nel 2012, quando viene organizzato un convegno in gran parte ad esso dedicato e pubblicato nel 2016,[6] il *César du Rhône* appariva ancor privo di quel bagaglio scientifico che caratterizza abitualmente la discussione e la divulgazione scientifica di un documento archeologico: un serio e solido inquadramento sul piano storico e storico-artistico.[7]

In questa prospettiva, non è un caso che la tavola rotonda organizzata al Museo del Louvre nello stesso 2012 intorno a questo ritratto[8] abbia visto la parteci-

---

[1] Che costituisce la traduzione italiana, con l'inserzione di aggiornamenti e di adattamenti sostanziali per la presente pubblicazione, di un articolo precedentemente édito in francese, vedi Denti 2016.

[2] Coarelli 1996.

[3] Denti 2008a; 2008b; 2014.

[4] Marc 2014.

[5] Long e Picard 2009.

[6] Gaggadis-Robin e Picard 2016.

[7] L'articolo di L. Long (che discuteremo in questa sede) aveva un obbiettivo puramente attribuzionistico; vedi Long 2009. Un solo serio tentativo di studio approfondito a carattere storico-artistico era stato proposto da E. Rosso, vedi Rosso 2010.

[8] Caratterizzata da un titolo a dir poco enigmatico, credo, per il grande pubblico, e in ogni caso incentrato sull'interpretazione

pazione esclusiva di specialisti — storici dell'arte — in ritrattistica (fatto in sé, naturalmente, assolutamente normale), lasciando tuttavia intenzionalmente fuori dalla discussione qualunque possibile approfondimento del contesto storico all'interno del quale la scultura fu realizzata. L'assenza di un settore della ricerca che avrebbe dovuto essere considerato, viceversa, come irrinunciabile, ha pesato notevolmente anche sull'altra componente di questo progetto, di evidenti dimensioni faraoniche — in quanto, come vedremo, considerato 'di interesse nazionale': la concomitante mostra parigina, in cui si rivendicava l'attribuzione del pezzo a Giulio Cesare.[9] Gli assi epistemologici sui quali la tavola rotonda è stata costruita, limitata a una discussione specificatamente storico-artistica e attribuzionistica, hanno così lasciato ai margini ogni possibile considerazione della sfera delle committenze, l'esame prosopografico delle élites locali che storicamente avrebbero potuto essere implicate in questa realizzazione scultorea, così come gli eventuali interessi politico-clientelari dei membri dell'aristocrazia urbana sviluppati nel territorio e nella città di Arles: una prospettiva metodologica che — insieme alle analisi storico-artistiche — avrebbe potuto metterci sulla buona strada nel processo di ricostruzione dell'orizzonte ideologico e del sistema politico-evergetico, come vedremo, che si trovava alla base dell'erezione di questa statua.

Per meglio comprendere le ragioni di questi avvenimenti, sarà necessario inserirli all'interno di un'analisi delle modalità di lettura messe in opera dagli studiosi e delle istituzioni che, in questa circostanza, si sono occupati del problema: modalità che riflettono — e che a loro volta costruiscono — una serie di categorie intellettuali e di prospettive visuali che alimentano, in questi primi decenni del terzo millennio, la nostra maniera di leggere e di osservare l'Antico. Si tratterà, dunque, non solo di affrontare i percorsi euristici che hanno consentito di presentare un'interpretazione 'preconfezionata' di questo particolare documento archeologico — un ritratto privato interpretato come la rappresentazione di un personaggio-chiave della storia antica (e moderna)[10] europea — ma di riconoscere le coordinate di una prospettiva più ampia: il tipo di esperienza ideologica e culturale, cioè, che gli studiosi e i professionisti delle discipline archeologiche vivono in quanto intellettuali che hanno

l'onere e l'onore di trattare i documenti dell'Antico, e di trasmetterne i significati alla comunità civica del loro tempo; e, di conseguenza, il tipo di esperienza ideologica e culturale che fanno vivere alla comunità civica, esperienza della quale occorre ricordare che essi portano tutta la responsabilità. Siamo infatti di fronte, in questo come in altri casi, a un'operazione squisitamente 'politica'.

Classicismo e sensazionalismo: due facce di una stessa medaglia

In luogo di un approccio critico, costruito secondo il canonico ricorso all'analisi tipologica, iconografica e stilistica, il ritratto del Rodano è stato immediatamente proiettato in una dimensione 'straordinaria'. Nel catalogo della mostra di Arles esso è stato presentato in termini entusiastici,[11] come una scoperta sensazionale, in quanto relativa a un pezzo considerato a priori come eccezionale (come vedremo, si tratta invece di una scultura di buona qualità, abitualmente documentata per l'epoca). Le nozioni di 'capolavoro', 'pezzo unico', 'tesoro', caratterizzano in modo significativamente ricorrente le introduzioni ufficiali al catalogo della mostra:

> Les fragments de mémoire arrachés en Arles aux eaux du Rhône par une plongée de vingt ans sont l'illustration même de ce *triomphe sur l'oubli*, [car il s'agit de] sortir des eaux *un trésor* des temps anciens [...] J'ai tenu à ce que *ce buste exceptionnel* soit exposé dans les salons du Ministère de la Culture et de la Communication au Palais Royal.[12]
>
> En remontant patiemment de la vase des objets modestes de la vie quotidienne, aussi bien que *les trésors les plus précieux, dont le buste de César reste l'emblème*.[13]

Perché il nostro ritratto risulta eccezionale? Perché esso, molto semplicemente, è un ritratto di Cesare. Anzi — come vedremo — *il vero* ritratto di Cesare: 'Avec le célèbre portrait de César en marbre et la statue de Neptune, d'autres *chefs-d'œuvre* occupaient la pente, entre 20 et 40 m du bord'.[14]

L'attribuzione al dittatore legittima l'eccezionalità della scoperta e — attraverso un ragionamento tipicamente circolare — viceversa. Ci ritroviamo, in questo quadro, all'interno della tradizione attribuzionistica tipica della storia dell'arte 'classica', che celebra i fasti della bellezza e dello statuto di eccezione di una grande

---

aprioristica del pezzo come Giulio Cesare: *Rendre à César...*, 20 giugno 2012.

[9] *Arles, les fouilles du Rhône. Un fleuve pour mémoire*, mostra al Louvre, 9 marzo-25 giugno 2012.

[10] Gentili 2008.

[11] Long e Picard 2009.

[12] Long e Picard 2009, 15 (Frédéric Mitterrand) (i corsivi sono miei).

[13] Long e Picard, 17 (Jean-Noël Guérini) (i corsivi sono miei).

[14] Long 2009, 25 (i corsivi sono miei).

'opera d'arte'. Di più: di un vero e proprio 'capolavoro'. Quest'attitudine, come scrive Jean-Paul Demoule:

> Constitue une régression, en ce sens qu'elle révèle une vision régressive de l'archéologie. On retombe là dans une conception ancienne pour laquelle l'archéologie est une branche de l'histoire de l'art, une discipline auxiliaire de l'histoire. Une conception collectionniste, issue de la Renaissance, celle des beaux objets et des chefs-d'œuvre, centrée sur l'époque gréco-romaine, qui n'étudie la société qu'à travers les objets de l'élite. Ce qui fait qu'on s'intéresse peu à la vie quotidienne.[15]

Queste osservazioni, certamente condivisibili, riflettono tuttavia una visione dicotomica fra l'archeologia di scavo da un lato (che si occupa tradizionalmente della cosiddetta 'cultura materiale') e la storia dell'arte dall'altro (considerata come disciplina che studia gli oggetti 'belli', 'les beaux objets'). Si tratta di una visione, oggi molto diffusa presso numerosi archeologi francesi (in particolare quelli attivi nell'ambito dell'archeologia preventiva), che dipende da paradigmi propri di una certa cultura archeologica degli anni '80, insistente su un'idea della ricerca storico-artistica come disciplina che potesse essere ancora concepita come recisa dalla storia socio-culturale e politica del mondo antico.[16]

In ogni caso, Jean-Paul Demoule ha fondamentalmente ragione. Proprio il modo in cui il ritratto del Rodano è stato presentato — contrassegnato, come abbiamo visto, da un preciso statuto di eccezionalità (sul quale dovremo ritornare) sul piano storico ed 'estetico' — finisce infatti per giustificare questo tipo di critica.

L'immediata attribuzione del nostro busto a Cesare si caratterizza inoltre come il riflesso di una concezione della ricerca archeologica in quanto attività finalizzata al ritrovamento di fatti sensazionali e di oggetti eccezionali.[17] Questa prospettiva è stata materializzata da una scelta mediatica fuori dal comune, a sua volta costruita sull'inserzione del documento archeologico portato alla luce nella sfera dell'eccezionalità, nello statuto di un vero e proprio capolavoro ('chef d'œuvre'). Si tratta di categorie concettuali reciprocamente dipendenti l'una dall'altra, entrambe sviluppate sulla forza ideologica che l'aura emanante dal pezzo scultoreo — elaborata ex novo — ha potuto instaurarsi a seguito dell'operazione fondatrice

di tutto il sistema: un'interpretazione aprioristica del ritratto come Giulio Cesare. Come vedremo, un vero e proprio, fragilissimo, castello di carte.

Appare davvero curioso osservare a che livello i paradigmi classicistici non smettono mai di rinascere, sotto forme apparentemente poco evidenti. Per meglio comprendere questo fenomeno, occorre ora affrontare il nodo che ne ha permesso lo sviluppo: l'ideologia archeologica francese a carattere nazionalista.

Un'archeologia nazionalistica

Il percorso attribuzionistico sul quale è stato costruito tutto il discorso di 'fondazione mitica' del 'César du Rhône' trova la sua più coerente spiegazione nel quadro dell'archeologia nazionalistica francese, all'interno della quale la categoria euristica di 'gallo-romanisme' si rivela una nozione ideologicamente ancor oggi attuale. Non è infatti un caso se le più alte istanze dello Stato hanno inteso figurare in prima linea in questa operazione. Ascoltiamole, nelle parole del Conservateur Général du Patrimoine au Département des Recherches Archéologiques Subaquatiques et Sous-Marines:

> Les pièces archéologiques ici présentées [...] sont surtout l'expression matérielle de notre histoire commune et l'on peut gager que chacun trouvera à se reconnaître un peu dans cette mémoire que le fleuve a su jalousement préserver et dont le Ministère de la Culture et de la Communication a souhaité voir l'exposition reconnue d'intérêt national. *Projet d'intérêt national, science du passé et histoire de nos vies...*[18]

Jean-Paul Demoule ci ha offerto, ancora una volta, alcune osservazioni molto pertinenti a questo proposito:

> On assiste à un vrai phénomène de société. Pour moi, avec ce marbre, c'est l'inconscient collectif et le mythe national qui ressurgissent des eaux et des boues du Rhône pollué. Cela revient à dire qu'avec la statue, on a trouvé une œuvre d'art, le buste d'un homme mythique dont le nom a traversé les siècles. César, celui qui a fait basculer la France de la Préhistoire dans l'Histoire [...] Avec César, c'est le mythe national qui ressurgit : celui de Vercingétorix, de Clovis et de Napoléon. Le buste serait un portrait de l'homme d'État réalisé de son vivant. Celui qui regarde le marbre a donc l'impression de l'avoir en face de lui. Cela a un aspect assez fascinant.[19]

---

[15] Intervista pubblicata nel WEB, vedi Demoule 2010.

[16] Ancora attualissime le osservazioni in merito di R. Bianchi Bandinelli, vedi Bianchi Bandinelli 1981.

[17] Una tendenza che vediamo oggi progressivamente diffusa, soprattutto in Italia, grazie a precise scelte politiche nella gestione del patrimonio storico-archeologico.

[18] Long e Picard 2009, 21 (Michel L'Hour) (i corsivi sono miei).

[19] Intervista pubblicata nel WEB, vedi Demoule 2010.

Nella dialettica concettuale che il termine 'gallo-romano' sottintende, è questa volta la figura storica 'negativa' operante all'interno del mito nazionalistico francese, a entrare in gioco. Il personaggio che attira le passioni del pubblico e dei ricercatori è, in questo caso, il conquistatore, non il conquistato; il romano, non il gallo; Cesare, non Vercingetorige. Ma si tratta dell'altra faccia di una stessa medaglia: una medaglia legittimante la costruzione del mito di una civiltà i cui caratteri sono ritenuti assolutamente peculiari, in quanto frutto di uno scontro / incontro storico fra 'Galli' e 'Romani', dotato di uno statuto di eccezione all'interno del mondo imperiale e invariabilmente interpretato alla luce di criteri etnici. È questa una categoria che semplifica e appiattisce la complessità delle relazioni storico-culturali che, nell'antichità greco-romana, si giocavano su ben diversi terreni rispetto all'esclusiva identità etnica, impedendoci di cogliere la complessità di un sistema politico e sociale in cui, quello che contava di più, era il valore dell'appartenenza a un orizzonte culturale e ideologico condiviso (nel nostro caso, l'ellenismo), concepito come preciso veicolo della costruzione del prestigio personale del cittadino, dell'integrazione nel sistema imperiale, della carriera politica dei notabili provinciali. Come sappiamo, peraltro, le stesse élite galliche di queste regioni erano state profondamente ellenizzate ben prima dell'arrivo delle armate di Giulio Cesare, avendo sviluppato il fenomeno (ben studiato, ormai) dell''auto-romanizzazione'.

Sull'altro versante (quello, diciamo, 'romano') occorre ribadire — perché ce n'è forse ancora molto bisogno — che l'impiego del soggetto storico 'i Romani', ricorrente anche in non poca letteratura specializzata, rimanda a una categoria generica, semplificatoria quanto banalizzante: costruita su una concezione etnica di tipo modernistico, questa formulazione non corrisponde in alcun caso a uno scenario che sappiamo non essere mai stato caratterizzato da un blocco storico uniforme e chiuso ('i Romani'), ma da una situazione mutevole, trasformantesi nei tempi lunghi e nei diversi spazi dell'impero, estremamente articolata sotto il profilo sociologico e politico. È questo il terreno di ricerca che noi dobbiamo decifrare se vogliamo capire il processo della monumentalizzazione di una colonia della tarda età repubblicana, come Arles, processo del quale il nostro ritratto non ne costituiva che uno degli ingredienti.

Tutti sappiamo che la diffusione dell'immagine di Vercingetorige come il capo supremo di una Gallia 'libera', che sarà sottomessa dall''invasore romano' (metto volutamente fra virgolette questi termini), riflette il paradigma nazionalistico proprio a un'ideologia e a una cultura poste al servizio della costruzione degli Stati nazionali. Il problema è che la forza inerziale di questo paradigma è ancora solidamente operativa nell'ambito della ricerca archeologica, così da rendere molto spesso opaca e fuorviante la nostra percezione del fenomeno della romanizzazione — e dell'ellenizzazione — di queste regioni dell'impero, riducendone notevolmente la complessità storica. Non dimentichiamo, in questo senso, che lo stesso Vercingetorige, alla metà del I secolo a.C., ci appare come uno dei protagonisti della storia del mondo ellenistico, un sovrano profondamente imbevuto di cultura greca (come le sue immagini monetarie, ad esempio, ci mostrano).

In questa prospettiva, dunque, un bel ritratto 'romano'[20] uscito dalle acque del Rodano ad Arles, all'inizio del terzo millennio, non poteva diventare che l'immagine di Giulio Cesare: *il vero* Cesare, che fino ad ora noi, evidentemente, non conoscevamo.[21] Un nuovo strumento, dunque, per la costruzione della *nostra* identità, un formidabile veicolo di legittimazione dell'appartenenza a un passato condiviso: 'l'expression matérielle de notre histoire commune', 'inscrit aujourd'hui dans un projet d'intérêt national, science du passé et histoire de nos vies', secondo le significative parole citate in precedenza.

Il modo stesso in cui la scultura è stata presentata al pubblico nella mostra si rivela del resto estremamente coerente con questa impostazione. Come è stato notato,[22] in questa esposizione la 'messa in scena' di un sistema visivo comprendente il presunto ritratto di Giulio Cesare, un presunto ritratto di Lepido e la statuetta in bronzo di un prigioniero, permetteva di consacrare definitivamente il paradigma storico-ideologico, in senso 'gallo-romano', della fondazione della colonia di Arles.

---

[20] Ancora una volta, utilizzo qui il termine 'romano' volutamente fra virgolette, nell'intento di suggerire tutta la problematica che emerge nel momento in cui noi scegliamo di descrivere questi prodotti scultorei impiegando il vocabolario mutuato da criteri etnico-nazionalistici. Cosa significano, infatti, l'aggettivo 'romano' e il sostantivo 'i Romani'? Tutto e niente. Nel busto del Rodano, infatti, chi vi è stato veramente rappresentato: un cittadino romano? Un membro dell'élite locale romanizzata? E, in entrambi i casi, un personaggio dotato di quale statuto politico? Se passiamo poi sul versante dell'artista che lo ha realizzato: lo scultore era un romano? O un greco? O, ancora, un greco che aveva lavorato a Roma, oppure direttamente ad Arles? Si cfr. le osservazioni sulla difficoltà nell'inquadrare la produzione figurativa ellenistico-romana attraverso criteri etnici, in Denti 2008a; 2008b.

[21] Long 2009.

[22] Rosso 2010, n. 9.

Tutti gli aspetti evocati fino ad ora non possono infine comprendersi pienamente senza interrogarci sul modo in cui questa scoperta è stata analizzata sotto il profilo scientifico, e più in particolare sul percorso intellettuale che ha condotto all'attribuzione del ritratto a Cesare. Vedremo così come un'attitudine di tipo emozionale — chiaramente dipendente da una miscela di romanticismo e di nazionalismo — si è coniugata a una vera e propria fede — egualmente irrazionale e modernistica — sul valore delle analisi 'scientifiche' copiosamente impiegate per confermare i risultati del percorso attribuzionistico iniziale, attraverso il ricorso a un ragionamento metodologicamente circolare e ideologicamente ben identificabile.

L'acquisizione, emozionale, di un 'pezzo unico'

Il percorso attribuzionistico che si trova all'origine del sistema interpretativo che ha accompagnato la presentazione al pubblico e la mediatizzazione di questo ritratto si è costruito intorno a un percorso euristico fondato su un approccio di tipo sostanzialmente emozionale, dichiaratamente 'intuitivo'. Nella primavera del 2009, Christian Goudineau, con 'une grande émotion', 'voit César devant lui'. Lo tocca, lo prende in mano, e dichiara:

> Evidemment, c'est César. J'ai passé des années avec lui, lisant et relisant ses écrits, écrivant à mon tour des commentaires sur les siens ! Une sorte de relation à la foi intuitive et charnelle se crée avec celui que l'on a fréquenté si longtemps. Un regard suffit. [...] J'ai vu César, j'ai vu Lépide.[23]

A questo punto, i giochi sono fatti: il ritratto rappresenta *a priori* Giulio Cesare. È infatti esattamente in questo modo che l'articolo di Luc Long, dedicato al ritratto in questione nel catalogo *César: Le Rhône pour mémoire*, prende avvio:

> La mise au jour en 2007, sur la rive droite du Rhône, à Arles, d'un portrait inédit [*sic*] de César, vraisemblablement exécuté de son vivant et qu'il faut considérer aujourd'hui comme un *unicum*, a constitué un événement archéologique d'une importance considérable.[24]

L'argomento che avrebbe dovuto costituire la conclusione di una ricerca — sviluppato sulla base di un lungo ragionamento scientifico — è qui presentato, nella prima riga dell'articolo, come un elemento già acquisito. In luogo di proporre una discussione su diversi inquadramenti *possibili* del personaggio all'interno delle serie iconografiche dei ritratti conosciuti per questa fase cronologica — seguendo cioè il protocollo abituale di qualunque analisi stilistico-iconografica — l'attribuzione aprioristica viene dichiarata come l'idea *primigenia*, dalla quale emanerà ogni altra successiva argomentazione.

Il riconoscimento del ritratto come immagine di Giulio Cesare viene in seguito sviluppato sulla base della proposta di una serie di somiglianze — del resto notevolmente ipotetiche — con i ritratti attribuiti al dittatore. Il problema, come si sa, è che questi ultimi costituiscono un corpo a) postumo, e b) già dubbio all'origine. Di conseguenza, l'operazione conduce inevitabilmente a constatare una serie di discordanze troppo importanti rispetto ai modelli attualmente conosciuti. Tali incongruenze, invece di essere esplicitate mediante una sana concessione al beneficio del dubbio, vengono infine rimosse grazie a una giravolta concettuale a dir poco sorprendente, di nuovo basata sulla nozione dell'eccezionalità del reperto archeologico: in mancanza, di fronte a ogni evidenza, di una tipologia scultorea definibile, se ne deduce che il nostro busto rappresenti finalmente un *unicum*, la più antica rappresentazione della serie dei ritratti di Giulio Cesare: *la più antica* attualmente conosciuta![25]

La categoria classicistica di 'pezzo unico' ha dunque strutturato e costruito lo sguardo che è stato posto su questa scultura.[26] Questo sguardo non si limita tuttavia alla percezione del nostro ritratto, ma finisce per alimentare tutta la logica della sua restituzione all'interno del relativo contesto storico-archeologico. La nozione di 'capolavoro' artistico, e dell'eccezionalità delle altre sculture associate a questa scoperta, ha necessariamente comportato il ricorso a una ricostruzione del contesto della città di Arelate attraverso una visione iperbolica e idealizzante dei fenomeni storici, i quali hanno finito per diventare essi stessi dei 'fatti unici'. È questa, come sappiamo, un'immagine molto lontana dal passato che noi siamo in grado di ricostituire per un tipo di contesto storico-monumentale come questo.

Per includere il nuovo ritratto di Arles in un quadro scientificamente corretto di quello che doveva apparire una colonia di diritto romano fra l'età tardo-repubblicana e gli inizi del principato, sarà sufficiente ribadire — a noi stessi, come al grande pubblico — che la natura di questa scultura non è quella di un capolavoro, di un *unicum*, l'immagine di 'César de son vivant' (datato peraltro

---

[23] Goudineau 2009, 25.

[24] Long 2009, 58.

[25] Long 2009; Johansen 2009, 80.

[26] Analoghe osservazioni sono state sviluppate in Rosso 2016, 52.

in una fase ben troppo antica, fra il 60 e il 40 a.C.).[27] Ma che si tratta, più semplicemente, di una delle numerose immagini onorifiche che, erette in uno degli spazi — verosimilmente pubblici — della città, riproducevano la fisionomia di un personaggio eminente. Si trattava di un esponente dell'aristocrazia senatoria dell'Urbs? Di un rappresentante dell'élite locale della colonia?[28] Allo stato attuale delle nostre conoscenze non ci è dato di saperlo, proprio perché gli studi in questa direzione non sono stati ancora sufficientemente approfonditi. Quello che sappiamo è che, in questo contesto storico-culturale, la colonia di Arelate si configurava, nel cuore della Gallia meridionale di età repubblicana, come un centro profondamente ellenizzato e culturalmente 'à la page' all'interno dell'orizzonte politico e ideologico — e dunque figurativo — del Mediterraneo romanizzato della seconda metà del I secolo a.C. (ritorneremo su questo aspetto più avanti).

Così, sarebbe stato più giudizioso affermare che la scoperta di un ritratto come questo ad Arles è un fatto che non ha nulla di eccezionale ma che, al contrario, rivela tutto il suo interesse in quanto testimonianza di un episodio storicamente normale all'interno degli standards dell'evergetismo tardo-repubblicano. Ricercandone un'attribuzione *possibile* — e non il suo riconoscimento *assoluto* — all'interno di questo fenomeno storico, noi contribuiremo a risistemare una tessera ulteriore nel mosaico della storia di una delle colonie dell'impero di Roma. Non del *nostro* passato gallo-romano.[29]

---

[27] Long 2009, 70. Cfr. le osservazioni in merito di E. Rosso, vedi Rosso 2010, 261.

[28] Secondo l'opinione di E. Rosso, vedi Rosso 2010, 300.

[29] Come è stato recentemente affermato (Rosso 2010, 292), la pratica consistente nell'attribuzione spasmodica di ogni ritratto conservato a celebri personaggi storici sembra costituire un'attività ben diffusa nelle ricerche sulla ritrattistica delle Gallie. La tendenza a mettere in rilievo 'l'empreinte arlésienne de César dans des témoignages indirects ou mutilés' (Rosso 2010, 298) è un fenomeno ricorrente soprattutto nella letteratura che si è occupata di Arles. Tuttavia, non credo che, nel caso specifico qui analizzato, l'attitudine emozionale e 'intuitiva' che ha caratterizzato l'attribuzione del nostro ritratto a Giulio Cesare possa dipendere da una 'justification toute à fait légitime', in quanto basata su una 'physionomie césarienne' (Rosso 2010, 290) certa — della quale non sono peraltro convinto. Questo processo attribuzionistico dipende, come abbiamo visto, da uno schema ideologico ben più complesso, nel quale storia 'nazionale', archeologia classicistica, lettura modernistica dei contesti storico-archeologici, interesse per il sensazionalismo, rappresentano gli ingredienti di un cocktail forse gustoso a un primo assaggio, ma piuttosto pericoloso, sulla lunga durata, per l'organismo intellettuale del pubblico a cui è dato di consumarlo.

Il mito delle analisi 'scientifiche' e i metodi di studio nella ritrattistica greco-romana

Un ultimo aspetto con il qualche appare utile confrontarci in questa sede è il ricorso alla dimostrazione dell'attendibilità dei risultati ottenuti dalla ricerca archeologica attraverso analisi proprie delle cosiddette 'scienze esatte'. Il percorso attribuzionistico a cui è stato sottoposto il ritratto del Rodano, che abbiamo sopra discusso, è stato infatti presentato come definitivamente confermabile dai risultati della modellizzazione digitale della scultura da un lato e dagli interventi di specialisti di medicina legale e di antropologia medico-legale nelle analisi dei tratti del volto della figura dall'altro:[30] due argomenti che sono stati prodotti come prova definitiva della consacrazione del riconoscimento del ritratto come Giulio Cesare. La procedura, peraltro metodologicamente criticabile in sé (come avremo meglio occasione di approfondire più avanti, discutendo della costruzione della struttura del volto del personaggio), è stata anche chiaramente manipolata da argomentazioni, ancora una volta, di tipo circolare, per la cui critica rinvio alle osservazioni già sviluppate da Emmanuelle Rosso.[31] All'interno di un atteggiamento intellettuale tendente a idolatrare le scienze cosiddette 'esatte', si è ricorso a un postulato marcatamente modernistico, mettendo in opera un cortocircuito metodologico che ha lasciato ai margini ogni solida analisi stilistico-iconografica del documento scultoreo, vera *condicio sine qua* per tentare di comprenderlo.[32]

Occorre qui ribadire, al contrario, tutto il peso e il valore di questo tipo di procedura: l'attribuzione di un nuovo ritratto a una serie tipologica conosciuta non può che costruirsi sull'esercizio di metodo e sull'applicazione dei criteri canonici allo studio della ritrattistica antica. Questi criteri si fondano, come noto, sulle conoscenze maturate durante lunghi anni di ricerca 'sul terreno' grazie all'acquisizione lenta e complessa di una familiarità diretta, materiale, nei confronti di una documentazione archeologica particolarmente difficile: su un'esperienza conoscitiva cumulativa, erudita, colta. Questi criteri presuppongono innanzi tutto la nostra capacità visiva (e intellettuale) nel riconoscere l'esistenza, o meno, della corrispondenza di un numero sufficiente di detta-

---

[30] Long 2009, 67.

[31] Rosso 2010, 292.

[32] In perfetta corrispondenza, del resto, con l'attuale diffusa richiesta istituzionale di ricorrere, in ogni progetto scientifico, all'adozione — molto spesso epistemologicamente sterile — di quello che il linguaggio alla moda chiama le 'tecnologie innovanti'.

gli fisiognomici fra due o più ritratti; ma, soprattutto, la nostra sensibilità nell'identificare la presenza, o meno, di un elemento-chiave in grado di farci stabilire ogni possibile riconoscimento iconografico: l'espressione del volto, il tipo di sguardo del personaggio rappresentato, la ricorrenza di quello 'schema mimico' che sia proprio al personaggio, che l'abbia reso unico e — di conseguenza — riconoscibile. Riconoscibile oggi, come agli occhi del pubblico ed esso contemporaneo.

Una delle più peculiari e preziose risorse degli scultori dell'antichità greco-romana risiedette, in effetti, in quella loro straordinaria capacità di far 'vivere' un personaggio nella sua rappresentazione statuaria, e di farlo vivere 'per sempre': attraverso la sua materializzazione in un'immagine 'pietrificata', realizzata in un materiale imperituro, inalterabile[33] (il marmo, il calcare, il bronzo, la terracotta ...). Vera e propria immagine fotografica a tre dimensioni della persona onorata, una statua-ritratto era dotata dello statuto di strumento privilegiato della trasmissione visiva di una serie di elementi propri del personaggio raffigurato: la sua qualifica a livello di rango sociopolitico, il suo modo di pensare e di porsi nella realtà del suo mondo, il suo ruolo di testimone di una storia passata che, rinnovandosi continuamente in quanto visualmente incarnata dall'immagine scultorea, diventava così contemporanea:[34] per questo doveva essere in grado di essere *riconoscibile*.[35] Tale 'processo identificatorio' veniva ottenuto grazie ad almeno tre elementi offerti allo spettatore antico, realizzati dall'artista attraverso un alto esercizio sul piano stilistico, iconografico ed epigrafico: il primo esercizio per ottenere un alto tasso di verosimiglianza della fisionomia, e dell'espressione, del volto; il secondo per descrivere con precisione analitica gli attributi che ne designavano il rango e la funzione; il terzo per fornire al pubblico l'opportunità di poter leggere, grazie all'iscrizione sulla base, il *cursus honorum* del personaggio. Tutto questo una statua-ritratto significava, e per questo i latini la chiamavano *signum*.

Il ritratto del Rodano non può appartenere all'iconografia di Giulio Cesare, per ragioni diverse e sostanziali che non abbiamo qui il tempo di elencare, ragioni che dipendono fondamentalmente dai criteri metodologici propri alla disciplina dello studio della ritrattistica antica. Ma vogliamo evocarne almeno una, accanto alla considerazione delle profonde divergenze riscontrabili nei

dettagli fisiognomici del dittatore (che si possono facilmente controllare sulle effigi monetali). Stiamo parlando di un altro grande assente nelle ricerche finora sviluppate su questo tema: la presa in considerazione dello sguardo, dell'espressione propria alla personalità dell'uomo rappresentato. Il tratto che, fondamentalmente, rende un personaggio unico (e, di conseguenza, immediatamente riconoscibile). E che, in nulla corrispondente a quello delle immagini del dittatore, potrebbe oggi guidarci lungo il cammino di una possibile identificazione del ritratto in questione.

Appare interessante osservare che questo elemento, se per un verso non ha ricevuto l'attenzione dovuta sul piano euristico, è stato per un altro paradossalmente evocato proprio nel titolo del principale articolo dedicato alla nostra scultura: 'Le *regard* de César. Le Rhône restitue un portrait du fondateur de la colonie d'Arles'.[36] Come abbiamo visto, l'evocazione dello sguardo del personaggio raffigurato sul ritratto del Rodano dipende, in questo contesto storiografico, da un'attitudine metodologica che ha conferito a questa scultura un'aura di tipo emozionale, finalizzata alla costruzione di un modello interpretativo fortemente ideologizzato. Al contrario, se correttamente utilizzato, questo stesso ingrediente avrebbe inevitabilmente finito per trasformarsi in uno degli argomenti-chiave per rivelare una delle differenze più evidenti fra i ritratti di Giulio Cesare attualmente conosciuti e il ritratto del Rodano.[37]

Note sul contesto storico-politico del ritratto del Rodano

È ora il momento di ritrovare insieme la strada di un percorso di ricerca in grado di cercare di ricostruire un quadro storico-archeologico corretto e verosimile per il ritratto emerso dalle acque del Rodano. Si tratta qui, semplicemente, di collocare quest'ultimo nel suo contesto, non solo in relazione alla storia del ritratto ellenistico-romano, ma della Storia stessa, attraverso un itinerario articolato in tre direzioni, fra loro dialetticamente intrecciate: l'analisi degli aspetti tecnici e stilistici della scultura, nell'obbiettivo di avvicinarsi per quanto possibile alla data e all'ambiente figurativo in cui esso è stato realizzato; lo studio del contesto archeologico-evergetico e storico-prosopografico che ne caratterizzava, all'epoca, il luogo della scoperta e lo spazio (possi-

---

[33] cfr. Bettini 1992.

[34] Pol. vi.53.

[35] È questo, ne sono convinto, il senso primo del realismo nella ritrattistica greco-romana.

[36] Long 2009 (il corsivo è mio).

[37] Come Paul Zanker (Zanker 2010) ha avuto l'occasione di sottolineare.

bile) della sua erezione; l'esame della rete delle immagini più vicine ad esso, documentate all'interno del mondo greco-romano per il periodo preso in considerazione, nell'obbiettivo di cercare di riconoscere ogni eventuale somiglianza fisiognomica e, nel migliore dei casi, di proporne un'attribuzione la più verosimile possibile. È in questa prospettiva che evocheremo ora, in modo molto succinto, alcune coordinate storico-politiche entro cui la scultura potrebbe essere inserita.

Abbiamo innanzi tutto in nostro possesso alcune utili notizie sull'attività dei membri dell'élite senatoria urbana nella nostra regione in età repubblicana. Al momento della fondazione di Arelate nel 46 a.C., come colonia di diritto romano,[38] Giulio Cesare invia in Gallia T. Claudius Nero,[39] presente ad Arles per i veterani della VIª legione, i *sextani*[40] (e a Narbonne per i veterani della Xª legione, i *decumani*). Il fatto che i *sextani* fossero originari dell'alto Lazio e del Sannio[41] costituisce un argomento di un certo interesse per l'identificazione della coloritura della formazione culturale dei coloni di Arelate.[42] Questo stesso anno, del resto, corrisponde significativamente a quello del consolato di Giulio Cesare e di M. Aemilius Lepidus, il triumviro:[43] quest'ultimo — pretore nel 49, governatore della Hispania Citerior nel 48–47 e console ancora nel 42 — diventerà nel 43 governatore della Gallia Narbonese.

In età imperiale, *patronus* della città è L. Cassius Longinus, console nel 30 d.C.[44] e marito di Julia Drusilla.[45] Potrebbe risultare di un certo rilievo sottolineare che la famiglia di quest'ultima possedeva numerose proprietà nella valle del Rodano.[46]

Augusto soggiornò ad Arles ben cinque volte. Una volta, durante tre anni (dal 16 al 13 a.C.).[47]

Il dossier relativo ai membri dell'élite locale di Arelate,[48] anche se piuttosto scarno, appare certamente notevole sotto il profilo politico. Pompeius Paulinus, 'un cavaliere di Arles' secondo Plinio, è prefetto dell'Annona tra il 48 e il 55 sotto Claudio[49] et suocero di Seneca, il quale gli dedicò il *De Brevitate vitae*.[50] Suo figlio, Pompeius Paulinus, console probabilmente nel 55, è *legatus* in Germania superior nel 56 e sarà chiamato da Nerone in una commissione di tre *consulares* con il compito di amministrare le entrate dello stato nel 62.[51]

Due sono le famiglie dell'aristocrazia arlesiana a noi note: i Mettii e gli Annii. Dei Mettii[52] conosciamo due prefetti dell'Egitto, un legato di Licia-Panfilia e un proconsole in Achaia.[53] Mettius Rufus è prefetto dell'Annona sotto Claudio, e in seguito prefetto dell'Egitto. Degli Annii, nel corso della seconda metà del I sec. d.C., A. Annius Camars è pretore e proconsole della provincia di Cipro, e infine legato del proconsole d'Africa.[54]

Un elemento intorno al quale occorrerà probabilmente lavorare ulteriormente è costituito dal fatto che tutti i membri delle due famiglie da noi conosciute, appartenenti all'élite locale di Arelate, sviluppino in modo ricorrente interessi in Asia Minore. La possibile origine del marmo del ritratto del Rodano (Dokimeion in Frigia)[55] potrebbe in tal modo ritrovare un interessante inquadramento geografico-politico.

Se il quadro prosopografico ora brevemente tracciato invita per un verso a interpretare l'orizzonte storico-politico arlesiano di età repubblicana (e in seguito, di conseguenza, alto-imperiale) come proprio di un centro urbano certamente non insignificante sul piano evergetico, siamo obbligati dall'altro a confrontarci con il problema dell'attuale assenza di una documentazione monumentale databile prima del principato augusteo.

---

[38] PW II, I, 1895, cc. 633–35.

[39] PW III, 2, 1899 cc. 2777–2778 n. 254. Alla metà del I secolo a.C. il personaggio aveva sviluppato interessi personali in Bitinia (Cic., *Fam.* XIII.64.1). *Quaestor* nel 48, comandante della flotta di Cesare nella guerra alessandrina, T. Claudio Nero propone nel 44 una ricompensa per i tirannicidi. *Praetor* nel 41, appoggia L. Antonius contro Ottaviano. Sposa Livia Drusilla, dalla quale avrà due figli: Tiberius, il futuro imperatore, e Drusus. Dopo il 39, Ottaviano lo persuaderà a divorziare da Livia; vedi Syme 1993, 152–53.

[40] Carcopino 1968, 543.

[41] Constans 1928, 14.

[42] Cfr. Rosso 2010, 300.

[43] PW n. 7. Syme 1993, 165–67; Monterosso Checa 2009, 94.

[44] PW III, 2, 1899, *c.* 1740 n. 67. Syme 1993, 258: appartenente all'antica *nobilitas* plebea.

[45] PW n. 567: seconda figlia di Germanico e di Agrippina.

[46] Gros 1987, 90 n. 86.

[47] Constans 1928, 18.

[48] Sui committenti, vedi Slavazzi 1996, 151.

[49] Gros 1987, 90 n. 87.

[50] Constans 1928, 21.

[51] Constans 1928, 20.

[52] PW XV, 2, 1932, cc. 1498–1503, 'Mettius': '[name] bei Osken wie bei Latinen'.

[53] Pflaum 1970.

[54] Constans 1928, 21.

[55] Secondo le analisi di Blanc e Bromblet 2009. In seguito a una personale osservazione autoptica del ritratto in occasione della mostra al Louvre, mi sono posto il dubbio se non poteva trattarsi di marmo pario.

Tuttavia, come si è visto, il quadro storico-prosopografico che caratterizzò la colonia di Arelate in età tardo-repubblicana sembra aver potuto difficilmente configurarsi come privo dei segni di una monumentalizzazione di un certo livello: i segni propri di qualunque altra analoga fondazione, e caratteristici in particolare di una colonia di diritto *romano*. Tale prospettiva euristica fa evidentemente ricorso a un modello puramente teorico, quello che ci è noto per questo tipo di deduzioni coloniarie, in quanto la documentazione monumentale di Arles a nostra disposizione non sembra risalire precedentemente agli anni 20 a.C.[56]

Questo iato fra la data di fondazione della città e l'avvio del processo della sua monumentalizzazione — una circostanza attualmente considerata come naturale e fisiologica — mi lascia tuttavia piuttosto perplesso.[57] Un intervento evergetico, sempre di alto profilo in termini quantitativi e qualitativi, appare in effetti documentato in maniera ricorrente negli anni *immediatamente successivi* alle deduzioni coloniarie conosciute, in particolare all'interno di contesti geografico-politici limitrofi ostili (pensiamo all'esempio di Cremona) così come nelle colonie *optimo iure*.[58] In questo quadro, in che misura noi dobbiamo ritenere certa una disparità di esiti e di comportamenti delle élites locali della Narbonnese rispetto, ad esempio, a quelle della Cisalpina? Sulla base di quali criteri? Un approccio 'gallo-romano' alla questione potrebbe di nuovo influire su questo tipo di visione? A che livello l'*argumentum ex silentio* — l'attuale assenza di documentazione — determina la nostra percezione del fenomeno?

Emblematica, in questo senso, si rivela la situazione storiografica del Nord-ovest della Gallia, una regione considerata, sino a poco tempo fa, come isolata e priva dei segni di una romanizzazione monumentale. Le recenti ricerche di Yvan Maligorne hanno consentito di rovesciare tale prospettiva, attraverso una lettura della documentazione nota che ha mostrato come le interpretazioni diffuse fossero sovente il risultato di precisi approcci ideologici.[59] Lo stesso si può affermare per quanto riguarda la Gallia Cisalpina, la visione della cui monumentalizzazione rimase, fino alla metà degli anni '80 del secolo scorso, completamente appiattita sull'immagine di un avvio del fenomeno non prima del regno di Augusto, considerandolo peraltro in senso sfavorevol-

mente 'provinciale'.[60] Ci sono voluti vent'anni di studi e di ricerche, costruite su una serie di trasformazioni metodologiche sostanziali, per far cadere questo preconcetto e poter finalmente mettere in valore la straordinaria ricchezza della documentazione di età repubblicana di questa regione, perfettamente ancorata sul piano cronologico e qualitativo alle coordinate formali, iconografiche e monumentali della produzione ellenistica internazionale del suo tempo.[61]

Credo che, per comprendere meglio situazioni come queste, occorra non lasciare ai margini la considerazione di un fenomeno più generale, che si colloca all'interno delle dinamiche relazionali fra Centro e Periferia fra tarda Repubblica e primo Impero. Mi riferisco — riassumendo — al fenomeno per il quale perché i gruppi dirigenti locali fossero in grado di far eleggere uno dei loro rappresentanti nel senato della Capitale, fosse necessario che almeno una (o anche due) generazioni *precedenti* la persona che ebbe accesso alle più alte magistrature, avessero partecipato ad almeno un'attività evergetica sufficientemente rilevante per riuscire a ottenere questo privilegio. Ora, se noi consideriamo le più antiche cronologie note dell'accesso alle magistrature urbane da parte dei personaggi di origine arlesiana (concentrate tutte intorno alla prima metà del I secolo d.C.), sembra legittimo non escludere un impegno politico-istituzionale da parte delle élites locali già al momento della deduzione coloniale. E, di conseguenza, un'attività evergetica piuttosto precoce nella loro città d'origine.

A conclusione del suo studio sulla scultura 'decorativa' della Narbonese, Fabrizio Slavazzi ha potuto osservare — all'interno di una datazione in ogni caso augustea delle più antiche testimonianze di copie di originali greci — come la regione fosse particolarmente vicina a Roma sul piano della qualità, della varietà e della diffusione di questo tipo di documentazione, anche in ragione di un assorbimento molto profondo della cultura della Capitale presso i gruppi dirigenti locali.[62] La definizione pliniana. *Italia verius quam provinciam*[63] dovrebbe dunque, in tale prospettiva, farci riflettere ulteriormente (considerando nel contempo la cronologia alta della probabile, anche se dibattuta, acquisizione dello statuto di provincia da parte di questa regione).[64]

---

[56] Gros 1987.

[57] Gros 1987, 89; Rosso 2010; Monterosso Checa 2009, 94.

[58] Denti 1991b, 183, con bibliografia precedente.

[59] Maligorne 2006.

[60] Mansuelli 1958; 1964; Chevallier 1983.

[61] Bandelli 1988; Denti 1991a; 1991b; Compostella 1996; Verzár-Bass 1996.

[62] Slavazzi 1996, 153.

[63] Plin., *HN*. III.4.31.

[64] Rinaldi Tufi 2000, 67.

Figura 10.1. Busto maschile in marmo, vista frontale, Arles, Musée départemental Arles antique. Da: Denti 2016, 93, fig. 5.

Figura 10.2. Busto maschile in marmo, lato, Arles, Musée départemental Arles antique. Da: Long e Picard 2009, 64.

Figura 10.3. Busto maschile in marmo, non finito, Aquileia, Museo Archeologico. Foto: Mario Denti.

Note su alcuni aspetti tecnico-stilistici del ritratto del Rodano

Lungi dal proporre in questa sede uno studio esauriente, cercheremo ora di seguire alcuni potenziali percorsi di ricerca in relazione agli aspetti tecnici, stilistici e iconografici del ritratto del Rodano,[65] scegliendoli fra quelli in grado di alimentare le problematiche in precedenza discusse.

In primo luogo, sarebbe opportuno che la scultura venga chiamata 'busto' e non 'ritratto' perché è questa l'esatta tipologia a cui essa appartiene, come ci indica la morfologia della parte inferiore del pezzo (Fig. 10.1). Si tratta di una tipologia ben diffusa nel corso della prima metà del I secolo d.C.[66]

Occorre inoltre sottolineare che il taglio verticale della parte posteriore del capo è stato realizzato *prima* della lavorazione dettagliata della superficie del marmo, come ci suggerisce inequivocabilmente la modellazione delle ciocche dei capelli intorno al profilo della parte posteriore della testa (Fig. 10.2).[67] In considerazione di tale foggia della parte posteriore del busto, ma anche delle proporzioni, piuttosto ridotte, del pezzo (h 39,5 cm), non è escluso che possa trattarsi di un'*imago clipeata*.[68] Questa tipologia, originaria con tutta probabilità dell'Oriente ellenistico, è attestata in particolare a Delo, da dove si diffonde in Occidente e, significativamente, in Italia settentrionale. Il più celebre esempio proveniente da quest'area è il busto repubblicano, non finito, di Aquileia (Fig. 10.3 e 10.4),[69] estremamente utile come confronto per la tipologia e la tecnica di costruzione del busto. Conosciamo inoltre alcune importanti ricezioni di questa tipologia anche presso gli ambienti delle committenze appartenenti all'élite locale della Cisalpina, testimoniate dal busto in calcare da Tarvisium

---

[65] Che necessitano, evidentemente, di un percorso di ricerca a sé stante — già in parte condotto da E. Rosso, vedi Rosso 2010.

[66] Un chiaro confronto, per la forma del busto, è con il presunto Lusius Storax, a Chieti; vedi Sanzi Di Mino e Nista 1993, 74 n. 20, datato al secondo quarto del I secolo d.C.

[67] Long 2009, 64 e 73. Cfr. il ritratto di Palestrina al Museo Nazionale Romano (h 38 cm), che presenta la parte posteriore tagliata (anche se il settore corrispondente alla nuca, in questo caso, dovette ricevere un'altra porzione di marmo per completare il pezzo), datato all'ultimo quarto del I secolo a.C.: Giuliano 1988, 75 n. R44.

[68] Questa ipotesi è stata formulata anche da E. Rosso, vedi Rosso 2010, n. 135. *Contra*: Baumer 2016, che vi ha visto un ritratto a rilievo decorante il monumento funerario di un liberto. L'ipotesi appare difficilmente sostenibile, in considerazione soprattutto dell'alta qualità formale e materiale (marmo greco) della scultura, eretta non in ambiente urbano.

[69] Denti 1991a, 63 n. 7, tav. XVI–XVII.

Figura 10.4. Busto maschile in marmo, non finito, lato, Aquileia, Museo Archeologico. Foto: Mario Denti.

Figura 10.5. Busto maschile in calcare, lato, Treviso, Museo Civico. Foto: Mario Denti.

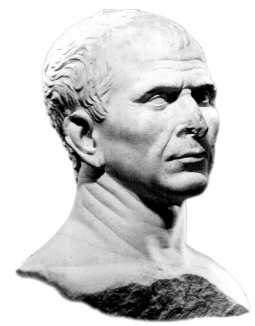

Figura 10.6. Busto maschile in marmo, vista da tre quarti da sinistra, Arles, Musée départemental Arles antique. Da: Long e Picard 2009, 75.

(Fig. 10.5),[70] che consente di cogliere notevoli somiglianze, in particolare nei dettagli tecnici applicati a una stessa tipologia, con l'esemplare di Arles.

Occorre egualmente notare che il punto di vista corretto per osservare il ritratto del Rodano non è quello assiale, ma di tre quarti da sinistra (dello spettatore). La circostanza appare immediatamente evidente osservando da vicino alcuni dettagli tecnici propri del lavoro dello scultore, e considerando nel contempo la costruzione dei volumi della testa: la parte destra della capigliatura (quella in tal caso meglio visibile per lo spettatore) appare molto più accurata di quella di sinistra, e la struttura dei volumi diventa correttamente percepibile solo se la si osserva dalla nostra sinistra (Fig. 10.6). Anziché dipendere da una deformazione fisiologica del cranio del personaggio, come è stato proposto,[71] è questo il frutto del modo di lavorare tipico degli scultori ellenistici, perfettamente in grado — grazie all'inserzione di sottili asimmetrie — di costruire e di adattare i volumi delle loro teste prevedendone con notevole precisione il luogo di esposizione, e dunque l'esatto punto di vista del pubblico.[72]

Per cogliere con esattezza questo fenomeno, e recuperare l'esposizione originale del busto, occorre semplicemente utilizzare il piano già esistente del taglio posteriore: è sufficiente arretrare leggermente la parte sinistra della scultura fino a sistemarne il retro contro un fondo, ed essa finirà automaticamente per corrispondere all'esposizione prevista al momento della sua realizzazione. La percezione della corretta morfologia dei volumi della testa ritroverà allora, naturalmente, tutta la sua coerenza (Fig. 10.6). Se ci sistemiamo, al contrario, in una prospettiva assiale, la figura rivelerà tutta una serie di asimmetrie: si noti in particolare la notevole diversità fra gli occhi (Fig. 10.1), la quale scompare completamente se li si osserva da sinistra (Fig. 10.6).

Si rivela significativo a questo proposito notare che, nella mostra del Louvre, il nostro ritratto è stato presentato frontalmente, girandolo fino a renderlo visibile in modo perfettamente frontale: attraverso dunque una prospettiva assiale, rispondente — di nuovo — a criteri visuali (e intellettuali) di tipo classicistico, incapaci di saper riconoscere, e sfruttare, la straordinaria ricchezza e complessità (filosofica, prima che formale) dell'arte ellenistica.

Ecco dunque un ulteriore argomento che conferma il tipo di approccio che ha caratterizzato il percorso dello studio e della presentazione al grande pubblico di questa scultura. Si tratta peraltro di un approccio che ritro-

---

70 Denti 1991a, 151 n. 2, tav. LI.

71 Long 2009, 58.

72 Denti 1991a, 54; 2004, 245.

Figura 10.7. Ritratto maschile in bronzo, Verona, Museo Archeologico al Teatro Romano. Foto: Mario Denti.

viamo molto spesso anche nella letteratura specializzata sulla ritrattistica greco-romana, in cui le fotografie delle teste sono prese quasi sempre da un punto di vista assiale (come si può facilmente verificare nella maggior parte dei cataloghi di scultura antica), con il risultato di deformare profondamente i principi dell'estetica e gli accorgimenti tecnici degli artisti ellenistici.

La disposizione assiale del nostro ritratto impedisce così non solo di cogliere le specifiche qualità del savoir-faire della migliore tradizione tecnico-formale degli atelier scultorei del mondo ellenistico-romano, ma finisce anche per giustificare una serie di argomenti — basati sull'asserzione di una presunta plagiocefalia —[73] destinati a inserire la sua iconografia all'interno della serie dei ritratti attualmente attribuiti a Giulio Cesare.

Per quanto riguarda infine la possibilità di identificare il personaggio rappresentato, come è stato notato da altri specialisti,[74] ogni percorso interpretativo dovrà tener conto delle caratteristiche di un tipo di immagine che rifletteva sia le coordinate figurative sia i modelli di comportamento propri dei protagonisti della storia politica nel momento del passaggio dalla Repubblica al Principato. In questo senso, senza aver bisogno di rincorrere a somiglianze (del resto notevolmente dubbie) con l'iconografia nota di Giulio Cesare, sarà sufficiente approfondire i percorsi tracciati dalle marcate corrispondenze che il nostro ritratto rivela con un buon numero di esemplari scultorei databili tra la fine dell'età repubblicana e gli inizi del regno di Augusto.[75]

Per farsene un'idea, la struttura della testa e alcuni elementi fisiognomici (profilo anteriore della capigliatura; forma del mento e della bocca, con le estremità rivolte verso il basso; presenza di due profonde rughe correnti obliquamente dalle narici alle estremità della bocca) si ritrovano ad esempio nella serie dei ritratti di Merida, databili all'ultimo quarto del I secolo a.C.[76] Un buon numero di affinità fisiognomiche emerge inoltre in maniera molto istruttiva con un ritratto in bronzo da Pestrino, nei pressi di Verona (Fig. 10.7):[77] struttura generale del volto; forma delle orecchie; costruzione della regione mento-bocca-naso; forma del naso; forma della fronte; struttura e dettagli della regione occhi-sopracciglia-zigomi. Si osservino, più in particolare, gli occhi, notevolmente ravvicinati fra loro: stesso profilo, stessa forma delle palpebre, identico disegno delle rughe alle estremità, senza parlare dell'espressione del viso, sorprendentemente analoga (Fig. 10.1 e 10.7). Tuttavia, se confrontiamo il profilo dei due ritratti, noteremo una marcata disparità nella morfologia del mento.

L'esempio qui preso in considerazione, nonostante le inequivocabili somiglianze fisiognomiche, ci dimostra comunque come un'attitudine a ogni costo attribuzionistica possa rivelarsi un esercizio estremamente rischioso, anche quando questo viene applicato a un contesto figurativo meno 'eccezionale' della serie cesariana, e forse più coerente sul piano storico: quello dell'*imagerie* dei gruppi dirigenti locali della fine della Repubblica.

Conclusioni

Le forme in cui sono stati condotti lo studio e la mediatizzazione della scultura venuta alla luce nelle acque del Rodano e glorificata come un nuovo ritratto di Giulio Cesare — forme che non rappresentano certo un caso isolato nell'attuale orizzonte della ricerca archeologica — riflettono una serie di percorsi metodologici e ideologici ben riconoscibili all'interno di buona parte della cultura accademica contemporanea.

Il ricorrente ricorso alla celebrazione di ritrovamenti 'unici', 'eccezionali', 'spettacolari' risponde a necessità e a strategie in cui — lo si sa — gli aspetti economici diventano oggi vieppiù determinanti. Questo fenomeno, tuttavia, si accompagna molto spesso (come nel caso qui esaminato, incentrato sull'immaginario cesariano) all'attri-

---

[73] Long 2009, 58 e 68.

[74] Cfr. le osservazioni di P. Zanker et di E. Rosso, locc. citt. *infra*.

[75] In questa stessa prospettiva si collocano le osservazioni di

Emmanuelle Rosso, vedi Rosso 2016.

[76] León 1980, tav. 36–44.

[77] Denti 1991a, 227, tav. LXX.

buzione di una particolare enfasi nei confronti di quelle scoperte archeologiche in grado di consolidare percorsi ideologici a carattere classicistico da un lato, etnico-identitario dall'altro, il tutto rinsaldato da una rinnovata fede 'scientista' che marginalizza definitivamente ogni traiettoria critica a carattere storico. In particolare Oltralpe, esso trova il suo fondamento nella frequentazione (più o meno cosciente) di ideologie fondamentalmente nazionalistiche, risorgenti in modo ricorrente dall'humus di una tradizione culturale che, nel milieu dell'archeologia francese, ha un nome preciso: archeologia gallo-romana.

L'immagine di Giulio Cesare si configura dunque di nuovo, all'interno di questa vicenda, come paradigma di una storia sentita come identitaria: uno schema, già tristemente noto nelle vicende storiche del Novecento europeo, che riemerge agli inizi del terzo millennio, in

significativa corrispondenza con un contesto politico e ideologico compatibile con la disinvoltura con cui scelte consimili vengono inerzialmente accolte, divenendo peraltro, con il tempo, vulgata dominante.[78] È questo, molto probabilmente, il rischio che corriamo oggi, se non ci poniamo nella condizione critica di riconoscere in maniera sufficientemente chiara i termini esatti di operazioni scientifiche e culturali che mai dobbiamo rinunciare a smascherare come non neutrali.

---

[78] Emmanuelle Rosso segnala (Rosso 2016, 58) la moltiplicazione dell'accoglimento dell'interpretazione del ritratto come immagine di Giulio Cesare nella letteratura archeologica francese: 'Ainsi se multiplient les effigies de César en Gaule, une identification douteuse servant de socle à une proposition plus fragile encore, en un étonannte surenchère'.

Bibliografia

Bandelli, G. 1988. *Ricerche sulla colonizzazione romana della Gallia Cisalpina: le fasi iniziali e il caso aquileiese* (Roma: Quasar).

Baumer, L. E. 2016. 'Forme, fonction, identité ? Une approche du "César d'Arles"', in V. Gaggadis-Robin e P. Picard (a cura di), *La sculpture romaine en Occident: nouveaux regards; actes des Rencontres autour de la sculpture romaine 2012* (Arles: Errance), pp. 75–81.

Bettini, M. 1992. *Il ritratto dell'amante* (Torino: Einaudi).

Bianchi Bandinelli, R. 1981. *Introduzione all'archeologia classica come storia dell'arte antica*, Universale Laterza, 334 (Bari: Laterza).

Blanc, P. e P. Bromblet. 2009. 'Déterminer l'origine des marbres sculptés', in L. Long e P. Picard (a cura di), *César: le Rhône pour mémoire; vingt ans de fouilles dans le fleuve à Arles* (Arles: Musée départemental Arles antique), pp. 84–87.

Carcopino, J. 1968. *Jules César*, 5th edn (Paris: Presses universitaires de France).

Chevallier, R. 1983. *La romanisation de la Celtique du Pô: essai d'histoire provinciale*, Bibliothèque des Écoles françaises d'Athènes et de Rome, 249 (Rome: École française de Rome).

Coarelli, F. 1996. *Revixit ars: arte e ideologia a Roma; dai modelli ellenistici alla tradizione repubblicana* (Rome: Quasar).

Compostella, C. 1996. *Ornata sepulcra: le 'borghesie' municipali e la memoria di sé nell'arte funeraria del Veneto romano* (Firenze: Nuova Italia).

Constans, L.-A. 1928. *Arles* (Paris: Les belles lettres).

Demoule, J.-P. 2010. 'Arles: quid de César?', 28 October 2010, <http://culture.france2.fr/patrimoine/actu/arles-quid-de-cesar-62042815.html?paragraphe=6> [assessed 23 February 2022].

Denti, M. 1991a. *Ellenismo e romanizzazione nella X Regio: la scultura delle élites locali dall'età repubblicana ai Giulio-Claudi* (Roma: Bretschneider).

—— 1991b. *I Romani a nord del Po: archeologia e cultura in età repubblicana e augustea* (Milan: Longanesi).

—— 2005. 'Trois statues de culte en Gaule cisalpine: artistes, commanditaires de l'urbs et clientèle locale à l'époque républicaine', in F. Trément, L. Lamoine e M. Cébeillac-Gervasoni (a cura di), *Autocélébration des élites locales dans le monde romain: contextes, images, textes, IIᵉ s. av. J.-C. – IIIᵉ s. ap. J.-C.* (Clermont-Ferrand: Presses universitaires Blaise Pascal), pp. 233–66.

—— 2008a. 'L'art du portrait en Grèce et à Rome, ou de l'approche ethnique et formaliste à un phénomène culturel et politique', *Perspective*, 1: 72–78.

—— 2008b. 'L'auctoritas du Classique dans la construction de la périodisation de l'art romain', *Perspective*, 4: 684–702.

—— 2014. 'Nuove prospettive e vecchi paradigmi negli strumenti della formazione universitaria contemporanea: considerazioni sulla manualistica di archeologia e storia dell'arte antica', *Revue archéologique*, 1: 89–99.

—— 2016. 'Idéologie et culture de la recherche sur le portrait gréco-romain: le "César" du Rhône', in V. Gaggadis-Robin e P. Picard (a cura di), *La sculpture romaine en Occident: nouveaux regards; actes des Rencontres autour de la sculpture romaine 2012* (Arles: Errance), pp. 83–95.

Gaggadis-Robin, V. e P. Picard. 2016. *La sculpture romaine en Occident: nouveaux regards; actes des Rencontres autour de la sculpture romaine 2012*, Bibliothèque d'archéologie méditerranéenne et africaine, 20 (Arles: Errance).

Gentili, G. 2008. *Giulio Cesare: l'uomo, le imprese, il mito* (Milan: Silvana).

Giuliano, A. 1988. *Museo nazionale romano: le sculture*, I.9.2.1: *Magazzini, i ritratti* (Rome: De Luca).

Goudineau, C. 2009. 'Arelate duplex, Arles la double', in L. Long e P. Picard (a cura di), *César, le Rhône pour mémoire: vingt ans de fouilles dans le fleuve à Arles* (Arles: Musée départemental Arles antique), pp. 22–27.

Gros, P. 1987. 'Remarques sur les fondations urbaines de Gaule Narbonnaise et de Cisalpine au début de l'empire', in *Atti del Convegno: studi lunensi e prospettive sull'occidente romano* (Luni: Quaderni del Centro Studi Lunensi), pp. 73–95.

Johansen, F. 2009. 'Les portraits de César', in L. Long e P. Picard (a cura di), *César: le Rhône pour mémoire: vingt ans de fouilles dans le fleuve à Arles* (Arles: Musée départemental Arles antique), pp. 78–83.

León, P. 1980. 'Die Übernahme des römischen Porträts in Hispanien am Ende des Republik', *Madrider Mitteilungen*, 21: 165–79.

Long, L. 2009. 'César, le Rhône pour mémoire', in L. Long e P. Picard (a cura di), *César: le Rhône pour mémoire; vingt ans de fouilles dans le fleuve à Arles* (Arles: Musée départemental Arles antique), pp. 58–73.

Long, L. e P. Picard. 2009. *César: le Rhône pour mémoire: vingt ans de fouilles dans le fleuve à Arles* (Arles: Musée départemental Arles antique).

Maligorne, Y. 2006. *L'architecture romaine dans l'Ouest de la Gaule* (Rennes: Presses universitaires de Rennes).

Mansuelli, G. A. 1958. 'Studi sull'arte romana nell'Italia settentrionale. La scultura colta'. *Rivista dell'Istituto nazionale di archeologia e storia dell'arte*, 8: 45–128.

—— 1964. *Arte e civiltà romana nell'Italia settentrionale dalla repubblica alla tetrarchia* (Bologna: Alfa).

Marc, J.-Y. 2014. 'Gaulois, Gallo-Romains et Romains vus du bord du Rhin', in G. Alberti, C. Féliu e G. Pierrevelcin (a cura di), *Transalpinaire: mélanges offerts à Anne-Marie Adam* (Bordeaux: Ausonius), pp. 23–49.

Monterosso Checa, A. 2009. 'M. Aemilius Lepidus. Hypothèse sur un portrait', in L. Long e P. Picard (a cura di), *César: le Rhône pour mémoire; vingt ans de fouilles dans le fleuve à Arles* (Arles: Musée départemental Arles antique), pp. 89–95.

Pflaum, H.-G. 1970. 'Une famille arlésienne à la fin du Ier siècle et au IIe siècle de notre ère', *Bulletin de la Société nationale des antiquaires de France*, 1: 265–72.

Rinaldi Tufi, S. 2000. *Archeologia delle province romane* (Rome: Carocci).

Rosso, E. 2010. 'Le portrait tardo-républicain en Gaule méridionale: essai de bilan critique', *Revue archéologique*, 2: 259–307.

—— 2016. 'César et le buste du Rhône, quatre ans après', in V. Gaggadis-Robin e P. Picard (a cura di), *La sculpture romaine en Occident: nouveaux regards; actes des Rencontres autour de la sculpture romaine 2012* (Arles: Errance), pp. 49–59.

Sanzi Di Mino, M. R. e L. Nista. 1993. *Gentes et Principes: Iconografia romana in Abruzzo* (Chieti: Pacini).

Slavazzi, F. 1996. *Italia verius quam provincia: Diffusione e funzione delle copie di sculture greche nella Gallia Narbonensis* (Perugia: Edizioni Scientifiche italiane).

Syme, R. 1993. *L'aristocrazia augustea* (Milan: Rizzoli).

Verzár-Bass, M. 1996. 'Spunti per una ricerca sulla politica religiosa in età repubblicana nella Gallia Cisalpina', in M. Cébeillac-Gervasoni (a cura di), *Les élites municipales de l'Italie péninsulaire des Gracques à Néron* (Napoli: Centre Jean Bérard), pp. 215–25.

Zanker, P. 2010. 'Caesars Büste? Der Echte war energischer, distanzierter, ironischer', *Süddeutsche Zeitung*, 17 May 2010 <http://sueddeutsche.de/wissen/caesar-bueste-der-echte-war-energischer-distanzierter-ironischer-1.207937> [accessed 30 June 2013].

NEW CONTRIBUTIONS ON CAESAR
AND HISTORIOGRAPHY

11. Julius Caesar and the Forum Caesaris: World History, Historiography, and Reception Investigated through Danish Biographies of Caesar from the Early Twentieth Century

Trine Arlund Hass

Linacre College, University of Oxford
(trine.hass@classics.ox.ac.uk/klftjah@cas.au.dk)

Rubina Raja

Centre for Urban Network Evolutions (UrbNet), School of Culture and Society,
Aarhus University (rubina.raja@cas.au.dk)

Introduction

Gaius Julius Caesar, perhaps the most notorious Late Republican statesman, tyrant, dictator, politician, rhetoric, general, (adoptive) father, husband, and lover of his time, has received extensive attention in history and remains an individual who fascinates and enthrals scholars and laypeople alike.[1] Today Caesar stands as a central individual in the complex process that led to the fall of the Roman Republic and its development into what effectively became a monarchy dominated by a single ruler, the Roman emperor. The first of these was his own adoptive son, Octavian, who was later given the name Augustus and who ruled the Roman Empire for decades, bringing peace and stability to the vast regions under Roman control, which had suffered from the impact of the Roman civil wars that to a large extent had been played out on foreign territory. While Caesar and his time have been studied in great detail from a variety of angles, there are still new perspectives to be brought to the forefront. One of these perspectives is the insights that can be gained through studying the reception of the man and his time as recounted in later periods.

Recently a surge in attention from the Danish side has spurred a revival of studies focusing on the time of Caesar and Caesar's person as well as his afterlife. This interest has been initiated through the new Danish-Italian excavations of Caesar's Forum, undertaken since 2018, of the until now unexplored parts of this forum located in the heart of Rome.[2] While this excavation project already has and currently is revealing new insights into both the post- and pre-Republican phases, the fact remains that the area owes its fame to the Late Republican phase when it became Caesar's public space, the Forum Caesaris, best known as the Forum Iulium, although this name was introduced only after the death of Caesar.[3] The new examinations of the area together with a string of affiliated research projects — including a project studying Caesar's Danish reception — provide the basis for this contribution.[4]

Bringing national narratives of Roman statesmen to the forefront, from immediately before and after World War I, allows — in hindsight, of course — for insights into the various national sentiments and their backgrounds, and possibly how the shocking event of the Great War influenced the contemporary view of the classical past — a past that always had been present in the European cultural sphere. The way in which Antiquity played a role in shaping discourses on politics and

---

* The authors' research is supported by Aarhus University Research Foundation, the Carlsberg Foundation, and the Danish National Research Foundation, grant DNRF119. We are grateful to these foundations for supporting this research as well as to our colleagues in the Caesar's Forum Project for input and discussions about the material presented here.

[1] Meier 1982; Billows 2009; Goldsworthy 2006; Griffin 2009.

[2] Jacobsen and others 2020, 36–51; see also Hass and Raja 2021.

[3] Forum Iulium was the name, which Augustus gave the space. It was not the original name of the space, which was Forum Caesaris, see Weinstock 1971, 81.

[4] Jacobsen and Raja 2018, 21–25; Jacobsen and others 2020; 2021a; 2021b.

national identity is noticeable and allows for a renewed understanding of the trajectories between national states and evolving national identities in a Europe that was in so many ways under pressure as a result of an accelerating globalization and shift in power structures. While the European biographies of Julius Caesar written in this period are not necessarily directly politically motivated, they were indeed indicative of a general surge in interest in Antiquity and the political and military leaders of that period, serving as a sounding board for current developments.

Caesar's time was one of great change — potentially some of the most deep-ranging changes in the European political and military sphere — bringing with it the abrupt transition from Republic to Imperial rule, and it thus remains a time that still today stands as complex and not entirely disentangled.[5] Caesar managed to contribute to shaping the way the history of his time and deeds was written, and the process of negotiating the narrative of the Late Roman Republic continued in the time immediately after his death. Such was the impact of his presence and deeds that hardly was he gone before borders between facts and fiction were blurred, and so the man and the facts were quickly lost in the ensuing myths. Suetonius, by including Caesar in his row of biographies of Roman emperors, firmly added to the picture of Caesar as emperor-material — projecting back into a time when a Roman emperor was not imaginable and the extreme grasp for power which Caesar undertook also became his downfall in the end, as we well know.

From his own time onwards, Caesar was used as a measuring rod, especially for leader figures, whether to suggest him as a good or bad example. Napoleon I and Napoleon III looked to Caesar in awe, as did Mussolini. All three admired him as a military leader as well as an intellectual figure and writer, while the French revolutionaries hailed Brutus and saw Caesar as the destroyer of liberty. Friedrich Schlegel found that Caesar, while incarnating greatness, lacked 'all subtle morality', but to Hegel, Caesar was 'the bearer of really distilled historical ideas'.[6] Caesar's general impact, however, shows that he was admired, discussed, and used in contexts way beyond war and politics. In the Middle Ages, pilgrims sought his alleged grave in Rome next to St Peter's Basilica for its supposed healing qualities.[7] Dante condemned Caesar's murderers to the innermost circle of hell, and Shakespeare discussed the dilemma of whether his murder could be defended due to its purpose in *The Tragedy of Julius Caesar*. Caesar has provided material for poetry and novels as well as for comics, plays, operas, movies, TV series, and computer games. And although President Trump's seeming reluctance to leave office and the resulting attack on the American Congress by Trump supporters in January 2021 almost made the Public Theater staging of Shakespeare's Julius Caesar in 2017, in which the title role was made to look like the president, too relevant, it underlines how Caesar and his deeds continue to function as vehicles for discussions of our contemporary politics — like it has been for more than two thousand years.

Imaginations and Excavations of the Forum Iulium

Denmark was never an integrated part of the Roman Empire. However, we can trace narratives back to the earliest written sources of Danish history of how attachments to Roman history have been perceived and shaped. Similarly to German medieval records, early Danish sources, such as the *Annales Ryenses* (*c.* 1288) and *Rimkrøniken* (The Rhymed Chronicle, 1495), state that Caesar visited the region.[8] This was dismissed long ago as a mythical narrative, and the story is nowadays generally forgotten, but the cultural attachment to Rome (and Greece) remains as strong in Denmark as in the rest of the Western world. When the biographies addressed in this article were written, Denmark and the Danes had recently been through a process of national redefinition. Danish territory had been reduced significantly due to the selling of most of the Danish colonies in 1845 and 1850 and defeats in war, especially the defeat in the war against Prussia in 1864. While Romanticism flourished, a democratic constitution was agreed upon in 1849 through a peaceful process. As a consequence of these matters, attention was directed inwards to Danish conditions, in a renegotiation of Danish identity prioritizing Danish language and history, to some extent at the expense of education in the classical languages. Classics did, however, still play a role, just like those who could, still went on the Grand Tour, which of course included going to Rome.

The two Danish biographies addressed here are both entitled *Cajus Julius Caesar*. The first announced itself

---

5 Beard and Crawford 1999; Zanker 1988, 5–32, 167–238.

6 Gundolf and Hartmann 1929, 287.

7 Osborne 2006, 102–04.

---

8 On the *Annales Ryenses*, see Gundolf and Hartmann 1929, 70; Kjær 2020, 169 and 276. On *Rimkrøniken*, see Hass 2019.

Figure 11.1. Photograph of Forum Romanum viewed from the east featured in Brandes's *Cajus Julius Cæsar*. According to Brandes, this is what it looked like after the excavations in 1872 (Brandes 1918, 1, pl. I.3).

as the first popular Danish biography of Caesar and was published in 1900 by Arnold Troels Lund Lobedanz (1861–1909) and Ove Malling Giersing (1813–1901 or 1846–1918). Lobedanz published two other works on historical figures, but neither he nor Giersing are well described in the Danish history of literature and publications. The opposite is the case with the author of the second biography, Georg Morris Cohen Brandes (1842–1927), who was a significant figure in the intelligentsia in Denmark and abroad.[9]

We shall return to the possible impact of World War I on Brandes's biography in the section 'Brandes on Caesar and the Forum Caesaris'. Here, it is important to underline that both biographies were written on the backdrop of what the Danish classicist Hartvig Frisch, who reviewed Brandes's biography and later wrote one about Cicero, called the 'hero-worship of Romanticism', of which he saw Brandes as an 'offshoot'.[10] Brandes, as well as Lobedanz and Giersing, looks backwards towards Niebuhr, Drumann, Boissier, and Mommsen,

[9] Brandes's biographies are generally not given much attention but see Jaurnow 1992; Krause 2000; Lundtofte 2000. In the USA, an abridged version of the biography was published in English in the series Little Blue Book, see Moritzen 1924. Several other works of Brandes came in similar adapted versions in this series. The biographies are briefly touched upon in Knudsen 2004 and Allen. Allen's work is the first and only biography of Brandes in English. A recent work on another aspect on the later phase of Brandes's works, to which the biographies adhere, is Banks 2020. Several of Brandes's

works are translated into English. The Danish Society for Language and Literature has published the digital research platform <https://georgbrandes.dk/front-page> providing research material as well as translations in several languages of Brandes's most influential work, *Hovedstrømninger* (Main Currents, 1871–1890). We have identified no critical scholarship on Lobedanz and Giersing's biography.

[10] Frisch 1946, 13–14, published in Danish as *Ciceros Kamp for Republikken* (Frisch 1942).

Figure 11.2. Reconstruction of the Forum Romanum as featured in Brandes's *Cajus Julius Cæsar* (reproduced from Brandes 1918, 1, pl. I.3).

rather than towards Ferrero's less accommodating analysis of Caesar.[11] It is no surprise that the works of both Napoleon I and Napoleon III on Caesar, as well as Stoffel's,[12] influenced Lobedanz and Giersing, the first of whom was an officer in the Danish army (the second was probably a physician), but Brandes, too, leans on them. The works were extremely popular towards the end of the nineteenth century,[13] and Brandes's reliance on them in 1918 is accepted and even commended by Frisch in his review of Brandes — he even compares Brandes to Napoleon.[14] Frisch, in general, commends Brandes for the number of sources used, but as his biography was aimed at a general readership, and since it was produced at the time it was, it does not feature references and consequently contains no bibliography. It, therefore, remains largely unknown how broad Brandes's reading had indeed been. Lobedanz and Giersing likewise do not give references, but they provide a list of what must be understood to be their primary sources (they add 'and more' at the bottom).[15]

As for their insight into the material aspect of Caesar's life and work, we do not know if Lobedanz and Giersing ever went to Rome, but Brandes did, in 1871. In a sense, this makes less of a difference for our general focus, given that the Forum Iulium had not been excavated at this time, although it was, of course, known where the forum was located through the detailed descriptions given in the ancient sources. The fact that it had not been excavated, however, makes it no less of a remarkable part of Caesar's architectural programme, one described in the literature of Caesar's time and consequently also in subsequent works. In fact, we work from the hypothesis that the biographers, having a more vague idea of what the forum might have been and what it looked like, compared to,

---

[11] Drumann 1834–1844; Boissier 1880; 1884; 1905; Niebuhr 1811–1832; Mommsen 1854–1856; Ferrero 1902–1907).

[12] Napoleon [I] and Marchand 1836; Napoleon [III] 1865–1866; Stoffel 1887, 67.

[13] Nicolet 2009, 410–17.

[14] Frisch 1918, 520; 1919, 267 and 270.

---

[15] For the content in the list, see below, in the section 'Lobedanz and Giersing on Caesar and the Forum Caesaris'.

11. JULIUS CAESAR AND THE FORUM CAESARIS

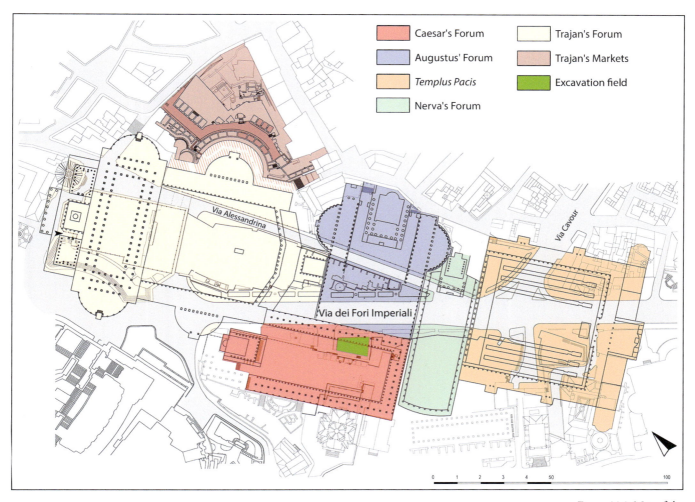

Figure 11.3. Map of the Imperial fora with the excavation field. Figure: the Caesar's Forum Project.

Figure 11.4. View of the Forum Iulium towards the south-west. Photo: Rubina Raja.

Figure 11.5. The demolition of the Alessandrino Quarter and the construction of Via dell'Impero, 1933.
Photo: Allinari Archives.

for instance, the Forum Romanum where some excavations had been undertaken and several structures were visible, needed to rely more on their own interpretation in their description of space and its role in Caesar's general political project, which included building projects in Rome (Figs 11.1–11.2). Thus, it is likely that examining the representation of Caesar's Forum in these texts is an effective way to determine the biographers' views on Caesar and his use of space, thus providing an even deeper historical foundation and holistic understanding for the current work undertaken there.

While Caesar financed several building projects in Rome, the Forum Iulium was the central and most programmatic of those initiated. Since the forum was not finished during his lifetime, it has in many ways been overlooked as an archaeological testimony of Caesar's own time and has much more often been viewed within the context of the Augustan building programme, pushed forward by his adoptive son and heir, first under the name Octavian and later as the first Roman emperor Augustus.[16] While there is certainly still much to be said on this matter — and much has been said already, the Forum Iulium from an ideological point of view stands as more significant and remarkable than eponymous building projects by Caesar's contemporaries, due to the position Caesar obtained within as well as after his lifetime.

Today two-thirds of Caesar's Forum have been uncovered through archaeological work undertaken until 2008 (Figs 11.3 and 11.4). The most extensive excavations were undertaken between 1930–1932 as part of the programme conducted during the reign of Mussolini, when the Via dell'Impero (later Via dei Fori Imperiali) was laid out (Fig. 11.5).[17] In the period 1998–2008 further excavations were undertaken on the occasion of the Great Jubilee in 2000.[18]

---

[16] Zanker 1988, 5–32, 167–238; Paterson 2009, 120–40.

[17] See Jacobsen and others 2020.

[18] La Rocca 2001, 174–84; Pinna Caboni 2008; Meneghini 2009; Delfino 2014.

Urban Archaeology and Danish Engagements with Rome

Urban archaeology is not simply focused on laying bare structures and understanding the overall layout of sites labelled urban and understood basically as organized conglomerations of people living together and structured by spatial layout. As a field it did not come into existence until after World War I when humanities research in numerous fields took new turns and a rejuvenation of international collaborations saw the light of day.[19] In an Italian context, the unification of the country in 1870 brought with it a new focus on the joint history — also through archaeology — of the region and its central site, Rome, which became the capital. In fact choosing Rome as the capital in 1871 also meant per se choosing Antiquity as a pivotal reference point. Through its new status as the main city of the country, Rome was intensely developed and archaeological services were put in place. Ancient monuments stood side by side with the new monuments of the late nineteenth century and linked the grandeur of past Rome with Rome of the present.[20] The extreme focus on Rome's classical heritage was continued and flourished during the reign of Mussolini. In the time immediately following Rome's announcement as capital up to 1914 and World War I, Stephen L. Dyson sees three matters to be significant with regard to archaeology and urbanization:

> The first was the 'purification' of monuments to enhance their visibility and their connection to ancient Roman greatness. The second focuses on the ways that the new urban environment and new structures from ministry buildings to the Victor Emmanuel Monument were designed to link the new with the city's classical past. The final, and in many respects the most depressing, narrative chronicles the impact of uncontrolled development on the overall archaeological record.[21]

The 'purification' Dyson relates primarily to the removal of Christian refigurations and redefinitions of monuments, exemplified with the removal of Bernini's bell towers from the Pantheon and the conversion of the Colosseum from a church into a secular space.[22] Actions like these were carried out with government-level intentions of furthering archaeological research and preservation of the ancient remains, as the establishment of the Commissione Archeologica in 1872 underlines. They are not incomparable to the Renaissance's wish to ignore the development between themselves and Antiquity, the era they idolized. The invasive placing of the monument in honour of King Victor Emmanuel II (1820–1878, king of Italy 1861–1878) constructed between 1885 and 1911 near the places of power of ancient Rome — the Imperial fora and the Capitoline Hill — is a most effective way of showing both the foundation and aspirations of the new united Italy.[23] This was also the heyday of agents and dealers soliciting archaeological objects for collectors of various nationalities, which eventually lead to modernizations of legislation on archaeological heritage in 1902, 1903, and 1909.[24] World War I meant an end to a broader European archaeological involvement in Rome, as well as the beginning of the use of Roman history in the national propaganda that Mussolini's fascist regime famously exploited, as it grew, nurtured by the despair of the population caused by the Great War.[25]

As mentioned, Danes, usually from the upper layers of society, had, like similar people of other nationalities, been travelling to Rome for centuries to experience the classical sites they had learned about during their education, to find inspiration for artistic practices or academic studies.[26] Experiencing Rome was central to the Grand Tour of Europe. Even as classical motifs went out of fashion in the late nineteenth century, Rome (and typically at least also Florence, Naples, and Pompeii — the classic stops of the Italian Grand Tours) still attracted the Danish artists. This trend was criticized by Brandes in connection with his own journey there in 1871, as he argued that the artists rather needed to look ahead and would find no inspiration to do so in Rome.[27] Furthermore, Brandes had confirmed that the Scandinavians in Rome, unlike himself, typically had not learned Italian and almost lived in a parallel society, engaging with each other rather than with the locals.[28] The Scandinavian Circle (Circolo Scandinavo), founded in 1860 and still in existence, did frame — to some extent still does, together with the Scandinavian Academies —

---

[19] Raja and Sindbæk 2020; 2021.

[20] For a general overview of the archaeology in Rome during the early decades of the national state, see Dyson 2019, 81–128.

[21] Dyson 2019, 101.

[22] Dyson 2019, 102–03.

[23] Dyson 2019, 103–06, on the Victor Emmanuel Monument.

[24] Dyson 2019, 143.

[25] Dyson 2019, 153.

[26] For key works on Danish–Italian/Roman relations, see Bobé 1935–1942; Moestrup and Nyholm 1989; Ritzau and Ascani 1982.

[27] Nyholm 1989, 218–19.

[28] Nyholm 1989, 218–19.

the Scandinavian artist milieus in Rome.[29] Rome was much sought for the ancient remains, but Christian sites and monuments were also visited, and several travel accounts report attending masses at St Peter's and audiences with various popes.

The surge of fascism in the 1920s both fascinated and alarmed the Danes who witnessed it. One of the central accounts is that of the above-mentioned Hartvig Frisch (1893–1950, classical philologist and Minister of Education in the Danish social democratic government 1947–1950), who in *Pest over Europa* (Plague over Europe, 1933) warned against the growing fascist movement he had experienced during his time spent in Italy and Rome at the beginning of the 1920s in connection with his studies. On the other side, pastor, poet, and playwright Kaj Munk (1898–1944) wrote of his fascination with Mussolini, whom he envisioned emerging from the ruins of Antiquity as a new Caesar, in an open letter to *il duce* printed in a Danish newspaper, encouraging him to discipline Hitler whose treatment of the Jews Munk found alarming.[30] Munk's fascination with fascism faded as he fervidly criticized the German occupation of Denmark, which led to his killing by the Gestapo in 1944.

The earliest Danish archaeological work and interest in Rome was that of agents and collectors, such as Georg Zoëga (1755–1809, agent, guided Bertel Thorvaldsen's use of classical art in his practice, studied classics in Göttingen); Friederich Münter (1761–1830, bishop, collector of antiquities, studied in Göttingen and Rome); Münter's sister, Friederike Brun (1765–1830), who lived in Rome and bought ancient objects there for her brother, Niels Iversen Schow (1754–1830). Zoëga, Münter, and Schow all studied classics, first in Göttingen and later in Rome, in order to study material remains first hand as well as texts.[31] Schow became the first professor of archaeology at the University of Copenhagen in 1805. Also, the brewers, collectors, and patrons of the arts Jacob Christian Jacobsen (1811–1887) and his son Carl Jacobsen (1842–1914) came to Rome, and especially Carl Jacobsen worked with agents, perhaps most importantly Wolfgang Helbig,[32] a central figure

in Rome, to build an exquisite collection of ancient art. Carl Jacobsen donated his collection to the Danish people in 1888, and it is still the core of the collection of the Ny Carlsberg Glyptotek in central Copenhagen. The establishing of the Scandinavian institutes in Rome became the foundation of excavation projects headed by Danish scholars — but only later than many other foreign missions. The first involvement of Scandinavians in excavations in Rome was in the excavations of the Temple of Castor and Pollux on the Forum Romanum, between 1983–1985 and in 1987.[33] The current Danish-Italian excavations on the Forum Iulium consequently add to the exploration of the core of the Roman world and, with the explicit angle of urban archaeology, consider the space of the Forum Iulium as an urban imprint across time.

The Forum Caesaris

Shaping the built environment and landscape has for a long time been acknowledged as a way to display power, identity, and wealth. The continuous shaping and reshaping of Rome and its developing urban landscape is no exception. The city can be viewed as one large entanglement of building projects that can often be traced back to individuals who we know held immense importance in ancient Rome. Building projects were frequently described and discussed by ancient writers. The projects and the nature of the buildings that individuals or groups wanted to sponsor, dedicate, and erect had to be approved officially, when they were constructed on public land. So the results — namely the building or the structure or monument — were outcomes of negotiations, which would have taken place before the projects could even have begun. The outcome — the monument — was a physical manifesto of the power, wealth, importance, and not least network of the sponsoring individual or group.[34] The urban fabric was one large organism, which was driven by private and public sponsorship, and the political and religious centre of Rome — the Forum Romanum — stood at the very core of Roman urban identity. Due to it being Rome's official centre for centuries, the large area of Forum Romanum was continuously developed and became more and more cluttered with buildings and monuments central to the Roman people,

---

[29] The Danish Academy in Rome was established in 1956, the Finnish Institute in 1954, the Norwegian in 1959, and the Swedish already in 1925.

[30] Munk 1938.

[31] On Zoëga, Münter, and Schow, see Mortensen and Raja 2019, 21–22.

[32] Moltesen 2012.

---

[33] Moltesen 1989, 104.

[34] See for example Thomas 2007, although it deals with a later period.

both with respect to religion and politics and the honouring of important individuals in the public sphere.[35] We hear of the Forum Iulium for the first time through Marcus Tullius Cicero, the Roman rhetor and politician, around the time of 1 July 54 BC.[36] He mentions the building project in the context of a broader description of a number of building projects, where more emphasis is also given to the basilica financed by Aemilius Lepidus Paullus:

> Itaque Caesaris amici (me dico et Oppium, dirumparis licet) <in> monumentum illud quod tu tollere laudibus solebas, ut forum laxaremus et usque ad atrium Libertatis explicaremus, centempsimus sescenties (cum privatis non poterat transigi minore pecunia); efficiemus rem gloriosissimam. Nam in campo Martio saepta tributis comitiis marmorea sumus et tecta facturi eaque cingemus excelsa porticu, ut mille passuum conficiatur.

> (And so we friends of Caesar — myself and Oppius I mean, though you may explode with wrath at my confession — have thought nothing of spending 60 million sestertii for that *monumentum* that you used to regard with praise, the extension of the *forum* and continuation of it as far as the Atrium Libertatis. We could not satisfy the private owners with less; but we will make it a most magnificent affair. In the Campus Martius we are going to make polling barriers of marble for the tribal assemblies [the Saepta Julia], roof them over, and surround them with a colonnade a mile in circumference.)[37]

Pliny the Elder and Suetonius, however, state a much higher price for the buying of the land, namely one hundred million sesterces.[38] No matter what the exact price was, it is certain that the layout of Caesar's forum was a prestige project, one which was conceived by Caesar and supported by his allies in order to underline his importance to Roman society and his power — both in terms of political and military but also financial power. Cicero writes that the new forum is to be seen as an extension of the Forum Romanum, a space that not only created a new space dedicated to the Julian family and which at its core celebrated Caesar and his achievements but also as an extension of the space for the entire Roman people. This is an aspect that has often been overlooked in scholarship, where Caesar's Forum is viewed as a separate building project intended to set Caesar's public space apart from the Forum Romanum. However, much more than doing this, the forum rather enlarged but also forced through a reorientation of an important part of the Forum Romanum upon which followed the moving of the entrance to the Curia, the meeting place of the Senate, which had until then been on the opposite side, but was now turned towards the new forum space. So while extending the Forum Romanum, Caesar's Forum did indeed draw attention towards this new space, which was inevitably tied closely to its sponsor, Gaius Julius Caesar.

Caesar's Forum is not to be viewed as a direct forerunner to the later Imperial fora since these were lavish closed spaces surrounded by colonnaded walls, conceived adjacent, and close to that of Caesar's Forum by the following emperors. In Caesar's design, there seems to have been no intention to entirely close off the space from the rest of the Forum Romanum, but for the space to function as an extension, with a strong emphasis on Caesar and his grand narratives. However, through its focus on one powerful individual, the space indeed came to inspire the later Roman emperors in the layouts of their fora.

Caesar's Forum was a building project of utmost prestige — along the lines of Pompey's building project, his theatre, which was so much more than just a theatre and also held a curia and a temple of Venus Victrix. This structure was completed in 55 BC, placed on the Campus Martius — and its curia was the location of Caesar's murder in 44 BC.

In order to construct Caesar's Forum, the domestic elite houses had to be demolished and cleared away, and the area, which was sloping, had to be levelled. The levelling of the area, which meant literally carving away parts of the Capitoline and Quirinal Hills, began in 54 BC.[39] The levelling involved removing partly a height difference of about 3–4 m. A rectangular square was created (measuring *c.* 115 by 30 m), and at one end of the complex, which was surrounded by colonnades on the remaining three sides, stood the temple dedicated to Venus Genetrix, the mythical ancestress of the *gens Iulia*.[40] Caesar did not live to see the forum finished.

---

35 Hopkins 2014, 29–61.

36 C. Morselli, *LTUR* II, 299–306 s.v. Forum Iulium. Also see Zanker 2009, 290–92. For a recent overview of the Forum Iulium in a historiographic perspective, see Sauer 2021; Ulrich 1986; 1993; 1994; Westall 1996; Maiuro 2010.

37 Cic., *Att.* IV.16.7. Transl. Loeb, adapted by Ulrich 1993, 54.

38 Plin., *HN* XXXVI.24.103; Suet., *Iul.* XXVI.2.

39 The limits of the levelling have been identified in the area towards the Clivo Argentario and behind the cella of the Temple of Venus Genetrix: Ammerman and Filippi 2000.

40 Smith 2010; Weinstock 1971; Grossi 1936; Strocka 2005, 153–67.

Although he inaugurated the temple in 46 BC, the complex as such was not completed until after his murder in 44 BC. Its construction was finalized much later by Octavian, Caesar's adoptive son, who also enlarged the forum square's original layout towards the south.[41] From written sources, we know that Caesar embellished the forum and the temple with a sculptural programme, which among other things, included a cult statue of Venus Genetrix and a statue of Cleopatra, standing in the temple cella together with Venus. Outside the temple in the open space in front of it stood an equestrian statue of Caesar as well as a statue of Caesar's horse, a gesture through which he drew a direct line to Alexander the Great, who was also known to have had a bronze statue cast of his favourite horse Bucephalus.[42]

There is no doubt that Caesar provoked many by extending the Forum Romanum through his new forum and thereby spurring the reorientation of the Curia.[43] Furthermore, the sculptural programme was noteworthy; especially the fact that Caesar set up a statue of Cleopatra, a foreign queen not particularly liked in Rome and Caesar's lover, who had come to Rome with their child, provoked people. Placing her statue together with the cult statue of Venus Genetrix inside the temple, thus aligning the two, would further have provoked Caesar's opponents and probably even some of his supporters. The Forum Caesaris was, despite the claim of being merely an extension of the Forum Romanum, just as much a space in which Caesar intended to create a closed setting where he could be represented as he saw fit — namely as the most important political and military leader of Late Republican Rome, while also underlining his divine descent from Venus.

This was the image of the forum conveyed to the Danish biographers through ancient sources. An image that was complex, attractive, and repulsive at the same time. A narrative of the creation of a central space in Rome that pointed to a future in which Rome would yet again be a monarchy and where one ruler would stand at the centre of power. This image fascinated Caesar's early twentieth-century biographers, not only through the shocking and provocative details of the narrative but also as an outcome of the developments in Europe in general in the nineteenth century. Societies were changing, and

so were political directions, and in this process upheaval moments from the past were once again conjured and reinterpreted.

Lobedanz and Giersing on Caesar and the Forum Caesaris

Lobedanz and Giersing's biography of Caesar is stated to be published on the occasion of the two-thousandth anniversary of Caesar's birth, on 12 July 1900 (set in black letter on the verso of the frontispiece). It is furthermore explained in the preface that this is the first biography of Caesar in Danish. The authors, Arnold Lobedanz and Ove Giersing, proclaim the work to be aimed at readers with interest in history but do list the sources on which their analyses are based (p. 4).[44] Neither of the authors were classics scholars: Lobedanz was a captain in the Danish army,[45] and Giersing was most likely a medical doctor (supposedly either Ove Malling Giersing (1813–1901) or his son by the same name (1846–1918)). The intended readers are described thus:

> For de Mange, der kun kende Cæsar fra den Tid, da hans *De bello gallico* voldte dem kvalfulde Timer i Skolen og for alle, der ere Yndere af historisk Læsning, vil der nu være Lejlighed til at lære denne 'Oldtidens Napoleon' at kende paa nært Hold.
>
> (For many who know Caesar only from the time his *De bello gallico* caused them hours of anguish in school and for all favouring historical reading, this is an opportunity to become intimately acquainted with the 'Napoleon of Antiquity'.)[46]

The initial labelling of Caesar as a Napoleonic parallel is telling. Lobedanz and Giersing's portrayal of Caesar is unmistakably marked by admiration and celebra-

---

[41] Delfino 2010, 335.

[42] Delfino 2010; Raja and Rüpke 2021; Smith 2010; Valenzani 2006.

[43] Billows 2009; Weinstock 1971; Wiseman 2009; 2014; 2016; 2019.

[44] The list mentions twenty-three works, of which four are ancient (by Caesar, Plutarch, and Sallust) and nineteen later works. Of the latter, five are focused on war and military aspects (Herchenbach, Fröhlich, Rüstow, Frölich, Galitzin), two on the bridge across the Rhine (Schleussinger and Poellnitz), three universal histories (Cantu, Dahlstrøm, and Böttiger). In addition to the works of the Napoleons, Mommsen, and Stoffel, they list works on Caesar and Rome by Thomsen, Schwanenflügel, Rheinhard, and Madvig.

[45] Lobedanz published two other historical works, *Heltene fra Napoleonstiden* (Heroes from Napoleon's Time) in 1896, translated into several languages, and *Mural og Hans Hustru* (Mural and his Wife) in 1899; Rockstroh 1976–1984.

[46] Lobedanz and Giersing 1900, 3: all translations from Danish are by the authors.

tion of his genius, and Caesar's military strategies and accomplishments seem to be of particular interest. With this said, their biography is not a hagiography. Caesar is described as having some flaws and making unwise moves, politically (e.g. not rising from his seat to receive those who come to celebrate him), personally (most noteworthy in his relationship with Cleopatra), and militarily (e.g. when he, at Dyrrhachium in 48 BC, acted recklessly by attempting to besiege Pompey in the city with his own tired troops).

The biography is divided into three parts and organized chronologically, beginning with Caesar's birth. Each part is subdivided into chapters. Illustrations occur in the shape of engravings of statues and coins as well as depictions of later representations of relevant people or material. There are no depictions of the area of the Forum Iulium.

Caesar's building programme and his forum features especially in three sections of the book's part three. We find the first in chapter 5, treating Caesar's arrival in Rome after defeating the last resistance at Thapsus and his triumphs. Here, it is underlined that Caesar made no reference to either Scipio or Cato.[47] Bridged by notions of how Caesar let hundreds of Romans dine for free during the days of his triumphs, Lobedanz and Giersing continue with a section on his reforms, likewise instigated with the aim of caring for the Roman people. They find that his primary focus is the reforms, which were 'almost all of them welcomed by the people' (saa godt som alle blev modtagne med Velvilie af Folket).[48] While the expectation would therefore be to hear of charitable reforms, the first mentioned is the reform of the calendar, and the next is the beautification of the city, beginning with his forum:

> Roms Forskønnelse laa Cæsar særlig paa Hjerte. Allerede i Aaret 54 havde han paabegyndt store Arbejder til Forums Udvidelse, men Borgerkrigen havde foreløbig standset Arbejdet. Han lod det nu genoptage og gjorde alt for at fremskynde det. Han vilde have, at hele Forum skulde være en Forhal til et mægtigt og pragtfuldt Tempel, som han agtede at bygge for at holde sit Løfte fra Slaget ved Farsalos om Oprettelsen af et saadant for *Venus Genetrix*, der havde været hans Skytsgudinde under Slaget.

> (Beautifying Rome was a case particularly close to Caesar's heart. Already in the year 54 BC, he had initiated great efforts to expand the Forum, but the civil war had

hitherto paused this work. He now recommenced it and did everything to hurry it on. He wanted the Forum in its entirety to be the vestibule of a mighty and splendid temple, which he intended to build in order to keep his pledge, made at the Battle at Pharsalus, to establish one such to Venus Genetrix, who was his patron goddess during the battle.)[49]

Caesar's architectural reforms of Rome are certainly understood as central to his general venture. However, it is noteworthy how the biography's narrative seems to lose sight of the theme of beneficial acts to the public — unless, of course, Caesar's beautification of Rome is found to be in the interest of the people in general. In the next section, following this first description of Caesar's forum and temple, it is stated that Caesar's building programme, along with his generosity, secured great support from the people, although it did also create enemies. The quoted passage above is followed by a description of the plans for decorations of the temple — how it was to be 'filled with images and statues from all over the world' and how 'no expenses should be spared to make it as pompous as possible'.[50] The plan to put a statue of Caesar's horse in bronze is mentioned before that of placing a golden statue of Venus there, and Caesar is said to have been impatient to get it all done, to a degree that he celebrated its opening when he only had a model ready. It is noted, too, that the initiation was 'of course' celebrated with a great party, in honour of his deceased daughter. This last piece of information, that the feast was given in honour of Julia, contrasts with the previous description's dwelling on Caesar's great desire for luxury items, marked especially by the highlighting of the statue of the horse. It could well be taken as an expression that Caesar's impatience to initiate the new space is a new outlet of his famous *celeritas*, a key aspect of his military success, also in the analysis of Lobedanz and Giersing — for instance, they describe the crossing of the Rubicon to be consistent with Caesar's daring and energetic nature and note that he often relies on his speed alone.[51]

It is not said in so many words, but one senses that there has been a development in Caesar's approach to the beautification of the space of the forum from before to after the Civil War. Rather than the war itself, however, Lobedanz and Giersing find another factor to have been

---

47 Lobedanz and Giersing 1900, 290.

48 Lobedanz and Giersing 1900, 291.

49 Lobedanz and Giersing 1900, 292.

50 Lobedanz and Giersing 1900, 292: 'Templet skulde fyldes med Billeder og Statuer fra alle Verdens Egne, og der skulde intet spares for at gøre det saa pompøst som muligt.'

51 Lobedanz and Giersing 1900, 230.

decisive to the building programme and Caesar's project in general. This becomes clear in the second treatment of Caesar's Forum in the work:

> Siden sit ophold i Ægypten, hvor Alexandrias mange pragtfulde Bygninger, brede, lige og rene Gader, umaadelige Torve, smukke Monumenter havde gjort et mægtigt Indtryk paa ham, var hans stadige Tanke at forskønne, berige og udvide det gamle Rom. Han satte derfor en Mængde Arbejder i Gang.

> (Since his stay in Egypt, where the many delightful buildings of Alexandria, the straight and clean streets, vast squares, and beautiful monuments had made a great impression on him, his constant thought was to beautify, enrich, and expand the old city of Rome. Therefore he initiated a number of projects.)[52]

While not denying that his fascination with Cleopatra would have been Caesar's reason to spend a couple of months in Egypt in 47 BC, Lobedanz and Giersing have underlined, at the beginning of part three's chapter four already that this was not time wasted, since he had made sure to put everything in order there.[53] This unwasted time appears to have included studies of architecture and city planning. As the narrative unfolds, the role of Cleopatra and especially her influence on Caesar does seem to have had negative effects, according to this analysis. It is said on page 298 that the year 46 BC was:

> et lykkeligt Aar for Cæsar. Han nød sine mange Triumfer og følte sig vel i sit kære Rom, men han savnede sin ægyptiske Veninde, sin elskede Kleopatra, for hvis Skyld han havde begaaet sit Livs største Letsindigheder. Minderne om de saa hastigt svundne Dage under Ægyptens Sol i Selskab med den vidunderlige Dronning blev ham for stærke og skød Blodet op i hans Kinder. Hans Længsel fik en saadan Magt over ham, at han brød alle Skranker og indbød hende til at gæste Rom [...] Cæsar lagde ikke Skjul paa sin store Kærlighed til hende og viste hende offentlig en Hyldest, som overskred alle Grænser. Hendes Statue i Guld lod han opstille i Venus-Templet ved Siden af selve Gudinden. Cæsars Lidenskab for den smukke Kvinde lod ham ganske overse, hvor galt han bar sig ad. Dels krænkede det mange, at Statens Overhoved viste en fremmed Dronning saa stor Hyldest, thi dette stred mod det gamle romerske Riges Stolthed, dels fandt mange det forargerligt, at Cæsar som Moralens Haandhæver, som

den, der atter vilde bringe Ro og Orden ind i det næsten opløste Samfund, afgav saa slet et Exempel for andre.

> (a happy year for Caesar. He enjoyed his many triumphs and felt well in his dear Rome, but he missed his Egyptian friend, his beloved Cleopatra, for whose sake he had committed his life's most unmindful acts. The memories of rapidly bygone days under the Egyptian sun with the wonderful queen became too strong and made his blood rise to his cheeks. His longing took such power over him that he broke all barriers and invited her to visit Rome [...] Caesar made no effort to hide his profound love for her and showed her a public tribute transgressing all boundaries. He had her statue, in gold, placed in Venus's temple, next to the goddess herself. Caesar's passion for this beautiful woman made him overlook completely how wrong his actions were. Firstly, many found it offensive that the head of state showed a foreign queen such great honours since it conflicted with the proudness of the old Roman realm, and secondly, many found it outrageous that Caesar as the guardian of morality, as the one who would again bring peace and order to this practically disarrayed society, set such a bad example for others.)[54]

Caesar's relationship with Cleopatra brings him off balance. While he had made laws to heighten morals in Rome, he himself compromised these moral standards. Egypt, and Cleopatra in particular, thus become a corrupting factor, and Caesar's Forum becomes the indicator of this; first in Caesar's eagerness to have it done, as the project is resumed, and next when he places a statue of his mistress next to the cult statue. In Lobedanz and Giersing's last mentioning of the Forum Iulium, it is the backdrop of the situation where Caesar receives the Senate, coming to bestow more honours on him, without rising from his seat. Their analysis of the situation is as follows:

> En saadan Ringeagt ligeoverfor det Senat, der i Forvejen var berøvet saa megen Magt og Anseelse, var en uklog Handling. Senatet var dog, naar alt kom til alt, Romernes Repræsentation og som saadan al ydre Agtelse værd, hvorfor Cæsar burde have været forsigtig og ikke overmodig. Ved saadanne Fejl fremskyndede han Katastrofen.

> (Such contempt for the Senate, deprived already of so much power and prestige, was an unwise act. The Senate was after all the representation of the Romans and as such worthy of all esteem, for which reason Caesar should have been careful and not arrogant. By such errors he spurred on the catastrophe.)[55]

---

[52] Lobedanz and Giersing 1900, 304.

[53] Lobedanz and Giersing 1900, 277: 'Tiden var ogsaa anvendt til andet end Fest og Kærlighed: alt var ordnet paa bedste Maade i det undertvungne Land.'

[54] Lobedanz and Giersing 1900, 296–97.

[55] Lobedanz and Giersing 1900, 308. Stoffel 1887, 167: 'Non

Caesar's corruption by Cleopatra and the development of an arrogant attitude to power is described as gradually increasing, and it is visible in the way the Forum Iulium is described and used in the biography. From wanting to create a place that highlighted the temple he had vowed — that is, from being an expression of piety — it gradually became a space to Caesar himself where he, led and accompanied by his Egyptian lover, took the role of the divinity celebrated.

Lobedanz and Giersing clearly admire Caesar, especially for his military successes, and to a great extent also for his moral character, visions, and genius, but they do point out his flaws and mistakes, although they trace them back to the exotic woman whom he loved. Thus their interpretation follows the well-established pattern of the corrupting woman going back to Eve tempting Adam and the following expulsion from Eden in Genesis 3.1–13, likewise showing their conception of Cleopatra to fit the bill of Said's Orientalism. Explaining matters thus, Lobedanz and Giersing seem to constitute a contradictory portrait of Caesar: the development of their narrative goes against their proclaimed loyalty to their protagonist, since they state, with reference to Mommsen, that 'Caesar was a passionate man, for without passion there is no genius; but his passion was never mightier than himself' (at Cæsar var en lidenskabelig Mand, thi uden Lidenskab gives der ingen Genialitet; men hans Lidenskab var aldrig mægtigere end han selv).[56] If we

were to take this statement, placed well before the other quotes presented here, at face value, it was not his love of Cleopatra that distorted Caesar and his project; it was an infatuation with the Egyptian way of ruling — but that is not unfolded directly in the text. Although only Mommsen is referenced, for Cleopatra's and Egypt's problematic role Lobedanz and Giersing rather seem to lean on Stoffel, who is found in their list of sources. On Caesar's intervention in Egypt, leading to his relationship with Cleopatra, he writes:

> Ainsi finit cette guerre d'Égypte à laquelle César se laissa entrainer sans motif valable. Elle fut une très grande faute; car elle donna au parti de Pompée le temps de réorganiser ses forces, releva ses espérances, et obligea César, comme on le verra, à faire deux autres guerres, l'une en Afrique, l'autre en Espagne.[57]

The quotation of Lobedanz and Giersing above (p. 309) is a paraphrase of Stoffel's rendering of Caesar's behaviour towards Cleopatra (see quotation in n. 57), following his announcement of Caesar's flaw to be his cultic admiration of beauty.[58] Lobedanz and Giersing do not go quite as far, but as already pointed out, they seem to find that Cleopatra did have an influence on Caesar and that it was she who led him astray and onto the path of defeat.

Brandes on Caesar and the Forum Caesaris

Literary critic Georg Brandes was a central figure in his day, in Denmark certainly but also beyond the Danish borders. Famous mostly for his introduction of modernity into literature (1872), the activism he advocated in art and literature also had a political dimension. He wrote a large biography of Caesar in two volumes, published in 1918 as part of what is generally considered the second phase of his oeuvre. Brandes was unequivocally against the world war, criticizing the parties for waging war on false premises,[59] and he refused to take sides, a stance that was criticized severely, not least by younger

---

seulement il l'admit, elle et le roi, parmi les amis et alliés du peuple romain, mais il fit encore placer sa statue en or dans le temple de Vénus, à côté de celle de la déesse. Ces honneurs, rendus à une reine étrangère, froissèrent tous ceux qui avaient conservé quelque chose de l'ancienne fierté romaine. On vit, il est vrai, la plupart des hauts personnages de Rome s'efforcer de plaire à Cléopâtre, mais non sans réprouver en secret les défaillances de celui qu'ils s'étaient donné pour maître. Et en effet, par sa coupable faiblesse, César s'attira le juste blâme de tout le monde, et désola ses partisans mêmes, en compromettant la dignité de conduite qui aurait si bien convenu au restaurateur de l'ordre. Surtout il méconnut une des premières maximes de gouvernement, c'est-à-dire l'influence des exemples partis de haut; il se déconsidéra et s'ôta l'autorité morale dont il aurait eu un si grand besoin, lui qui s'était imposé comme tâche de régénérer une société tombée en dissolution.'

56 Lobedanz and Giersing 1900, 217. See Mommsen 1862–1866, 451: 'Caesar was a man of passion for without passion there is no genius; but his passion was never stronger than he could control. He had had his season of youth, and song, love, and wine had taken joyous possession of his mind; but with him they did not penetrate to the inmost core of his nature.' Mommsen follows up on the next page, addressing the particular relationship to Cleopatra thus: 'But however much, even when monarch, he enjoyed the society of women, he only amused himself with them, and allowed them no

manner of influence over him. Even his much-censured relation to Queen Cleopatra was only contrived to mask a weak point in his political position.'

57 Stoffel 1887, 67.

58 Stoffel 1887, 166: 'César, tout en présentant un admirable équilibre des qualités de l'intelligence et de celles du caractère, rendait à la beauté une sorte de culte: ce fut là son imperfection, ou la marque par où se révélait chez lui l'infirmité humaine.'

59 Bendtsen 2020, 121.

members of the Danish intelligentsia, who looked up to Brandes. The Danish defeat to Prussia in 1864 directly defined the view of many Danes of the elder generation on the parties of World War I, while many of the younger generation proclaimed to favour the German side.[60] Brandes's production at this time is described thus by Julie Allen, Brandes's first English biographer:

> Many scholars have interpreted the shift in Brandes's focus during this period as confined to the literary sphere, involving a turn from critiquing individual literary texts to writing biographies of prominent historical figures. While it is true that Brandes produced a large number of biographies during this period, his literary endeavours took on a much more pronounced political tone than previously, and he devoted increasing amounts of time and energy to political journalism.[61]

Brandes had been *the* intellectual frontrunner, bringing modernism to Danish literature and art. In the 1870s, he introduced naturalism, termed Det Moderne Gennembrud (The Modern Breakthrough) in Denmark, aiming to create art that would provoke debate on the situation of the lower classes of society, including women's rights. However, the so-called Morality Feud in 1885–1887 caused a development in Brandes's position, as seen in the article 'Aristocratic Radicalism', published in 1889, in which Brandes declared to agree completely with Nietzsche's democratic criticism.[62] In the following years, Brandes published biographies of several great men: Nietzsche (1889), Shakespeare (1897), Goethe (1915), Voltaire (1916), Napoleon (1917), Julius Caesar (1918), and Michelangelo Buonarotti (1921). Allen says that 'the unifying theme in these texts is Brandes's admiration of his subjects' radical individualism and his conviction that all decisive change is accomplished by individuals rather than broad social movements'.[63]

According to Knudsen, author of a biography of Brandes in five volumes, the last four of Brandes's biographies present an attempt to let 'the great spirits meet across time', aiming to show alternatives to the events of his present day, which Brandes continued to problematize:[64]

Biografierne er fire eksempler på den enhed af liv og værk, der er de store menneskers særkende, og som også var hans personlige ambition: Den stærke personlighed realiserer sine muligheder, folder sig ud på alle felter, I kunst, politik og privatliv. Til inspiration og provokation for en tid, hvor skillet mellem at synes og at være, mellem offentlig og privat, var den bekvemme norm. Det er Brandes' brud med denne norm, der er kernen i hans virke og en væsentlig forklaring på samtidens vrede reaktioner. Kravet om at være menneske i ét stykke er en bombe under det moralistiske samfund.

(The biographies are four examples of the unity of life and work characteristic of great men, as well as Brandes's personal aspiration: strong personalities realize their options, unfold themselves in every field, in art, politic, and in their personal lives. As inspiration and provocation for a time, in which the divide between seeming and being, between public and private, was the convenient norm. Breaking away from this norm is at the centre of Brandes's work and a significant explanation for the angry reactions of his contemporaries. The demand to be a human being in one piece is a bomb under the moralistic society.)[65]

Knudsen finds that Brandes, in his late years, returned to the heroes of his youth, considering how his own life might have been different, had he taken their paths instead. Brandes was politically engaged and had a loud, important voice, and although associated with the Danish liberal party *Venstre* he was never a member of this or any other party. But with the biography of Caesar, he seems to consider what it might have been like to aim for political power, had he had the chance to do so in an empire rather than the 'doghole' fate had placed him in (Knudsen cites one of Brandes's letters for this particular expression).[66]

As the following will show, Brandes — building to a large extent on Mommsen, Napoleon, and Stoffel — found Caesar was practically the image of the perfect man, politician, and leader. Caesar was to him a genius, and he found that all his deeds were well-considered. This shows in Brandes's descriptions and analyses of Caesar's Forum, its purposes, organization, and decorations.

Brandes mentions the establishing of the Forum Iulium in his introduction, at the beginning of his general presentation of Caesar. The motivation for creating a new forum is practical: the old forum had become too

---

[60] Bendtsen 2020, 126–28.

[61] Allen 2013, 95.

[62] Brandes 1889, 565–613; Busk-Jensen 2006–2009.

[63] Allen 2013, 95.

[64] Knudsen 2004, 440: '[D]e store ånders møde hen over tiderne.' Translation by the authors.

---

[65] Knudsen 2004, 441.

[66] Knudsen 2004, 442.

11. JULIUS CAESAR AND THE FORUM CAESARIS

small, but this observation is embedded in Brandes's presentation of Caesar's divine lineage:

I Hovedslagene ved Farsalos og Munda valgte Cæsar sin Ætmoders, sin Gudindes, Navn til Feltraab for sine Soldater: *Venus Genitrix.* Han bar hendes billede i sin ring. Han satte senere hendes billede paa sine Mønter. Han opførte et Tempel for hende som Midtpunkt paa det Forum, han lod bygge, da Forum Romanum var blevet for snevert. Han satte Kleopatras Statue af Guld ind deri ved Siden af Gudindens. Kleopatra blev i hans sidste Leveaar for ham, hvad Aspasia i lang Tid var for Perikles, en Genstand for hans Kærlighed og en Forargelse for hans Misundere. Der var i Cæsars Dyrkelse af Venus en dybere Mening: Ved sit Væsens Ynde, ved sin uimodstaelige Elskværdighed var han i Virkeligheden Venus's Ætling. Paa St Helena sagde Napoleon om ham (14. December 1816); 'I Modsætning til Alexander begyndte Cæsar sin Løbebane sent; men efter en ørkesløs og udsvævende Ungdom lagde han den mest virksomme, højsindede og skønne Sjæl for Dagen. Jeg anser ham for en af Historiens mest elskværdige Karakterer.' Den Juliske Æt vilde den Dag idag være glemt, som saa mange andre romerske Slægter, om ikke Cæsar havde gjort Navnet Julius udødeligt i Forening med sit eget, dette Navn som (i det tredie aarhundrede efter vor Tidsregning) af Spartianus Ælius med Rette blev kaldt varigt, saa længe Verden staar (*clarum et duraturum* cum *æternitate mundi*).

(In the main battles at Pharsalus and Munda Caesar chose his female ancestor's, his goddess', name as the battle cry for his soldiers: *Venus Genetrix.* He carried her image in his ring. He later put her image on his coins. He built a temple for her as the centre of the forum he built when Forum Romanum had become too cramped. He put a statue of Cleopatra in gold next to that of the goddess. In his last years, Cleopatra became to him what Aspasia had for a long time been to Pericles, an object of his love and of indignation for those who envied him. There was a deeper meaning to Caesar's idolization of Venus: by the refinement of his being, by his irresistible grace, he was really Venus's kin. On St Helena, Napoleon said about him (14 December 1816): 'as opposed to Alexander, Caesar began his career late; but after a trivial youth, he demonstrated to have the most effective, nobleminded, and wonderful soul. I consider him to be one of History's most graceful characters.' The Julian line would have been forgotten today, as so many other Roman families, had Caesar not made the name Julius immortal in junction with his own, this name which (in the third century, according to our reckoning of time) Spartanius Ælius said would last eternally, as long as the world exists (*clarum et duraturum cum æternitate mundi*).)[67]

---

67 Brandes 1918, i, 2.

Brandes seems to accept Caesar's relation to Venus, but in a reimagined form, so as to be a spiritual relation by character and nature rather than a literal relation by blood, quite similar to the way Brandes saw the great men of history to be spiritually connected, himself included. The point of this section is to demonstrate Caesar's creation of eternal fame for his family. Brandes does mention Caesar's placing of a statue of Cleopatra next to that of the goddess in the temple, that which attracted Lobendanz and Giersing's attention and in their work became an ominous action, paving the way for Caesar's defeat by his enemies. Brandes, however, bypasses it quickly, justifying Caesar's relationship with Cleopatra by comparing it to that of Pericles to Aspasia.

Brandes repeatedly states the focal point of the forum to be the temple to Venus, but does give a more 'secular' description of Caesar's architectural plans of Rome, including the establishing of a new forum — at least it begins as such:

Til den aandelige Omformning af Rom svarede den arkitektoniske. Forum Romanum, hvor Valgmøder afholdtes, Domme afsagdes Forretninger afgjordes og Lediggængere voldte Trængsel, frigjorde Cæsar baade for Comitier og for Tribunaler, idet han henviste Folkeforsamlingerne til de Skranker til Brug for Stemmegivningen som han havde ladet opføre paa Marsmarken (*Sæpta Julia*) og henviste Retsforhandlingerne til sit nye Torv (*Forum Julium*) mellem Capitolium og Palatinerbjerget [...] Havde Cæsar ikke den Tro, der flytter Bjerge, saa havde han den Vilje, der flytter Floder. Hans forudseende Visdom vilde ændre Rummet som den havde ændret Tiden. Roms hidtil uforanderlige *Pomerium* (det fri Rum indenfor Bymuren) blev flyttet, Naturen overvundet Klimaet forbedret. Cæsar blev for den romerske Menigmand den guddommelige Personlighed, *Divus* Julius, som forvandlede Alt. Den afrikanske Giraf holdt sit Indtog i Rom sammen med den indiske Elefant. Circus omdannedes til en Sø, og der fandt Søslag Sted paa Landjorden: Naturen syntes ude af Stand til at afslaa Cæsar noget. Skulde da Menneskene negte ham noget, ham, den bestandig overdaadige Giver!

(The architectural reshaping of Rome corresponded to the spiritual. Caesar liberated Forum Romanum — where election meetings were held, judgements passed, businesses settled, and where unoccupied people caused congestion — from Comitia and tribunals, referring the popular assemblies to the counters used for voting erected by him in the Field of Mars (*Saepta Julia*) and litigations to his new square (*Forum Julium*) between Capitolium and the Palatine Hill [...]. If Caesar did not have the kind of faith that moves mountains, he surely had the kind of will that moves rivers. His foreseeing wisdom wanted to

Figure 11.6. Anaglypha Traiani (from the south). Historical reliefs found on Trajan's Forum in 1872 featured in Brandes's *Cajus Julius Cæsar*. Brandes uses them to describe the area of the fora around the time of Caesar (reproduced from Brandes 1918, I, pl. I.4).

change space like it had changed time. Rome's hitherto immutable *Pomerium* (the free space behind the city wall) was moved, nature overcome, the climate improved. To the common man, Caesar became the divine personality, Divus Julius, who changed everything. The African giraffe entered together with the Indian elephant. The circus was turned into a lake, and naval battles were carried out on land. Nature seemed incapable of denying Caesar anything. Should, then, humans deny something to him who continued to give lavishly.)[68]

Caesar's changes to the cityscape of Rome are undisputedly positive and pragmatic. Brandes does not talk of moving the centre to his own new space and of celebrating Caesar but of taking the stress off Forum Romanum by distributing its functions in new areas designed by Caesar. With his pun on the saying that faith moves mountains, Brandes elevates Caesar: Caesar does not believe and hope, he wants, does, and acts — like the gods. From a pragmatic description of city planning, Brandes's description turns into a confirmation of how Caesar must have come across as a godly figure to the common, contemporary Roman. A seed is planted here to see his deification not just as a propagandistic stunt but legitimized by the people, based on their witnessing of Caesar's power and abilities to turn the world upside down and shape it according to his will. Nonetheless, Brandes defends the viewpoint that Caesar's work was balanced and purposeful beyond his personal interests, as he moves on to talk about costs:

> Med uhyre Midler begyndtes Roms Ombygning og Forvandling. Templer var ikke mere Hovedsagen, men verdslige Bygninger, om end Opførelsen af Templer ikke blev forsømt. Da Forum Romanum var blevet for snevert for Domssagerne (Appian II.02) besluttede Cæsar at indrette et Forum Cæsaris. Oppius og Cicero fik det Hverv at opkøbe hvad Privatbygninger der stod i Vejen, indtil Libertas-Templets Forhal, for 60 Millioner Sestertser (12 Millioner Kroner) og selv dette viste sig, ikke at være nok. Grunden alene kostede 20 Millioner Kroner. Det var den, som smykkedes med Templet for Venus Genetrix og som blev indviet sammen med dette, Aar 46.

> (At extreme costs, the remodelling and transformation of Rome began. Temples were no longer the main objective but secular buildings, albeit the erection of temples was not neglected. When Forum Romanum had become too small for litigations to be held there (Appianus II.102), Caesar decided to organize a Forum Caesaris. Oppius and Cicero were charged with the task of buying whichever private buildings were in the way, up until the vestibule of the Libertas temple at the cost of 60 million sestertii (12 million Kroner), and even that proved not to be enough. The land alone cost 20 million Kroner. This he adorned with the Temple for Venus Genetrix inaugurated together with the forum together in year 46.)[69]

---

[68] Brandes 1918, I, 33–34.

[69] Brandes 1918, I, 49.

Figure 11.7. Anaglypha Traiani (from the north). Historical reliefs found on Trajan's Forum in 1872 featured in Brandes's *Cajus Julius Cæsar*. Brandes uses them to describe the area of the fora around the time of Caesar (reproduced from Brandes 1918, I, pl. I.4).

The economic costs of establishing his forum are yet another sign of the lengths Caesar will go through to carry out his plan — to improve Rome. It is not about himself but functionality especially yet also religious piety: the temple is highlighted again as the justification for the cost and sanctioning of Caesar's efforts. The price is brought up again in Brandes's volume two, where he points out that the Gallic campaigns funded the building project. Here, he furthermore elaborates on Cicero's involvement by mentioning how he by all means strove to please Caesar and cement their good relationship. Brandes likewise mentions that the great orator had plans to write a piece on the campaign and that Caesar was kind enough to politely praise some verses Cicero had sent to him — although Brandes adds in brackets that they were probably horrible,[70] and elsewhere how Cicero borrowed money from Caesar and that it was no wonder Caesar eventually grew tired of him.[71]

Like the common people of Rome, Brandes seems genuinely amazed by the works erected and the celebrations given by Caesar. He describes the festivities at the inauguration of the temple in great detail. Here, it suffices to quote the introduction:

> Efter Tempelindvielsen gav Cæsar Kamplege og Teaterforstillinger til Ære for sin Datter Julias Minde. Et mægtigt Indtryk gjorde det, da Tilskuerne omkring den Skueplads, Cæsar midlertidigt lod opføre paa Forum, ved et udspændt *Silkesejl* blev skærmede imod Solen. Dion moraliserer (43.24) over Blødagtigheden hos de Barbarer, der frembragte slige Stoffer, en Blødagtighed, der nu forplantedes til Rom.

> (After the inauguration of the temple, Caesar gave games and theatre performances in honour of his daughter Julia's memory. It made a great impression that the audience encircling the temporarily erected scene on the Forum was shielded from the sun by an awning in *silk*. Dion moralizes (43.24) over the softness of the barbarians who procured such fabrics, a softness now spreading to Rome.)[72]

Brandes does not himself cast judgement, although he includes Cassius Dio's. Having completed the list of measures taken to make the occasion splendid, including the number of animals brought in for the games and the innovative games mentioned above,[73] he again gives voice to criticism in order to reject it:

> Var mange Romere henrykte over den Luksus, der ved disse Festligheder blev udfoldet, saa var der naturligvis ogsaa andre, hvem Overdaadigheden var imod, og som mente, Pengene kunde være anvendte bedre, navnlig saa de var komne dem selv til Gode.

> (While many Romans were delighted at the luxury displayed at these celebrations, there were, of course, others who frowned upon the opulence and found that the money could have been better spent, especially in ways benefitting themselves.)[74]

---

70 Brandes 1918, II, 123–24.
71 Brandes 1918, I, 260.
72 Brandes 1918, II, 358.
73 Brandes 1918, I, 33–34.
74 Brandes 1918, II, 358.

Although Brandes would, as mentioned, have been unable to see the Forum Iulium and its surroundings, since they were not excavated at the time he wrote his biography, he attempts a description of it based on the reliefs found in 1872 on Trajan's Forum, the so-called Anaglypha Traiani:

> Curia Julia blev bygget til Erstatning for det ældste Raadhus *Curia Hostilia*, hvis Opførelse tillagdes Kong Tullus Hostilius. Nord derfor anlagde Cæsar den af Søjler omgivne Plads *Forum* Julium, indviet 26. September 46, med Venus Genetrix s Tempel og hans egen Rytterstatue, hvor Hesten var en tro Afbildning af hans Yndlings-Stridshingst, en Sammensætning, der kom til at angive Typen for ethvert nyt Forum under Kejserne. Med disse Bygninger fortrængte han det gamle republikanske Comitium, der fik ny Plads paa Marsmarken, og med den indsnevrede han det gamle Forum paa den sydlige Langside. Samtidigt gav han *Circus maxmius* kunstnerisk Form, saa det kunde optage 150,000 Tilskuere. Relieferne paa de lange Marmorskranker fra Trajans Tid der i 1872 blev fundne paa Forum, fremstiller som Baggrund for historiske Scener Forum selv, som det tog sig ud, mens Cæsars Frembringelse endnu var friske og urørte. Paa Østskranken ses Cæsartemplet, opført paa det Sted, hvor Cæsars Lig blev brændt; paa Vestskranken ses Concordiatemplet. Vi genkender Basilica Julia og det hellige Figentræ, Symbolet paa Byens Grundlæggelse; ved dets Side Marsyasstatuen, Sinbilledet paa Byens Frihed. Vi finder her Talertribunen med Skibssnablerne, det synligste og mest fejrede Mindesmærke paa Forum, som Cæsar otte Aar før sin Død lod flytte noget i den Hensigt at udvide Forum i Retning af Marsmarken, paa hvilken samtidigt den Pragtbygning blev rejst, der kaldtes Sæpta Julia, Afstemningspladsen af Marmor for Centuriatcomitierne, en mægtig fri Plads, omgivet af Søjlehaller.

(Curia Julia was built to replace the oldest city hall *Curia Hostilia*, the erection of which was attributed to King Tullus Hostilius. North of this Caesar placed the square of Forum Julium, surrounded by columns, inaugurated 26 September 46, with the Temple of Venus Genetrix and his own equestrian statue, of which the horse was modelled after his favourite war stallion, a composition that would serve as model of any new forum under the emperors. With these buildings, he displaced the old republican Comitium, for which a new location was provided at the Campus Martius, and with it he narrowed the old forum on the southern longitudinal side. At the same time, he gave the *Circus Maximus* an artistic shape enabling it to contain an audience of 150,000 people. The reliefs on the long marble balustrades from Trajan's time found on the Forum in 1872 [i.e. *the Anaglypha Traiani*], render the Forum in the background of historical scenes, as it looked when Caesar's creations were still new and untouched. On the eastern balustrade we see the Temple of Caesar erected on the spot where Caesar's body was burned [see Fig. 11.6]; on the western balustrade we see the Temple of Concordia [see Fig. 11.7]. We recognize the Basilica Julia and the holy fig tree, the symbol of the city's foundation; next to it the statue of Marsyas, the image of the city's liberty. Here we find the speakers' tribune with the beakheads, the most visible and most celebrated memorial of the Forum, which Caesar had moved slightly eight years before his death, intending to expand the Forum towards the Campus Martius where, at the same time, the magnificent building called Saepta Julia was erected, the voting space in marble for the Centuriate Assembly, a great open space surrounded by porticos.)[75]

The culminating description is connected directly to Brandes's political interpretation of Caesar's spaces; how they are the symbol of the political changes effected by Caesar. He is replacing and displacing buildings representative of Republican functions while his way of organizing the space in his own name, with a temple to his god and an equestrian statue of himself, becomes a new norm. Brandes's familiarity with the city of Rome becomes clear in the 'guided tour' he gives the reader, based on the reliefs from Trajan's Forum. The rather detailed description of the ancient remains continues for some time in the work (and Brandes later returns to it, going into more detail about the decoration, naming artists as well as costs of individual objects).[76] Brandes never loses sight of Caesar but generally uses him as a prism to look into various aspects of ancient Rome — from the physical display of the city, as here, to the life and role of women in Caesar's time.

That Caesar was a model for the emperors to come is a recurrent theme, particularly how Augustus modelled himself and his deeds on Caesar's example. Brandes's judgement of Augustus is hard and negative, and it seems paramount to him to set in stone that Augustus by no means measured up to Caesar. In his introductory chapter, he states Caesar to be by nature a brave lion, while Augustus was a cunning fox, reaping everything that Caesar had sown.[77] Architecturally, too, Brandes finds that Augustus, the first to imitate Caesar, did so with negative intent:

> Senatet, der koldsindigt havde været Vidne til Cæsars Mord, oprettede for Augustus *Ara Pacis Augustæ*, en med Relieffer af Carrakisk Marmor smykket Alterbygning midt i en Søjlegaard ved den Gade, som nu hedder corso. Augustus lod en Mængde gamle Bygninger, deri-

---

[75] Brandes 1918, I, 54.

[76] Brandes 1918, II, 358, with reference to Plin., *HN* IX.116.

[77] Brandes 1918, I, 12.

blandt 82 Templer, istandsatte. Under Skin af Omsorg for Cæsars Minde stræbte han at overbyde hans Foretagender, som da han klods op ad Forum Julium opførte det langt større Forum Augustum. Cæsars Navn har dog overstraalet hans.

(The Senate, having cold-bloodedly witnessed Caesar's murder, erected the *Ara Pacis Augustae* in Augustus's honour, an altar building decorated with reliefs in Carrara marble placed in the middle of an atrium by the street nowadays called the Corso. Augustus had a great number of old buildings restored, among them 82 temples. Under the guise of caring for Caesar's memory he aimed to outbid his doings, like when he erected the much larger Forum Augustum right next to Forum Julium. Caesar's name, however, has outshined his.)[78]

Perhaps it is the mentioned difference in size that spurred the insertion of Brandes's comparison and judgement of the two here, in the description of Caesar's building projects.

Summing up

Caesar had, on reoccurring occasions, been a central figure in European literature and history writing. His character and deeds, so closely entangled in what turned out to be profound changes, making Rome the defining Western power, had fascinated and inspired biographers, historians, and statesmen alike for centuries throughout European tidal waves of political change. The treated Danish biographies of Caesar's life and deeds must also be seen in light of societal change on the one hand and literary tradition on the other. The biographies take two different approaches in their understanding of the Forum Caesaris, its role, and meaning. The earliest from 1900 by Lobedanz and Giersing focused on the ambitious individual and Caesar's fascination with Cleopatra, which they held to be of a degenerated nature, thus to some extent exempting Caesar's person from blame for his mistakes. The biography was written before World War I in a time of deep tensions in Europe and beyond. Austria-Hungary in 1908 annexed Bosnia and Herzegovina, which had been Ottoman territory since 1878. This annexation brought tensions between Austria-Hungary and Serbia and therefore also the Pan-Slavic and Orthodox Russian Empire, which backed Serbia. Furthermore, the 1911–1912 Italo–Turkish War, which brought to the forefront deep nationalistic tendencies in the Balkan states, also became a precur-

sor of World War I and spurred the Balkan Wars. The strong nation states of Europe contributed to keeping the Balkan conflicts at bay, but the assassination of the Archduke Franz Ferdinand of Austria in Sarajevo in 1914 became the last spark to ignite the fire that would spread throughout Europe and beyond and become known as World War I. The turn of the twentieth century was, so to say, one of immense political and military tensions, characterized by strong personalities across Europe, who had deep-rooted national interests. Thus, focusing on Caesar as a negative role model at this time could be a way to indirectly question agendas of contemporary leaders. In Lobedanz and Giersing, we may see the beginning of such, as they explore the wrong steps Caesar took — of which his forum was the most striking — although they do much to pardon his behaviour.

World War I and its devastating impact on Europe, its populations, and lands plunged European identities into a deep crisis, which was made more severe through the raging pandemic we know as the Spanish Flu. Europe was not a united continent when Brandes wrote his Caesar biography, but rather a dispersed landscape of nations in crisis. Turning to Antiquity's strong men and the figure of Caesar was one way of framing ideal leadership in a time of aftermath of war and financial crises. Brandes's description of Caesar as a powerful leader, Caesar's interest in landscape, as well as his love for Cleopatra as positive — or at least not negative — were in many ways a romanticized description. However, when seen in the light of the events of the preceding decades, the recent end of World War I and the raging pandemic, Brandes's biography also opens another perspective, namely that of the human leader with feelings and empathy — a leader who could be moved but still led the people with a firm hand and only the best intentions. A fantasy, perhaps, of a leader with unmistakable insight into the right path to take.

Caesar's Forum holds a place in both biographies as a central location, working as an indicator of Caesar's personality and his politics as well as his way of representing himself to the Roman people. Again the biographies take diverging perspectives on Caesar's intentions with the space, reflecting their overall account of him as a leader, tyrant, dictator, politician, lover, and almost divine statesman. While the biographers relied on the ancient descriptions of Caesar's Forum, they added their own interpretations of the space to their biographies and in this way allowed for their contemporary society to see Caesar in a different light — as a competent leader who lost his focus, or as the best leader the world had ever seen.

---

[78] Brandes 1918, I, 54.

Works Cited

Allen, J. 2013. *Icons of Danish Modernity: Georg Brandes and Asta Nielsen* (Seattle: University of Washington Press).

Ammerman, A. J. and D. Filippi. 2000. 'Nuove osservazioni sull'area a nord del Comizio', *Bullettino della Commissione archeologica comunale di Roma*, 101: 27–38.

Banks, W. 2020. *Human Rights and Oppressed Peoples: Collected Essays and Speeches* (Madison: University of Wisconsin Press).

Beard, M. and M. Crawford. 1999. *Rome in the Late Republic*, 2nd edn (London: Duckworth).

Bendtsen, B. S. 2020. 'Colour-Blind or Clear-Sighted Neutrality? Georg Brandes and the First World War', in J. den Hertog and S. Kruizinga (eds), *Caught in the Middle: Neutrals, Neutrality and the First World War* (Amsterdam: Uitgeverij Aksant), pp. 121–38.

Billows, R. A. 2009. *Julius Caesar: The Colossus of Rome* (London: Routledge).

Bobé, L. 1935–1942. *Rom og Danmark gennem tiderne*, 3 vols (Copenhagen: Levin & Munksgaard).

Boissier, G. 1880. *Promenades archéologiques: Rome et Pompei* (Paris: Hachette).

—— 1884. *Ciceron et ses amis: étude sur la société romaine du temps de César*, 2nd edn (Paris: Hachette).

—— 1905. *La Conjuration de Catilina* (Paris: Hachette & Cie).

Brandes, G. 1889. 'Aristokratisk Radikalisme', *Tilskueren: Maanedsskrift for Litteratur, Samfundsspørgsmaal og Almenfattelige Videnskabelige Skildringer*, 7: 565–613.

—— 1918. *Cajus Julius Cæsar*, 2 vols (Copenhagen: Gyldendal).

Busk-Jensen, L. 2006–2009. 'Brandes' kursændring', *Dansk Litteraturs Historie* <https://dansklitteraturshistorie.lex.dk/Brandes'_kurs%C3%A6ndring> [accessed 25 January 2021].

Delfino, A. 2010. 'Il primo Foro di Cesare', *Scienze dell'antichità*, 16: 335–47.

—— 2014. *Forum Iulium: L'area del Foro di Cesare alla luce delle campagne di scavo 2005–2008; le fasi arcaica, repubblicana, e cesariano-augustea*, British Archaeological Reports, International Series, 2607 (Oxford: Archaeopress).

Drumann, W. 1834–1844. *Geschichte Roms in seinem Übergang von der republikanischen zur monarchischen Verfassung oder Pompeius, Caesar, Cicero und ihre Zeitgenossen*, 3 vols (Königsberg: Bornträger).

Dyson, S. L. 2019. *Archaeology, Ideology, and Urbanism in Rome from the Grand Tour to Berlusconi* (Cambridge: Cambridge University Press).

Ferrero, G. 1902–1907. *Grandezza e decadenza di Roma*, 4 vols (Milan: Fratelli Treves).

Frisch, H. 1918. 'Georg Brandes: Caius Iulius Cæsar', *Tilskueren: Maanedsskrift for Litteratur, Kunst, Samfundsspørgsmaal og almenfattelige videnskabelige skildringer*, 35.2: 520–26.

—— 1919. 'Georg Brandes: Caius Iulius Cæsar II', *Tilskueren: Maanedsskrift for Litteratur, Kunst, Samfundsspørgsmaal og almenfattelige videnskabelige skildringer*, 36.1: 266–75.

—— 1942. *Ciceros Kamp for Republikken: Den historiske Baggrund for Ciceros filippiske taler* (Copenhagen: Hirschsprungs).

—— 1946. *Cicero's Fight for the Republic: The Historical Background of Cicero's Philippics* (Copenhagen: Gyldendal).

Goldsworthy, A. K. 2006. *Caesar: Life of a Colossus* (New Haven: Yale University Press).

Griffin, M. T. (ed.). 2009. *A Companion to Julius Caesar* (Malden: Wiley-Blackwell).

Grossi, O. 1936. 'The Forum of Julius Caesar and the Temple of Venus Genetrix', *Memoirs of the American Academy in Rome*, 13: 215–20.

Gundolf, F. and J. W. Hartmann. 1929. *The Mantle of Caesar* (London: Grant Richards).

Hass, T. A. 2019. 'The Meaning of *jul* (Christmas) according to Pontanus, Vedel and Worm: Etymology, Controversy and Stories of the Danes', *Analecta Romana Instituti Danici*, 44: 217–38.

Hass, T. A. and R. Raja. 2021. *Caesar's Past and Posterity's Caesar* (Turnhout: Brepols).

Hopkins, J. N. 2014. 'The Creation of the Forum and the Making of Monumental Rome', in E. C. Robinson, *Papers on Italian Urbanism in the First Millennium B.C.* (Portsmouth, RI: Journal of Roman Archaeology), pp. 29–61.

Jacobsen, J. K. and R. Raja. 2018. 'A High-Definition Approach to the Forum of Caesar in Rome: Urban Archaeology in a Living City', in R. Raja and S. Sindbæk (eds), *Urban Network Evolutions: Towards a High-Definition Archaeology* (Aarhus: Aarhus University Press), pp. 21–26.

Jacobsen, J. K. and others. 2020. 'Practicing Urban Archaeology in a Modern City: The New Excavations of the Alessandrino Quarter in the Heart of Rome', *Journal of Field Archaeology*, 46: 36–51.

—— 2021a. 'Excavating Caesar's Forum: Present Results of the Caesar's Forum Project', *Analecta Romana Instituti Danici*, 44: 239–45.

—— 2021b. 'High-Definition Urban Narratives from Central Rome: Virtual Reconstructions of the Past and the New Caesar's Forum Excavations', *Journal of Urban Archaeology*, 3: 65–86.

Jaurnow, L. 1992. 'Heltebilleder: Et Danskspeciale om Georg Brandes' Biografier over Shakespeare, Goethe, Voltaire, Cæsar og Michelangelo' (unpublished doctoral dissertation, University of Copenhagen).

Kjær, L. 2020. 'Cæsar i Middelalderen: Cæsars Ånd', in T. A. Hass and S. G. Saxkjær (eds), *Cæsar: Manden og Myten* (Aarhus: Aarhus University Press), pp. 167–84.

Knudsen, J. 2004. *Georg Brandes: Uovervindelig taber 1914–27* (Copenhagen: Gyldendal).

Krause, S. 2000. 'Georg Brandes' Shakespeare-Biographie', *Tijdschrift voor Skandinavistiek*, 21: 81–105.

La Rocca, E. 2001. 'Il foro di Cesare', *Römische Mittelungen*, 108: 174–84.

Lobedanz, A. 1896. *Heltene fra Napoleonstiden* (Copenhagen: Gyldendal).

—— 1899. *Mural og Hans Hustru* (Copenhagen: Gyldendal).

Lobedanz, A. and O. Giersing. 1900. *Cajus Julius Cæsar* (Copenhagen: Hagerup).

LTUR = Eva Margareta Steinby (ed.). 1993–2000. *Lexicon topographicum urbis Romae*, 6 vols (Rome: Quasar).

Lundtofte, A. M. 2000. 'Pointing Fingers at Genius: Reading Brandes Reading Kierkegaard', *Tijdschrift voor Skandinavistiek*, 21: 149–63.

Maiuro, M. 2010. 'What Was the Forum Iulium Used for? The Fiscus and its Jurisdiction in First-Century CE Rome', in F. De Angelis (ed.), *Spaces of Justice in the Roman Empire* (Leiden: Brill), pp. 189–221.

Meier, C. 1982. *Caesar: A Biography* (New York: Basic Books).

Meneghini, R. 2009. *Fori Imperiali e Mercati di Traiano: storia e descrizione dei monumenti alla luce degli studi e degli scavi recenti* (Rome: Libreria dello stato).

Moestrup, J. and E. Nyholm. 1989. *Italien og Danmark: 100 års inspiration* (Copenhagen: Gad).

Moltesen, M. 1989. 'Danske Udgravningsprojekter i Italien', in J. Moestrup and E. Nyholm (eds), *Italien og Danmark: 100 års inspiration* (Copenhagen: Gad), pp. 96–107.

—— 2012. *Perfect Partners: The Collaboration between Carl Jacobsen and his Agent in Rome Wolfgang Helbig in the Formation of the Ny Carlsberg Glyptotek 1887–1914* (Copenhagen: Ny Carlsberg Glyptotek).

Mommsen, T. 1854–1856. *Römische Geschichte*, 3 vols (Leipzig: Reimer & Hirzel).

—— 1862–1866. *The History of Rome*, 4 vols (London: Bentley).

Moritzen, J. 1924. *Life of Julius Caesar (as Seen by Georg Brandes)* (Girard: Haldeman-Julius).

Mortensen, E. and R. Raja. 2019. 'Introduktion: Om store danske arkæologer, fortidens byer og tilblivelsen af en humanistisk disciplin', in E. Mortensen and R. Raja (eds), *Store danske arkæologer: På jagt efter fortidens byer* (Aarhus: Aarhus University Press), pp. 9–39.

Munk, K. 'Aabent Brev til Mussolini', *Jyllandsposten*, 17 November 1938.

Napoleon I and M. Marchand. 1836. *Précis des guerres de César: suivi de plusieurs fragments inédits* (Paris: Chez Gosselin).

Napoleon III. 1865–1866. *Histoire de Jules César*, 2 vols (Paris: Henri Plon).

Nicolet, C. 2009. 'Caesar and the Two Napoleons', in M. T. Griffin (ed.), *A Companion to Julius Caesar* (Malden: Wiley-Blackwell), pp. 410–17.

Niebuhr, B. G. 1811–1832. *Römische Geschichte*, 3 vols (Berlin: Realschulbuchhandlung).

Nyholm, E. 1989. 'Danske Malere og Italien i Årene mellem 1870 og 1920', in J. Moestrup and E. Nyholm (eds), *Italien og Danmark: 100 års inspiration* (Copenhagen: Gad), pp. 218–45.

Osborne, J. 2006. 'St Peter's Needle and the Ashes of Julius Caesar', in M. Wyke (ed.), *Julius Caesar in Western Culture* (Malden: Blackwell), pp. 95–109.

Paterson, J. 2009. 'Caesar the Man', in M. T. Griffin (ed.), *A Companion to Julius Caesar* (Malden: Wiley-Blackwell), pp. 120–40.

Pinna Caboni, B. 2008. 'Il foro di Cesare: Aspetti della decorazione architettonica', in G. Gentili (ed.), *Giulio Cesare: l'uomo, le imprese, il mito* (Milan: Silvano), pp. 57–59.

Raja, R. and J. Rüpke. 2021. 'Creating Memories in and of Urban Rome: The Forum Iulium', in T. A. Hass and R. Raja (eds), *Caesar's Past and Posterity's Caesar* (Turnhout: Brepols), pp. 53–66.

Raja, R. and S. M. Sindbæk. 2020. 'Biographies of Place: An Introduction', *Journal of Urban Archaeology*, 2: 11–14.

—— 2021. 'Urban Networks and High-Definition Narratives: Rethinking the Archaeology of Urbanism', *Journal of Urban Archaeology*, 3: 173–86.

Ritzau, T. and K. Ascani. 1982. *Rom er et fortryllet bur: Den gyldne epoke for skandinaviske kunstnere i Rom* (Copenhagen: Rhodos).

Rockstroh, K. C. 1976–1984. 'Arnold Lobedanz', *Dansk biografisk leksikon* <https://biografiskleksikon.lex.dk/Arnold_Lobedanz> [accessed 25 January 2021].

Sauer, N. 2021. 'The Forum of Caesar: A Historiographical Review', in T. A. Hass and R. Raja (eds), *Caesar's Past and Posterity's Caesar* (Turnhout: Brepols), pp. 213–41.

Smith, C. J. 2010. 'Caesar and the Early History of Rome', in G. Urso (ed.), *Precursore o visionario?* (Pisa: ETS), pp. 249–64.

Stoffel, H. 1887. *Histoire de Jules César: guerre civile*, II: *De la bataille de Pharsale à la mort de César* (Paris: Imprimerie nationale).

Strocka, V. M. 2005. 'Das Fassaden–Motiv des Venus Genetrix-Tempels in Rom: Bedeutung und Nachwirknung', J. de Waele and S. T. A. M. Mols (eds), *Omni pede stare: Saggi architettonici e circumvesuviani in memoriam Jos de Waele* (Naples: Electa), pp. 153–67.

Thomas, E. 2007. *Monumentality and the Roman Empire: Architecture in the Antonine Age* (Oxford: Oxford University Press).

Ulrich, R. B. 1986. 'The Appiades Fountain of the Forum Iulium', *Römische Mitteilungen*, 113: 405–23.

—— 1993. 'Julius Caesar and the Creation of the Forum Iulium', *American Journal of Archaeology*, 97: 49–80.

—— 1994. *The Roman Orator and the Sacred Stage: The Roman 'Templum rostratum'* (Brussels: Latomus).

Valenzani, R. S. 2006. 'The Seat and Memory of Power: Caesar's Curia and Forum', in M. Wyke (ed.), *Julius Caesar in Western Culture* (Oxford: Wiley), pp. 85–98.

Weinstock, S. 1971. *Divus Julius* (Oxford: Clarendon).

Westall, R. 1996. 'The Forum Iulium as Representation of Imperator Caesar', *Römische Mitteilungen*, 103: 198–224.

Wiseman, T. P. 2009. *Remembering the Roman People: Essays on Late-Republican Politics and Literature* (Oxford: Oxford University Press).

—— 2014. 'The Many and the Few', *History Today*, 64: 10–15.

—— 2016. *Julius Caesar: Pocket Giants* (Stroud: History Press).

—— 2019. *The House of Augustus: A Historical Detective Story* (Princeton: Princeton University Press).

Zanker, P. 1988. *The Power of Images in the Age of Augustus* (Ann Arbor: University of Michigan Press).

—— 2009. 'The Irritating Statues and Contradictory Portraits of Julius Caesar', in M. T. Griffin (ed.), *A Companion to Julius Caesar* (Malden: Wiley-Blackwell), pp. 288–314.

12. Past Research Perspectives and Narrated Space: The Incident When Caesar Did Not Rise for the Senate, according to Georg Brandes (1918) and Hartvig Frisch (1942)

Trine Arlund Hass

Linacre College, University of Oxford (klftjah@cas.au.dk/trine.hass@classics.ox.ac.uk)

Introduction

Most historical accounts of the life and deeds of Gaius Julius Caesar render a remarkable encounter between Caesar and the Roman Senate, a sort of stand-off between the old and new power, and many accounts place this situation at the Forum Julium. The main events go as follows: at a point in time in 44 BC, Caesar was at the site of his new forum. Having decided to grant him new honours, the Senate approached him there to present him with these, but Caesar did not rise to receive the Senate although this would have been protocol. According to one account of the event, he even remarked that it would have been better to reduce his honours than enhance them. Caesar's reaction caused much disturbance in Rome, and many analyses find that it spurred on the opposition against Caesar that led to his assassination that same year.

This essay examines two Danish treatments of the episode as part of a larger study of Danish receptions of Caesar and Roman culture. The first is by the literary critic Georg Brandes (1842–1927); it occurs in his massive two-volume biography of Caesar published in Danish in 1918 and intended for a wider readership. The second is by the Danish classicist and social democratic politician Hartvig Frisch (1893–1950), found in his scholarly work *Cicero's Fight for the Republic* that sets out to examine the backdrop of Cicero's *Philippics*. The work was published in Danish in 1942 (*Ciceros Kamp for Republikken*) and in English translation in 1946 (hence referenced Frisch 1942/46a), the latter as the first volume in Humanitas, a series of English translations of Danish scholarship in classical studies founded by Frisch and professor of classical philology at the University of Copenhagen, Carsten Høeg. Frisch's account is found in his chapter on Caesar's end, 'Idus Martiae'. He treats the episode again in the work *Cicero and Caesar* (pub-

lished in Danish only, as *Cicero og Cæsar*, 1946), aimed at a wider readership. This volume presents sources in Danish translations on the two great men and their relationship, with explanations by Frisch.

Frisch and Brandes are directly connected in the sense that Frisch reviewed Brandes's work when it first came out.[1] Following the reviews the intellectual friendship between the promising young philologist and the elderly critic blossomed; they remained in vivid contact until Brandes's death. In his review of the first volume, Frisch praises and characterizes Brandes's approach to his historical topic, saying:

> Saaledes lever Historien — som til alle Tider Menneskenes Sagn har levet — ved at *siges*: hver Tid faar sin Fortæller, Bøgerne på Hylden gør det ikke. En speciel Interesse, en stor Viden eller faglig Dygtighed slaar ikke til for det, jeg hér mener; ved alt dette forberedes et Værk, der siger de kendte Ting paa ny, men det skabes ikke. Hvad der brænder et saadant Stof sammen, er den hede Ild, vi kalder en Karakter.[2]

---

* This article was written during my transition from a postdoctoral fellowship at the Danish Academy in Rome and Aarhus University, funded by the Carlsberg Foundation, via my employment at Centre for Urban Network Evolutions (Aarhus University Research Foundation and the Danish National Research Foundation, grant DNRF119), to my Carlsberg Foundation Junior Research Fellowship at Linacre College, University of Oxford. The role of the Forum Iulium in Danish biographies of Caesar is treated in Hass and Raja elsewhere in this volume. While benefitting from the results produced there, this is an independent study. I am grateful to Marianne Pade and Nikoline Sauer for reading and commenting on my text.

[1] Frisch 1918; 1919.

[2] Frisch 1919, 266; Christiansen 1993, 70–71.

(Thus history lives on — in the way humans' stories have always lived on — by being *told*: each era has its own narrator; the books on the shelf will not do it. A particular interest, a great amount of knowledge, or professional skill will not suffice for what I mean here; through all of the above, a work stating the familiar anew is prepared but not created. What forges matter of this sort together is the ardent fire that we call a character.)[3]

The appreciation expressed here of Brandes's own life experience comes back to a point made at the very beginning of Frisch's review of how any biographer of Caesar should have ample experiences in life and thereby be of a certain age, but he points explicitly to Brandes's aptitude as a narrator too. On this, he later elaborates with more direct reference to Brandes's style: 'This great master *is within* his work, indeed, in every line, and hence one reads the book on Caesar just as one experiences a play — you do not leave it until the drama has played out.'[4] According to Frisch's own biographer, Christiansen, it must be implied in Frisch's insisting on narrative quality as an indispensable requirement of historical works that Frisch himself is capable of writing in this style too. Christiansen indeed sees the reviews of Brandes's biography of Caesar as programmatic of Frisch's own works.[5]

In this understanding of biography and history writing, narrative qualities are bound to mark renderings of episodes such as the one treated in the present study, in that they are, to use Frisch's terminology, mosaics composed of tesserae (understood as the sources from various points of time in Antiquity), and that the laying of these mosaics relies on the author/narrator, while they are dependent also on accounts by other historians and biographies from later periods than the events and people treated. To recognize this aspect of their renderings of Caesar, I will examine Brandes's and Frisch's accounts of the episode in question as narratives, attempting to discern how the composition of these narratives contributes to establish an image of Caesar and what role his spaces, the Forum Julium and the Temple of Venus Genetrix, are made to play. For this, terminology from narrative theory will prove useful, especially the narratological concept of *focalization*. This term was coined by Genette, who was among the first to distinguish between narrative voice (who speaks?) and the point of view from which the narrated is experienced (who sees?).[6] When a character focalizes, we experience events through their eyes, although the narrative is not necessarily told in this character's voice; the degree to which we are granted access to the inner reflections of the focalizer may vary. The terminology of character analysis as proposed by Phelan, who suggests narrative character balances *mimetic*, *synthetic*, and *thematic* functions, will be used too.[7] *Mimetic* is understood, in the Aristotelian tradition, as the realistic aspect of a character, that which furthers the conception of the portrayed as an autonomous person; the *thematic* qualities of a character represent a particular idea or ideology; and the *synthetic* qualities relate to the way a character is instrumental in bringing forward the plot. Each character in a narrative contains elements of all three qualities, but in varying quantities. For the episode in question, the thematic aspect of Caesar's character would be ambition, while the synthetic reflects the role of this episode in the story of Caesar's life and death in general. As to the mimetic aspects, it will be discussed whether the interpretations of Caesar presented in relation to this particular episode are concurrent with the general understanding and presentation of his character in the work in question.

The primary object is thus to examine how Caesar's character is narrated and if and how the Forum Julium plays a role in the displayed understanding of his character. To contextualize the Danish accounts, they will be held against international historical works on Caesar, of which some can be identified as direct models of the Danish versions, while others are rather representative of attitudes which may have shaped them.

Ancient Accounts of the Incident

In the literature discussed, the following accounts are mentioned: Suet., *Iul.* LXXVIII; Nicolaus of Damascus (Nic. Dam.), *Life of Augustus* LXXIX; Liv. CXVI.2, Eutr. VI.25; Cass. Dio XLIV.7; Plut., *Caes.* LX; and App. II.107. Reference practice is different in the various works; Brandes gives none while Frisch discusses some treatments and references others. In the international accounts, references are more consistently applied, although here too not all the ancient treatments are referenced by all. To indicate which information is found

---

[3] This and subsequent translations are by the author, except from Frisch 1942/46a, which is quoted from the published English translation.

[4] Frisch 1918, 525: 'Denne store Mester *er i* sit Værk, ja i hver Linie, og man læser derfor Bogen om Cæsar, ligesom man betragter et Skuespil — man gaar ikke derfra, før Dramaet er udspillet.'

[5] Christiansen 1993, 70–71.

[6] Genette 1979.

[7] See e.g. Phelan and Rabinowitz 2012.

Table 12.1. Ancient accounts of the incident.

	App.	Cass. Dio	Eutr.	Liv.	Nic. Dam.	Plut.	Suet.
The incident is located at the a. Forum Julium b. by the Temple of Venus Genetrix c. by the Rostra	c	b		b	a	c	b
Caesar's business is specified to be the tenders of the Forum Julium					x		
The honours are inscribed on silver tablets with gilded letters and laid down at the Capitoline		x					
The procession: members of the procession are specified a. with regard to offices, b. Mark Antony is mentioned, c. the accompanying crowd is mentioned	a				a, c	a, (c)	
Caesar's remark is referenced						x	
Explanations of or excuses for Caesar's reaction are treated: a. he did not notice the procession, b. Balbus held Caesar back, c. Trebatius advised Caesar to rise, d. illness/disease, e. response to Pontius Aquila's behaviour at his triumph, f. Caesar realizes his mistake		d			a	f, d, b	b, c, e

where, a schematic survey of the ancient sources is presented above. It is not the aim here, however, to scrutinize the relationship between the ancient and the later historical accounts of the episode, for which much besides the mere taking over of information would deserve treatment (Table 12.1).[8]

Brandes and Frisch's Reviews

Georg Morris Cohen Brandes (1842–1927) played an important role as a literary critic in Denmark and from 1901 as professor of literature at the University of Copenhagen, a position he pursued, upon encouragement, already thirty years earlier but did not get at that time, probably due to his liberal ways of thinking.[9] He is most famous for introducing naturalism, the so-called Modern Breakthrough, to Danish literature and art in a lecture series presented at the University of Copenhagen in 1871. Here, Brandes encouraged the use of literature to raise debate on social problems especially, moving literature and art in a new direction and making Denmark a front runner internationally. Brandes was a key figure in the Danish intelligentsia and received much international attention as well. In his later years, he wrote several biographies of great men. Besides Caesar (1918), he wrote of Nietzsche (1889, an introduction to the philosopher

rather than a biography), Shakespeare (1895–1897), Goethe (1915), Voltaire (1916), Napoleon (1917), and Michelangelo Buonarotti (1921). According to Jørgen Knudsen, Brandes's biographer, the biographic studies might well have been written to show Brandes's contemporaries exemplary ways to follow.[10] As such, Brandes's works follow in the tradition of Thomas Carlyle, who found the history of the world to be comprised of the lives of great men.[11] Brandes surely celebrates Caesar as one of history's greatest men and moral examples.

Despite their good relationship, Brandes and Frisch do not see completely eye to eye when it comes to history. Frisch's view on Brandes's work is generally positive, especially in the review of the first volume, but he does voice some criticism, most importantly of the way Brandes portrays Caesar's opponents. In the introduction of Frisch's review of Brandes's first volume, he states that it takes an elderly man to write about Caesar; the young like himself should read and cultivate Caesar's works instead.[12] He returns to this point towards the end, in a general characterization of Brandes's familiarity with the classical texts, which Frisch describes as characteris-

---

[8] For some important treatments of the incident in the classical texts, see Dobesch 2001; Pelling 2011; Toher 2016; Weinstock 1971.

[9] The only English biography of Brandes is Allen 2013.

[10] Knudsen 2004, 440; Hass and Raja (in this volume).

[11] Possing 2017, 73–75; Carlyle 1841.

[12] Frisch 1918, 520: 'Cæsar beundrer man et helt Liv igennem, der vokser lutter Bekræftelser paa hans Færd og Gerning af det, der møder en selv i Livets Spil. Men netop derfor bør den, der skriver Bogen om Cæsar, ikke være nogen ung Mand. Lad os unge læse ham, dyrke hans Liv i det enkelte og arbejde paa at fuldkommengøre vor Viden om denne skabende Kraft!'

tic of his grandparents' generation. They approached the classics without any learned apparatus 'but with all the more sense of the humane of this occupation'.[13] Frisch finds that Brandes's work becomes the tangible evidence of his generation's intimate knowledge of Roman literature, which would otherwise have been unattested, and he proclaims it a stroke of luck that it was captured by the pen of the last person left who happened to also be the greatest.[14]

Frisch places Brandes in the tradition following Mommsen and Drumann, with the notable difference that World War I lies between him and their Romanticist point of departure.[15] Brandes's accounts of the wars in Gaul in the second volume of the biography Frisch defines as informed by the works of the Napoleons and Henri Stoffel.[16] Guglielmo Ferrero alone is mentioned as an example of the contemporary attempts to reconsider Caesar's opponents, and him Brandes rejects. The above-mentioned is placed at the beginning of the first review but coincides with Frisch's criticism, voiced in the review of volume two, of Brandes's unnuanced approach to Caesar's opposition, on which Frisch develops both in connection with his depiction of the Gauls and the Roman opposition. This is particularly noteworthy since Frisch in his review of the first volume found it to be a quality and addition to the research on Caesar that Brandes evaluated his life and deeds based on Caesar's own circumstances, those which he finds are treated especially in the biography's first volume.[17] This novelty and quality is, in a sense, the root of Frisch's main objection as well, since he finds it unfair that Caesar's opponents have not been viewed on the backdrop of their particular circumstances. Frisch finds this motivates a new great work on Caesar and his time taking a different point of departure. Whether he feels that is what he himself offers in his work of Cicero, we can only speculate. In any case, it may speak to the weight of Brandes's biography that it took more than seventy years before a new Danish biography of Caesar was published.[18]

The Incident at the Forum Julium according to Brandes

As said, Brandes's biography of Caesar is divided into two volumes, comprising 363 and 607 pages respectively. In this way, it is slightly reminiscent of Napoleon III's *Histoire de Jules César* (1865–1866) in two volumes, although this was followed up by a third volume in two parts by Stoffel in 1887, treating the wars in Gaul and the remaining part of Caesar's life, which is the subject of Brandes's second volume. The conceptual organization of the material is, as indicated above, such that the first volume deals with Caesar's youth and much serves to give context by accounting for Rome, the empire, and society at this time, while the second begins with the wars in Gaul and ends with Caesar's death. The episode in question here is found towards the end of volume two:

> En Dag, da han havde taget Plads paa det nye Forum og fordelte Arbejdet til de dèr forsamlede Arkitekter og Kunstnere, gik alle Roms mest fremragende Mænd i højtideligt Optog ud til ham for at overrække ham Dekretet med de sidste Udmærkelser, Senatet havde tildelt ham. Marcus Antonius skred i sin Egenskab af Consul i Spidsen med sine Lictorer foran sig. Ham fulgte Prætorerne, Folketribunerne, Quæstorerne og alle de andre Øvrighedspersoner. Saa kom Senatet *in corpore* ledsaget af en umaadelig Folkemasse. Hele Rom talte i en Maaned ikke om andet end om at Cæsar havde taget saa ringe Notits af denne Hyldest, at han end ikke havde rejst sig fra sit Sæde. Dette blev udlagt som en Forhaanelse af Roms Senat og Folk, *Senatus populusque Romanus*, hvortil Historien ikke kendte Mage. Værre endnu var det, at Imperatoren, istedenfor at takke, blot havde svart, at man vilde gøre bedre i at indskrænke de Æresbevisninger, man havde skænket ham, end i yderligere at forøge dem. Den Ringeagt, der laa i dette Svar, var ikke til at misforstaa, og blev ikke misforstaaet. Den var visselig fortjent, men det havde været klogt at fortie den. Modet var her et Øjeblik svulmet til et Overmod, der ytrede sig som Ironi.[19]

(One day when Caesar had gone to the new Forum and was distributing tasks to the architects and artists gathered there, all of Rome's most splendid men came to him in solemn procession to present him with a decree containing the latest honours awarded to him by the Senate. Mark Antony pushed forward in front, in his capacity of consul, his lictors before him. After him followed the praetors, the tribunes of the people, the quaestors, and all the other public officials. Then came the Senate *in corpore*, accompanied by an immense crowd of people. For a month, all of Rome talked of nothing else but how little notice Caesar had taken of this celebration, that he

---

[13] Frisch 1918, 525: 'men med saa meget større Sans for det menneskelige ved denne Beskæftigelse.'

[14] Frisch 1918, 525.

[15] Frisch 1918, 520 and 522.

[16] Frisch 1919, 267.

[17] Frisch criticizes him exactly for not approaching Caesar's opponents in a similar matter, see more on this in Hass and Raja (in this volume).

[18] Ørsted 1994.

---

[19] Brandes 1918, II, 529–30.

had not even risen from his seat. This was interpreted as an insult to the Senate and People of Rome, *Senatus Populusque Romanus*, of which history knew no parallel. Even worse was the fact that the imperator, instead of thanking them, had merely answered that they would do better to diminish the honours it had granted him rather than extend them further. The contempt implied in this answer was impossible to misunderstand and was not misunderstood. Indeed, his contempt was just but it would have been wise to suppress it. Confidence had, in this instance, swelled to overconfidence, expressing itself as irony.)[20]

In Brandes's account, the first subject we meet is Caesar. He is located in the Forum Julium, and we are informed about his business: he is putting to work those who are going to realize the amazing space he has conceived, but this is presented in a subordinate clause. The key 'action' of the first period is introduced when the main clause interrupts the subordinate, just like Caesar is interrupted by the arrival of the procession of officials, described in the main clause to have come to present the decree announcing his new honours. The description of the procession is meticulous in that the narrative zooms in on its members and renders their order, as if pointing them out on the spot.

Surprisingly, just as Brandes has lowered the pace of the narrative — stretched the narrative time, so to speak — the chronological narrating of the event is abruptly cut off. Having ended his description of the procession by mentioning the immense crowd following the officials, Brandes jumps to describing their general subsequent reaction to Caesar receiving the procession without rising. An element of focalization is at play here, in the rendering of the topic of the talk of the town in indirect speech: 'how Caesar had taken such little notice of this celebration that he had not even risen from his seat.' Then follows Brandes's analysis: he finds that the indignation relies on the conception of the Senate body as representative of the Roman people. Consequently, Caesar has insulted not those who some might term the oligarchs of Rome but all Romans, which is more concerning to Brandes.

With this organization of his account, Brandes avoids present Caesar in this precarious situation in his first-person narrator's voice, letting it be presented only through the focalized general crowd. Furthermore, the authoritative narrator's evaluation that follows exempts Caesar from this general verdict in judging his view of

the decision to grant him more honours to be correct. Caesar's fault is thereby made smaller: it was unwise to let his confidence get the better of him and express his (correct) opinion. Here too, Brandes avoids presenting Caesar as the direct object of blame, by assigning the blame to an aspect of Caesar's character, his confidence, giving it a life of its own or at least the power to cloud Caesar's judgement, which is otherwise sound.

The detailed description of the procession makes clear the solemnity of the act it is coming to carry out, but dwelling on it also makes us see how this clashes with Caesar's mood, perhaps his character altogether. Caesar is in that situation acting as an entrepreneur on a construction site. He is busy, effective, making things happen on the forum — characterized by the general qualities associated with him, his *celeritas* and what Brandes finds especially characteristic, his *energy*.[21] While the officials are moving slowly, in procession — it takes several lines to describe them — Caesar is effectively drawn in a single line. While Caesar is an entrepreneur on a building site, they are in the process of carrying out a solemn ritual appropriate to the ceremonial space the Forum Julium is to become. Caesar is in a different place and role and has no time for empty rituals. This is what makes him fail to recognize the general acceptance of his project, which the people understands the awarding of honours to represent.

Consequently, we can say that Brandes's portrayal of Caesar in this version of the episode must be understood as weighing the *mimetic* aspect of his character, as Caesar's character is what explains his behaviour. It is not that he is arrogant; he is simply too efficient to play along with the rituals. The Forum Julium here helps further the general understanding of the different positions of Caesar and the approaching procession as well as the crowd: to him, the site is under construction, as are his own position and general project. To the other group, the space already holds the meaning Caesar intends for it, just like the Senate and people are on board with his project and want to be allowed to play their part, to sanction it formally. If we extend the reading to include the synthetic aspect too, this episode would point to Caesar's inability to rest on his laurels — to recognize his own success and allow the rest of Rome to play out their role in acknowledging it and make it seem like a team effort.

---

20 All translations of Brandes are by the author.

21 Cf. esp. Brandes 1918, I, 14–18.

Brandes in Context: Mommsen and Drumann

Brandes does not discuss other treatments of the incident at the Forum Julium, yet prompted by Frisch (above) I will nonetheless set his account against Drumann's, since Brandes discusses other of Drumann's analyses, after some brief remarks on Mommsen, whom Brandes praises elsewhere. Mommsen does not treat the episode but states in his presentation of Caesar's architectonical programme that Caesar did not build temples and similar splendid structures but structures that were purposeful for the Romans (he explicitly mentions taking the stress off the forum, as well as creating new assembly and court sites). This, according to Mommsen, showed 'the love of building of a Roman and of an organiser'.[22] The concise description rather complies with Brandes's depiction of Caesar, who is if not literally getting his hands dirty then certainly directly involved in the organization of his forum and its construction. One remark in Mommsen's text is probably to be traced back to our episode. It relates how Caesar conducted himself in official contexts:

> Caesar appeared in public not in the robe of the consuls which was bordered with purple stripes, but in the robe wholly of purple which was reckoned in antiquity as the proper regal attire, and received, sitting on his golden chair and without rising from it, the solemn procession of the senate.[23]

By considering the behaviour, which is traditionally problematized with reference to one particular incident, to be a general practice, Mommsen normalizes it, making any treatment of a particular situation irrelevant, although he thereby also does not document the claim that this was Caesar's habit.

Drumann treats the specific episode and rather extensively in the third volume of his *Geschichte Roms*.[24] He introduces it in a section opening with the declaration that Caesar deserved the highest praise since he had given the gift of peace to Rome. Drumann notes that the Senate especially thanked Caesar through celebrations and dedication of honours but also by raising him to a special status: declaring him to be sacrosanct (*unverlet-*

zlich) and letting every member of the Senate swear on their life to protect him.[25] This, Drumann concludes, means that the Senate had become Caesar's bodyguard, recognizing Caesar to be mortal while at the same time raising him to the gods and enlarging the distance between him and the people. Drumann uses this as an occasion to discuss the use of religion in politics. Next, he describes how Caesar's house was practically turned into a temple, how his ancestors were honoured with games, how Caesar himself was called Jupiter and was promised a temple in that capacity together with his Clementia. This was furthermore to have a priesthood under the leadership of Mark Antony, so that like there were colleges of *luperci* and *fabii*, there was to be a college of *julii*. Then follows Drumann's rendering of our episode:

> So wanden sich die Senatoren, den Königsnamen zu umgehen, weil sie ihn haßten oder das Äußerste noch nicht wagten; das Königtum wurde durch ihre Beschlüsse ein rechtlicher Zustand und sogar erblich, aber sie mochten ihr Werk nicht deuten und überreichten das Diadem in unzähligen Teilen. Als sie mit den wichtigsten unter diesen Verordnungen, welche mit goldenen Buchstaben in silberne Tafeln eingegraben und im Kapitol niedergelegt wurden, in der Halle seines Venustempels vor dem Diktator erschienen, empfing er sie sitzend und äußerte nur, man habe ihm schon so viel Ehre erwiesen, daß sie eher vermindert als vermehrt werden müsse. Wenn Pompeius an seiner Stelle so gehandelt hätte, so würde man die Ursache in dessen Unbehilflichkeit finden; der schlaue und gewandte Caesar bewegte sich in jeder Rolle mit Leichtigkeit; er war auch zu selbständig, als daß der ältere Balbus ihn zu dem Mißgriffe verleiten konnte, und ein Anfall von Krankheit wurde offenbar später erdichtet, als man den ungünstigen Eindruck bemerkte; da ihm bekannt war, was man brachte und — nicht brachte, so mag dies die Ungebühr veranlaßt haben.[26]

Drumann sees the Senate's distribution of honours as a way to avoid naming Caesar king — or, as it is stated, to hand him the diadem, the symbol appropriate for the position he held de facto. Hence, when Caesar receives and answers the Senate as he does, he is calling them out: all the honours are excuses. Drumann draws on Pompey for a hypothetic comparison: had he been the one acting as Caesar did in that particular situation, it would be thought of as nothing but characteristic of his general character, which Drumann finds to be clumsy.

---

[22] Mommsen 2010, 504. Here and in the following I use the reprint of the English translation of volume four in the Cambridge Library Collection Classics series. The translation was first published in 1866 and follows the fourth edition of the German third volume.

[23] Mommsen 2010, 474.

[24] This was first published in 1837, but I quote from the second edition of 1906.

[25] Drumann 1906, 598–99.

[26] Drumann 1906, 600–01.

Caesar, on the other hand, sharply reads the situation, as he always does, and reacts. Thereby he is calling a bluff rather than losing his temper. Drumann is consequently using Caesar's character as an argument in his reading of the episode, rather than using the episode as a window into it. In this respect, his narrative is similar to Brandes's and his Caesar comparable to the matter-of-fact, effective character Brandes sees. However, their understandings of the intentions behind the procession and consequently the event in its totality are clearly very different.

Brandes explicitly states elsewhere in his work that he disagrees with minor and major aspects of Drumann's account of Caesar's life and deeds,[27] but even so mentions his high regard for him.[28] Evidently the two also disagree on Caesar's approach to kingship. Drumann's opinion is clear from his version of the episode; Brandes found claims that Caesar strove for the title of king to be slander caused by his opponents in order to stir up opposition against him.[29] Hence, when Frisch states that Brandes represents the same view of Caesar as Mommsen and Drumann, this is not always the case, but it is when it comes to Caesar's character.[30]

Frisch, his Cicero Book, and the Danish Context

Frisch states in his preface that the purpose of his book is to reassess Mommsen's and Drumann's evaluations of Cicero, which had been dominant and which he finds Brandes follows completely.[31] Frisch was not alone in feeling this urge to re-establish Cicero, and even the rela-

tively small classics environment in Denmark produced several works on Cicero in the 1940s.[32] In the same year as Frisch's work came out, his colleague in Copenhagen, Professor Carsten Høeg, published an introduction to Cicero. They were reviewed together by Docent Adam Afzelius, their colleague at Aarhus University, who was professor of classical philology there from 1946.[33]

Frisch directly relates his own urge to redeem Cicero to the pressing political conditions of his own time — Denmark was under German occupation 1940–1945:

> Now that we have gained new experiences, have seen all the blessings of liberty subverted which in the 19th century were acknowledged as matters of course, even by Reaction, it is natural that the judgement of Cicero, the republican and parliamentarian, the philosopher and publicist, should be made the subject of a renewed examination.[34]

Being an active politician himself is, however, perhaps just as much the reason — this is his reviewer's hypothesis[35] — and it is said to be characteristic of all of Frisch's work on the ancient world that he compares it to his own.[36] Frisch played a central role in the Danish social democratic party and was appointed Secretary of State for Education in 1947.

Christiansen, in his biography of Frisch, points out that Frisch's praise of Brandes's abilities as a biographer, which we treated above, also contains criticism of the generation of classicists that were Frisch's teachers. While Brandes wrote in the spirit of Johan Nicolai Madvig (who like Frisch was both a politician and a classical philologist, perhaps the greatest Denmark ever saw), those who had studied with Madvig mostly

---

[27] In Drumann's acceptance of Suetonius's claim that Caesar was behind Vettius (Brandes 1918, I, 217), in his and Mommsen's view that Caesar had conceived a plan for his doing from the onset (Brandes 1918, I, 358), and in his evaluation of Dumnorix (Brandes 1918, II, 31).

[28] Brandes 1918, I, 217: 'en fremragende moderne Historiker som Drumann' (a splendid modern historian like Drumann). Brandes 1918, I, 358: 'Saa fremragende tyske Historikere som Mommsen og Drumann' (such splendid historians as Mommsen and Drumann).

[29] See e.g. Brandes 1918, II, 529 (on Caesar's rejection of the title of *rex* on his return from the Alban Mountains), and Brandes 1918, II, 560 (on the 'acclaimed' sibylline oracles regarding the defeating of the Parthians).

[30] Repeated in Frisch 1942/46a, 14.

[31] Afzelius does point out that the new, more favourable view of Cicero was preceded by Boissier 1870. Frisch mentions Boissier once in his review of Brandes, but Brandes does not himself mention Boissier, and Boissier does not seem to treat the episode in Caesar's life, with which we are concerned here.

[32] Besides the above-mentioned also Foss, Frisch, and Høeg 1945; Frisch 1946b; Foss 1947.

[33] Afzelius 1942.

[34] Frisch 1942/46a, 7.

[35] Afzelius 1942, 561: 'Udredningen af Periodens storpolitiske Spil, Kampen mellem de forskellige Arvtagere til Diktaturet og Forsøget paa at benytte denne Kamp til at genoprette Senatesvældet, maa have været en Ønskeopgave for en Mand, der som Frisch paa een Gang er Videnskabsmand og Politiker. Dette maa være Forklaringen paa, at Forf. har kunnet præstere en saa omfattende og vel gennemarbejdet Bog paa saa kort Tid' (Unravelling the power play in high politics of this era, the fight between the various heirs to the dictatorship and the attempt to use this fight to reinstate the Senate as the ruling power must have been a dream job for a man who like Frisch is at the same time a scholar and a politician. This has to be the explanation why the author was capable of issuing such an elaborate and thorough work in such short time).

[36] Christiansen 1993, 75.

concerned themselves with petty questions of textual criticism. Christiansen understands this passage as an explanation of Frisch's unconventional career path: although everyone found him to be an exceptional talent and expected him to pursue an academic career, he only did so after twenty-five years as an upper secondary school teacher. In 1941, he obtained both the higher doctorate degree with a thesis on Pseudo-Xenophon's *Constitution of the Athenians* and a position as full professor at the University of Copenhagen.[37] As mentioned, Christiansen finds Frisch's review of Brandes to be somewhat programmatic of his own scholarly programme and finds that Frisch possesses the acclaimed competencies of a narrator of history.[38] Afzelius surely recognizes Frisch 1942/46a as standing out from the typical works of his time, describing Frisch's venture as 'halfway philological and predominantly historical'.[39] Frisch 1942/46a is clearly a scholarly work but nonetheless marked by this narrative quality: 'the style almost has the character of drama' — which as Christiansen mentions might well also be the effect of the book building on a lecture series.[40]

In Frisch's work on the political context of Cicero's *Philippics*,[41] we find a more explicit critique of Brandes, most likely rooted, at least to some extent, in the flourishing Nazism.[42] Frisch repeats his critique by quoting the relevant passage of his own review and expands it further so that it becomes the transition to his recounting of Caesar's murder, which concludes the chapter 'Idus Martiae'.[43]

The volume as such begins with the triumvirate and Caesar's death. Hence, while Cicero is the main concern, Caesar's role in shaping the political landscape receives ample treatment as well. Frisch focuses more directly on Caesar in the work *Cicero og Cæsar* (1946b), an antho-

logy of texts, mainly letters and excerpts from *De bello civile*, in Danish translation and with introductions and short explanations by Frisch, aimed at a broader readership. In the preface, he points out connections to his work of 1942, and it is quite clear that the analyses presented in the new work are consistent with the former. Nonetheless, something might be gained from considering how he has trimmed the material and adapted it to the new context. Both works are therefore considered in the following, although our main interest lies with Frisch 1942/46a.

Caesar's urban planning is barely mentioned in Frisch 1946b, and Cicero's role in purchasing land for the Forum Julium not at all. Caesar's and Cicero's dealings in 54 BC are described in relation to the meeting in Lucca, Cicero's political turnaround, and his borrowing of money from Caesar.

In Frisch 1942/46a, the relevant chapter is much concerned with examining Caesar, first with regard to his character, next and more extensively with regard to his approach to and management of his role as dictator up until his death. Frisch discusses historical approaches to Caesar, opening with a short categorization of Caesar's *De bello civile* as a work created during war and thereby forever to be subject of dispute, while Suetonius's biography is better in the sense that it voices all the different opinions about Caesar. Frisch uses this as a steppingstone to discuss later historians, specifically Ferrero's characterization of Caesar's character and deeds. According to Frisch, Ferrero finds Caesar to be no statesman but the greatest demagogue the world had ever seen.[44] This judgement is set against Mommsen's view of Caesar, as 'thoroughly a realist and a man of sense'.[45] Frisch references Caesar's own works as proof of this analysis and gives as a concrete example a passage of *De bello civile*,[46] which leads him to speak of Caesar as dictator.

Frisch finds proof in the sources that Caesar had no plans to abolish his dictatorship and that 'he did not act as a partisan, but as a ruler on a grand scale'.[47] Before zooming in on the episode at the Forum Julium and unfolding his own analysis, Frisch asserts that most historians of the nineteenth century agree with Mommsen that victorious revolutionaries do not remain leaders of their parties and will find that both members of their

---

[37] See e.g. Christiansen 1993, 77–79 for Frisch's views on and ideas of education and formation based on Plato.

[38] Cf. Christiansen 1993, 70–71 and Frisch 1918, 525, quoted above.

[39] Afzelius 1942, 560: 'halvvejs filologisk: at skildre de philippiske Taler og deres Baggrund, og en overvejende historisk: at behandle Ciceros Indsats' (halfway philological: to render the Philippics and their background, and predominantly historical: to treat Cicero's efforts).

[40] Christiansen 1993, 200. All translations of Christiansen are by the author.

[41] Frisch 1942/46a.

[42] Christiansen 1993, 199 and Frisch quoted above.

[43] Frisch 1942/46a, 37–41.

---

[44] Frisch 1942/46a; Ferrero 1907.

[45] Frisch 1942/46a, 26; Mommsen 2010, 452.

[46] Caes., *B Civ.* III.17.

[47] Frisch 1942/46a, 27.

12. PAST RESEARCH PERSPECTIVES AND NARRATED SPACE

own party and those they have vanquished will turn against them rather than accept that they are striving towards the common good.

Next, Frisch describes how the immediate reaction from those around Caesar was to bestow honours on him, to a degree that Frisch finds would have caused ordinary people to stop and question what had happened:

> No wonder that normal people of the time reacted against these quite immoderate marks of honour, which blurred the difference between divine and human and pointed towards the monarchy which was so detested by the Romans. And her[e] it seems that Caesar's usual rational clear-headedness failed. It is not only obscure to us, but must have been so to the contemporaries, whether Caesar himself wanted these marks of honour or no[t].[48]

Frisch relies on what he considers to be the public opinion and reaction to Caesar's behaviour, which one must understand to show how Caesar loses his ability to sense the mood of those opposed to him.[49] This is where he inserts the familiar two examples, first of how Caesar reacted to being called *rex* at his return from the Alban festival and secondly (and more extensively) on the incident in question. The general analysis is that Caesar's way of reacting reflects 'an act of the arrogance of absolutism'.[50] That Frisch understands average person to have found the honours bestowed on Caesar to be excessive is concurrent with the emphasis placed on the crowd's reaction in his presentation of the event.

The Incident at the Forum Julium according to Frisch

Both Frisch 1942/46a and Frisch 1946b mention the Forum Julium only once in connection with our incident. In Frisch 1946b, this episode occurs in the introduction to the chapter 'Caesar's Death and Legacy'[51] as one of two peculiar episodes following a listing of honours granted to Caesar that year. The first is how Caesar inscribed his rejection of the royal diadem presented to him by Antony in the *Fasti*; then follows the incident at the Forum Julium:

Hele scenen vakte umaadelig Opsigt, ligesom Cæsars Holdning overfor Senatet da dette i højtideligt Optog overbragte ham nogle Sølvtavler hvorpaa alle de vedtagne Æresbevisninger var optegnet med Guldskrift; Cæsar var beskæftiget med Licitationerne til det planlagte Forum Iulium, og til alles Forbløffelse modtog han Optoget siddende og bemærkede ganske tørt at det snarere var en Indskrænkning end en Forøgelse af Æresbevisningerne der var paakrævet — men han blev siddende![52]

(This entire scene attracted immense attention [i.e. the above-mentioned rejection of the titulation *rex*], as did Caesar's attitude towards the Senate when arriving in solemn procession it presented him with silver tablets on which honours were inscribed in gold; Caesar was busy with the tenders for the planned Forum Iulium, and to everyone's astonishment, he received the procession seated and remarked in a quite dry manner how it was rather necessary to reduce than expand his honours — but he remained sitting!)[53]

The presentation relies on the narrator's authority. It is in a résumé style and narrated in a relatively neutral way, except for the adversative of the last phrase and the exclamation mark following it, which is the closest we come to dramatization and focalization in this treatment. The wording of Caesar's remark on the new honours bestowed on him can be understood to be quite humble in this rendering, but the noting of Caesar's lack of display of respect by not getting up from his seat to receive the Senate, as well as the tone, underlines that Caesar's reaction is considered an expression of arrogance. Describing Caesar as absorbed in the plans to realize a forum in his own name underlines this further. The episode is presented in more detail in Frisch 1942/46a:

> Just as enigmatic is the scene at the new *Forum Iulium* in the place where the Temple of *Venus Genetrix* was to be built. While Caesar was sitting here, fully occupied by the tenders submitted for the new temple, a ceremonious procession made its appearance. In front of it went Antonius, his colleague, carrying some silver tables with gold script on which were written all the last great honours voted by the Senate. On either side marched lictors, who swept aside the crowd, and behind followed all the praetors, tribunes, and quaestors and the other officials, being followed by the senators in ceremonial dress, and the procession was hedged by a huge crowd. The wonder and expectation of the people were great, *but Caesar remained sitting*. Occupied as he was, and with his eyes turned towards those with whom he was negotiating just

---

[48] Frisch 1942/46a, 30.

[49] Cf. Frisch 1942/46a, 26: 'To this intellectual lucidity of his also belonged this faculty of seeing the point of view of the other side, a quality which has a refreshing effect in our times, satiated with propaganda.'

[50] Frisch 1942/46a, 30.

[51] Frisch 1946b, 78: 'Cæsars død og eftermæle'.

[52] Frisch 1946b, 78.

[53] Translation by author.

beside him, he did not at first see the procession, but continued that which he had on hand. Only when somebody had called his attention to the procession did he lay aside the writing-tablets, and when he had heard the message of the procession, he drily remarked that a reduction rather than an increase of honours was called for. *But he remained sitting during the whole scene.*[54]

The general structure is the same: Frisch begins by placing Caesar at the scene, and not just at the Forum Julium but at the spot where the temple was to be. Caesar is not only busy with the tenders, we are also told that he is sitting down — this is, of course, central for what happens later, but nonetheless renderings of the episode do not often mention it from the onset. Then comes the procession, described in more detail than in Frisch 1946b, beginning with the man in front, Mark Antony, whom Frisch identifies to be Caesar's colleague, thus underlining the close bond between them, and then the officials in order of appearance. Like in Brandes, it is as if we were standing on the forum seeing the spectacle ourselves — which of course explains why Frisch finds it important that we know how to imagine Caesar too: seated, in the spot of the temple. The senators are said to be in ceremonial dress, thus underlining the ritual nature of the intended event. Like in Brandes's case, the description of the procession ends by mentioning the accompanying crowd and then transitions to focalize them, rendering their mood: great wonder and expectation, turning into frustration when Caesar does not react. Here, Frisch's version deviates from Brandes's because it can be understood to keep focalizing the crowd, in dragging out the waiting, while excitement turns to wonder, astonishment, disappointment, and offence, as they see how Caesar does not even look up but keeps on discussing the tenders. The narrator is, however, able to provide the information that Caesar actually had not even noticed the procession and crowd approaching, making use of the powers of the omniscient narrator to discern thoughts and motivations (or, in Genette's terminology, the 0-focalized narrator, who has access to the inner life and thoughts of all characters). The general focus, however, remains with those who arrive at the Forum Julium, most notably so by the repeating of the phrase in italics that, due to both repetition and formatting, becomes their silent roars.

Placing Caesar in the exact spot where the temple to Venus Genetrix was to be erected is central for the interpretation of Frisch's account — he indeed calls this epi-sode 'the scene at the Temple of *Venus Genetrix*' on the following page.[55]

The way Frisch portrays Caesar in his account of this episode serves to explain the rising opposition against him. The synthetic aspect is thus significant here too — again, Caesar's behaviour on this occasion is understood to spur on his fall — but the thematic aspect of character is quite remarkable, not least compared to Brandes. Frisch 1942/46a seems even keener to present Caesar's behaviour as outrageous than Frisch 1946b, although one might have expected the reverse, considering the intended readers of the two works. Caesar is presented as completely caught up in overconfident self-assertion, and his dry remark becomes utterly arrogant — he is the image of the tyrant corrupted by power. Frisch makes no excuse for Caesar's behaviour, that is, he does not present it as atypical of Caesar, whereby he must find it to be consistent with Caesar's character, in the Aristotelian sense. The mimetic aspect is consequently in no way played down, meaning that not only in this particular instance but generally Caesar is arrogant, self-absorbed, fully conscious and confident about the amount of power concentrated in his person — and what is perhaps worse, it does not trouble him to show it off. It is likewise noteworthy that Frisch attributes the negative reaction to Caesar's behaviour to everyone else present and how the narrator prefers to stand with them, not just to see the scene with them but feel it with them and them alone. It seems reasonable to expect the person who makes Caesar aware of the procession to be someone close to him, although it is not specified. Similarly, Frisch's narrative choice here includes Caesar's followers among the astonished — just like presenting Mark Antony, not as consul, but as Caesar's colleague underlines this which is only implied wherever else Mark Antony is mentioned by name: that it seems like the presentation of honours might very well have been staged by Caesar's closest supporter. Unlike Brandes, Frisch does not talk of the connection between Senate and people; on the contrary, his description might well be taken to indicate how it was clear to all that Caesar was going too far.

Frisch in an International Context

As mentioned, Frisch's stated purpose is to reassess Mommsen and Drumann's view of Cicero, but in his treatment of Caesar's final days and death, he further discusses several international treatments. Of those,

---

[54] Frisch 1942/46a, 31, original emphasis.

[55] Frisch 1942/46a, 32.

Pais (1918), Meyer (1918/1922),[56] and Adcock (1932) render the incident of concern to our study and will be examined with regard to it here.

Pais and Meyer

In his discussion of the incident at the Forum Julium, Frisch references Ettore Pais, whose analysis he characterizes as original but implausible.[57] Pais finds that Caesar is mirroring the situation at his latest triumph where the tribune Pontius Aquila notably did not rise from his seat for the *triumphator* (as presented in Suet., *Iul.* LXXVIII, whose treatment Pais follows). That episode is pivotal to the first part of Pais's treatment of 'L'aspirazione di Cesare al trono e l'opposizione tribunicia durante gli anni 45–46 A.C.', while our incident is treated in the second.[58] Pais's rendition, which will only be treated briefly here since Frisch seems unaffected by it, emphasizes Caesar's elevated religious status. In the discussion of the relationship between it and the incident with Aquila, he notes how both the Senate and Caesar himself realized that he had overstepped, that Caesar 'se ne addolorò e dette in smanie'[59] and that the scandal was large enough to provoke excuses of a rather ridiculous sort.[60]

Frisch rejects that Caesar's reaction could be provoked by Aquila due to the distance in time between the two episodes: although it cannot be fixed precisely in time, he notes the ancient historians agree on the incident at the Forum Julium taking place soon before Caesar's death while the triumph in question took place in October 46 BC. Pais, on the other hand, reckons there to be just five months between the two incidents and underlines that Aquila was among Caesar's assassins.[61]

Frisch next discusses whether Caesar was a victim of 'gross flattery',[62] and before moving on to Eduard Meyer, he states that the Stoics of Caesar's own time were certain of Caesar's intention to impose monarchy on the Roman realm, which concurs with Suetonius, Plutarch, Appian, and Cassius Dio — as well as Shakespeare's tragedy, which is discussed at some length.[63]

Eduard Meyer is, to Frisch, 'the scholar who has most boldly defended the assassination'.[64] Like the Stoics of Antiquity, he believed Caesar to strive for monarchical power and his murder to be ideologically motivated. Frisch notes this to be Pais's opinion too, but remarking how Pais finds Cleopatra and the oriental influence to be a central factor as well.[65] For this view, he likewise references Jérôme Carcopino,[66] who understands Caesar as thereby resting on his descent from Venus and the old Roman kings, but Frisch does reveal his own view of this theory. Meyer's account of our episodes goes as follows:

In der Tat war für Caesar alles, was ihm bewilligt wurde, unzureichend. Wie für Napoleon das lebenslängliche Consulat, so war für ihn die lebenslängliche Dictatur nur die Vorstufe für die offen anerkannte Monarchie. Wie er seine Stellung auffaßte, wurde aller Welt deutlich, als der Senat in feierlichem Zuge, unter Vortritt des Consuls Antonius und der übrigen Beamten mit ihren Lictoren, ihn aufsuchte, um ihm die neuen Ehrenbeschlüsse zu überbringen, die dann auf silbernen Tafeln mit goldenen Buchstaben eingegraben und zu Füßen des capitolinischen Juppiter aufgestellt werden sollten. Er selbst saß auf seinem goldenen Stuhl beim Tempel der Venus Genetrix; und als der Senat erschien, stand er nicht auf, sondern nahm die Ehren, darunter die lebenslängliche Dictatur, sitzend in Empfang. Das machte ungeheures Aufsehen und schuf eine tiefgreifende Erbitterung, und so wurde zu seiner Entschuldigung behauptet, er sei unwohl gewesen, oder er habe, mit den Bauten beschäftigt, das Nahen des Senats nicht bemerkt. Diese Absurditäten bedürfen keiner Widerlegung; eben so verkehrt aber ist es, in seinem Verhalten eine Anwandlung von Sultanslaune zu sehn. Vielmehr hat Caesar den Anlaß benutzt, um seine Stellung zum Senat ganz deutlich zu manifestieren: der göttliche Monarch empfängt in der öffentlichen Staatsaktion seinen Staatsrat sitzend, wenn dieser ihm seine Huldigung darbringt. Viel eher glaublich ist die Erzählung, daß er habe aufstehn wollen, aber Balbus, der Minister, der seine Gedanken am besten kannte, ihn zurückgehalten habe, oder daß Trebatius, der leutselige Jurist, ihn gemahnt habe, aufzustehn, er aber diesen unfreundlich angeblickt habe. Jedenfalls wußte Caesar

---

56 I here use the 2011 reprint of the third edition of 1922 published in the Cambridge Library Collection referred to as Meyer 2011.

57 Pais 1918.

58 Pais 1918, 313–35.

59 Pais 1918, 327.

60 Pais 1918, 327.

61 Pais 1918, 324.

62 Frisch 1942/46a, 32.

63 Frisch 1942/46a, 33: 'In later literature, this view is

---

subscribed to by Shakespeare himself, with the characteristic addition that his "Caesar" is decrepit, not only suffering from the historically authenticated epilepsy, but also being deaf of the left ear, superstitious without admitting it, suspicious of lean men, insatiable of flattery, if only the person in question constantly assures him that he is immune from it, and revealing his inner anxiety by the very fact that he incessantly states that he fears nothing in the world.'

64 Frisch 1942/46a, 33.

65 Pais 1918, 329. For this see also Yavetz 1983, 29.

66 Carcopino 1936.

auch hier genau, was er tat. Aber es ist natürlich, daß der Senat sein Verhalten nur als eine schwere Beleidigung ansehen konnte.[67]

Meyer begins with the description of the procession and to some degree focalizes it by rendering the intention motivating its approach, not failing to mention either the gold-inscribed silver tablets with the decrees that are to be laid down on the Capitoline Hill, at the feet of Jupiter's statue. The narrative style is, however, dominated by the authoritative narrator's own voice and judgement of matters. When focus is directed towards Caesar, he is placed by another temple, his own to Venus Genetrix, on a golden throne. Meyer makes it explicit that Caesar remained seated even though one of the decrees was the remarkable granting of life-long dictatorship. The following description of the outrage caused is not attributed to any subject and thereby implied to be general, which is supported by the stated attempts to excuse Caesar's behaviour. Now the narrator slides from authoritative description into interpretation, making even more manifest his authority and stance by judging the excuses to be so absurd that they need no treatment. The narrator's authoritative opinion would mix in with the general feeling of the crowd, senators, etc. (*ungeheures Aufsehn, Entschuldigung*), were it not for his call to moderation, in that he states it unfair to understand Caesar's behaviour as indicative of an unstable tyrant (*Sultanslaune*). Previously in his work, Meyer determined that Caesar saw straight through 'die Scheinlegitimität, die den Senat umgab';[68] it is this view that Caesar makes manifest here, along with his own much more powerful and higher-ranking position.

Meyer's description sets the Temple of Jupiter on the Capitoline Hill against the Temple of Venus in the Forum Julium. Placing Caesar by the latter makes the Temple of Venus both mirror and rival the Temple of Jupiter, just like Caesar, replacing the cult statue of Venus, rivals Jupiter's statue and position. Caesar is acting like the divine monarch, as whom he wants to be recognized by the Senate, according to Meyer's introduction to the episode. Meyer does leave open the possibility of Balbus or Trebatius playing a role but concludes that Caesar knew what he was doing. Meyer's analysis again finds that Caesar would not have reacted in affect or by accident, although he is not, like Drumann, explicitly using Caesar's character as an argu-

ment. This is a general point at which Meyers's approach differs from Drumann and, more explicitly in the work itself, from Mommsen. Meyer has moved beyond the idea of the great characters and strives to inscribe events into a general context,[69] which Frisch determines relates to 'constitutional problems'.[70]

Juxtaposing the Capitoline Temple of Jupiter, where the Senate intends to lay down their decree, and the Temple of Venus Genetrix, where Caesar sits as the main authority instead of the cult statue, delineates the Forum Julium as the new centre of power. While Frisch may, in placing Caesar in the temple space of the Forum Julium, be inspired by what we see here, his use is more moderate: Frisch's Caesar is not sitting on a throne, and he does not parallelize Caesar and Jupiter, nor his forum and the Capitoline Hill.

Frisch and Rostovtzeff against Adcock, Brandes, Mommsen, and Drumann

Against the tendency described above and exemplified by Meyer, Frisch mentions Mommsen and Drumann, as well as Brandes. Yet, before discussing Brandes further, he moves on to Sir Frank Ezra Adcock, who has written on Caesar in the *Cambridge Ancient History* and whom he finds represents the British understanding of Caesar.[71] Frisch describes that Adcock takes a middle position 'though it is written with great sympathy for Caesar and keeping aloof from Ed. Meyer'.[72] Of Adcock's viewpoints, he highlights how Caesar's divinization is put down as 'an invention of Dio Cassius'' since only he talks of *Jupiter Julius*.[73] Adcock's rendition of our episode is consistently free from religious allusions and unfixed in space; it is brief, in résumé style, and embedded in discussions of Caesar's manners, which Adcock finds are generally tactful but with occasional slips.

> Although in general he was possessed of rare tact and polished manners, servility aroused in him moments of arrogance. When early in 44 BC, the *patres* went in procession to announce to him a new grant of honour, he failed to rise at their approach, and the excuses advanced for this behaviour cannot have satisfied those who were ready to be affronted. His ceaseless clear-headed activity

---

[67] Meyer 2011, 518–19. Quoted after the reprint of the third printing of Meyer's work of 1922 in the Cambridge Library Collection Classics series.

[68] Meyer 2011, 333; Krist 1994, 162.

[69] For a characterization of Meyer's approach with regard to Caesar in particular, see Krist 1994, 155–65.

[70] Frisch 1942/46a, 14.

[71] Adcock 1932.

[72] Frisch 1942/46a, 34.

[73] Frisch 1942/46a, 34.

till the end disposes of the legend of him as the pathological study in diseased greatness which Shakespeare has read out of his Plutarch, but in small matters he yielded now and then to vanity which would have been harmless except in one whose position challenged the traditional pride of an aristocracy. An enemy attributed to him the saying that the Republic had become a form without substance; and it was perilously near the truth. He had drained the life-blood of the State into his dictatorship — 'dictaturam' wrote Cicero 'quae iam vim regiae potestatis obsederat'.[74]

Episodes like the one concerned here are considered rare exceptions that do not justify diagnosing Caesar with 'diseased greatness'.

Frisch further underlines how Adcock finds most of the honours granted to be understood as excessive recognitions, yet not of a religious sort, and he argues, with Napoleon, that Caesar was unlikely to have planned on installing a new constitutional order so shortly before the planned campaign against the Parthians, which would entail a longer period of absence. The omen stating that the Parthians could only be defeated by a king would have put Caesar in a difficult position, Adcock admits, but this Caesar would have solved by becoming king in the provinces alone. Lastly, regarding the murder, Frisch notes how Adcock finds it rooted in much idealism although manifested in a perverted way. The central takeaway from Adcock's analysis Frisch finds to be that the British seemed against the idea that Caesar was mixing the humane and divine.[75]

It is made clear that Frisch disagrees with this downplaying of the religious aspects when he brings Michael Rostovtzeff into the discussion. The main point here, according to Frisch, is that Caesar was leaning not only on his army but on the people believing that he was a higher being.[76] Placing Caesar in the spot of the temple at the Forum Julium in his own rendition of the incident shows exactly how Frisch finds the religious aspect to play an active role in Caesar's appearance and representation. He furthermore calls it 'very sensible' when Rostovtzeff considers Caesar to have underestimated the nobility, who proved to cling onto their power, to the extent that Frisch adds further arguments in favour.[77]

Frisch first inserts Augustus's organization of power and next provides an example from his local context:[78] he compares the Roman nobility to the Danish before absolute monarchy was instated in 1660, in that the Danish nobility viewed the fiefs as their *praedia*. He likewise finds the connotations attributed by the Roman nobility to the title *rex* would have compared to those attributed by the Danish to the term *tyrant*. Although the Danish example may come off as less persuasive in the English translation, it is retained, which can be taken to underline how Frisch strives to place his view on these matters in the Danish discourse, which Brandes must be understood to have defined.

The correspondence between Frisch's and Rostovtzeff's views is clear when Frisch concludes:

> The bold man who stirred up such a hornets' nest, knew the sting of these insects, and must know what he was doing. Least of all Caesar could expect this race of gentlemen to become employees; they followed him as long as they thought that this led to their own objectives (and everybody had his own), but not a moment longer.[79]

Here, Frisch's analysis and discussion indeed return explicitly to his dialogue with Brandes, as it is here he inserts the passage of his review criticizing Brandes's lacking understanding of the conditions of Caesar's opponents:[80] opportunism is one central explanation of why several of those conspiring against Caesar's life had been generals in his army or in other ways his allies.

God, Tyrant, or Entrepreneur?
Concluding Remarks

Caesar's reshaping of Rome is indisputable, although his impact on politics often outshines his impact on the physical shaping of the city of Rome in accounts of his accomplishments. This might have been different, had he lived to follow through his plans to renew the city — but he did initiate the construction of the Forum Caesaris. In the episode treated here, we see various understandings of an incident in which we can almost say that man and space interact. The understanding of the space and the meaning Caesar is presumed to install in it, as well as the general response to both, are almost as disputed as Caesar himself. While we might have expected the Danish tradition to be rather uniform based on Frisch's

---

[74] Adcock 1932, 733–34.

[75] Frisch 1942/46a, 35: 'The English do not like a mixing together of gods and human beings.'

[76] Rostovtzeff does not render the episode, with which we are concerned here.

[77] Frisch 1942/46a, 36.

[78] Frisch 1942/46a, 36.

[79] Frisch 1942/46a, 37; Frisch 1919, 274.

[80] Frisch 1942/46a, 37.

positive review of Brandes's influential work, Brandes and Frisch are far from blind to the complexity inherent to this incident, to which Caesar's reaction adds further, and represent different understandings of the event as well as the motivations of Caesar and the function and meaning of his space.

Brandes, like Mommsen, understands the Forum Julium as a fully realized space to those participating in the procession as well as the accompanying crowd — to the Roman people as such. Caesar, on the other hand, is not yet considering it as a ceremonial space. This renders the encounter as a misunderstanding making Caesar's reaction justified although it is found to be ill conceived. Caesar is thereby hardly demonstrating a character flaw, since arrogance and religious aspirations have no place in Brandes's view of his reaction. To him, Caesar remains true to his character — the mimetic aspect of character is only somewhat counteracted by the remark, in the sense that it was uttered and not suppressed — there is little if any difference between the energetic general, who builds bridges and leads battles in Gaul and the energetic renewer of the capital. In Drumann's account, on the other hand, Caesar has been transformed; he is now sacrosanct and divine and ought to have been named king, and Caesar's reaction makes manifest his status and claim. While he is no longer the enterprising general, his sharpness remains the same, as he sees through the pretence and schemes of the Senate.

To both Drumann and Brandes, explaining the episode so that it concurs with Caesar's character is key, character becomes the central argument, which is indicative of their general approach to history. Brandes says elsewhere: 'since the ancient historians are generally in complete disagreement on the actual nature of the transmitted matters, we can only approach the truth by leaning on our estimation of the characters of those acting.'[81]

That Brandes judges it unwise of Caesar to not see and value the recognition of the Roman people and hence failing to allot a role to it, shows Brandes to believe in a somewhat balanced power system, not tyranny, despite his praise of Caesar. But there is no negative judgement of the space created by Caesar; it is an extension of the idea of Caesar's entrepreneurism and rendered as practical above all.

Frisch shares with many others a disgust with Caesar's arrogance towards the Senate and crowd that Brandes is not completely blind to but finds less offensive and downplays in his rendering of the episode. Frisch, on the other hand, dwells heavily on the remarkability of Caesar's reaction.

We saw how Frisch seems to be inspired by Meyer with regard to the emphasis placed on Caesar sitting in the temple space and in a sense replacing the cult statue. Frisch's account is, however, more moderate than Meyer's. He does not explore the parallelization of Caesar in the Forum Julium with Jupiter and his temple at the Capitoline Hill, and Frisch seems less occupied with character than Meyer, Brandes, and Drumann. He might well have prioritized countering Brandes's account. While Brandes can be understood to find Caesar is uncorrupted by his status so that he sees through the empty rituals, Frisch sees matters from the other side, wondering at how Caesar could fail to notice the population and institutions of the city. His conclusion diametrically opposes Brandes's: he finds that Caesar is exactly caught up in the space made to celebrate himself and set him apart from everyone else. His emphasis on the religious aspect of Caesar's self-fashioning in the Forum Julium is underlined when he counters Adcock's dissociation of Caesar's ambitions from religion. Frisch presents Caesar as relying on religion to raise him to a higher status in the view of the people in general. However, when explicitly speaking against Brandes by citing the critical part of his review, it relates to the Roman nobility. To Frisch, the core of the problem with Caesar's behaviour, which ultimately comes to haunt him, boils down to the disrespect he showed those from his own class by not rising to receive them, the opportunistic nobility, of whose shifting mindset Frisch says Caesar must have been aware.

This leaves considering whether Frisch's analysis is then not fairly close to Brandes's when it comes to discerning why this incident became catastrophic for Caesar: Brandes is more inclusive in talking about the Senate and people — *Senatus Populusque Romanum*. To him, the Senate represents the people as such, while Frisch singles out the nobility, those who occupied the offices of the Roman system, as the problem. Even so, Brandes's and Frisch's ways of rendering the treated episode make it a vehicle of two very different narratives of Caesar, his ambitions, his mistakes, and the use and purpose of his forum.

---

[81] Brandes 1918, I, 216: 'Eftersom Oldtidens Historikere i Reglen er fuldstændigt uenige om de overleverede Træks egentlige Væsen, kan vi kun tilnærmelsesvis finde Sandheden ved at gaa ud fra vort Skøn om de Handlendes Karakterer.'

Works Cited

Adcock, F. E. 1932. 'Caesar's Dictatorship', in S. A. Cook, F. E. Adcock, and M. P. Charlesworth (eds), *Cambridge Ancient History*, IX: *The Roman Republic, 133–44 B.C.* (Cambridge: Cambridge University Press), pp. 691–740.

Afzelius, A. 1942. 'Review of Carsten Høeg, Introduktion til Cicero (Kbh. 1942, 328 Sider). – Hartvig Frisch: Ciceros Kamp for Republikken (Kbh. 1942, 327 Sider)', *Historisk Tidsskrift*, 10: 553–66.

Allen, J. 2013. *Icons of Danish Modernity: Georg Brandes and Asta Nielsen* (Seattle: University of Washington Press).

Boissier, G. 1870. *Ciceron et ses amis: étude sur la société romaine du temps de César*, 2nd edn (Paris: Hachette).

Brandes, G. 1889. 'Aristokratisk Radikalisme' *Tilskueren: Maanedsskrift for litteratur, kunst, samfundsspørgsmaal og almenfattelige videnskabelige skildringer*, 6: 565–613.

—— 1895–1896. *William Shakespeare*, 3 vols (Copenhagen: Gyldendal).

—— 1915. *Goethe*, 2 vols (Copenhagen: Gyldendal).

—— 1916. *Francois de Voltaire*, 2 vols (Copenhagen: Gyldendal).

—— 1917. *Napoleon og Garibaldi: Medaljer og Rids* (Copenhagen: Gyldendal).

—— 1918. *Cajus Julius Cæsar*, 2 vols (Copenhagen: Gyldendal).

—— 1921. *Michelangelo Buonarotti*, 2 vols (Copenhagen: Gyldendal).

Carcopino, J. 1936. *La république romaine de 133 à 44 avant J.–C., César*, Histoire romaine, 2.2 (Paris: Presses universitaires de France).

Carlyle, T. 1841. *On Heroes, Hero-Worship, and the Heroic in History* (London: James Fraser).

Christiansen, N. F. 1993. *Hartvig Frisch: Mennesket og politikeren; En biografi* (Copenhagen: Christian Ejlers).

Dobesch, G. 2001. 'Nikolaos von Damaskos und die Selbstsbiographie des Augustus', in H. Heftner and K. Tomaschitz (eds), *Gerhard Dobesch: Ausgewählte Schriften*, I: *Griechen und Römer* (Cologne: Böhlau), pp. 205–73.

Drumann, W. 1906. *Geschichte Roms in seinem Übergange von der republikanischen zur monarchischen Verfassung, oder Pompejus, Caesar, Cicero und ihre Zeitgenossen*, III, ed. P. Groebe (Leipzig: Verlag von Gebrüder Borntraeger).

Ferrero, G. 1907. *Grandezza e decadenza di Roma*, 5 vols (Milan: Fratelli Treves).

Foss, O. 1947. *Cicero og Catilina: Romersk politik i teori og praksis* (Copenhagen: Gyldendal).

Foss, O., H. Frisch, and C. Høeg. 1945. *En Cicero antologi: Danske oversættelser med vedføjet latinsk tekst og noter* (Copenhagen: Gyldendal).

Frisch, H. 1918. 'Georg Brandes: Caius Iulius Cæsar', *Tilskueren: Maanedsskrift for litteratur, kunst, samfundsspørgsmaal og almenfattelige videnskabelige skildringer*, 35.2: 520–26.

—— 1919. 'Georg Brandes: Caius Iulius Cæsar II', *Tilskueren: Maanedsskrift for litteratur, kunst, samfundsspørgsmaal og almenfattelige videnskabelige skildringer*, 36.1: 266–75.

—— 1942. *Ciceros kamp for republikken: Den historiske baggrund for Ciceros filippiske taler* (Copenhagen: H. Hirschsprungs).

—— 1946a. *Cicero's Fight for the Republic: The Historical Background of Cicero's Philippics* (Copenhagen: Gyldendal).

—— 1946b. *Cicero og Cæsar* (Copenhagen: Gyldendal).

Genette, G. 1979. *Narrative Discourse: An Essay on Method* (Ithaca: Cornell University Press).

Hass, T. A. and R. Raja. 2023. 'Julius Caesar and the Forum Caesaris: World History, Historiography and Reception Investigated through Danish Biographies of Caesar from the Early Twentieth Century', in J. K. Jacobsen, R. Raja, and S. G. Saxkjær (eds), *Caesar, Rome, and Beyond*, Rome Studies, 4 (Turnhout: Brepols), pp. 189–210.

Høeg, C. 1942. *Introduktion til Cicero* (Copenhagen: Gyldendal).

Knudsen, J. 2004. *Georg Brandes*, V: *Uovervindelig taber 1914–27* (Copenhagen: Gyldendal).

Krist, C. 1994. *Caesar: Annäherungen an einen Diktator* (Munich: Beck).

Meyer, E. 2011. *Caesars Monarchie und das Principat des Pompejus: Innere Geschichte Roms von 66 bis 44 v. Chr.* (Cambridge: Cambridge University Press).

Mommsen, T. 2010. *The History of Rome*, IV.2, trans. W. P. Dickson (Cambridge: Cambridge University Press).

Napoleon III Bonaparte, C. L. 1865–1866. *Histoire de Jules César*, 2 vols (Paris: Henri Plon).

Ørsted, P. 1994. *Gajus Julius Caesar: Politik og moral i det romerske imperium* (Copenhagen: Gyldendal).

Pais, E. 1918. *Dalle guerre puniche a Cesare Augusto: indagini storiche, epigrafiche, giuridiche* (Rome: Nardecchia).

Pelling, C. 2011. *Plutarch 'Caesar': Translated with an Introduction and Commentary* (Oxford: Oxford University Press).

Phelan, J. and P. J. Rabinowitz. 2012. 'Characters', in D. Herman and others (eds), *Narrative Theory: Core Concepts and Critical Debates* (Columbus: Ohio State University Press), pp. 111–18.

Possing, B. 2017. *Understanding Biographies: On Biographies in History and Stories in Biography* (Odense: University Press of Southern Denmark).

Rostovtzeff, M. 1928. *A History of the Ancient World*, II: *Rome* (Oxford: Clarendon).

Stoffel, H. 1887. *Histoire de Jules César*, 2 vols (Paris: Imprimerie nationale).

Toher, M. (ed.). 2016. *Nicolaus of Damascus: 'The Life of Augustus' and 'The Autobiography'* (Cambridge: Cambridge University Press).

Weinstock, S. 1971. *Divus Julius* (Oxford: Clarendon).

Yavetz, Z. 1983. *Julius Caesar and his Public Image* (London: Thames & Hudson).

INDEX

Personal, Divine and Mythological Names

Adcock, Frank Ezra: 221–24
Adonis: 14, 31, 36
Aegyptus: 35
Aemilius Lepidus Paullus: 197
Aeneas: 35, 39
Afzelius, Adam: 217–18
Agrippa: 22, 28–29, 39, 41, 109
Agrippina: 180
Ajax: 38
Alexander the Great: 21, 31, 33, 38,
    109–10, 198, 203
Ammianus Marcellinus: 30
Amor: 37
Andromeda: 15
Annona: 180
Aphrodite: 38
Apollo: 9, 17, 28, 32, 34–35, 37, 40, 42
Appian: 20, 157, 204, 221
Appius Claudius Caecus: 38
Arcesilaus: 38
Argus: 37
Aristotle: 12
Asinius Pollio *see* Gaius Asinius Pollio
Aspasia: 203
Ateius Captio: 109
Atia: 32
Augustus, emperor of Rome *alias* Caesar
    Augustus (Augusto): 2, 8, 22, 27–43,
    88, 90, 109, 120, 122, 127–28,
    154–55, 157, 169–70, 180–81, 184,
    189, 194, 206–07, 223
    see also Octavian
Aulius Annius Camars: 180
Aulus Gabinius: 110

Balbus: 28, 39, 213, 216, 221–22
Belides: 34–35, 37
Belus: 35
Boissier, Gaston: 191–92, 217
Brandes, Georg Morris Cohen: 3, 191–92,
    195, 201–07, 211–18, 220, 222–24
Brun, Friederike: 196
Brutus: 170, 190
Buonarotti, Michelangelo: 202, 213

Cadmus: 31
Caesar *see* Gaius Julius Caesar
Caius Aiedius: 169
Callimachus: 38
Camerius: 31
Carlyle, Thomas: 213
Cassius Dio: 20, 39–41, 43, 110, 213,
    221–22
Cassivellaunus: 104, 106–08, 112
Cato the Younger: 109–10, 199
Catullus: 29, 31, 109
Ceres: 34
Cetus: 15
Cicero: 14, 17, 19, 98, 102, 110–11, 122,
    141, 169, 191, 197, 204–05, 211, 214,
    217–18, 220, 223
Claudius, emperor of Rome (Claudio):
    109, 180
Cleopatra, queen of Egypt: 21, 35, 37–38,
    40, 198–201, 203, 207, 221
Concordia: 8, 10, 34, 206
Constantine, emperor of Rome: 40
Constantius, emperor of Rome: 30

Danaids: 35–36
Danaus: 35
Dante Alighieri: 190
Diocletian, emperor of Rome: 37, 127
Diodorus Siculus: 111
Diviciacus, king of the Suessiones: 99
Divus Iulius: 31
Domitian, emperor of Rome: 38
Drumann, Wilhelm: 191, 214, 216–17,
    220, 222, 224
Drusus: 180

Epaphus: 37
Eratosthenes: 111
Eros: 15
Europa: 31
Evander: 30, 39

Ferdinand, Franz: 207
Ferrero, Guiglielmo: 214, 218, 192
Florus: 13, 110
Frisch, Hartvig: 3, 191–92, 196, 211–14,
    216–24

Gaius Asinius Pollio: 21, 72
Gaius Caecilius Metellus Caprarius: 10
Gaius Claudius Pulcher: 15
Gaius Julius Caesar (Giulio Cesare, César):
    1–4, 7–8, 10, 17, 19–22, 27, 29,
    31, 33–34, 36–39, 41–42, 51–52,
    55–61, 64, 66, 71–72, 86, 90, 97–113,
    119–23, 126–27, 129–30, 132, 137,
    141, 153–55, 157, 161–62, 164–69,
    173–80, 184–85, 189–92, 194,
    196–207, 211–24
Gaius Oppius *see* Oppius
Gaius Valerius Catullus *see* Catullus
Galli, priests: 14
gens Barronii: 168
gens Iulia: 197
gens Metella: 36
Germanicus (Germanico): 180
Giersing, Ove Malling: 191–92, 198–201,
    203, 207
Gnaeus Flavius: 10
Gnaeus Pompeius Magnus *see* Pompey the
    Great
Goethe, Johann Wolfgang von: 202, 213
Gracchi: 8, 10

Hegel, Georg Wilhelm Friedrich: 190
Helbig, Wolfgang: 196
Hercules: 13, 17, 31, 154, 161, 164
Hirtius: 52
Hitler, Adolph: 8, 196
Høeg, Carsten: 211, 217
Holmes, Thomas Rice: 97–98, 101
Horace: 29
Hypermnestra: 35

Io: 37

Jacobsen, Carl: 196
Jacobsen, Jacob Christian: 196
Julia: 19, 199
Julia Drusilla: 180
Julia Minor (Iulia Minor): 29, 41–42
Julius Caesar *see* Gaius Julius Caesar
Jupiter: 8–9, 20, 33, 36–37, 216, 222, 224
Juvenal: 12

Kangxi, emperor of China: 134, 136

Labienus: 52, 106
Latona: 35
Livia: 28–30, 34–35, 37, 180
Livia Drusilla *see* Livia
Lobedanz, Arnold Troels Lund: 191–92, 198–201, 207
Lucan: 72, 112
Lucius Caecilius Metellus Delmaticus: 10
Lucius Caecilius Metellus Diadematus: 10
Lucius Cassius Longinus: 180
Lucius Cornelius Sulla *see* Sulla
Lucius Licinius Crassus: 15
Lucius Licinius Lucullus *see* Lucullus
Lucius Mummius Achaicus *see* Mummius
Lucius Opimius: 10
Lucullus: 110, 112
Lysippus: 21, 33, 38

Madvig, Johan Nicolai: 198, 217
Maecenas: 29
Mandubracius: 104
Manius Curius Dentatus: 13
Marcellus: 21, 28, 31, 33, 35, 39
Marcus Aemilius Lepidus (Marco Emilio Lepido): 88, 168–69, 176, 180
Marcus Aemilius Scaurus: 15
Marcus Barronius Sura: 168
Marcus Claudius Marcellus: 13, 33
Marcus Junius Brutus *see* Brutus
Marcus Lentulus Spinther: 19
Marcus Licinius Crassus (Crassus): 109–10
Marcus Porcius Cato *see* Cato the Younger
Marcus Scribonius Curio: 7
Marcus Tullius Cicero *see* Cicero
Marcus Vipsanius Agrippa *see* Agrippa
Mark Antony (Marcus Antonius): 35, 37, 40, 169, 213–14, 216, 219–21
Marsyas: 206
Martial: 12, 32
Maxentius, emperor of Rome: 127
Medea: 38
Mettius Rufus: 180
Meyer, Eduard: 221–22, 224
Michele Bonelli, Cardinal *alias* Cardinal Alessandrino: 132
Mithridates VI: 109–10, 112
Mommsen, Theodor: 97, 191–92, 198, 201–02, 214, 216–18, 220, 222, 224
Mummius: 13
Munk, Kaj: 196
Münter, Friederich: 196
Muses: 17, 31–32
Mussolini, Bernito: 1, 119, 130, 190, 194–96

Napoleon I: 190, 192, 202–03, 213–14
Napoleon III: 2, 22, 52, 97, 190, 192, 214
Nero, emperor of Rome (Nerone): 34, 180
Nerva, emperor of Rome: 38, 122, 166–67
Nicolaus of Damascus: 212
Niebuhr, Barthold Georg: 191
Nietzsche, Friedrich: 202, 213
Nike: 132
Niobe: 35
Niobids: 35

Octavian (Ottaviano): 2, 27, 35–37, 108–09, 154–55, 168–70, 180, 189, 194, 198
see also Augustus
Oppius: 122, 197, 204
Ovid: 27–30, 32–43

Pais, Ettore: 221
Pericles: 203
Phidias: 33
Pliny the Elder (Plinio): 16–17, 20, 32–33, 111–12, 122, 197
Plutarch: 51, 71, 110, 198, 221, 223
Polybius: 89
Pompeius Paulinus: 180
Pompey the Great (Pompeius Magnus): 7, 10, 15–22, 27–33, 36–39, 51, 72, 109–12, 165–68, 197, 199, 216
Pontius Aquila: 213, 221
Pope Giulio III: 132
Pope Leone X: 132
Posidonios: 111
Praxiteles: 33
Propertius: 27–28, 35, 42
Pseudo-Xenophon: 218
Ptolemy XII Auletes, king of Egypt: 110
Publius Barronius Barba: 168
Publius Clodius: 19
Publius Cornelius Scipio Nasica: 14
Publius Popilius Lenas: 88
Pytheas: 111

Quintus Caecilius Metellus Numidicus: 10
Quintus Lutatius Catulus: 10

Ramses II, pharaoh of Egypt: 40
Remus: 72
Romulus: 39, 72
Rostovtzeff, Michael: 222–23

Sappho: 31–32
Schlegel, Friedrich: 190
Scipio: 199
Schow, Niels Iversen: 196
Seneca: 180
Septimius Severus: 33
Sethi I, pharaoh of Egypt: 40
Sextus Pompeius: 157
Shakespeare, William: 190, 202, 213, 221, 223
Speer, Albert: 8
Statilius Taurus: 28, 40
Statius: 38

Stephanus: 38
Stoffel, Henri: 192, 198, 201–02, 214
Strabo: 108, 141
Suetonius: 20, 66, 71–72, 122, 190, 197, 217–18, 221
Sulla: 14–15, 39, 71–72, 90

Tarquinius Priscus, fifth king of Rome: 39
Tarquinius Superbus, seventh king of Rome: 39
Tatianus: 32
Thorvaldsen, Bertel: 196
Tiberius Claudius Nero: 180
Tiberius, emperor of Rome: 180
Tigranes, king of Armenia: 110, 112
Timomachus: 21, 38
Titus Pomponius Atticus: 31
Titus Tatius, king of the Sabines: 39
Trebatius: 111, 213
Tullus Hostilius: 206
Tutmoses III, pharaoh of Egypt: 40

Vedius Pollio: 34, 38
Velleius Paterculus: 20, 40, 169
Venus: 36, 38, 40, 43
Venus Genetrix: 21, 37–39, 112–13, 122–23, 126, 197–201, 203–04, 206, 212–13, 219–22
Venus Victrix: 7, 10, 197
Vercingetorix (Vercingetorige): 52–53, 175–76
Vespasian, emperor of Rome: 35
Victoria: 17
Virgil: 27, 30
Vitruvius: 157
Voltaire: 202, 213
Volusenus: 102

Yongzheng, emperor of China: 134, 136

Zoëga, Georg: 196

INDEX

People and Ethnic Groups

Aduatuci: 56–58, 60
Ambiani: 99
Ambivariti: 59
Ancalites: 112
Apulians: 13
Arpinate: 169

Batavians: 61–62
Belgae: 55
Bellovaci: 100
Bibroci: 112
Boii: 88
Britons: 98, 101–02, 104–09, 111–13
Bruttians: 113

Cassi: 112
Cenimagi: 112
Coriosolites: 100

Danes: 190, 195–96, 202

Eburones: 56, 60, 64–65, 67

Gauls (Galli): 13, 52, 55, 76, 89, 97, 101, 112, 114, 176
Germans: 59, 101, 110

Jews: 36, 196

Ligurians: 88
Lucanians: 13

Macedonians: 13
Meldi: 103
Menapii: 58, 60
Molossians: 13
Morini: 60

Parthians: 41, 91, 109, 217, 223
Persians: 20

Roman people *see* Romans
Romans (Romani): 12–14, 17, 20, 56, 58, 76, 101, 105–08, 110, 176, 196–97, 199–200, 205, 207, 215–16, 219, 224

Sabines: 13, 39–40, 43
Samnites: 13
Scythians: 109
Segontiaci: 112
Senones: 89
Suebi: 58
Suessiones: 99
Sugambri: 60

Tencteri: 56, 58–60, 67
Thessalians: 13
Trinobantes: 104, 107–08, 112

Usipetes: 56, 58–60, 67

Veneti: 98, 100–01, 104
Volscians: 13

Topography and Geographical Places

Ad Confluentes: 75, 88, 90
Ad Statuas: 80
Adriatic: 74, 87–89, 91, 110
Africa: 180
ager Aquinas: 169–70
Ager Decimanus: 89
Alesia: 52–53, 55, 79, 105–06
Alessandrino Quarter: 119, 130, 132, 136–37, 194
Alexandria: 200
Almería: 58
Alps: 71, 90, 109, 111
Apennines: 71, 88
Aquileia: 91, 182
Aquino: 144–45
Aquinum: 3, 141–48, 152–58, 161–62, 164–65, 167–69
area Capitolina: 10
Arelate: 177–78, 180–81
Argiletum: 38
Ariminum: 88–90
Arles: 3, 173–74, 176–81, 183
Armorica: 98–100, 103
Arno, River: 71
Arrabona: 80
Arx: 8, 10, 14, 21
Asia Minor: 180
Austria-Hungary: 207
Aventine Hill: 7, 39, 120

Balearic Islands: 58
Belgium: 55, 57, 62, 64, 97
Biesmelle, River: 57
Bigbury: 105–06
Black Sea: 29
Bosnia: 207
Boulogne: 101, 106
Brentford: 107
Brigentium/Bregenz: 84
Britain: 3, 51, 76, 97–101, 103–13
Britannia: 66, 98
British Channel *see* English Channel
Brundisium: 110
Bussy Hill: 52

Campania: 155
Campus Martius: 20, 22, 30–31, 33, 36, 40–41, 197, 206
Canterbury: 105–07
Cap Gris Nez: 106
Capitol *see* Capitoline Hill
Capitoline Hill: 1, 7–8, 11, 14–15, 109, 120–22, 195, 197, 213, 222, 224
Capua: 158
Cassino: 145, 165
Castrocielo: 141–42, 145–48, 158
Celtic territory: 76–77
Cesenatico: 87–88
Channel Islands: 100
Chichester: 100

Col de Panissars: 111
Cologne: 62, 64
Compito: 74, 88, 90
Corinth: 13
Cornwall: 99–100
Cremona: 181
Crete: 109
Croton: 17
Curva Caesena: 90
Cyprus: 109
Cyrene: 109

Dacia: 82, 91
Dalmatia: 91, 167
Dangstetten: 84–85
Deal: 101–02, 105
Denmark: 3, 190–91, 196, 201–02, 213, 217
Demer, River: 62–64
Dokimeion: 180
Dover: 100–02, 110
Dover, Strait of: 100, 110
Dover, White Cliffs of: 101–02
Dura-Europos: 36
Dyrrhachium: 199

East Anglia: 107
Ebbsfleet: 105–07
Egypt (Egitto): 19–20, 35–27, 40, 109–10, 180, 200–01
Emona *see* Ljubljana
England: 99–100, 108
English Channel: 51, 98–101, 104
Esino, River: 89
Esquiline Hill: 121
Etruria: 126
Europe: 52, 78, 111, 174, 185, 190, 195–96, 198, 207

Fiumicino, River: 87, 89
Fortin de l'Épineuse: 52
France: 52, 97, 101, 107, 110, 175
Frigia: 180

Gaul (Gallia): 19, 51–53, 55–56, 59–60, 62, 64, 66, 72, 76, 79, 84, 97–100, 103–06, 108–11, 176, 178, 180–81, 214, 224
  Gallia Cisalpina: 103, 181
  Gallia Comata: 51
  Gallia Narbonese (Transalpine Gaul): 110, 112, 180
Gergovia: 52, 55
Gergovie: 76
Germania: 58, 60, 180
Gönyű: 80
Greece: 8, 190

Heliopolis: 40
Hermeskeil: 54–55, 68
Herzegovina: 207
Hesbaye/Tongeren region: 64
Hispania Citerior: 180
Hispania Ulterior: 111
Hungary: 80, 84, 207

230 INDEX

Iberia: 51, 58, 66, 100
Iberian Peninsula *see* Iberia
Interamna Lirenas: 168
Ireland: 98
Israel: 31, 36
Italy: 7, 40, 57, 66, 71, 75, 88, 90, 124, 157, 195–96

Kent: 100, 105–08
Kessel-Lith: 58–59
Kingsdown: 102

La Chaussée-Tirancourt: 84
Latium: 124, 126
Lautagne: 84
Lavinium: 33
Le Câtillon: 100
Lea, River: 108
Les Laumes: 52
Liane at Boulogne: 106
Limburg: 55
Liri Valley: 168
Lizard Peninsula: 100
Ljubljana: 79
London: 107
Luxembourg: 52, 97
Lydden Valley: 102, 105

Macedonia: 13
Marche: 89
Marecchia Valley: 90
Marecchia, River: 75, 88
Marne, River: 103
Mauchamp: 55
Meaux (Seine-et-Marne): 103
Mediterranean (Mediterraneo): 12–13, 103, 110, 112, 178
Meuse, River: 58–59, 62–64
Minturnae: 157
Mont Réa: 52
Monte de' Cenci: 40
Montecassino: 145
Montone, River: 89
Mount Perticara: 87
Mount Strigara: 87
Murcia: 58
Mutatio Competu: 90

Near East: 36
Netherlands: 55, 59, 62, 97
Nijmegen: 82, 84–85
Nile, River: 36, 109, 112
Norfolk: 107
Noricum: 76, 91
Normandy: 100
North Bersted: 100
Novae: 84
Numidia: 19

Oberaden: 84–85
Oppian Hill: 34, 36
Ostia: 36
Ottoman territory: 207
Otzenhausen: 55

Palatine Hill: 10, 13–15, 30, 35–36, 39, 120, 203
Palestrina: 166–67, 182
Pannonia: 91
Paris: 8, 22, 103
Pegwell Bay: 105–07
Phoenicia: 36
Piacenza/Placentia: 88
Piazza del Popolo: 40
Piazza San Giovanni: 40
Piazza Venezia: 1, 129, 132, 136
Pisciatello, River: 87–88
Po Valley: 71, 88, 91
Pompeii: 19, 31, 37, 40, 195
Pontus: 19
Porolissum Fort: 83
Prussia: 190, 202
Puig Ciutat: 51
Puy d'Issolud: 52
Pyrenees: 111

Quirinal Hill: 121–22, 197

Ravenna: 71–72, 88–91
Red Sea: 112
Rhine, River: 55, 58–60, 62, 64, 76, 84, 101, 103–04, 109–12, 198
Rhône, River (Rodano): 3, 112, 173–80, 182–84
Riccione: 74
Rigoncello, Canal: 89
Rigossa, Canal: 89
Rimini: 71–72, 75, 78, 86–91
Rödgen: 84–85
Romagna area: 75, 91
Rome (Roma): 1–4, 7–8, 9–10, 12, 14–15, 17, 19–21, 27–30, 34, 36, 38–40, 42–43, 60, 66, 71–72, 75, 89, 91, 97, 99, 103–04, 108–12, 119–22, 129–32, 137, 157–58, 165–68, 176, 178, 181, 189–90, 192, 194–96, 198–201, 203–07, 211, 214–16, 223
Rubicon, River (Rubico Flumen): 2, 3, 71–73, 75, 86–91, 199
Russian Empire: 207

Sacra Via: 20
Salla/Zalalhövö: 80, 84
San Vito: 87–88
Santarcangelo di Romagna: 87–88
Sassina: 90
Savignano sul Rubicone: 72, 87–88
Savio Valley: 74
Scheldt, River: 62–64
Sena Gallica: 89
Sentino, River: 89
Serbia: 207
Sikyon: 15
Snettisham: 107
Somme Valley: 99
Spain: 51, 58, 104, 111
Subura: 36–37
Switzerland: 97

Tarentum: 13
Tarvisium: 182
Thames, River: 106–07
Thanet, Isle of: 105
Thuin: 56–58
Tiber, River: 7, 13, 22, 71, 131
Titelberg: 52
Tomis: 29
Trans Tiberim: 27, 30, 41
Tyre: 20

Ulia/Montemayor: 51
Urgon, River: 87
Ushant (Île d'Oussant): 100
Uso, River: 87–89
Uxellodunum: 52

Valgirmes: 84–85
Valkemburg: 84
Vallis Murcia: 39
Verona: 184
Verucchio: 74–75
Verulamium: 107
Via Aemilia Militaris, *Rubicon area*: 88
Via Aemilia, *Rubicon area*: 75, 87–88
Via Alessandrina, *Rome*: 132
Via Appia, *from Rome to Brindisi*: 38, 157
Via Bonella, *Rome*: 132
Via Campo Spinello, *Aquinum*: 147
Via Civita Vetere, *Aquinum*: 147
Via Cremona, *Rome*: 132, 137
Via dei Fori Imperiali, *Rome*: 1, 120, 137, 194
    see also Via dell'Impero
Via del Confine, *Rubicon area*: 88
Via del Teatro, *Aquinum*: 144, 148, 150, 152–54
Via dell'Impero, *Rome*: 1, 119, 137, 194
    see also Via dei Fori Imperiali
Via della Palestra, *Aquinum*: 144, 147
Via della Salara Vecchia, *Rome*: 132
Via delle Terme, *Aquinum*: 148–49
Via Domitia, *from Rome to Gaul*: 111
Via Emilia, *Rubicon area*: 88
Via Latina, *from Rome to Benevento*: 143–45, 147–48, 152–53, 156–58, 161
Via Montana, *Aquinum*: 147, 152
Via Pasquale Villari, *Rome*: 37
Via Popilia, *Rubicon area*: 75, 88
Via Praetoria, *Rubicon area*: 83–84
Via Prenestina, *Rome*: 166
Via Santa Maria Maddalena, *Aquinum*: 147
Via Saudoni, *Aquinum*: 147
Via Tecta, *Rome*: 7, 14
Vigna Barberini, *Rome*: 36

Wallbury: 108
Walmer: 101–02
Wantsum, Channel: 105
Watling Street, *from Canterbury to London*: 107
Wheathampstead: 105
Wissant: 106
Worth: 102, 105

INDEX

Monuments

Adonaea: 28, 36
Anaglypha Traiani: 204–06
Aqua Alsietina: 41
Aqua Appia: 38
Aqua Marcia: 13, 38
Ara Pacis Augustae: 206–07
Augustus's Forum *see* Forum of Augustus

Basilica Julia: 206
Baths of Trajan: 34

Caesar's Forum *see* Forum of Caesar
Capitolium of Aquinum: 143, 145, 147, 157
Circus Flaminius: 21, 40
Circus Maximus: 14, 18, 20, 28, 30–31, 39–40, 206
Cloaca Maxima: 129, 131
Colosseum: 1, 137, 195
Curiae:
    Curia Hostilia: 206
    Curia Iulia: 33, 38, 126, 197–98, 206
    Curia Octaviae: 33
    Curia Pompeia: 19, 31, 197

Domus Augustana: 36
Domus Aurea (Nero's Golden House): 34
Domus Publica: 20

Fora/forums:
    Forum Augustum *see* Forum of Augustus
    Forum Boarium: 9, 76
    Forum Caesaris *see* Forum of Caesar
    Forum Iulium *see* Forum of Caesar
    Forum of Augustus: 27, 28, 29, 33, 35, 41, 43, 120, 122, 127, 128, 207
    Forum of Caesar: 1–4, 7, 18, 20–21, 27–29, 37–38, 40, 42–43, 112, 119–23, 126–27, 129–30, 132, 137, 189–92, 194, 196–98, 200–02, 204, 206–07, 211, 219, 223
    Forum of Nerva, Nerva's Forum: 130
    Forum of Trajan: 1, 130
    Forum of Vespasian *see* Templum Pacis
    Forum Romanum: 1–2, 19, 40–41, 129, 191–92, 194, 196–98, 203–04

Gardens of Caesar (Horti Caesaris): 27, 41
Garden of Adonis: 36

Horologium Augusti: 28, 40
House of Augustus: 28, 37
House of Livia: 37

Imperial fora: 122, 137, 193, 195, 197
Iseum Campense: 28, 36–37
Iseum Metellinum: 28, 36–37

Misenum, Augusteum of: 38

Navalia: 7, 8, 13
Nerva's Forum *see* Forum of Nerva

Obeliscus Augusti: 40
Obeliscus Constantii: 40

Pantheon: 28, 41, 195
Portico of Pompey: 27, 31–32, 36
Portico of the Danaids: 35–36
Porticus Aemilia: 7
Porticus duplex of Aquinum: 143, 153–57, 161–63
Porticus of Livia (*Porticus Liviae*): 28–30, 34–36, 42
Porticus of Octavia (*Porticus Octaviae*): 28–30, 33

Roman Forum *see* Forum Romanum
Rostra: 213

Sanctuary of Juno Sospita: 33
Sanctuary of Magna Mater: 7, 11, 14,
Sant'Omobono: 9
Santa Maria sopra Minerva: 36
Saepta Julia (Saepta Iulia): 28, 40–41, 197, 203, 206
St Peter's Basilica: 190

Tabularium: 8
Temples:
    of Apollo Medicus: 9
    of Apollo Palatinus: 28, 34–35, 37, 40
    of Apollo Sosianus: 28, 35
    of Bellona: 9
    of Caesar: 206
    of Castor and Pollux: 8, 11, 196
    of Concordia: 8, 10, 206
    of Diana: 143, 150, 152–53
    of Elagabal: 28, 36
    of Fortuna Respiciens: 13
    of Hercules Victor: 13
    of Isis: 28
    of Isis in Pompeii: 37
    of Juno Moneta: 10
    of Juno Regina: 33
    of Jupiter Optimus Maximus: 8–9
    of Jupiter Stator: 22
    of Mars Ultor: 27, 41
    of Portunus: 9
    of Saturn: 9
    of Venus Genetrix: 21, 37–39, 112–13, 122–23, 126, 197–201, 203–04, 206, 212–13, 219–22
    of Venus Victrix: 7, 10, 197
    Temple A at Largo Argentina: 9
Templum Pacis: 35, 122, 131
Terme Vecciane (Vecciane Thermal Baths): 140, 143, 147–49, 152–53
Theatres:
    Marcus Aemilius Scaurus' theatre: 16
    Marcus Scribonius Curio's theatre: 16
    Pompey's Theatre-Portico Complex: 7, 10, 15–21, 27–28, 31–33, 36, 39, 197
    Theatre of Balbus: 28, 39
    Theatre of Marcellus (Theatrum Marcelli): 21, 28, 31, 33, 35

Written Works

(author listed in brackets)

Amores (Ovid): 35, 40, 42
Annales Ryenses: 190
Ars amatoria, Art of Love (Ovid): 2, 27–29, 31, 34, 40–43

Cajus Julius Caesar (Lobedanz and Giersing): 190
Cajus Julius Caesar (Brandes): 190–91
Carmen (Catullus): 32, 109
Cicero og Caesar (Frisch): 211, 218
Cicero's Fight for the Republic, Ciceros Kamp for Republikken (Frisch): 211
Commentarii de bello gallico, Caesar's commentaries (Caesar): 51–52, 55, 97–99, 111
Constitution of the Athenians (Pseudo-Xenephon): 218

De bello civili, De bello civile (Caesar): 71, 218

Elegiae (Propertius): 35

Fasti (Ovid): 29, 34, 43, 219

Geschichte Roms (Drumann): 216

Library of History (Diodorus Siculus): 111

History (Cassius Dio): 36,
History (Posidonios): 111
Histoire de Jules César (Napoleon III): 214

Metamorphoses (Ovid): 36

On the Consular Provinces (Cicero): 110
Oratio ad Graecos (Tatianus): 32

Philippics (Cicero): 211, 218
Plague over Europe, Pest over Europa (Frisch): 196

Res gestae divi Augusti (Augustus): 41, 91, 108
Rimkrøniken: 190

The Tragedy of Julius Caesar (Shakespeare): 190
Tristia (Ovid): 27, 29, 35, 42

Periods and Chronology

Antiquity: 56, 60, 66, 104, 122, 162, 189–90, 195–96, 207, 212, 216, 221
    Late Antique period: 130
    Late Antiquity: 72, 91
Archaic: 10, 12, 119, 121, 123–27, 129, 137
Augustan: 29, 30–31, 33–34, 36–39, 42–43, 61–62, 64, 81–82, 84, 87–90, 128, 155, 157–58, 166, 169, 194
    Early Augustan: 81

Bronze Age
    Recent Bronze Age: 120
    Late Bronze Age: 119

Caesarian/Caesarean: 19, 51–52, 54–56, 60–62, 64, 67, 72, 76, 81, 84, 89, 91, 106–07, 128, 129, 165, 167, 169
Classical: 97, 189, 196
    Late Classical: 32
Claudian: 62, 64, 104,

Enlightenment: 12
Eneolithic: 73–74

Flavian: 36–37

Hellenistic: 32, 157, 161, 165, 167–68
    Late Hellenistic: 30, 33

Imperial (imperiale): 1, 7, 8, 12, 35, 39, 41, 66, 86, 91, 122, 130, 137, 141, 176, 180, 190, 193, 195, 197
    Early Imperial (primo Impero): 66, 79, 82, 128
    Late Imperial: 141

Iron Age: 74–75, 99–101, 106, 108, 122
    Early Iron Age: 122
    Late Iron Age: 56–57, 59–65, 76, 100–01

La Tène: 58–59, 62, 64

Medieval: 1, 33, 72, 101, 105–07, 119, 123, 127–32, 190
    Early Medieval: 129–31, 137, 141, 145, 190
Middle Ages *see* Medieval

Neolithic: 74

Prehistoric: 8, 56, 72, 74
Protohistoric: 74

Regal period: 8, 42
Renaissance: 2, 127, 130–33, 175, 195
Republican (repubblicana): 7–8, 10, 41–42, 58, 78–79, 82, 87–88, 97, 105–06, 122–23, 128, 167, 178, 180–82, 206, 217
    Late Republican (tardo-repubblicano/ repubblicana): 2, 7–8, 14, 19, 22, 60, 66, 81, 89, 104, 119, 122, 128, 155, 161, 165, 167, 169, 173, 176–78, 181, 184, 189, 198
Roman period: 62, 64, 72, 76, 82, 86, 131
    Early Roman period: 57, 62–63, 76

Third Reich: 8
Tiberian: 61, 64
Twentieth Century: 3, 137, 198, 207

Villanovan: 74–75

General Index

Battles:
    Battle of Actium: 41
    Battle of Ilerda: 51
    Battle of Naulochus: 170
    Battle of Pharsalus: 38
    Battle of Philippi: 169
    Battle of Salamis: 41
Breakthrough, The Modern: 202, 213

clementia: 29, 216

damnatio memoriae: 34, 37, 60, 169
domus solarate: 130
domus terrinee: 123, 127, 129–31, 137

Empire, Roman: 1, 29–30, 33, 35, 62, 71, 83, 89–90, 109, 161, 189–90, 214
Empire, Russian Orthodox: 207

Floralia, festival: 19
focalization: 212, 215, 219

genocide: 51, 55, 58, 60, 67

Lex Iulia: 21, 34, 42, 132
Lex Trebonia: 109
Ludi:
    ludi Apollinares: 31
    ludi Megalenses: 19
    ludi scaenici: 17
    ludi saeculares: 33

Megalesia, festival: 14

naumachia, naval combat games: 28, 30–31, 40–41

Portraits:
    of Alexander the Great: 38
    of Augustus: 154, 157
    of Cleopatra: 39
    of Caesar: 3, 21, 38, 141, 153–55, 162, 165–69, 174–75, 177, 179, 201
    of Nerva: 167
    of Pompey the Great: 31
portraiture, Roman: 3, 165, 167, 169

reception: 3, 189, 211
Republic, Roman (Repubblica): 189, 184
    Late Republic: 51, 190
Romanization: 76, 89–90
Romanticism: 190–91

Senate, Roman: 3, 7, 9–10, 14, 19, 31, 33, 71–72, 109–10, 197, 200, 206–07, 211, 214–17, 219–22, 224
Siege of Alesia: 53
Spanish Flu: 207
Statues:
    of Alexander on Bucephalus: 21, 38, 198
    of Cleopatra: 21, 38, 198, 203
    of Jupiter: 222
    of Pompey: 31
    of Sappho: 31–32
    of Venus Genetrix: 198–99, 222
    of Venus Anadyomene: 38
    of Vercingetorix: 53
suggrundaria: 121

Tabula Peutingeriana: 88–89

Wars:
    Caesarian war in Gaul: 84, 89
    Civil wars: 14, 51, 66, 72, 108, 189, 199,
    Gallic wars: 2, 51–53, 55, 57–58, 65–66
    Italo-Turkish War: 207
    Second Punic War: 13
    Sertorian Wars: 111
    World War I: 189, 191, 195, 202, 207, 214
    World War II: 97–98

ROME STUDIES | ARCHAEOLOGY, HISTORY, & LITERATURE

All volumes in this series are evaluated by an Editorial Board, strictly on academic grounds, based on reports prepared by referees who have been commissioned by virtue of their specialism in the appropriate field. The Board ensures that the screening is done independently and without conflicts of interest. The definitive texts supplied by authors are also subject to review by the Board before being approved for publication. Further, the volumes are copyedited to conform to the publisher's stylebook and to the best international academic standards in the field.

Titles in Series

Caesar's Past and Posterity's Caesar, ed. by Trine Arlund Hass and Rubina Raja (2021)

In Preparation

Foro di Cesare. I materiali ceramici dallo scavo del 1998–2000, a cura di Jan Kindberg Jacobsen, Claudio Parisi Presicce, Rubina Raja, e Sine Grove Saxkjær

Scavi dei Fori Imperiali. Il Templum Pacis (1998–2015), a cura di Antonella Corsaro e Roberto Meneghini